Predictability of Financial Crises

The Impact of Fundamental, Policy-induced and Institutional Vulnerabilities on China Compared to other Emerging Markets

Sebastian Petric

ISBN: 978-0-578-57686-2

Due to the dynamic nature of the internet, any web addresses or links contained in this book may have changed since publication and may no longer be valid. The views expressed in this work are solely those of the author.

Contents

Part 1: Introduction 1

Part 2: Conceptual Section 11

2. A) Fundamental Vulnerabilities 12

a) Growth and Fundamental Change 13

i) Factor Endowment and the Changing Distribution of GDP 14

ii) The Credit Impulse and Debt Financing 15

b) Balance-of-Payment (BoP) Dynamics 22

i) Current Account, Exports and FX Valuation 23

ii) Financial Account, FX Reserves and Errors and Omissions 28

c) Early Warning Literature 32

2.B) The Policy Dimension 35

a) Development Policies 36

i) Policy Experimentation 37

ii) Population Control and Urbanisation 42

iii) Poverty Reduction, Inequality and Stability 47

b) Monetary Policy 51

c) Fiscal Policy and the Debt Binge 56

d) Soft Factors 62

i) Legitimacy and Status 62

ii) Ideational Factors 64

2.C) Institutions 68

a) Liberalisation 73

i) Liberalisation – Economic Transition and Price Liberalisation 73

ii) Liberalisation – Capital Flows and Capital Controls 80

iii) Liberalisation – Interest Rates, the Banking Sector and Capital Market Development 87

b) FX Regime – Internationalisation, the Onshore/ Offshore Market and the FX Basket 95

c) The International Monetary System 103

i) International Financial Institutions 104

ii) Further Institutions 107

iii) Voting Systems 108

d) Institutions, Governance and the Rule of Law 112
e) The State-owned Enterprise Sector 118
f) Technology and Productivity 123
g) Remarks 128
2.D) FX Crises and Early Warning Systems 129

Part 3: Historical Background Section 137
3. A) Crises in Perspective 138
a) Introductory Note 138
b) Definition of Crisis 139
c) Historical Crisis Episodes 142
i) The Global Crisis of the 1980s 142
ii) The Asian Financial Crisis of the 1990s 146
iii) Transition Economies 152
iv) The Global Financial Crisis of 2008 157
d) Early Warning Systems and Historic Crisis Episodes 163
3.B) China's Economic Empowerment 167
a) Introduction 167
b) Historical Background: Pre-1949 168
i) The Traditional Economy 168
ii) External Pressure and Humiliation 170
iii) China's Failure to Adopt 173
iv) Early Industrialisation 176
v) World War II and the Aftermath 177
c) Historical Background: 1949-1978 179
i) The People's Republic of China 180
ii) China's Development Strategy 182
iii) Cycles during the Maoist Period 184
iv) The Great Leap Forward 186
v) Further Policy Uncertainty 188
d) The Transition Period between 1978 and 2008 190
i) The Transition Period between 1978 and 1993 193
ii) The Student Protests of 1989 200
iii) The Transition Period between 1993 and the 2000s 202
iv) China's Isolation and Emergence 205
e) The Financial Crisis of 2008, Prelude and Aftermath 208

i) The Effect of the Global Crisis on China 208
ii) China's Response to the Challenges of 2008 and 2009 210
iii) China's Growth and the Global Recovery 210
3.C) China's Growth Model 212

Part 4: Case Study 225
4. A) Qualitative Analysis of China's Vulnerabilities in the Second Half of 2015 and 2016 226
a) China's Current Fundamental Vulnerabilities 227
i) Growth, Fundamental Change and the Build-up in Debt-to-GDP 230
ii) Balance-of-Payment Dynamics, FX Reserves and FX Valuation 239
China's Saving Rate 239
FX Valuation 242
China's FX Reserves 245
b) The Policy Dimension 248
i) Development Policies 249
Policy Experimentation 249
Population Control and Urbanisation 250
Poverty Reduction, Inequality and Stability 254
ii) Monetary Policy 256
iii) Fiscal Policy as well as Creditability Issues 259
iv) Soft Factors that Generate Tangible Outcomes 262
Legitimacy and Status 262
Ideational Factors 266
c) Institutional Weakness 268
i) Internationalisation of the RMB and Capital Account Liberalisation 271
ii) A New Basket Exchange Rate and the Beginning of 2016 275
iii) Sources and Sizes of China's Capital Outflows and Capital Account Tightening 277
iv) Further Notes on Financial Liberalisation 279
v) The International Monetary System 280
vi) Institutions, Governance and the Rule of Law 281
vii) SOE Reforms 283
viii) Technology and Productivity 286
d) Remarks on the Qualitative Analysis 288
4.B) Quantitative Part of the Case Study 290

a) The Events of 2015 and 2016 293
b)Research Strategy 298
c) Independent Variables 300
i) Fundamentals 300
ii) Policy-induced Weaknesses 305
iii) Institutional Factors 309
d) Principal Component Analysis and the Logit Model 313

Part 5: China in Constant Transition – The Aftermath and the Path Forward 317
a) Fundamental Vulnerabilities• 318
i) Reversion to the Mean 318
ii) Risks 323
iii) Further Facts 328
b) Policy-induced Fragilities 332
i) Development Policies 332
ii) Fiscal and Monetary Policy 336
iii) Soft Factors 340
c) Institutional Weaknesses• 341
i) Economic Transition 341
ii) Liberalisation 347
iii) FX Regime 352
iv) State-owned Enterprises, Governance and the Rule of Law 359
v) Technology and Productivity 364
Part 6: Concluding Remarks on this Book 365

List of Abbreviations 367

Bibliography 373

Chief Witch: Yes that's right.
Macbeth: I understand you can foretell the future.
BBC Radio Programme, 1968

Whatever moves is moved by another.
St. Thomas Aquinas

Thou this be madness, yet there is method in it.
Hamlet, Shakespeare, 1601

Part 1:
Introduction

This book is about an expanded conceptualisation of vulnerability to financial crises which will be applied to China's struggles in the second half of 2015 and 2016. A crisis is defined as an underlying vulnerability in combination with a specific crisis trigger (Ghosh and Ghosh 2003; Ghosh et al. 2008; Chamon et al. 2012) with the triggering event being endogenous to the underlying vulnerability (Chamon et al. 2012: 3). This shows that the key to predicting as well as preventing financial crises is to address the underlying vulnerabilities. Until now, research on financial crises in emerging markets has foremost focused on fundamentals, defined as economic and financial fragilities (Goldstein et al. 2000: 1-2). Certainly, fundamental vulnerability is one key dimension to predicting and preventing these outcomes. However, by expanding the conceptualisation of vulnerability to financial crises, in particular to currency crises as laid out below, I show that outcomes can be predicted to a higher degree. In fact, by understanding the expanded set of dimensions, corrective measures can be taken more effectively. In general, a different conceptualisation of vulnerability provides for a different response to the fundamental question: How to predict financial crises to a higher degree and thus, to preventatively address a country's vulnerability in order to avoid the damaging outcomes?

This research creates awareness of the different forms of vulnerability which must be taken into account in predicting financial crises in addition to weaknesses in a country's fundamentals. To start with, I add a dimension related to policy-induced weakness. Additionally, one category with respect to institutional fragility complements the theoretical framework. Consequently, I construct the analytical section using this expanded set of dimensions, which should help to gain an improved understanding of the key drivers of outcomes. By detaching the discussions of financial crises from the limitations of pure fundamental variables and using an expanded framework to predict outcomes, I encourage stakeholders to acknowledge the multiple forms of vulnerability to financial crises. Indeed, these multiple forms of vulnerability are present simultaneously. The expanded approach towards predicting currency crises provides a framework for integration, on the one hand, by underlining the distinct types of vulnerability to financial crises and, on the other hand, by highlighting the interconnectedness of the different dimensions. The different types of vulnerability should not be seen as competing concepts as laid out in the theoretical section, but rather as different forms of vulnerability which, nevertheless, are related to each other. For instance, the conceptual framework allows stakeholders to see how inclusive institutions positively influence fundamental trends in a country resulting in a lower vulnerability to financial crises across various variables. The three dimensions are distinct from each other, though positive trends in one category reinforce positive developments in other variables as well and vice versa.

I use the aforementiond three dimensions to build a theoretical framework, which helps me to analyse China's recent struggles. The expanded scope of the concept of vulnerability to financial crises will be applied in detail to China's state in the second half of 2015 and in 2016. Firstly, however, I will analyse why China was less severely affected by historic financial crises over the past forty years relative to other emerging markets and thus, the country's rise did not get derailed. By drawing on lessons from past financial crises, I shed light on the notion that China had advantages along the three dimensions – fundamental, policy-induced, institutional – of the analytical framework which made the country less vulnerable to financial crises, in particular to excess volatility in China's currency. I hypothesise, however, that certain variables of these dimensions have changed, thus leading to increased fragilities of China in the second half of 2015 and 2016. Therefore, the question I seek to answer in this book is: *"Analysis of China's rise by applying a theoretical framework of fundamental, policy-induced and institutional vulnerabilities of emerging markets. How did China manage to continue its steep rise over the last forty years while other emerging markets were derailed by financial crises and what caused the country's struggles in the second half of 2015 and 2016?"*

Based on my practical experience as an emerging market investor and strategist in international banking as well as my prior research, I find that three broad categories of fragilities exist, namely fundamental, policy-induced and institutional, which are the basis for the theoretical framework. Empirical analysis so far has mainly focused on fundamental vulnerabilities of countries, which is certainly a key dimension of explaining emerging market crises. However, I believe that one dimension is insufficient to explain outcomes and therefore, by adding a policy-induced and institutional category, the predictability of outcomes can be greatly increased. In fact, the limitation of the fundamental dimension with respect to political and institutional drivers was identified as a gap in the literature on emerging market crises, for instance by Reinhart's comment on Drazen's paper 'Political Contagion in Currency Crises' (2000). Also, Goldstein et al. (2000) attribute the limitation of financial and economic indicators to predict financial crises to the importance of political drivers for outcomes. In addition, Reinhart and Rogoff (2009) mention in their review of early warning systems (EWS) that the literature on early warnings is still quite incomplete, leaving out many crisis episodes as well as primarily looking at financial and economic indicators to predict financial crises. With an extended analytical framework, I will seek to close this gap.

To analyse fragilities of emerging markets I distinguish between fundamental, policy-induced and institutional vulnerabilities. Existing research focuses mainly on the fundamental side of these countries. Indeed, by focusing only on one dimension, foremost on fundamental weaknesses, research is quite susceptible to an omitted variable problem. Acemoglu (2004: 19) names the omitted variable problem as one of the key pitfalls in predicting outcomes. He describes this in the context of econometric analysis in which key interfering variables are skipped and thus, the analysis is rendered insufficient. Therfore, the model would be biased because by omitting important predictive factors, the effect of the applied variables would be overestimated. I tackle this issue by expanding the conventional set of analytical variables by two dimensions and show that policy-induced as well as institutional weaknesses have a crucial impact on crises, meaning these have to be considered in future research with respect to financial crises. By applying an expanded conceptualisation of vulnerability, I have a higher degree of predictability while also countering the aforementioned omitted variable problem.

The debate on vulnerability and financial crises in emerging markets often is limited conceptually to financial and economic drivers of outcomes. Indeed, in the historical background section, I explain that many of the discussions of past crisis episodes have focused on fundamental variables. However, I will show that observers of financial crises must work with multiple concepts of vulnerability to better accomplish their task of predicting financial crises in emerging markets. In this book, in particular in the case study on China's struggle in the second half of 2015 and 2016, I will show how the consideration of the multiple character of vulnerability of a country to financial crises will significantly improve the understanding and subsequently the predictability of outcomes. In fact, there is a widely accepted conceptualisation of vulnerability, which foremost takes into account a country's fundamental weaknesses. This limitation can be interpreted as a disciplinary attachment of the observers of financial crises, which leads to the tendency to see a country's weaknesses primarily through a financial and economic lens. Thus, attempts to operationalise vulnerability mainly follow this definition while other forms of vulnerability have been neglected. In the case study, I will show that the approach should be different. Indeed, the failure to develop alternative concepts of vulnerability to financial crises and apply these when predicting outcomes, has led to a myopic view on this topic. The failure to develop and apply alternative conceptualisations of vulnerability to predicting financial crises limits the understanding of outcomes and how countries are enabled as well as constrained by these factors. The starting point for the theoretical framework is to identify the critical dimensions that make up for the conceptualisation of vulnerability. In general, vulnerability can be viewed as an imbalance, which needs to adjust over time either through corrective actions or, as often observed, more disruptively adjusts automatically via a financial crisis.

Indeed, the concept of vulnerability is central to predicting financial crises. Yet, discussions primarily tend to focus only on one specific, albeit significant, form, namely fundamental weaknesses. I argue that multiple concepts of vulnerability should be developed and subsequently, applied to predicting financial crises. This extended analytical framework should encourage increased and proper attention to the different forms of vulnerability. In fact, most analyses focus on fundamental variables, defined as economic and financial drivers of outcome. The lack of political and institutional drivers of prior research will be outlined in the historical background section as well as in the case study. These omitted dimensions generally contribute significantly to crisis by either triggering or reinforcing certain events. If the fundamental analysis is rendered insufficient, a simple solution is usually put forward, namely institutions, without people knowing what this is about. 'Institutions are the rules of the game in a society or, more formally, are the humanly devised constraints that shape human interaction' (North 1990: 3). Indeed, good institutions are not only associated with a higher level of income but also with less output volatility. The latter point also explains well the difficulty in predicting economic activity in developing countries. The poor quality of institutions in developing countries makes them very susceptible to all types of crises and thus, reflects a key vulnerability. As a matter of fact, the causality runs from institutions to outcomes as shown by Feenstra and Taylor (2014: 427). While fundamental variables enable institutional factors tend to constrain countries in their actions. To understand institutions, Acemoglu (2004: 2) argues that political power dynamics must be analysed, which leads to the policy dimension. Thus, it is not sufficient to implement international best practices. The question of policy is less related to what institutions should be built-up, but rather to 'how existing, and initially deficient, institutions can be put to work, transformed, or replaced for economic and social development in an open-ended process of institutional innovation that is based on locally generated solutions rather than on imported policy recipes' (Heilmann 2008: 3). Indeed, all three dimensions, fundamental, policy-induced, institutional, are important drivers of outcomes and none should be neglected as touched upon by Acemoglu (2004) in his omitted variable critique. I urge observers not to see the different forms of vulnerability as competing concepts, but rather see the connections between the dimensions in order to generate a more sophisticated understanding of outcomes. Yet, these dimensions are dynamic and to make the predictability of outcomes valid empirical continuities and breaks have to be taken into account, which I will describe among others below.

After the analytical section is laid out, the historical background section sets the scene for the subsequent application of the conceptual framework to the case study. On the one hand, I examine past crisis episodes and on the other hand, the history of China more specifically. These historical demonstrations are necessary in order to have a better understanding of present circumstances. I begin with defining which events I would like to explain before laying out historical crisis episodes and how China was influenced by these. Indeed, it must be defined which events said vulnerabilities can warn of. In this book, I particularly focus on currency adjustments. FX crises often precede other types of financial crises. For instance, Reinhart (2002) put forward that in 84 percent of the observed examples a debt crisis is preceded by a currency crisis. Moreover, among the first researchers who analysed currency crises in more detail were Jeffrey Frankel and Andrew Rose. They defined crashes as a depreciation rate of 25 percent per annum (Frankel and Rose 1996). FX reserve losses as well as sharp increases in local interest rates often accompany these currency crashes. In contrast, Reinhart and Rogoff (2009: 6) define a currency crash as depreciation of the local exchange rate versus the US dollar in excess of 15 percent per annum. In this book, I go one step further, as the definition is not generalised, but rather individual circumstances of a country are taken into account and thus, a currency crash is defined relative to the currency's own history versus the US dollar. In addition, with every definition of crisis, whether quantitative or qualitative, empirical breaks have to be taken into account. As research by Sharma (2016) among others shows, emerging markets experienced such a break in the early 2000s. Therefore, contemporaneous predictability analysis should be conditioned on this time horizon. Given this definition of a currency crisis, which will be laid out in more detail in the case study on China, two incidences with respect to China's exchange rate are noteworthy, namely the end of the nominal exchange rate peg of the Chinese exchange rate to the US dollar in 2005 as well as the exchange rate volatility in August 2015 and its aftermath. Given that the former resulted in an appreciation of 2.1 % against the US dollar (Lardy 2012: 101), the event does not fall into the definition of an exchange rate crisis. Therefore, since the early 2000s China experienced only one disruptive exchange rate event, namely the

1.9% devaluation in August 2015 and the volatile months that followed the event. As a matter of fact, the global financial crisis of 2008 did not trigger an exchange rate crisis in China. China stopped the appreciation of the renminbi in 2008 and re-pegged the currency versus the US dollar for about 22 months until June 2010 (Lardy 2012: 104). While other emerging market currencies severely depreciated versus the US dollar and FX pegs got dissolved during the great financial crisis, investors in the Chinese currency would have been relatively safe. Hence, this period does not fall into the definition of an FX crisis in China and in the case study particular attention will be devoted to the second half of 2015 and 2016, as it was a quite unique period in China's history. Nevertheless, historical financial crisis episodes are examined in more detail to draw lessons for China today as the country's transition continues. Therefore, I try to answer the following sub-question in this part of the historical background section, *"What are the lessons from past financial crises and how was China able to come out of those crises in a better state than other emerging markets?"* which is a puzzle that helps to answer the questions of this book. I will draw lessons from historic episodes of crises and analyse why China was able to dodge these financial crises. So, what did China do differently to other countries that its rise did not get derailed? By developing a deep understanding of the drivers of crises, I will reflect on China's rise as well as on the country's troubles in the second half of 2015 and 2016.

In addition, by speaking of historical crises one cornerstone in the academic literature is: 'This time is different: Eight centuries of financial folly.' by Reinhart and Rogoff (2009). However, another event which often leads to financial crises, is a country's transition from plan to the market in many former communist countries. These transitions are often accompanied by severe economic distortions and thus, have frequently led to financial crises. The transition economic literature is not covered by Reinhart and Rogoff (2009) and thus, another section must be added to the analysis of historic crisis episodes. Indeed, some FX crises are related to economic transitions, for instance the RUB crisis of 1998. Also, China is a so-called transition economy and therefore, to shed light on this perspective the following sub-question should be answered in the historical background section, *"China is a transition economy - why was China able to circumvent a stark economic downturn as it happened in other transition economies in Central and Eastern Europe as well as in the former Soviet Union?"*.

Subsequently, in the historical background section I show the main inflection points in China's history, which have an influence on today's actions. Indeed, history plays a significant role how a country's strengths and weaknesses are perceived and thus, addressed or simply ignored. The framework for analysing vulnerabilities is often defined within the historical context and thus, a country's memory determines a nation's strategy today, which makes the historical background section inevitable for understanding current debates (Gong 2001: 53). Indeed, China's history defines its identity and therefore influences the present and channels the nation's perceptions of its strength and weaknesses (Gong 2001: 45). Historic humiliations, for instance, give China a particular sensitive feeling for topics such as growth or opening to the outside world. The country's history is determined by foreign threats and invasion, which significantly curtailed the country's sovereignty in the eyes of the Chinese. These historic real and perceived humiliations are a powerful driver of today's actions (Hurrell 2014: 88). Without the historical background section, these issues cannot be understood. The historical context provides the basis for the application of the analytical framework on China and therefore, the following sub-question *"What are the distinct properties of Sino-capitalism?"* should be answered.

While it is necessary to understand the history of China as well as preceding financial crises, the lack of literature on crises in China is noteworthy. In historic episodes, such as in the Asian financial crisis, China is often left out due to the country not having experienced the exchange rate volatility of the affected Asian Tigers. This is because China was able to prevent disproportionate exchange rate volatility and thus, was able to independently manoeuvre through the crisis, although with the option to devalue the exchange rate (McNally and Gruin 2017: 12). FX reserves served as a vital buffer for the country to pull through the crisis and closed capital as well as financial accounts and inconvertibility of the local exchange rate hindered disproportionate outflows in times of global market stress (Goldstein 1998: 30). Indeed, this historic absence of excess exchange rate volatility has led to a lack of literature regarding China and vulnerabilities, in particular with respect to FX crises. This also contributed to the surprise effect that the devaluation of the Chinese renminbi had in August 2015. The lack of historic precedence and therefore, the inexistence of research further contributed to the global uncertainty regarding China in the second half of 2015 and 2016. With this book, I aim to shed light on these events from a different angle than that taken on previous historic crises, namely with an extended framework as laid out above and a new data set as described below.

China is at the heart of the case study due to its unique growth trajectory over the past decades, in particular relative to other emerging markets and developing economies. In addition, China's troubles in the second half of 2015 and 2016 form an excellent test for the analytical framework in explaining the drivers of the volatility experienced by the country in this period. The goal is to analyse China's trajectory by applying the theoretical framework to the struggle the country faced in said time period. To put it differently, I show how the extended analytical framework serves to examine China's troubles in the second half of 2015 and in 2016 and leads to a better understanding of crises. In short, the country sent global shockwaves through capital markets and thus, the following sub-question should provide another brick in addressing the main research question, *"Why did China become the source of global uncertainty in the second half of 2015 and 2016?"* Indeed, China's transition is not yet completed and in 2017, many observers were surprised by the recovery of the country and the stability China provided on a global basis. Thus, I will use the results of the analysis to answer the following sub-question, *"How will China manage its transition going forward?"*, which should round up the prior research and give the reader an outlook on China's further trajectory.

Part 2:
Conceptual Section

2. A) Fundamental Vulnerabilities

The dependent variable in this research is the debasement of the Chinese yuan, which took place in August 2015, together with the revision and the subsequent alterations in the exchange rate regime as well as the entailed capital market volatility. The independent variables are the three dimensions – fundamental, policy-induced and institutional vulnerabilities of China. In the analytical section, these concepts are examined in detail and will be subsequently applied in the case study.

There is a strong focus on fundamental vulnerabilities in research and thus, it is this dimension that the conceptual section begins with. However, it will be shown that a more complete framework by incorporating two additional dimensions, namely policy-induced and institutional fragilities, leads to a better understanding of outcomes. The expanded early warning approach towards explaining currency crises provides a framework for integration, on the one hand, by underlining the distinct types of vulnerability to financial crises and, on the other hand, by highlighting the interconnectedness of the different dimensions. The types of vulnerability should not be seen as competing concepts as laid out in this theoretical section, but rather as different forms of vulnerability which, nevertheless, are related to each other.

I will start out by discussing the key fundamental variables. The intervening properties of certain variables help to narrow down and identify the relevant mechanism and help to understand the properties of these variables (Mahoney and Terrie 2008: 741-749). As shown in the conceptualisation of the idea of an early warning system as well as in the historical background section, fundamental variables play a key role in vulnerability analysis. In this section, I describe the theoretical connection between fundamental vulnerabilities and financial crises, particularly FX distortions, which is illustrated in the case study on China. Research, most famously by Goldstein et al. (2000), focuses on fundamental variables, defined as economic and financial drivers of outcome. In general, crises have severe impacts on countries in many ways, most notably in a loss in living standards for the local population.

The negative repercussions a financial crisis has on the various spheres of a country should not be underestimated and thus, the predictability of crises must be prioritised by policymakers. Contractionary monetary policy, a drag on the fiscal balance, distortions in the foreign exchange market as well as lower growth momentum are only a few negative effects a financial crisis can have on a country (Goldstein at al. 2000: 1-2). The limitations of the analysis of Goldstein et al. (2000) with respect to a lack of political and institutional drivers considered will be shown. These dimensions significantly contribute to crises by posing severe vulnerabilities and were clearly identified as a gap in the literature on early warning systems. The unified framework helps stakeholders to better understand the holistic picture of China's unfinished transition and demonstrates that policy efforts of China should aim at addressing underlying vulnerabilities.

The fundamental part is inevitably linked to the review of the early warning literature in the section 'Crises in Perspective'. In the analytical section, the concepts will be discussed in detail from a theoretical perspective before these are applied in the case study to China's troubles in the second half of 2015 and in 2016. I demonstrate the different concepts of vulnerability in order to understand financial crises, defined as currency distortions, to a higher degree. Subsequently, this is shown with the examination of over five hundred research reports as well as with the help of a logit model in the case study. Before laying out more details on the case study, the different dimensions of the unified framework must be described. I start with the fundamental dimension.

a) Growth and Fundamental Change

To begin with, I discuss how to think about growth as economic variables are among the key predictors of early warning systems. What are the growth determinants of an emerging country? The question is tackled from an input factor perspective; however, how the different input factors generate output is treated in the institutional section. First, the concept of growth accounting is explained. This is inevitably linked to the Solow model. In this respect, capital accumulation plays a crucial role, which leads us to the discussion of the investment driven growth model of China and the decreasing returns per unit of input factor such an approach yields over time. Second, the discussion of growth also must tackle the impulse given by credit stimulus and thus, the build-up of debt. While credit is often used to smooth fluctuations, the build-up of debt depicts important long-term features as well. In general, the conceptual section serves as a guideline and sets the scene for the specific application of the theoretical framework in the case study.

i) Factor Endowment and the Changing Distribution of GDP

For a relatively long period in history, population and output increased at approximately the same rate. This type of growth is known as extensive growth with the increase in output being fully absorbed by population growth. In contrast, intensive growth can be characterised by population growth as well as rising living standards. Historically, an extensive growth phase always preceded an intensive growth phase. The switch between the two phases can be regarded as a turning point. The most famous proponents of this are Lewis (1954) and Rostow (1956). Generally, the periods in which population and output are increasing at the same speed are quite long (Reynolds 1983: 943). The main feature of turning points from extensive to intensive growth is export-driven growth; however, the nature of exports depends on the country (Reynolds 1983: 959). Indeed, the global boom years between 1945 and 1973 were driven by a spurt in world production as well as global trade. Thus, on the economic side, 'the turning point is usually associated with a marked rise in exports' (Reynolds 1983: 963). In addition, the establishment of manufacturing after a turning point depicts certain features, namely agricultural production tends to adjust according to a country's factor endowment and rural industries form the basis of the manufacturing sector initially. This is valid for China as is described in the historical background section (Reynolds 1983: 967). When thinking about the distinction between extensive and intensive growth, inevitably the Soviet model of development comes into mind. In the early decades of the Soviet Union, it succeeded in industrialising the economy. While Western economies were fighting with the Great Depression, the Soviet

Union's manufacturing output increased rapidly between 1928 and 1940. However, this was mainly due to a speedy increase in input factors. 'The Soviets, in other words, could move resources into the factories, but they could not maintain the efficiency with which they were used' (The Economist 2017d). In general, the Soviet approach towards development consisted of three cornerstones, namely said Big Push industrialisation, abundant labour on the countryside and the collectivisation of farming. In hindsight, the latter contributed to the most significant distortions across communist countries (Allen 2003). As laid out in the historical background section, this development model greatly resembles the East Asian economic model. Factor accumulation was the driver of growth for the Asian tigers, not efficient use of resources. Also, China's growth model is partly driven by surplus workers moving from the countryside to urban areas. However, China's distinct approach towards transition also allowed the country to reap the benefits from more efficient allocation of resources (The Economist 2017d, Yueh 2013). The role of factor accumulation is examined in detail below as growth dynamics are crucial in current research on early warning systems and thus, for explaining currency distortions.

Before touching upon the Solow model and growth accounting, it has to be mentioned that the Malthus model described historic facts well over long periods of time. Indeed, before the Industrial Revolution growth patterns hardly differed across countries. The main sector was agriculture. Population growth was matched by changes in production and thus, no significant improvements in living standards could be observed. This is the main prediction of the Malthus model. However, the model neglects capital accumulation as well as technological progress and thus, the Industrial Revolution proved this model wrong (Williamson 2014: 253). Indeed, the classical inputs of the growth equation for a country are capital and labour. Solow (1957) decomposed growth into these two factors plus a residual, which refers to technological progress. This relates to the question of how much output can be generated with the factors of production?

How can technology be defined? In this book, a broader definition of technology is applied - not only it refers to the blueprints for a range of products and the production technologies - but also to the organisation of the economy and to the rule of law and its enforcement as well as the political system (Blanchard and Johnson 2013: 217-218). Given the aforementioned, over time, growth defined as output per worker can either come from more capital per worker or from improvements in technology. However, capital accumulation itself does not lead to sustained growth due to decreasing returns. The factors of production depict decreasing returns per additional unit of input. More and more inputs would be needed and at some point, saving and investment in an economy cannot be expanded anymore and output per worker will not further increase. Thus, a higher savings rate does not raise the growth rate of output sustainably but nevertheless leads to a higher level of output as it entails higher growth of output per worker for a certain time. Therefore, only technological growth can lead to sustainable improvements in a country's growth trajectory (Blanchard and Johnson 2013: 218-221). In the long run, the country with the highest growth rate in technology will be the first among equals.

Capital accumulation can be broken down into human and physical capital accumulation. With human capital accumulation, what comes to mind is education. However, on the job training should also be included, which is a direct substitute for more formal education. Therefore, a higher savings rate or increasing the fraction of income spent on education or training raises the level of output of an economy, but only technological progress can lead to sustainable growth. Thus, whether technology is related to the aforementioned factors or what is driving technological progress must be examined in detail (Blanchard and Johnson 2013: 243-244), which is laid out in the institutional section. Furthermore, Syrquin and Chenery (1989) perform a cross-sectional country analysis of the determinants of growth in light of structural transformation. 'We analysed processes that are commonly used to define structural transformation: accumulation of physical and human capital; shifts in the composition of demand, trade, output, and factor use' (Syrquin and Chenery 1989: 145). In line with the above, the researchers find that the most significant category of growth performance is the difference between the countries that are open to trade, and those pursuing an inward orientated strategy. Trade openness can be defined as exports plus imports in percentage of output and should not be confused with the opening of the capital and financial accounts. Based on data for 1950 to 1983 the annual growth rate differs by 1.4 percentage points between the outward and the inward-orientated groups (Syrquin and Chenery 1989: 100). How is this related to China's growth trajectory? China's economic performance was foremost driven by growth in total factor productivity between the start of the reform period and the mid-1990s (World Bank 1997). After the second period of transition began in the mid-1990s, growth can be foremost related to increased factor accumulation, mainly of capital (Zheng and Hu 2006; Zheng et al. 2009). With China's accession to the WTO a new era of openness began, which spurred the country's economic performance as well as led to global imbalances in China's favour (Yueh 2013). How this is related to China's troubles in the second half of 2015 and 2016 is examined in detail in the case study.

ii) The Credit Impulse and Debt Financing

'The failure of understanding revealed by the present crisis demands that we humbly return to macroeconomic and financial history', as Schularick and Taylor (2012: 1) noted on the financial crisis of 2008. Only in the 1980s, the perspective that credit has real influences gained attention. Proponents of the view that quantities of credit matter are Mishkin (1978) and Gertler (1988) among others. Indeed, leverage and its composition have implications for macroeconomics. An increase in credit tends to be analysed from two different perspectives. First, from a financial accelerator effect (Bernanke and Blinder 1988) and second, the effect on a country's fragility or as Minsky (1977) and Kindleberger (1978) put it, a financial crisis can be regarded as credit booms turned into busts. Indeed, Schularick and Taylor (2012: 5) show that lagged credit growth is a significant predictor of financial crises, which is in line with prior descriptions of emerging market crises by McKinnon and Pill (1997) and by Kaminsky and Reinhart (1999), which is examined in more detail below. 'In terms of lessons for policymakers and researchers, history demonstrates that they ignore credit at their peril. The behaviour of credit aggregates contains valuable information about the likelihood of future financial crises' (Schularick and Taylor 2012: 29).

In line with the above, Panizza and Presbitero (2012) analyse whether high levels of public debt entail a slowdown in economic growth. Indeed, empirical analyses has mostly confirmed this view, expressed as a negative correlation coefficient between economic growth and public debt. In this respect, research was performed by Reinhart and Rogoff (2009), Kumar and Woo (2010) and Checherita and Rother (2010). In addition, Panizza and Presbitero (2012: 2-3) include FX effects on foreign currency denominated debt in their analysis. This is in line with prior research on financial crises, which particularly highlights the negative effects of balance sheet mismatches on the probability of a stress event. The researchers do not find any threshold debt level to be particularly relevant for triggering a growth slowdown, which stands in stark contrast to prior research, for instance by Kumar and Woo (2010). The latter show nonlinearities with increases in higher levels of initial debt entailing a disproportionally larger negative effect on subsequent economic performance. Thus, credit growth and the build-up in debt matter to the dependent variable – the currency debasement of the Chinese yuan, which took place in August 2015, together with the revision and the subsequent alterations in the exchange rate regime as well as the entailed capital flow volatility - because of the indirect effects via growth as well as the direct impact on financial stability, which is laid out below.

The Economist (2017b) cites a recent paper from the IMF (2017) in which the effects of increasing household debt on economic growth is analysed. While in the short-term increased borrowing leads to increased economic growth and constant unemployment rates, these effects reverse over the mid-term. 'The IMF study found that a five-percentage-point increase in the household debt-to-GDP ratio over three years tends to result in a 1.25-percentage-point decline in real growth three years in the future' (The Economist 2017b). And a rise of a single percentage point in household indebtedness raises the likelihood of a financial crisis by the same degree. In addition, the problem is that monitoring costs are high and thus, the Chinese government often fails to control the build-up in debt (The Economist 2017a). Given the increased leverage in the economy, risks are on the rise. As a matter of fact, the former head of the Chinese Central Bank, Zhou Xiaochuan, routinely warned of the hidden risks in the Chinese economy (The Economist 2017c).

The IMF noted in its report on 'Global Financial Stability' from October 2017 that 'it is during times of easy financial conditions that vulnerabilities build' (IMF 2017: ix). This is in line with the comments from Zhou Xiaochuan (The Economist 2017c). In particular, a low volatility environment can increase a system's susceptibility to shocks as investors as well as the real economy is incentivised to take on leverage. In addition, the global financial crisis of 2008 and the response to the downturn has led to an unprecedented build-up in debt in many economies, foremost in China though. Credit has regularly served the Chinese government to smooth economic volatility at the cost of being vulnerable to a burst of the debt bubble. This coincided with increases in real housing prices (Fuster et al. 2010; Shiller 2005). As laid out in the section on historical crisis episodes, debt frenzies in combination with run-ups in real asset prices have a tendency to end badly when the tide turns, and the bubble deflates. The sharp fall in asset prices tends to have spillover effects to the real economy and thus, a vicious spiral starts which usually can only be escaped with the help of an independent circuit breaker (IMF 2017: 37). In addition, private sector credit increases the probability of financial crisis at the same time as it depressed economic performance. However, it has to be distinguished between the short-term and the mid-term. Whereas in the short-term changes in credit are associated with faster growth, the picture does reverse in the three to five-year period. Institutions can mitigate these negative effects and the specific features of the debt binge matter. 'Even in countries where household debt is high, the growth-stability trade-off can be significantly mitigated through a combination of sound institutions, regulations, and policies' (IMF 2017: 53). This hints at the interconnectedness of the three dimensions which I lay out in the analytical section.

High indebtedness can be related to significant costs in case a country experiences an external negative shock. Indeed, historic crisis episodes, in particular the great financial crisis of 2008, has shown that high indebtedness can be a significant vulnerability for a country, which may entail prolonged economic downturns (Mian and Sufi 2011). Further studies point to the direct risks of financial crisis in relation to high levels of debt (Jordà et al. 2016; Mian et al. 2017). However, 'emerging market economies may be less prepared to deal with the consequences of a household deleveraging process because of limited institutional capacity' (IMF 2017: 54). Research finds that the level of the private sector debt matters in the sense that if a threshold is crossed, growth slows down (Sahay et al. 2015). In addition, macro-financial stability is also negatively influenced by leverage in light of constraints on borrowing, negative externalities or certain biases. These market imperfections lead to indebtedness being a vulnerability to a country. For instance, an adverse shock may lead to declining collateral values triggering constraints on borrowing and thus, leading to a vicious cycle (Eggertsson and Krugman 2012; Korinek and Simsek 2016). In addition, research shows that strong credit expansions serve as direct predictors for asset price crashes (Baron and Xiong 2017), which makes this variable a crucial driver of uncertainty.

In addition, the household debt is negatively correlated to the current account, which hints to the fact that excess consumption is the reason for most debt sprees (Mian et al. 2013). The IMF uses quantile regressions to evaluate their sample. Regarding the specific debt level when growth is on average negatively affected, the report puts forward that a leverage in excess of 30 percent of GDP with respect to household debt is related to negative economic growth effects. 'The presence of this nonlinearity is consistent with recent findings of a bell-shaped relationship between financial deepening and long-run growth' (Sahay et al. 2015 quoted in IMF 2017: 63-65). Furthermore, the report notes that changes in household debt are a good early warning signal. To prove this, a logit model is applied. It is shown that at high levels of household debt – above 65 percent of GDP – the likelihood for a financial crisis is increased significantly. Compared to the weak macroeconomic performance, the higher threshold related to crisis hints to the severe nature of these events. Furthermore, 'increases in the household debt ratio predict negative equity excess returns' (IMF 2017: 67), which hints to the systemic nature of this variable. Moreover, capital account openness together with a fixed exchange rate further increase the risks associated with high household debt levels, which is mainly related to capital flow volatility (Calvo and Reinhart 2000) as well as to bad incentives, which is discussed in detail in the institutional section.

Sharma (2016) pays particular attention to the five-year increase in private credit relative to the growth rate of GDP. 'First, it identifies a point of no return, past which private credit has risen so fast over five years that a financial crisis is very likely. Second, [...] past the point of no return, the economy is not only likely to suffer a financial crisis but is virtually certain to suffer a sharp economic slowdown' (Sharma 2016: 300). In many historical debt binges, the turn for the worse came after the fifth year in which the spurt in private credit hit the threshold of about 40 percentage points (Sharma 2016: 301). While the threshold seems somehow arbitrary, the analysis shows that it is crucial to keep a close eye on credit binges particularly relative to GDP growth. Often authorities try to counteract the trend in credit growth by increasing regulations. However, this hardly reins in the momentum in debt growth as people, more often than not, find ways to circumvent these. The turn of the cycle is often related to the central bank being forced to increase interest rates in order to reduce these excesses. This results in severe problems for the private sector, which tend to be the originator of crisis episodes. Given the close connection to policy-induced uncertainty, the five-year cycle found by Sharma (2016) can be put into perspective. In general, the global debt burden increased from 269 percent in 2007 to 286 percent in 2015 with one third of the increase being associated to China (McKinsey Global Institute: 2015). This is due to China's response to the global financial crisis of 2008 as laid out in detail in the historical background section. Not only was the increase in debt substantial, but it also entailed a boom in property prices. 'Lacking much choice in a country where the stock market is still underdeveloped, a few well-heeled Chinese were buying as many as thirty to forty homes as investments' (Sharma 2016: 311). Nonetheless, the real estate boom seemed to peak in 2014 while credit was still increasing. The excess money went into stock markets, which was supported by the Chinese state. This triggered a spurt in Chinese equity markets. 'There are four basic signs of a stock market bubble: prices rising at a pace that can't be justified by the underlying rate of economic growth; high levels of borrowing for stock purchases; overtrading by retail investors; and exorbitant valuations' (Sharma 2016: 313). Chinese equity markets started to crash in June 2015, which was one of the indications of the troubles China should face over the subsequent months. This, in particular the distortions in the Chinese foreign exchange market, is analysed in detail in the case study of this book. China's debt binge is unprecedented for the GDP per capita category China is currently in. There was no recession in China 2015 and 2016. However, as noted above, capital market volatility significantly increased and the exchange rate recorded a one-off event which is examined from three different angles in this book.

b) Balance-of-Payment (BoP) Dynamics

As will be pointed out in the review of early warning systems, Goldstein et al. (2000) identify deviations from the trend in the exchange rate as one of the best monthly indicators for predicting crises. The overvaluation of exchange rates often dissolves itself in times of high volatility as the market wants to enforce an adjustment of the exchange rate in times of crisis. Apart from the latter, the top annual, fundamental variables for currency crises are the following: 'The current account balance as a share of GDP, the current account balance as a share of investment, and the overall budget deficit as a share of GDP' (Goldstein at al. 2000: 56). The indicators give a warning signal if an unusual deviation from its trend occurs and thus, the signals depend on the history of the indicators. With respect to the monthly time series, the real exchange rate is identified as the best indicator for crises. As a matter of fact, strong deviations from historic trends in the real exchange rate are associated with excessive capital flows. Moreover, most of the annual indicators identified by Goldstein et al. (2000) are related to the balance-of-payments and thus, provide a warning against premature liberalisation which will be analysed in detail under the roof of the policy-induced and institutional dimensions. However, the connection between liberalisation and the volatile nature of capital flows links the former also to the fundamental section and it will be thus also touched upon below.

i) Current Account, Exports and FX Valuation

Inevitably a country's openness is related to its current account. Most definitions take the sum of exports and imports as a percentage of GDP to define openness. Thus, also factors outside the developing country's influence have an impact on the country's interest rates, exchange rates as well as prices (DeRosa 2009: 39). A nation's exports of goods and services less its imports are known as the main components of the current account. For instance, if a country imports more than it exports the current account depicts a deficit, which represents a drag on the GDP and thus, also has effects on employment. Moreover, the current account balance also represents how much a nation borrows or lends internationally. A country can only import more than it exports by building its foreign debt (Krugman et al. 2015: 352-353). To put it differently, the current account balance is equal to its difference between output and the sum of consumption, investment and government spending. Thus, by running a current account surplus, a country is building its net foreign wealth. The difference between foreign assets and liabilities is known as a nation's net international investment position (Feenstra and Taylor 2014: 582). Globally, the world's current account balance can neither depict a surplus nor a deficit and if it does it is due to errors in the statistics, most likely due to the mismeasurement of international investment income (Krugman et al. 2015: 357). Accordingly, a country's current account balance can be split into three categories, namely goods trade, services and income with the latter category mainly being made up of interest and dividend payments as well as foreign earnings from local companies (Krugman et al. 2015: 361). Whether the current account depicts a surplus or a deficit has a significant influence on the vulnerability of a country to FX crises, which is partly self-correcting. 'Signals of a turn for the worse flash when the current account deficit has been rising for about four years and hits a single-year peak of 5 percent of GDP. Soon after exceeding that level, the deficit typically tends to reverse and to fall naturally, simply because business and investors lose confidence in the country's ability to meet its obligations, and they pull out money. That undermines the value of the currency and forces locals to import less. The current account deficit then starts to narrow, and the economy slows significantly until falling imports bring the current account back into balance' (Caroline Freund 2000 quoted in Sharma 2016: 269). However, it must be mentioned that not all transactions of the balance-of-payments, namely between the residents of the local country and the rest of the world, have an effect on the exchange rate as these transactions might be conducted in the same currency. In general, the balance-of-payments must always balance as it is a system of double counting, namely accounting of debit and credit. On the left-hand side, the current account is divided into visible and invisible transactions. The visible part is made up of the trade balance while the invisible part is comprised of services (Beavan 2013). A current account deficit reflects investment or consumption over saving and vice versa and the deficit must be financed, namely via capital inflows. One statistic which captures the sustainability of the balance-of-payment dynamics is the basic balance, which is the sum of the current account balance and the long-term capital inflows, namely foreign direct investments. If the basic balance is negative, the country under observation is in external short-term financing needs (Feenstra and Taylor 2014: 590-593). The latter can be regarded as a vulnerability as the nation would be susceptible to so-called hot money (Sharma 2016: 276). This should result in an upward pressure on refinancing rates for a country as well as on potential depreciation pressure of the foreign exchange rate (Beavan 2013). In general, many developing countries run a current account deficit as those countries are in need to finance their long-term growth. This is one point that will be examined in more detail in the subsequent chapters.

What are the accompanying features of a current account deficit? Most notably, it is a vulnerability for a country as it needs to attract foreign capital flows. Thus, strong growth and the potential for high returns in developing countries can lead to inflows of capital and not lead to an immediate depreciation pressure on the currency. However, when the tide turns, these countries are particularly susceptible to crises.

Thus, apart from the global environment, the sustainability of a current account deficit depends on a country's external debt level as well as its ability to finance it (Sharma 2016: 287). In this respect, valuation effects in large external assets and liabilities could play an important role (Feenstra and Taylor 2014: 597). Moreover, demographic factors play a role in a country's balance-of-payment dynamics as an ageing population may imply that a country runs down its foreign savings and thus depicts a current account deficit which reflects the capital inflows on the other side of the balance of payments (Beavan 2013). This forms a clear vulnerability for a country and highlights the connectedness between the different dimensions. The repercussions of population control are also visible in fundamental variables, which underlines the influence of policy choices.

How do balance-of-payment dynamics influence exchange rates? Traditionally, current account deficits are associated with strong economic growth and weak currencies. However, the strong growth can lead to capital inflows according to the asset market approach, which are lured by the prospects of high returns, and thus, the exchange rate might appreciate. The latter often results in an unsustainable build-up of vulnerabilities. Other significant factors related to the points made above are monetary and fiscal policy. Tight monetary policy tends to squeeze imports and attracts foreign capital and vice versa. A tighter fiscal policy, irrespective of any response by the central bank via monetary policy, tends to improve the current account (Beavan 2013). The policy dimension is addressed separately from the fundamental variables, although the multiple forms of vulnerability are connected. In general, the end of the Bretton Woods system in 1973 led to the era of different exchange rate systems. Floating exchange rates are important inputs for the comparison of goods and services in different countries. A depreciation in the local exchange rate makes imports more expensive and exports cheaper and vice versa. Thus, the exchange rate is crucial for a country's trade balance. As a matter of fact, these effects help to explain why local manufacturing industries complain when foreign countries decide to weaken their currencies. Therefore, a downturn in economic growth often goes hand in hand with a weaker currency, which is sometimes known as competitive devaluation (Krugman et al. 2015: 374-379). However, many currencies in developing countries are not freely convertible, which means that the local currency is not freely exchangeable in international markets. Most local currencies are evaluated against the US dollar as about 80 percent of FX trading is done via buying or selling USD against another currency (DeRosa 2009: 60). For instance, the Chinese renminbi can be traded within China's borders but is restricted from trading outside of China because the local government curtails the free purchase of the renminbi by non-residents. Still, non-deliverable forward (NDF) contracts, whereby the balance is settled in US dollars, can be used to gain or hedge exposures (Krugman et al. 2015: 385). Another point worth mentioning is that when a country experiences a balance-of-payment crisis and the IMF intervenes, one of the first steps is the devaluation of the local exchange rate in developing countries. This leads to imported inflation and thus, the IMF programme tries to dampen demand by raising interest rates, which leads to a recession in the affected country. Imports contract, exports eventually recover, and the current account rebalances, which helps the economy to bounce back. Also, in the US, even though the situation is unique due to significant advantages of seigniorage, variations in the current account deficit and swings in the USD trade-weighted index comove (Beavan 2013). The influence of the exchange rate and its valuation on the BoPs is examined in detail below.

'If the country has an overpriced currency, it will encourage both locals and foreigners to move money out of the country, eventually sapping domestic economic growth' (Sharma 2016: 263). One concept closely related to FX valuation is the law of one price, which means that in case of open as well as costless trade, identical goods in different countries have to have the same price in the same currency, otherwise arbitrage would occur. This is further connected to the purchasing power parity (PPP), which relates the exchange rate of two countries to the ratio of their price levels (Krugman et al. 2015: 447). The purchasing power parity is a long-run relationship, nevertheless it can give an indication whether an exchange rate is over-, under- or fairly valued. Deviations from PPP can be long-lasting. In general, the relationship works better for small open economies with close geographical neighbours. Deviations in PPP would imply shifts in real exchange rates (RER) and thus, people try to model the RER. Attempts to model the real exchange rate were made by Clark and MacDonald (1999) with the so-called Behavioural Equilibrium Exchange Rate (BEER), which takes into account different economic variables such as productivity, terms of trade or international investment positions. Moreover, Williamson (1985) came up with the Fundamental Equilibrium Exchange Rate (FEER) which takes into account the internal, full employment, and the external, sustainability of the current account, equilibrium. In addition, 'there are some competing measures that try to adjust the value of the currency based on different measures of inflation, such as producer prices, or labour costs, or the rate of increase in per capita income' (Sharma 2016: 265), which is the basis of the Balassa-Samuelson approach. With respect to the latter, differentials in GDP per capita growth rates serve as proxies for differences in productivity.

Empirically seen, PPP is not effective in explaining movements in exchange rates. This is most likely due to trade barriers as well as transportation costs invalidating the law of one price (Krugman et al. 2015: 457). Moreover, as prices are sticky, PPP has to be a long-run relationship, if it holds at all. In case the central bank increases the money supply, the exchange rate jumps. According to Dornbusch (1976), this jump is larger than the long-run depreciation and thus, the currency overshoots. This excess volatility is a consequence of the sluggish adjustment of economic variables, most notably the price level (Krugman et al. 2015: 435-436). As indicated above, related to the PPP is the real exchange rate of a country, which measures the relative prices of two country's goods and services. In general, the real exchange rate is based on the nominal exchange rate and the price levels (Krugman et al. 2015: 463-465) and if the modelling of the nominal exchange rate fails, academia and practitioners usually try to use the real exchange rate as an alternative concept for predicting exchange rate movements. Why is the above so important? Chamon et al. (2012: 12) find that vulnerabilities related to the external sector have the best predictive power among fundamental variables. An overvaluation of the exchange rate as well as a deteriorating debt-to-export ratio were the most significant indicators in their analysis signalling an adjustment of the foreign exchange rate. More details on this and China's exchange rate valuation is given in the historical background section.

ii) Financial Account, FX Reserves and Errors and Omissions

The financial and the capital accounts are the counterbalance to the current account. The three accounts should add up to zero. Any discrepancies are recorded in the net errors and omissions (E&Os) section (Feenstra and Taylor 2014: 590), which can be a symptom of disguised capital flows as argued in the case study on China's troubles in the second half of 2015 and 2016. 'Rich locals and corporations can also slip money out of troubled countries through illicit channels that show up only in the "errors and omissions" column of the balance of payments' (Sharma 2016: 282). For instance, in China research showed that E&Os surpassed USD 80 billion in the first quarter of 2015, which is a record level for an emerging market. 'This means that outflows through the murky errors and omissions channel were running at an annual rate of $320 billion, or more than 3 percent of China's GDP – an alarming signal' (Sharma 2016: 283). In general, the capital account shows asset transactions for capital goods with non-residents. Often people refer to the capital account as the sum of the financial and the capital account according to the IMF definitions (DeRosa 2009: 40). The same analogy is applied in this book, if not specified otherwise. With respect to the latter, the financial account records the sale or acquisition of assets by foreigners and is generally divided into portfolio investment, which are rather short-term in nature, foreign direct investment, long-term, and changes in FX reserves according to the IMF definition of 2008. It must be noted that an increase in FX reserves enters the balance of payments with a negative sign (Beavan 2013). International reserves are held by the local central bank, which is the institution that has the task of managing a country's money supply. In addition, FX reserves held by the local central bank also aim at balancing capital flight in times of market stress. However, 'the bank spends billions of dollars from its reserves to buy its own currency, hoping to "defend" the currency, but this ends up draining the reserves and achieving only a temporary pause in the currency's slide. That gives investors a chance to flee the country with partial losses, but their flight keeps exerting downward pressure on the exchange rate. Many currency traders joke that "defending the currency" really means "subsidizing the exit" of foreign investors' (Sharma 2016: 292). In case the chosen FX regime of a country is not a floating one, the currency peg might require the central bank to intervene regularly in the FX market (Krugman et al. 2015: 364), which is a topic for the institutional section.

Windows for capital flows usually open when a country starts with liberalisation. 'A more damaging view of foreign capital is that when it flows in, it leads to overvalued exchange rates, and further reduces the profitability of investment, beyond any constraints imposed by an inadequate financial system. Indeed, by stifling the growth of manufacturing exports that have proved so crucial to facilitating the escape of many countries from underdevelopment, the real exchange rate overvaluation induced by foreign inflows can be particularly pernicious' (Prasad et al. 2007: 7). Capital flows play a crucial role in vulnerability analysis. One of the key pieces of academic literature analysing the nature of capital flows is Kaminsky et al. (2004) in which the researchers point out stylised factors with respect to capital flows. First of all, the researchers point out the procyclicality of capital flows which means that economic success attracts capital to emerging markets and vice versa, which reinforces either stage of the cycle and might lead to exuberances. Second and third, monetary as well as fiscal policy is mostly unable to decouple itself from the patterns described in the first point and thus, both monetary and fiscal policy tend to be procyclical. Fourth, the reinforcing states of the three points mentioned leads to a high covariance with the business cycle which reinforcement leads to a when-it-rains-it-pours problem in emerging markets. Emerging markets which were more successful historically were able to escape the procyclicality of policy, aiming for a neutral, but at best a countercyclical monetary and fiscal policy (Kaminsky et al. 2004: 32), which can be described as a Keynesian approach towards policy-making. The build-up of savings during the boom years could serve as a vital buffer and buy some time during crises. In contrast to this, the empirical positive covariance between the business cycle and capital inflows, as defined by Kaminsky et al. (2004: 3-4), hints to weaknesses in fundamentals. In a good state, low global interest rates fuel inflows into emerging markets and depress risk premia in these countries and thereby leading to a misallocation of resources. Often the latter fuels a boom in consumption in emerging markets as could have been observed in Latin America in the 1980s encouraging a pattern of dissaving behaviour (Kaminsky et al. 2004: 6) and ultimately, leads to capital flow reversals.

Moreover, Milesi-Ferretti and Razin (1998) analyse capital reversals and find that these stops and reversals are more likely in case a country runs a high current account deficit as well as a low level of central bank reserves. However, the researchers also associate a high degree of openness with a lower probability of capital flow reversals. Nevertheless, it clearly depends on the definition of openness. If openness is defined as the sum of imports and exports as a percentage of GDP, then openness plays a positive part in the development trajectory of a country and should not be interpreted as vulnerability. However, if openness refers to the financial and capital accounts more caution is warranted as these factors are empirical predictors for crises as shown in the historical background section. In fact, capital flows can lead to asset price bubbles as well as to a sharp increase in domestic credit according to Calvo et al. (1994: 54), which both can have severe destabilising effects on an economy once the tide turns and the asset price bubble deflates as well as credit growth contracts. Therefore, 'capital flows are often associated with inflationary pressures, a real exchange rate appreciation, a deterioration in the current account, and a boom in bank lending' (Calvo et al. 1994: 54). As could be observed historically many capital flow cycles ended in tears as it was in the case in the 1980s in Latin America (Calvo et al. 1994: 55) and is described in detail in the section 'Crises in Perspective'.

One way to deal with the volatility of capital flows is to increase the burdens to these free flows and therefore, counteracting the problem of pro-cyclicality. Capital controls would be one way how to deal with excessive capital flow volatility. Calvo and Reinhart (2000: 25) point out that capital controls not only stabilise capital flows but also change the composition of the flows. As a matter of fact, short-term flows tend to be substituted with long-term investments in case of the introduction of capital controls. Nevertheless, it is pointed out that capital controls are not a long-term solution to certain problems but should be rather used tactically to dampen the pressure in the foreign exchange market and allow a country to pursue a more autonomous monetary policy (Calvo and Reinhart 2000: 25). Moreover, a coherent regulatory framework can also reduce the risks of excessive flows and thus, can help to dampen the destructive forces of capital. However, these factors are analysed in more detail in the sections on policy-induced and institutional weaknesses. It will be shown how strength and credibility in these two dimensions can significantly reduce any blowbacks from capital flows and thus can reduce the risk of crisis as well as allow a country to harvest the benefits of openness.

Capital account openness is an important factor in any vulnerability analysis, interconnected with policy-induced and institutional weaknesses of a country. In general, it can be said that the smaller and less open a country is, the less susceptible the country is to global shocks and thus to crises. This degree of illiquidity is costly for emerging markets in good times (Goldstein et al. 2000: 76) but serves as a vital factor during times of crisis. Indeed, the critical items of the balance of payments are the capital and the financial accounts as those are driven mostly by expectations from investors. Moreover, capital flows are related to institutional factors such as taxes and capital controls (DeRosa 2009: 50-51). Many of the problems described above refer to the impossible trinity, namely a fixed exchange rate, an independent monetary policy, and openness to capital flows. A country can only have two sides of the triangle and attempts to have all three sides usually result in a build-up of significant vulnerabilities, which leads to a collapse of the system at some point (DeRosa 2009: 45-47). As a matter of fact, Mundell (1961, 1963) held the conviction that capital mobility entailed various policy options for the central bank regarding monetary policy as well as the regime of the exchange rate. However, capital mobility comes at a high cost of crisis if the set-up is not appropriate for the country. One example of this flow problem happened in Latin America in the 1980s and on a global scale after a further dismantling of capital controls in the 1990s (DeRosa 2009: 98). In fact, large capital flows have the potential to distort monetary policy as well as lead to an overheating of the local economy as well as to an appreciation of the exchange rate (DeRosa 2009: 99). The negative side of the coin comes apparent when a sudden stop in capital inflows or even a reversal of the flows happens.

c) Early Warning Literature

The aim is to analyse the determining drivers of financial crises, particularly of foreign exchange crises, to increase the understanding about these events as well as derive implications for the prevention of these harmful outcomes. In this respect, early warning systems deal with the empirical analysis of currency distortions, foremost capturing fundamentals defined as economic and financial determinants. The underlying events that early warning systems aim to predict are currency crises (Ghosh et al. 2009). The first step is to determine the crucial variables from which the likelihood of excess FX volatility can be deducted. In practice, foremost, a logit or probit model is used to assess early warning indicators. This method tries to determine whether certain vulnerabilities can be also interpreted as crisis determinants and thus help to predict outcomes well ahead before these occur (Goldstein et al. 2000: 15). The IMF makes use of the Developing Country Studies Division (DCSD) model which does include five independent variables. These are the real exchange rate, current account, FX reserves, exports as well as short-term debt to FX reserves. The likelihood of a financial crisis is determined from a probit model and a threshold is set to convert the probabilities into a binary crisis indication (IMF 2002: 50). It must be mentioned that FX reserves enter the model two times, first directly and second, in the form of the short-term debt to FX reserves ratio. This is econometrically not clear-cut as similar variation of each indicator could lead to the problem of multicollinearity. An extension of the DCSD model is the Policy Development and Review (PDR) model by Mulder et al. (2001), which mainly adds debt variables to the above-mentioned factors.

Furthermore, the IMF applies the KLR Crises Signals model (Kaminsky et al. 1998) to predict financial crises, which extends the above-mentioned set of variables by the ratio of FX reserves to M2, credit growth as well as output among others. The threshold approach applied in this model is set via optimising the percentiles, which makes the analysis susceptible to an in-sample problem. This approach is also used by Reinhart and Rogoff (2009). The researchers examine the early warning literature in their book 'This Time is Different' and try to find the crucial drivers of certain types of financial crises. Reinhart and Rogoff (2009: 279) mention that the literature on early warning system is still quite incomplete as these leave out many historical crisis episodes as well as only focus on a particular set of variables, namely fundamental drivers of financial crises. This represents a gap in the literature, which I aim to close with this research.

In general, what is daunting is that China is often left out in the analysis of historic crisis episodes. This can be partially attributed to the lack of exchange rate volatility, particularly during the time of the Asian financial crisis as is laid out in the section 'Crises in Perspective'. China was able to prevent any devaluation of its local exchange rate and thus, had the possibility to independently decide on the country's future, although with the option to devalue its currency (McNally and Gruin 2017: 12). The country's foreign exchange reserves served as a crucial buffer in times of market stress in addition to the closed capital and financial accounts of China during that period (Naughton 2007). Thus, the inconvertibility of the exchange rate prevented a disproportionate devaluation of the renminbi in difficult times (Goldstein 1998: 30). Consequently, the historic absence of exchange rate volatility in China has led to a gap in the literature regarding the assessment of China's vulnerabilities, in particular with respect to FX crises. This explains the global surprise effect the Chinese devaluation of the renminbi triggered in August 2015. The missing historic precedence and thus, the gap in the literature contributed to the global level of uncertainty with respect to China in the second half of 2015 and 2016.

Scholars and financial market practitioners foremost drew lessons with respect to economic and financial variables from historic crisis episodes. Therefore, in many analyses determinants from the growth literature (Solow 1957; Reynolds 1983), credit booms (Minsky 1977; Kindleberger 1978; Schularick and Taylor 2012), external sector variables (Dornbusch et al. 1995; Goldstein et al. 2000), banking sector problems (Kaminsky and Reinhart 1999), variables related to the capital and financial accounts (Calvo et al. 1994; Kaminsky et al. 2004) as well as general macroeconomic performance (Krugman 1979) are applied. These economic variables are among the most commonly used predictors for financial crisis. As is shown in the historical background section, research regarding historical crisis episodes mainly points to these variables as determinants of harmful outcomes, foremost of the global debt crisis of the 1980s, of the Asian financial crisis of the 1990s as well as of the global financial crisis of 2008.

As aforementioned, by speaking about historical crisis episodes it is inevitably to leave out the research by Reinhart and Rogoff (2009). Apart from the crises listed above, which are also covered in their research, one must add financial crisis related to economic transformations. The transition from plan to market often resulted in severe disturbances in a country's economic performance as well as in asset prices such as in a nation's exchange rate (Kornai 1994). The literature on transformation is not covered by Reinhart and Rogoff (2009). As China's transition is not yet completed, I also draw on knowledge from the literature on the transition period. As a matter of fact, some of the most severe currency crashes occurred because of certain approaches towards transforming a country's economy, for instance the RUB crisis of 1998 (Roland 2000). With respect to economic transformation the research by Brüggemann and Linne (2002) is particularly relevant as the vital drivers of transformational recessions and disturbances in a country's asset prices are determined. The most important variables, which serve as predictors for said troubles, are an overvalued exchange rate, weak exports as well as declining FX reserves. The findings of the researchers are in line with the research on previous crisis episodes.

To sum up, the primary economic drivers of historic crisis episodes were summarised in this section. However, with my research I aim to shed light on China's troubles in the second half of 2015 and 2016 from a different angle than has been applied to previous crises. The currency debasement of the Chinese yuan in August 2015, the change in the FX regime and the frequent revisions of this as well as the entailed capital outflows in 2015 and 2016 have not received appropriate attention from an early warning analysis perspective. Closing the gap and discussing these events from a different perspective than is usually applied is the aim of this book.

2.B) The Policy Dimension

In this section I expand the conventional way of describing vulnerabilities to financial crises by one dimension, namely by policy-induced fragilities. The pure focus on fundamental variables from an early warning perspective represents conceptual favouritism. The failure to develop and apply multiple concepts to explaining and predicting financial crisis, defined as an FX crisis in this book, limits the understanding of outcomes and how China is enabled and constrained by these factors. In this regard, policy-induced weaknesses and strengths are crucial and thus, I examine topics such as development policies, monetary and fiscal policy as well as soft factors such as status and ideational factors as significant drivers of outcomes from an early warning perspective.

With respect to policy-induced weaknesses, policy experimentation, population control and urbanisation as well as poverty and inequality are among the most important development policies. Policy experimentation is one means for institutional innovation, population control refers to the Chinese one-child policy, urbanisation is related to the so-called Lewis Turning Point and, last but not least, inequality deals with the negative side-effects of China's rapid development. Apart from development policies, monetary and fiscal policies are examined in detail. Due to the independent variable, an FX crisis, both policies are of crucial interest. The former is very much related to movements in the exchange rate, while the latter is partly responsible for the severe vulnerability related to the build-up in debt, which is analysed in detail in the section on fundamentals of this book. The last determinants of the policy section are soft factors as vital drivers of outcomes. In the case study it will be made clear why these largely unobservable forces such as the demand for status and ideational factors generate observable outcomes. These determinants are part of the unique features of the Chinese trajectory and should help to better explain the dependent variable in the case study.

I demonstrate the different concepts of vulnerability and the determining factors in order to understand currency crises to a higher degree. This is shown with the examination of over five hundred research reports as well as with the help of a logit model in the case study. However, not all factors of the policy-induced dimension are traceable in the logit model and hence, soft factors are examined qualitatively with the help of the research reports to better understand the events of 2015 and 2016, which has not been done yet from an early warning perspective. As mentioned, the expanded early warning approach towards explaining currency crises provides a framework for integration, on the one hand, by underlining the distinct types of vulnerability to financial crises and, on the other hand, by highlighting the interconnectedness of the different factors and dimensions. The policy category is one dimension among the three categories of the unified analytical framework – fundamental, policy-induced, institutional - that is applied in the case study to China's troubles in the second half of 2015 and 2016 and thus helps to better understand the crucial determinants of the currency debasement of the Chinese yuan, the change in the FX regime and the frequent revisions of this as well as the subsequent capital outflows.

a) Development Policies

What is meant by the term development policies? In general, development refers to the capacity of a national economy, which means that development policies aim at improving a country's economy (Todaro 2000: 14). However, the term economy is too limited; in fact, development policies aim at improving the economic, political as well as institutional mechanisms of a country. While a variety of policies, which aim at improving the lives of the local population, exist, the most important and sometimes controversial approaches, as shown in the historical background section, are policy experimentation, population control and urbanisation as well as the reduction in inequality. Unique to the Chinese approach towards development is policy experimentation. The country's opening was pursued with a focus on local development of certain areas, which gave the Chinese leadership the benefit of experimenting with certain policies before implementing it or rather stop pursuing the experiments. In contrast to the latter, population control is a double-edged sword as a spurt in short-term development comes at a long-term cost for a country. In addition, the causality between the short-term development and lower population runs two ways as development leads to a reduction in child mortality, which tends to be accompanied with a decline in fertility in developing countries. The controversy is particularly relevant in China today as the country was forced to reverse part of its development policies enforced in the early reformist era. Moreover, urbanisation is another crucial topic in development, which is closely linked to inequality given the rural-urban divide. The above is described in detail below. In comparison to many fundamentals, these factors are slow-moving, but still can hint to significant inflection points in a country's trajectory. Thus, conditioning the analysis on these policy-variables can add significant benefits for predicting and, over the long run, preventing crises.

i) Policy Experimentation

Policy experimentation is one means that should help to facilitate institutional innovation. Avoidance of entering unknown territory has substantial value-added for reformists. The trajectory of China shows that the transformational change can be induced via policy experimentation. These measures ultimately led to large-scale economic expansion by supporting new types of economic activities via the opening of the country, which is inevitably linked to the dependent variable. In the case study, I apply the theoretical knowledge laid out below to the currency debasement of the Chinese yuan, which took place in August 2015, together with the revision and subsequent alterations in the exchange rate regime as well as the entailed capital flow volatility.

China is a transition economy and thus the ultimate question is how to facilitate the shift from plan to market, which started at the end of the 1970s. This transformation of the economy is not yet complete due to China's incremental approach towards transitioning. As mentioned in the respective section, this process has to be understood as large-scale institutional change (Roland 2000). The question is how to facilitate the transformation in the presence of severe opposition to reforms? This should not be simply done via imports of foreign blueprints, which ignore local idiosyncrasies (Evans 2004). One of the strengths of the Chinese political economy is its ability to find creative solutions that help the country to forego some of the crises other transition economies experienced. China's adaptive capacity in the absence of property rights and the rule of law has made for a success story (Mukand and Rodrik 2002). North (2006) notes that China's approach enables the country to overcome some of the most difficult impediments in a country's shift from plan to market better than other emerging markets. This happens even though the Communist Party has ruled the country since the establishment of the PRC in 1949 (Bunce 1999). However, policy experimentation should not be confused with simple trial and error. 'It is a purposeful and coordinated activity geared to producing novel policy options that are injected into official policymaking and then replicated on a larger scale, or even formally incorporated into national law' (Heilmann 2008b: 3). This is usually related to demonstration projects which are not strictly controlled by Chinese policymakers but allow for a certain leeway to explore novel paths to contemporaneous challenges. In contrast to the conventional model in which the incorporation of certain policies into law would happen ex ante, in China the innovation is first tried out before any further steps are made, which significantly facilitated institutional innovation (Rawski 1995; Cao et al. 1999; Roland 2000). China's gradual transition process allowed for sufficient time to experiment with certain practices and institutions. Heilmann (2008a) notes that the Chinese Communist Party follows the strategies of 'proceeding from point to surface' and only 'in accordance with local circumstances'. The tools for policy experimentation in China are threefold, namely experimental regulation, experimental points as well as experimental zones. With respect to the former, the central government was given the right to establish interim regulation for the purpose of policy experimentation in 1985, which does not represent formalised law, but rather helps policymakers to bypass legislative bodies in order to implement their experimental approach. This was partially abolished with China's accession to the WTO. Regarding experimental points, experimentation is limited to certain pre-defined areas or sectors. It serves the purpose of trying out certain measures before these are either universalised or abolished. With respect to the last tool, experimental zones refer to geographical units or certain jurisdictions being assigned to certain powers (Heilmann 2008b: 5-7). The most notable experimental zones are SEZs, which are described in detail below.

After the death of Mao, China established the first SEZs in 1979 and 1980, which can be interpreted as signs of the opening of the country. In the decades to follow, every round of liberalisation was preceded by the establishment of SEZs. The first policymakers, who requested such economic zones with certain extended rights, were officials in Guangdong in 1978 (Yueh 2013: 257). The endorsement of SEZs by Deng Xiaoping in 1979 marked the beginning of the Chinese commitment to opening the country. As laid out in the historical background section, the involvement of foreign companies in Chinese affairs is generally seen as critically given the experience of the century of humiliation. Therefore, the opening of restricted areas to the outside world served as a powerful tool for the country's growth strategy without touching upon the critical topic of sovereignty. These zones provided the Chinese credibility in its efforts of opening the country and every time the nation faced resistance to its strategy the Chinese leadership could resort to these special economic zones. For instance, Deng Xiaoping's tour to the Shenzen SEZ in 1992 preceded a wave of liberalisation after the dark years following the Tiananmen interlude (Naughton 2007: 406-410). In addition, the establishment of SEZs feature the crucial characteristics of the first phase of reforms in China, namely 'dual-track, incremental reforms that started by creating a new system alongside, or in the interstices of, the existing one' (Naughton 2007: 407). Moreover, these areas were mostly autonomous regions as these served as windows to the outside world. The SEZs were export-processing zones that served the purpose of international trade and investment (Lardy 1998). These areas can be regarded as research laboratories with respect to economic reforms. 'The introduction of market forces into SEZs allowed the government to experiment with a limited degree of opening' (Yueh 2013: 24). A detailed history of SEZs is given in the section 'China's Economic Empowerment'.

In China, implementation before establishing the innovation in the legislation is the de facto policy cycle. In the case of Guangdong, the experimental approach is in many cases driven by local policymakers who try to address certain problems in their provinces. However, these initiatives always have to be backed by higher-level advocates. As Heilmann (2008b: 9) describes 'in a hierarchical system, bottom-up experimentation goes nowhere without higher-level patrons'. At the same time, decentralised policy generation plays a crucial role (Meyer 2008). 'The combination of decentralized experimentation with ad hoc central interference, which results in selective integration of local experiences into national policymaking, is a key to understanding how a distinctive policy process has contributed to China's economic rise' (Heilmann 2008b: 23). Furthermore, the researcher describes the Chinese approach with respect to policy experimentation in various case studies, namely state-owned enterprises, private business, foreign investment and trade, the stock market and social goods and societal participation. In the historical background section, these topics are laid out in detail, in particular with respect to the state-owned enterprise reforms and the emergence of private business. With respect to the former, the Chinese government relied on an experimental approach towards reforming the SOE sector given the significant problems this sector faced due to the transition from plan to market. The introduction of additional incentives as well as greater autonomy, are among those steps taken by the Chinese leadership to improve the performance of the SOEs. The avoidance of political and ideological controversies was only possible due to policy experimentation, which made the gradual approach towards transformation possible (Heilmann 2008b: 14). Similar obstacles were present with respect to the emergence of private business in China, which severely contrasted the socialist ideology (Naughton 2007: 95). Regarding foreign investment and trade, Deng Xiaoping launched a wave of opening in 1992 with his tour to the Shenzen SEZ. However, this became even more prominent in China with the extension of the economic opening from the coastal lines to the inner regions in the second phase of the reform era (Yang 1997). With the proclamation of a socialist market economy, China aimed at transforming the system, which triggered a wave of experimentations by local policymakers. In this respect, special zones with preferential conditions for trading with the outside world were particularly favoured by local officials (Zweig 2002). The increased economic exchange with the outside world also led officials to support more market-orientated reforms in China (Shirk 1994). These special zones for trade and investment went far beyond the usual controlled experimentations and became crucial for the successful trajectory of China (Yang 1997). Regarding the development of the stock market since the early 1990s, Walter and Howie (2006: 4) note that it had to be 'squeezed into an economy still based on state planning and the absence of private ownership'. Furthermore, Heilmann (2008b: 18) remarks that 'insiders from China's newly emerging financial industry, using their excellent connections to top national policymakers, had launched the policy initiative to establish stock exchanges in a socialist economy on an experimental basis. [...] Stock market history in China overall is marked by a series of experimental schemes. Most important are the repacking of SOEs into listed shareholding companies (early 1990s), selected transfers of legal person shares to new owners (1992), Hong Kong listings of SOEs (1993), the creation of "national champions" (from the second half of the 1990s), and several attempts at reducing the holdings of state shares (1999, 2001, and 2005). The two stock exchanges were classified as "experimental points" from 1990 to 1997'. Thus, policy experimentation played a crucial role in the development of local stock exchanges, which should not be confused with a trial error approach as noted above. While in the above-mentioned cases policy experimentation significantly helped China in its successful trajectory, experimentation did not significantly further the provision of public goods such as health care in China. Nonetheless, China's approach towards policy experimentation represents a suitable alternative to importing international best practices as it helps to tap local knowledge and mobilises bottom-up initiatives (Meyer 2008). The role of policy experimentation versus blunt trial and error is examined in the case study with respect to China's troubles in the second half of 2015 and 2016.

ii) Population Control and Urbanisation

'China is on the eve of a demographic shift that will have profound consequences on its economic and social landscape. Within a few years the working age population will reach a historical peak, and will then begin a precipitous decline. The core of the working age population, those aged 20-39 years, has already begun to shrink. With this, the vast supply of low-cost workers – a core engine of China's growth model – will dissipate, with potentially far-reaching implications domestically and externally' (Das and N'Diaye 2013: 17). As is shown in the case study, China's demographics are closely linked to fundamental variables such as the current account and thus, play a crucial role in understanding the country's external balances. A lower dependency ratio is connected to a higher current account surplus and vice versa. As external variables are among the key predictors in early warning systems, it is inevitably to understand the slow-moving long-term trends that determine these variables.

Aging will pose a challenge for societies as the median age is rapidly on the increase in many countries. Standards of living will be hard to sustain while countries with a more youthful population can still profit from the demographic dividend. Economic growth will be spurred if the young population can be encouraged to actively contribute to the society. In contrast, in aging societies, countries in which no spike in fertility takes place, the working age population will automatically decline dragging down economic growth and violating the social contract between the generations. Thus, population control is a double-edged sword with some short-term benefits at the cost of endangering a country's long-term trajectory. It is inevitable that these states will have to undergo reforms of their health and pension systems to sustain and improve the standards of living (NIC 2012: 20; Todaro 2000). As is laid out in the case study, population control sometimes backfires. The Economist (2013) commented on this as follows: 'For more than three decades the bureaucrats who enforce China's one-child policy have been among the most ubiquitous, and the most despised, in the country'. Why are policy-makers so obsessed with population control in emerging markets? The answer is related to the working age population. Generally, children and elderly people depict a very low level of labour force participation and thus, the share of the local population that works is greatly influenced by the share of the people that is in working age. Therefore, many developing countries implement population control measures, which help those countries to temporarily increase the fraction of working age population and thus lower the dependency ratio, at the cost of the long-term growth trajectory of a country (Weil 2008: 140).

With respect to population growth and economic performance, Sharma (2016) mentions the declining supply of the labour force as one determinant of the downward trend in global growth. In many countries the low labour force growth rate, which effectively relates to growth in the working age population, people between the age of 15 and 64, poses a significant drag on economic growth. In the decades after World War II, global population grew approximately by 2 percent every year, which represented a baseline rate. However, in the early 1990s global population growth declined to about 1 percent, which accumulated to significant loss in output over time. The full effect of the declining population growth rate is yet to show. The fall in the rate can be associated with the delayed effect of birth control measures in emerging markets. Apart from direct population control measures, the declining birth rates in said countries were also related to a higher level of development. In general, basic shifts in fertility and mortality rates account for changes in population growth. 'The period since 1960 has also been a global baby bust, as the average number of births per woman has fallen from 4.9 to 2.5 worldwide' (Sharma 2016: 26). The replacement rate is about 2.1; below this rate the global population shrinks. Thus, in contrast to popular belief, for most countries the primary economic threat is too few people, not too many.

Workers are the crucial drivers of economic growth and thus, it has to be monitored what a country is doing to address the issue of slowing population growth. Apart from the question of population growth, topics such as more women in the labour force as well as migration could alter the negative population trend growth rate in order to stabilise a country's outlook. Sharma (2016: 29) analyses 'how fast the working age population needs to grow to raise the likelihood of an economic boom, it turns out 2 percent is a good benchmark'. Indeed, in China the working age population is actually shrinking due to the one-child policy introduced in the 1970s. As a matter of fact, the realisation that a slowdown in population growth poses a severe risk for a country has led to a variety of nations to implement measures that boost their fertility rate. For instance, Singapore already launched a campaign in this respect with the slogan 'Have three, or more if you can afford it' (Hopper 2015). China only acknowledged the problems caused by the one-child policy around 2013 with the announcement of the ending of the measure in 2015. Indeed, this policy contributed significantly to China's aging problem as well as to its skewed gender balance (Sharma 2016: 35). However, it also has to be noted that the population control measures initially led to a growth spurt in East and Southeast Asia, generally known as a demographic dividend (Mason 2005). Sharma (2016: 39) notes on the benefits of a growing population that 'in recent years countries with faster-growing populations have also tended to exhibit faster productivity growth. As the dependency ratio declines, with more people entering the workforce and earning an independent living, a country's income increases, and that creates a greater pool of capital, which can be used to invest in ways that further raise productivity'. A growing population helps to avoid the social burden of aging and leads to a more dynamic and a more highly productive society. This is very much linked to the talent pool a nation has available to foster its progress.

China's deceleration in population growth has contributed significantly to the global slowdown in demographics. As a result of the birth control measures introduced in the 1970s, China is facing a drag due to population aging as well as due to the resulting social burden to the society. To start with, two terms have to be distinguished – the birth rate as well as the total fertility rate. The former refers to the number of births in percentage points of the total population and the latter relates to the number of children a woman will have during her life. In China, the end of the war period and the take-over of the Communist party led to a significant decline in deaths as well as to improvements with respect to sanitation and food supply among others. In general, two factors constrain birth rates as a country develops. First, as infant survival rates increase with the stage of development, fewer births are required to reach the wished-for family size. Second, social changes such as more accessible education and higher educational standards tend to lead to smaller families (Naughton 2007: 161-163). Thus, the stage of a country's development is linked to birth and total fertility rates.

With respect to China's trajectory, birth rates were relatively high from the early 1950s to the introduction of population control measures in the 1970s. The peak in the rate occurred in 1963. As a matter of fact, 'consistently high birth rates combined with steadily declining death rates meant that the population was growing extremely rapidly' (Naughton 2007: 166). In contrast to these decades of increased population growth, the 1970s depicted a sharp decline in these growth rates, mainly due to population growth measures as is described below. The Great Leap Forward (GLF) had many Chinese officials convinced that the country should establish family-planning policies. The first phase of this planning system lasted from 1971 to 1978 and the measure was coined as the "Later, Longer, Fewer" policy. The policy can be regarded as a success for the Chinese planners as the total fertility rate was cut from 5.8 percent in 1970 to 2.7 percent in 1978. At the end of the 1970s, China introduced the one-child policy, which was controversial from the start. The policy was formally adopted in September 1980 and the initial implementation was very strict, which led to a high level of resentment in the Chinese population. Indeed, the policy had to be relaxed in 1984, but, still, the top-down pressure to implement the one-child policy was enormous (Naughton 2007: 167-169). Critics of the policy argue that the measure was neither appropriate in scope nor necessary at all. Indeed, Bongaarts and Greenhalgh (1985) note that more moderate measures would have been more effective regarding the aim of population control.

The decrease in the dependency ratio since the 1970s spurred output in China. The dependency ratio dropped significantly over the last decades while the ratio with respect to seniors has yet to pick-up. The latter poses a future vulnerability to China given an increased social burden as well as the general disadvantage of an old population. During the initial years, China profited from the demographic dividend (Mason and Kinugasa 2005). The relative growth advantage of the working age population to the population as a whole leads to a declining dependency ratio, which goes in hand with improvements in material living standards. This allowed the Chinese population to save and invest more. 'China's extremely high domestic saving and investment rates in recent years [...] can be plausibly linked to the low dependency ratio' (Naughton 2007: 174). In more recent times, these measures created strains for the social system. Naughton (2007: 175) commented on this as follows, 'an aging population will create substantial strains on China's social system. Particularly after 2015, rapid aging will require an effective response as the age structure of the country will place greater burdens on those currently employed'.

Thus, demographic patterns drastically shape the global environment. In this respect, various trends are identified by the NIC report (2012: iv), namely aging, a shrinking number of youthful countries and growing urbanisation among others. Regarding the latter, about 50 percent of the world population lives currently in urban areas. The report estimates that this number will increase to about 60 percent by 2030. This stands in sharp contrast to the share of the population that lived in cities in 1950, which is about 30 percent. Currently, nearly 50 percent of all urban dwellers live in Asia. In fact, about 80 percent of economic growth is created in cities globally as cities are hubs of productivity. Indeed, urbanisation drives various positive developments for these nations, namely, for instance, better education and smaller families, which boosts Asia's competitiveness (NIC 2012: 26-29). The question of population growth and urbanisation is inevitably linked to the Lewis Turning Point. Das and N'Diaye (2013) analyse the topic with respect to China. The researchers put forward that China will reach the Lewis Turning Point between 2020 and 2025 with demographics being the driver of the depletion in surplus labour. This is related to the question whether the era of cheap labour in China and whether the urbanisation trend witnessed since the reform period started at the end of the 1970s is coming to an end. 'For China, this would mean that the current extensive growth model that relies so heavily on factor input accumulation could not be sustained and that China would need to invest less, but in better, capital. It would imply switching to a more 'intensive' growth model with a greater reliance on improving total factor productivity (TFP)' (Das and N'Diaye 2013: 3). The topic first came up in 2004 as labour shortages in China's coastal regions, which focus on export-orientation, were reported. Nonetheless, government policies could lead to an improvement of the picture. For instance, the hukou reform could lead to more rural workers moving to the city and thus postponing the Lewis Turning Point (Das and N'Diaye 2013: 7). These topics are analysed in detail in the case study on China's troubles in 2015 and 2016.

iii) Poverty Reduction, Inequality and Stability

The present level of inequality is intolerable or unsustainable according to Atkinson (2015: 9), which does not mean that a certain difference in rewards is not justifiable. In general, the author distinguishes between inequality of opportunity and inequality of outcome. The former refers to when circumstances such as family background do not contribute significantly to determining the winner of the race, while the latter is related to the actual outcome. 'Inequality of opportunity is essentially an ex ante concept – everyone should have an equal starting point – whereas much redistributional activity is concerned with the ex post outcomes' (Atkinson 2015: 10). Why does inequality of outcome matter when a level playing field via equality of opportunity is created? There are various reasons for this. First, those for whom the outcome is related to hardship cannot be simply ignored. Second, the unequal distribution of prizes matters even if the race is a fair one. Third, inequality of outcome today leads to inequality of opportunity tomorrow, i.e. for the next generation. What are the effects of an increased level of inequality? Research by Stiglitz (2012) associates a high level of inequality with a lack of social cohesion, high levels of crime or ill-health. Furthermore, Christine Lagarde noted on the subject in her speech at an annual meeting of supranational organisations in 2012 that 'recent IMF research tells us that less inequality is associated with greater macroeconomic stability and more sustainable growth' (Lagarde 2012 quoted in Atkinson 2015: 12). A proposal by former Labour Chancellor of the Exchequer, Hugh Dalton, illustrated his thoughts on inequality with the notion of transferring GBP 1 from a rich to a poor person and by doing this reducing inequality as well as raising the overall level of utility for the society. The economist, Arthur Okun, asked the question, "What if part of the sum got lost during the transfer?". Nonetheless, the thought experiment gives a powerful picture on the topic of addressing inequality (Atkinson 2015: 12-13). Indeed, inequality has become an issue again as 'the share of the top 1 per cent has returned to its value of 100 years ago' (Atkinson 2015: 19). In addition, globally, poverty fell until the late 1960s and since then hardly any improvements, except for China, were made.

As mentioned above, there exists a distinction between inequality and inequality of opportunity. While the former is related more to outcomes as people are differing, for instance, in income or health services they consume. The latter notion is connected to the initial conditions people are finding themselves in, which refers to job opportunities or education and training for example (Spence 2008: 61). In general, what can be said about capitalism is that markets do not lead to equality. With respect to the management of an economy, free markets have long been considered as the most efficient approach (Smith 1776). This was the prevailing view, particularly in the 1970s; only a minor role for the government is foreseen in said approach. However, the flaws of this became very much visible during the financial crises over the last decades (Hardoon et al. 2016; Stiglitz 2008) as well as in the rise of inequality to extreme levels today.

The aforementioned is per se not a good feature of markets. Inequality was compared by Albert Hirschman (1981) to a two-lane traffic jam. 'If one lane begins to move, drivers in the other at first take comfort, inferring that their lane will also move soon. But the longer they remain stuck, the more frustrated they will become. The other lane becomes a provocation, not a consolation' (Albert Hirschman 1981 quoted in Spence 2008: 61). In fact, tax programmes and government spending programmes can mitigate the latter, which is vital for social cohesion and therefore, for a country's sustainable growth path. With respect to inequality of opportunity, the situation is more dangerous. The systematic denial of opportunities to certain groups related to religion, ethnic origin or gender can indeed be toxic for a society. Social disorder and political change are often entailed by a high degree of inequality of opportunity (Spence 2008: 62). Equality is one variable of the policy-induced dimension that is interlinked with fundamental and institutional factors. Robert Solow (2008) put the issue as follows, 'in many ways, the more equitable the growth the more sustainable it's likely to be, because there will be less controversy, less disagreement, less resistance, and also there's an enormous amount of talent in populations that needs to be tapped. Excluding some parts of the population, whether by gender, age, or ethnicity, from the benefits of growth loses the talents that they have. So, in my view, it is not only desirable that they go together, it's useful that they go together' (Robert Solow quoted in Spence 2008: 62). How can equality of opportunity be improved? Access to public services as well as education and training should be provided by the government as well as supported by the private sector. In addition, the infrastructure of the capitalist system must be improved, for instance by securing property rights of the poor as brought forward by Hernando de Soto (1993). Moreover, financing for small enterprises should be improved to tackle the issues shown by Banerjee et al. (2015). Indeed, Carin Jämtin (quoted in Spence 2008: 63) notes on the topic, that 'there is no contradiction between equality, redistribution and growth. Quite the contrary. Prosperity that is shared is not only morally right, it also gives people a chance to lift themselves out of poverty, creates legitimacy for responsible economic policies and can have an enhancing effect on long-term growth and prosperity'.

Another point which is closely connected to inequality is globalisation, which started with the fall of the Berlin Wall and was interrupted by the global financial crisis. Many people accuse the current high level of inequality to this era of internationalisation. This was examined in detail by Milanovic (2016). The researcher showed that foremost the Asian economies, predominantly China, were the main beneficiaries of globalisation during said period. Measured in relative terms, the people in the middle of the income distribution benefited most from this trend. 'The two median deciles (fifth and sixth) in urban China and rural China had their real per capita income multiplied by 3 and about 2.2, respectively, between 1988 and 2008' (Milanovic 2016: 19). This trend coined the term "emerging global middle class"; however, these people are still relatively poor in comparison to Western standards. Measured in absolute terms, the highest incremental change was made by the top 1 percent, which dominates today's discussion on inequality. Even though the distribution of absolute gains is skewed, the relative emergence of the middle-income layer of the Asian nations is a fact (Milanovic 2016). Nonetheless, the absolute level of global inequality challenges leaders around the world as laid out above and below.

As Hardoon et al. (2016) note 'growing economic inequality is bad for us all – it undermines growth and social cohesion. Yet the consequences for the world's poorest people are particularly severe'. In the report it is put forward that inequality is closely related to the higher returns of capital than to labour. This has been identified as market fundamentalism and indeed is connected to the high level of inequality visible today. An OECD (2012) report related an oversized financial sector to higher instability – thus, financial crisis – as well as to inequality, which threatens social cohesion as well as endangers economic performance. In addition, the responses to the global financial crisis contributed to the widening gap between the rich and the poor as well as to inequality related to different groups in a country, such as the urban-rural divide in China. Even the IMF admitted that inequality not only has dire consequences for the poorest people but also for the health of an economy and thus for the risk of crisis (Dabla-Norris et al. 2015), which is examined with respect to China in the case study.

b) Monetary Policy

As shown by Krugman et al. (2015), exchange rates depend on two components, namely on interest rates yielded by deposits of the currency pairs as well as on expected changes in the future exchange rate. To better understand exchange rate crises, it has to be understood how interest rates and expectations are determined which leads us to the topic of monetary policy. First, the effect of local money supply on aggregate output and other macroeconomic variables as well as of the demand for a country's money on local interest rates and the FX has to be examined. 'Because exchange rates are the relative prices of national monies, factors that affect a country's money supply or demand are among the most powerful determinants of its currency's exchange rate against foreign currencies' (Krugman et al. 2015: 411). Indeed, developments on the monetary side of a country have influence on both interest rates as well as expectations and thus, influence exchange rates via both channels. Nonetheless, expectations of the exchange rate also depend on many other factors than money, which is examined in detail in this book.

In this section of the analytical framework, I describe local money markets and how interest rates are determined, how this feeds into foreign exchange rates and I point to the necessity to distinguish between the short and the long run. To start with, the purpose of money and what counts for money supply have to be defined. Money serves as a medium of exchange, as a unit of account and as a store of value. The latter is related to the transfer of purchasing power from one period to the next. The benefit of money in comparison to other assets is that it is liquid, which means that it can be transformed into other goods and services without the occurrence of relative high transaction costs. Money supply is often referred to as M1, which is the sum of currency and checking deposits held by households and companies. A broader measure of money would be M2, which includes time deposits in addition to the determinants of M1. A country's money supply is controlled by its central bank (DeRosa 2009: 18-19; Feenstra and Taylor 2014: 691-694; Krugman et al. 2015: 412-413). For China, the definition of money supply diverges slightly from the conventional way of defining M1 and M2, which is examined in detail in the case study. What determines the demand for money by individuals or, more generally, for an asset? This is related to three components, namely the expected return, the riskiness of an asset as well as its liquidity. The interest rate is often related to the yield on government bonds and it can be said that the higher the yield the lower is the demand for holding money as the yield can be seen as an opportunity cost. However, if the increase in the yield of an asset is related to its riskiness, the demand for money must not necessarily be influenced by this. Furthermore, when the liquidity of assets shrinks than the demand for money generally rises. In addition to the above, the aggregate demand for money is determined by the interest rate, the price level as well as by the real national income. Rising price levels mean that households and companies need more money to purchase goods and services and thus, have to hold a higher money supply. The same view is held with regard to rising real national income (Krugman et al. 2015: 414-416). How does the money supply influence interest rates? Higher money supply leads to lower interest rates and vice versa. Again, this also holds for the real output as higher growth raises interest rates. Now, we determine the effect on the exchange rate and have to distinguish between the short and the long run. In the former case, an increase in a country's money supply leads to a depreciation of the local exchange rate and vice versa. In the latter case, higher money supply leads to an increase in a country's price level (Feenstra and Taylor 2014: 691-694). Generally, 'an economy's long-run equilibrium is the position it would eventually reach if no new economic shocks occurred during the adjustment to full employment. You can think of long-run equilibrium as the equilibrium that would be maintained after all wages and prices had had enough time to adjust to their market-clearing levels' (Krugman et al. 2015: 426). In contrast to the short-run, a change in money supply does not alter interest rates or output in the long-run; only the price level changes. In case of a permanent higher money supply, a proportional long-run decrease in a country's exchange rate occurs (Krugman et al. 2015: 429). One crucial point has to be mentioned with respect to the aforementioned, namely that prices are rigid in the short-run and flexible in the long-run. This is due to the fact that many prices are incorporated in long-run contracts and thus cannot be changed immediately. One example of this would be wages of workers. Even though there is short-run price stagnation, an increase in money supply creates immediate pressure that ultimately leads to the future increase in the price level. This pressure gets translated into the foreign exchange market, which leads to the phenomenon of exchange rate overshooting and is closely connected to FX crises (Dornbusch et al. 1995; Eichengreen et al. 1994, 1995; Krugman et al. 2015: 430-435). With respect to the above, it has to be mentioned that developed countries mainly target interest rates directly instead of the money supply. This is not yet the case for many developing countries.

The main monetary authority of a country is its central bank as it conducts monetary policy and creates money via currency and reserve deposits of commercial banks. As mentioned above, the monetary base of a country is its currency plus reserve deposits, which is also referred to as high-powered money. This leads us to broad-based aggregates such as M2, which is generally defined as 'the sum of currency in hands of the public, demand deposits, and savings account deposits' (DeRosa 2009: 18-19). Among the main goals of central banking is the containment of excessive inflation, which is mainly done with the help of targeting money supply in emerging markets. An additional means to controlling the level of inflation can be the establishment of a fixed exchange rate regime. To direct monetary policy, central banks have various tools at hand, foremost the variation of reserve requirements, open market operations, repurchase agreements, foreign exchange interventions and sterilisation among others. Reserve requirements refer to the regulation of the money multipliers and refer to the link between the level of the base money and monetary aggregates (DeRosa 2009: 20-21). Open market transactions are related to the purchase and sale of domestic assets which entail alterations in the monetary base. Repurchase agreements, which are generally known as repos and reverse repo agreements, are additional means to regulate the monetary base. FX interventions by the central bank are carried out via buying or selling hard currency in order to alter the level of the local exchange rate. This is related to sterilisation, which is performed by a central bank as a consequence of FX interventions in order to keep the monetary base approximately constant. There are four monetary policy channels, namely the interest rate channel, the domestic asset price channel, the exchange rate channel as well as the credit channel. These are described in detail by Kamin et al. (1998). Mostly, monetary policy aims at the interest rate channel. However, emerging markets usually have a monetary regime in transition. One primary sign, that an emerging market is migrating from managing the quantity of money to the targeting of short-term interest rates, is the increased use of repo or reverse repo transactions (DeRosa 2009: 22-27). Substantial literature exists on the limitations of targeting the money supply in circulation.

In general, the limitations of monetary policy are severe in emerging markets, which is mostly related to the weaknesses of the local financial system. This is examined in detail in the institutional section. Further aggravating factors are the lack of independence of the central bank as well as a historic bad track record with respect to managing price stability. Monetary policy management still has a long way to go in emerging markets (DeRosa 2009: 32), particularly in China. One important factor with respect to the transmission of monetary policy to prices in China is price reform. Even though the reform era brought various changes with respect to this, the Chinese state continued to influence monetary policy as well as price setting with respect to a number of strategic goods and services. Foremost, factor prices such as capital, fuels and electricity as well as water and land face a distorted pricing scheme (Lardy 2002, He and Kujis 2007). These factors, for which the Chinese government continues to be involved in the price setting mechanism, were and still partially are underpriced, which helped foremost to foster the manufacturing sector and contributed to China's tremendous economic rise over the previous decades. Not only cheap capital, but also fuel and electricity, contributed significantly to the high competitiveness of the Chinese exports at the cost of a distorted chain of production (Bergsten et al. 2008; Lardy 2012: 106). Changes in the exchange rate 'and appropriate pricing of factor inputs are highly complementary since they both would raise the cost of producing tradable goods relative to non-tradables, thus leading to a reduction in China's global surplus and a restructuring of its GDP' (Lardy 2012: 112). These distortions were partially removed with China's goal of rebalancing the economy.

In this respect, one crucial topic in emerging markets, which is closely related to monetary policy, is financial repression. Indeed, in some countries an interest rate ceiling for loanable funds hinders the adjustment of local rates to a normal level. The distorting impact of fixing the ceiling below the market-clearing level can be severe. As shown in the historical background section, however, this was one of the main development strategies of China. Instead of relying on private sector investment decisions, the country mainly accrued government savings and thus, investment decisions were centrally made. One important point with respect to this is the control of corruption in the banking sector. Commercial banks mainly allocated available credit to large enterprises, resulting in severe distortions of the system. This topic is analysed with respect to state-owned enterprises in the institutional section as well as in the case study (Todaro 2000: 666-667). As mentioned above, monetary policy has severe limitations in emerging markets. In general, the level of interest rates in developed countries is associated with investment decisions. This does not hold for many emerging markets as other factors than the level of local interest rates significantly influence the investment decisions as well. In history, many emerging markets pursued expansionary monetary policy regardless of the stage of the cycle. The idea behind this policy was that negative real interest rates should encourage investments. However, this usually backfired and resulted in inflation rather than in the desired growth spurt. Hence, the political influence of the central government must not be underestimated (Todaro 2000: 659-661). The topics of financial repression and interest rate liberalisation are dealt with in detail in the institutional section. These are crucial determinants of a country's exchange rate.

Furthermore, Pesenti and Tille (2000) examine exchange rate crises and the theoretical models that explain these events. Many models associate these bouts of volatility with unsustainable economic policy, i.e. in the case of the Asian financial crisis as laid out in the section 'Crises in Perspective'. 'A more comprehensive view of the turmoil in Asia takes into account the interaction of policy and volatile capital markets. Weak policy makes a country vulnerable to abrupt shifts in investor confidence; the sudden rise of investor expectations of a crisis can force a policy response that validates the original expectations' (Pesenti and Tille 2000: 3). The currency crisis in Asia in the 1990s had particularly dire effects on the affected economies. In this respect, one example of the workings of the so-called first-generation models, which will be examined at a later stage, is given as follows: In case of expansionary monetary policy combined with a fixed exchange rate regime, a country has to deplete its FX reserves in order to balance the foreign exchange market. In the long run, this scenario leads to a weaker local exchange rate, even though in the short-run any depreciation can be stopped via the sale of FX reserves. Market participants observe the expansionary monetary policy and assume the unsustainability of this together with a fixed exchange rate regime will trigger a speculative attack on the local exchange rate, which is related to the second-generation models. 'The interaction between expectations and actual outcomes is at the core of the second-generation models of crises, in which market expectations directly influence macroeconomic policy' (Pesenti and Tille 2000: 5). One way to see a currency crisis is as a shift in expectations towards a faster depreciation or devaluation of the local exchange rate. In this respect, two forms of volatility have to be distinguished, namely one associated with financial markets and the other with macroeconomic variables. In case of an FX crisis, the former tends to exceed the latter. Market sentiment related to sudden changes in expectations, as also pointed out in the institutional section, play a significant role in the determination of an FX crisis.

c) Fiscal Policy and the Debt Binge

The dissolution of financial repression leads to the increased importance of fiscal policy, which relates to government taxation as well as managing expenditure. The crucial connection between the two types of policies, as described above, is the abolishment of the interest rate ceiling. In a system of financial repression revenues accrue automatically to state-owned enterprises, which in itself do not have a profitability goal, but instead form the base for government expenditure in a repressive system. In case of the dissolution of financial repression via the abolishment of interest rate ceilings, the government has to build a tax base in order to avoid a fiscal crisis. In the past, this was not always possible as I show in the historical background section. The gradual dissolution of financial repression in China helped to avoid a severe output loss as could be observed in many other transition countries. Still, the country faced repeatedly severe fiscal strains over the last decades. This highlights the importance of building a substantial tax base which helps to mitigate the negative effects of changes in policy. At the same time China tries to rebalance its economy, which partially means to empower individual households via fiscal policy (Lardy 2012). Nevertheless, in developing countries a broad-based tax system is difficult to establish, because it makes no sense to levy taxes from the poor. One means of introducing taxation, by avoiding aggravating the situation for the poor, is to levy property taxes (The Economist 2017b). Another problem with building an efficient tax system in emerging markets is the enforcement, which tends to be very expensive. This is related to the administrative capabilities, which can be a strength as well as a weakness of a country. As shown in the historical background section, the Chinese Communist Party made efficient use of the national planning capabilities built up by the Nationalist Party. Furthermore, after the death of Mao Zedong in 1976 the reformists did not try to change the system from one day to the next, as was done by other transition economies, which famously became known as the big bang approach (Todaro 2000: 674-676). Instead, the Chinese leadership under Deng Xiaoping decided for a gradual shift in policies, which helped to avoid the collapse in output experienced by other transition economies. This is described in detail in the historical background section.

As indicated, the topic of state-owned enterprises is crucial in this respect. SOEs are public corporations owned by the government. Thus, any profit that accrues to SOEs is government income (Lardy 2012). Particularly, strategic sectors such as natural resources and defence are in the interest of the leadership of emerging markets. These enterprises have come under increased scrutiny for inefficient resource usage.

Many emerging markets have historically relied on privatisation to raise revenues as well as to address this problem (Todaro 2000: 680). However, this partially failed as laid out in the section on transition economies. Instead of leading to an improved resource allocation the privatisation simply helped to enrich a few at the cost of many. Particularly, the failed privatisations of state-owned enterprises in Central and Eastern Europe as well as in the former Soviet Union should lead us to question this. In contrast to these failures, the Chinese approach to transition from plan to market has not yet received sufficient attention. Instead of relying on destruction, "growing out of the plan" (Naughton 1996) was the main policy pursued by the Chinese leadership in the first decades of the reform era.

With respect to raising revenues, a progressive taxation system does not exist yet in many emerging markets. Apart from simple tax avoidance by the beneficiaries of the privatisations, no coherent tax system exists yet which would alter the situation in the foreseeable future. Unfortunately, in most emerging countries the reform era must be classified as a period with losers (Naughton 2007). As is addressed in a subsequent section, emerging market institutions were not able to deal with the change from plan to market effectively and thus, the repercussions for the local population caused by these policies were severe. In addition, these changes often led to a build-up in debt in emerging markets (The Economist 2017a). In many communist countries it was quite unusual to rely on debt as a source of financing growth. It was only over time as benefits of economic activity started to accrue to the private sector, the state indebtedness became a problem (Todaro 2000). None of the emerging markets, which relied on consumption as a driver of growth, were able to catch up with developed nations. As a matter of fact, these countries were enticed to import products from advanced economies leading to debt binges historically resulted in financial crises. This is described in detail in the historical background section and becomes particularly critical in the case study on China. As a matter of fact, the global crises of the 1980s are examples of the failure of consumption driven development.

Zhou Xiaochuan, the former head of the Chinese Central Bank, noted that the massive debt binge is 'the root of weakness in China's macro financial system' (The Economist 2017b). While the build-up of debt per se is a fundamental vulnerability of China, the causes of this can be partially attributed to bad policy, particularly in relation to fiscal policy. In this regard, the dysfunctional connection between central and provincial government plays a crucial role, which resulted in an unprecedented build-up in debt. While the central government tried to resolve the issue by changing the law, the problem remains virtually unresolved. Under the Chinese fiscal law, local governments have very little power to raise revenues themselves. Furthermore, until 2014 the issuance of debt or outright borrowing from banks was forbidden at all and thus local governments strictly were dependent on their share of the taxes: '50% of value-added tax, for example, and 40% of personal income tax' (The Economist 2017b). However, this is not sufficient to cover the spending of the Chinese provinces and consequently local governments are also dependent on transfer payments from Beijing, which gives the central government a greater say in local matters. It goes without saying that local governments try to avoid this and thus, investment companies, which are under control of local authorities and generally known as local government financing vehicles (LGFVs), were founded in the 1990s to raise funds. These vehicles were largely unregulated and counted mostly as state-owned enterprises, which facilitated the borrowing for these. In comparison to other forms of debt, local government debt is still rather limited in amount as laid out in the section on fundamentals of this book. However, most borrowing via these vehicles was done off-budget and remains unreported. In 2014, Beijing restricted this kind of money raising and requested that these vehicles get refinanced via local bond issuances. No LGFVs debt other than bonds should exist anymore, which substantially would increase the transparency of the issue. In addition, the central government imposed borrowing ceilings on the provinces, which should help address the debt problem. However, in July 2017, the Chinese President, Xi Jinping, admitted that the solutions to the problem are flawed. 'Local-government debt was still one of the two biggest threats to China's financial stability (the other was debt built up by state-owned enterprises). The problem was that local governments were still using every trick in the book to disguise their shenanigans' (The Economist 2017b). One solution to the problem would be to clearly distinguish between the tax-raising powers of the central government and of local provinces. Furthermore, a property tax proposal from 2013 would help to mitigate the dire funding situation for local governments. However, the trust deficit between the different Chinese entities is severe, which clearly hampers any progress. Indeed, local governments have only very limited tax-raising powers themselves (The Economist 2017a), which is at the root of the disharmony between Beijing and local authorities. Apart from the introduction of a property tax, the central government has to make clear who is responsible for what spending. Indeed, the reforms of 2014 requires all authorities to publish their budgets, which brings some light to the difficult situation.

With respect to rebalancing the economy, Lardy (2012) suggests various options, namely higher government outlays for health, education and pensions as well as raising dividends paid by state-owned enterprises to the government among others. Regarding the latter, increasing corporate taxes via higher dividends payable to the state would reduce the corporate savings rate and enable the Chinese government to use the funds for urgently needed social programmes. As mentioned above, in the early years of the reform period, the Chinese government and SOEs took over most health care costs, not individuals. Over time the contribution from households had to be raised due to the restructuring of the state-owned enterprise sector and the subsequent shortfall in revenues for the Chinese government. Households contributed about one third of the total health care costs by the early 1990s. 'After the aggressive restructuring, downsizing, and bankruptcy of many state-owned corporations in the mid-1990s, the personal share of health care outlays grew rapidly' (Lardy 2012: 69). In this respect, higher outlays for health and pensions would reduce the household savings rate significantly and thus help the Chinese economy to rebalance (Barnett and Brooks 2011). Regarding the government's goal of reducing the imbalances in the economy, various tax and expenditure policies were implemented to support the Chinese households. For instance, the agricultural tax was abolished in 2007. Furthermore, taxes on interest rate income on savings deposits were severely cut for households and as a matter of fact, totally eliminated in 2008. With these measures the Chinese government raised household disposable income by about 1 percent of GDP per year (Bergsten et al. 2008: 121). However, it has to be mentioned that the scope for reducing direct taxes such as the agricultural tax as well as personal income taxes is rather limited. 'China's Ministry of Finance (MOF) relies very heavily on indirect taxes, such as the value-added tax, rather than direct taxes, to finance government expenditures' (Lardy 2012; 70).

While tax policy has been on the weaker side, as described above, government expenditure initiatives have been more successful. On the one hand, the Chinese government is contributing to the build-up of a social safety net in urban areas, which had suffered due to the restructuring of the economy, particularly since the start of the second reform phase in the early 1990s as laid out in the historical background section. On the other hand, the Chinese government is trying to provide social services to those layers of the population, who had received close to nothing in the past. In rural areas, the cooperative medical insurance scheme is the most notable innovation. The scheme kicked off in 2003 and is a voluntary health insurance programme funded by contributions from various stakeholders. Health care costs are partially reimbursed by this scheme (World Bank 2008: 89). Outlays for this programme from the side of the central government increased steadily since its initiation and more rapidly since the mid-2000s. In addition, the Chinese government aims at building a pension system. A pilot programme was launched in 2008 with participation being voluntary. The funding for this programme also comes from various stakeholders, among others from the Chinese state. When the retirement age is reached, the scheme allows for monthly contributions to individuals, which is a fraction of the accumulated funds, plus a contribution from the government. Further to the aforementioned social schemes, the Chinese government eliminated tuition for millions of Chinese students in rural areas in 2006 and 2007. In urban areas, the restructuring of the SOE sector left many workers without any social safety net. To address this issue, the Chinese government launched a basic health insurance programme for individuals in 2007 (Lardy 2012: 73-76). The goal of all these reforms is to provide Chinese citizens with adequate social security, which should be partially funded by the state in order to decrease the household savings rate and facilitate the rebalancing of the Chinese economy.

d) Soft Factors

For the soft factors used in this book, no quantification is deducted. Nonetheless, these variables, namely legitimacy and status as well as ideational factors, are assessed with the help of the examination of over five hundred research reports. In the case study, the reports serve to reconstruct in great detail the events that took place in China in 2015 and 2016. A qualitative assessment is of equal importance to a quantitative analysis.

i) Legitimacy and Status

The Chinese people hold a strong belief that the future will be better than today is (Jianmin 2015). This belief entails the question what will happen if the Chinese people get disillusioned and lose trust in their leadership? As a matter of fact, financial crises not only entail severe economic losses but also lead to political turmoil, which often entails a change in leadership. For instance, Frankel (2005: 6) names the example of Indonesia in 1997 to illustrate the high political costs of a currency crisis: 'How is it that a strong ruler like Indonesia's Suharto can easily weather 32 years of political, military, ethnic, and environmental challenges, only to succumb to a currency crisis?'. The political costs entailed by a financial crisis are mainly due to the economic costs incurred by the country in question. The leadership's legitimacy in developing countries is often linked to the economic success of a nation. A crisis can severely harm the beliefs of the local population and thus, a change in leadership is often demanded. After the leadership's legitimacy has become tarnished, political change often becomes inevitable (Feenstra and Taylor 2014: 761). This is why many policymakers in emerging markets have a strong emphasis on upholding their legitimacy via the generation of economic growth.

In this regard, another important factor is status; this is closely related to other concepts such as 'prestige, esteem, honor, standing, rank, and face' (Wohlforth and Kang 2009: 3). As a matter of fact, even though material rewards would point in a different direction, status by itself is a means and can lead to an outcome that would not maximize the actor's wealth. For instance, a country's status entails value for the leadership, not only on an absolute basis, but also relative to others. Thus, status in itself is a crucial driver for actors or as Wohlforth and Kang (2009: 13) put it, it is 'an underlying, unobservable force that generates observable causal effects'. Hence, status entails significant value-added for actors. What determines a country's status? According to Hurrell (2009: 5), a country's status can be mainly attributed to its legal as well as its political standing. In addition, certain associations with international organisations or other groups can entail significant status for a country. Particularly, recognition by formal bodies such as the United Nations or the OECD plays a key role for developing countries (Wohlforth and Kang 2009: 16). The idea of leaving past stigmas behind and being recognised by or joining the international community can certainly spur countries into actions.

Furthermore, Robert Gilpin (1983) analyses prestige in light of the perceived humiliation developing countries experienced in the past. This plays a particularly important role in terms of China's policy-making as shown in the historical background section and in the case study. The decades of humiliation after the opium war led to the inward orientation of the country after the civil war. It was only at the beginning of the 1970s as China relaxed the relations with foreign powers and the gradual opening of the country under Deng Xiaoping further improved the latter. This is laid out in detail in the historical background section. Recognition by international bodies helps these countries to escape the stigmas of their past and gain a more prestigious standing in the global environment (Hurrell 2014: 88). Ultimately, this is related to the inclusiveness of the international institutional set-up. Only gradually the international community accepted particularities of certain countries and thus, could attract rather than repel these nations. The international institutional set-up is addressed in the institutional section of this book.

To conclude, the search for legitimacy and status can lead to policy-induced uncertainty and thus, forms a vital dimension of the theoretical framework. It is crucial for countries to balance their demand for these soft factors with local stability in economic and social terms. This framework should serve towards better decision making in this regard. In the case study, I show that the demand for status in relation to the SDR inclusion of the Chinese renminbi led to significant policy-induced vulnerability. This is qualitatively assessed with the examination of over five hundred research reports. It is argued that soft factors had a considerable influence on the currency debasement of the Chinese yuan, which took place in August 2015, together with the revision and the subsequent alterations in the exchange rate regime as well as the entailed capital flow volatility. I demonstrate that soft factors represent one determinant of the policy-induced dimension that helps to understand said events to a higher degree.

ii) Ideational Factors

'Over the long term, particularly when policy-makers confront conditions of uncertainty, where the previous orthodoxy has been delegitimized by financial crisis, agents' conceptions of their long-term interests are determined by theories concerning exchange rate management, and shared causal beliefs about theories in particular' (Wright 2009: 26-27). This situation is particularly valid for China in 2015. The stock market crash that preceded the change in the FX regime in August 2015 had delegitimised the prior system and thus, the Chinese leadership had been strongly influenced by ideational factors regarding exchange rate flexibility. This has to be seen in light of the potential SDR inclusion of the Chinese RMB at that point in time. In particular, prior comments by the IMF regarding the lack of exchange rate flexibility played a crucial role in this respect. In addition, in the thesis of Wright (2009), lessons were drawn from the Asian financial crisis of the 1990s. Prior financial crises play a vital role in formulating today's policy choices (Minkin and Lau 2013). This also holds true for the change in the FX regime in August 2015. In particular, currency and maturity mismatches of debt were addressed by China prior to the devaluation of the RMB.

This can be regarded as one lesson drawn from historic crisis episodes. In addition, ideas regarding a more flexible exchange rate that would address the macroeconomic slowdown and the misvaluation of the RMB were other factors playing a crucial role in the decision to alter the exchange rate regime. However, a more flexible exchange rate system is not the same as a more efficient one, as can be seen in the subsequent months after the devaluation. Frequent changes in the fixing mechanisms are symptoms of this misguided belief. A more holistic picture has to be drawn in order to understand this, which I try to do with the expanded conceptual framework consisting of fundamental, policy-induced, and institutional vulnerabilities. Ideational factors are one variable of the analytical framework, which help to explain the dependent variable of this book.

Two conditions are often ignored by comparative statistics, namely 'the type of uncertainty faced by agents and the set of ideas available to them' (Blyth 2002: 8). Situations of crisis are characterised by Knightian uncertainty. These are 'situations regarded by contemporary agents as unique events where the agents are unsure as to what their interests actually are, let alone how to realize them' (Blyth 2002: 9). Static models tend to eliminate Knightian uncertainty through the means of institutions. However, in the presence of uncertainty, two conditions change. First, agents' interests need to be explained rather than used as an independent variable. Second, the definition of crisis becomes crucial to the analysis of the situation. 'Crises need to be narrated and explained' as they are not self-apparent phenomena (Blyth 2002: 9). The destabilisation of institutions may result in uncertainty, which in return leads to currency collapses or rising prices. However, both the causes of and the solutions to such uncertainty cannot be simply identified by examining the collapse itself. 'Crises thus becomes an act of intervention where sources of uncertainty are diagnosed and constructed. Given this, the set of available ideas with which to interpret the environment, reduce uncertainty, and make purposeful collective action possible becomes crucially important in determining the form of new institutions' (Blyth 2002: 10). The identification of a situation as a crisis by a particular set of ideas makes the perceived uncertainty explicable, manageable, as well as actionable. 'Therefore, in periods of economic crisis, it is imperative to attend to the economic ideas that key economic agents have' (Blyth 2002: 10). The same holds for financial crisis, in particular, for exchange rate crisis. Static accounts generally tend to neglect the crucial role of uncertainty and ideational factors in determining the trajectory of institutional change. Ideas serve as an interpretive framework by defining interrelations describing the workings of an economy. Thus, ideas can specify how elements in an economy should be constructed and can, therefore, serve as blueprints for institutional change. 'Such an analysis of institutional change suggests that the reduction of uncertainty, the specification of causes, and the actual supply of new institutions are parts of a temporally distinct sequence of events where ideas have different effects at different junctures' (Blyth 2002: 11). In this book, a crisis is defined as an underlying vulnerability in combination with a specific crisis trigger (Ghosh and Ghosh 2003; Ghosh et al. 2008; Chamon et al. 2012) with the triggering event being endogenous to the underlying vulnerability (Chamon et al. 2012: 3). This shows that the key to predicting, as well as preventing crises, is to address underlying vulnerabilities. Ideational factors are one variable of the analytical framework, as mentioned above.

Chwieroth (2007) analyses the role of ideas in the spread of liberalising policies in his paper, 'Neoliberal Economists and Capital Account Liberalization in Emerging Markets'. Evidence from past crisis episodes in Chile, as well as in Malaysia, show that capital controls can be an effective means with respect to containing volatility. Nonetheless, some countries decide to liberalise their economies in order to be able to pursue an independent monetary policy. The fact that policymakers mediate is often overlooked. In addition, these decisions are surrounded by significant uncertainty. 'For instance, domestic financial intermediaries in emerging markets are often uncertain as to whether they stand to benefit from the increased opportunities for intermediation that can accompany liberalization or whether they stand to be harmed from the possibility that liberalization will precipitate a banking crisis due to the legacies of financial repression and poor prudential supervision that typically characterize emerging markets' (Chwieroth 2007: 444). The accompanied uncertainty leads to interest groups not being effective. Nonetheless, existing explanations of capital account liberalisation often do forego the crucial roles ideas play in this process. Furthermore, Wright (2009) describes in his book the factors that explain China's abandonment of its long-term exchange rate peg vis-à-vis the US dollar in July 2005. It is argued that the main drivers behind this were ideas within international financial institutions regarding FX policy, which emerged in the aftermath of the Asian financial crisis of the 1990s, as well as China's evolving self-perception as a responsible stakeholder in the global system. As a matter of fact, the ideational factors significantly altered China's interests in the long-term. Traditional political economy approaches focus on the influence of interest groups or the pressure from other states. However, Wright (2009) and Minkin and Lau (2013) show that the informal international consensus regarding flexible exchange rates propagated by international financial institutions provided Chinese policymakers, foremost in the PBoC, with the opportunity to push for change and present it as congruent with China's emerging trajectory as a normal state in the global system. Indeed, China's exchange rate reform has been a non-linear process with the above-mentioned factors being crucial drivers of the pace, as well as the direction of market-orientated reforms.

To sum up, in this section I lay out the specific factors of the policy-induced dimension that determine the currency debasement of the Chinese yuan in August 2015, the change in the FX regime and the frequent revisions of this as well as the subsequent capital outflows in 2015 and 2016. The policy-induced section includes factors such as development policies as well as monetary and fiscal policy and soft factors which encompass the demand for status and ideational factors driving outcomes. Soft factors are only examined qualitatively with the help of over five hundred research reports, while all other factors are also used as part of the logit model in the case study. Indeed, the events, which unfolded in China in 2015 and 2016, have not received appropriate attention from an early warning perspective. With the expanded conceptualisation of vulnerabilities, I try to close this gap in the literature.

2.C) Institutions

A pure focus on fundamentals leads to a myopic view on the topic of financial crisis. An expanded conceptualisation of vulnerability – fundamental, policy-induced, institutional – is necessary to better understand and thus, predict these outcomes from an early warning perspective. In this book, financial crises are defined as currency crises. By detaching the analysis from one specific dimension, I encourage scholars and market observers to acknowledge the multiple forms of vulnerability to financial crises. Hence, this book proposes a unified framework for modelling currency crises along the three analytical dimensions.

In this section of the analytical framework, I will focus on the conceptualisation of the institutional dimension. By expanding the conventional set of fragilities, a better understanding of outcomes should be derived. In practice, one often speaks of a weak institutional set-up without knowing what it is about. 'Institutions are the rules of the game in a society or, more formally, are the humanly devised constraints that shape human interaction' (North 1990: 3). Indeed, output volatility and economic performance are inevitably linked to the quality of an institutional set-up. This is one reason why many fail to predict financial crisis. It is a misguided belief in economic and financial drivers as the sole explanatory factors of outcomes. Foremost, the weakness of institutions in developing countries make them particularly vulnerable to financial crises and thus, the institutional dimension is one key determinant of the analytical framework. Given historical examples, this category is a crucial factor in analysing financial crises. Institutional strengths and weaknesses make a difference in the long-run trajectory of a country as these variables set the guidelines for the growth trajectory of a nation through both the effective accumulation of productive factors and through the prevention of diversion and predatory rent-seeking. Thus, institutions form the backbone of sustainable growth (Ngai 2015). Indeed, according to Olson (1996: 20), poor institutions is the single most important factor holding back developing countries from catching-up with the developed world. Moreover, growth accounting points to differences in income between countries due to variations in technological progress and therefore, also raises the awareness of the importance of setting up an effective institutional framework. Consequently, it is vital for a society to discourage predatory behaviour and foster an environment of inclusive growth by establishing good institutions.

As pointed out in the section on fundamentals, factor accumulation is an important driver of a country's growth rate. Capital accumulation is related to investment while labour growth rate is foremost dependent on population growth as well as on the labour force participation rate, and human capital relates to education and training. Moreover, total factor productivity or technology relates to the effectiveness of the factor inputs to generating output. The question is why does the growth trajectory of many countries significantly diverge? Part of the puzzle is related to institutions (Ngai 2015). For instance, Weil (2008: 193) attributes the Asian growth miracle primarily to factor accumulation, namely high investment rates directed by a strong state-sector, as well as decent population growth. However, factor accumulation by itself does not lead to a sustainable growth path due to diminishing marginal returns. As the total factor productivity in Asia is by far lower than in developed countries, the growth trajectory might slow down at some point unless the region finds a way to engage in effective technological progress. Therefore, the build-up of inclusive institutions is key for this region, as well as fostering innovation and entrepreneurship (Ngai 2015). Indeed, the institutional system of a country can determine whether the nation ends up in poverty or prosperity or suffers from political turmoil. Empirical research links the quality of institutions to the income of a country and the effects are non-negligible. The quality of institutions in developing countries is particularly poor and thus the gap between advanced economies and the latter is often termed 'The Great Divergence' (Kaufmann et al. 2006). However, it takes a relatively long period of time to build an inclusive institutional system and local governments play a crucial role in this respect.

China's rise does not fit well into most studies regarding institutions and growth due to the fact that the Chinese Communist Party has governed the country since the establishment of the PRC in 1949. Thus, it might not be surprising that formal market-supporting institutions remain weak. In the absence of this, it is particularly surprising that China was among the most successful economies over the last forty years. This has been named the China Paradox (Yao and Yueh 2009; Lu and Yao 2009) as it partially contradicts the academic body of knowledge and understanding. Therefore, the application of the theory on institutions on China's rise is fairly complex. The predominant view is that market-supporting institutions and an effective rule of law support a country's trajectory in the long run (La Porta et al. 1997, 1998 and Acemoglu et al. 2005). In general, China is excluded from many of these studies. As a matter of fact, Allen et al. (2005) note that China makes for 'a counterexample to the findings in law, institutions, finance and economic growth literature'. In contrast to this, Hasan et al. (2009) analyse provincial data in China with respect to financial sector development, the establishment of legal institutions as well as regarding political pluralism. In a study between 1986 and 2006, these researchers associated higher quality institutions with stronger economic development across a sample of 31 Chinese provinces. This study showed that regions with better rule of law, property rights, and higher levels of political pluralism depict stronger economic growth. While this study associates institutional quality with growth, China must be classified as a counterexample to the Coasian economic model (Coase 1937) due to the fact that although high transaction costs distort economic efficiency, the country has still been successful in its rise. Nonetheless, the process of transition, which started in China at the end of the 1970s, as well as the importance of institutions such as the exchange rate regime, capital flows and controls, financial repression, international institutions, governance and the rule of law, SOEs as well as technology and productivity must not be underestimated. China's status as 'a transition economy that is also a developing country' (Yueh 2013: 23) contributes to the uniqueness of its trajectory.

Questions relating to institutions, which I answer in this book, include why China's trajectory can be classified as successful, particularly in relation to other transition economies such as Russia, or why China continued its rise in the 1980s and 1990s while other emerging markets were derailed by crises. These questions are analysed in the historical background section and relate to fundamental, policy, and institutional determinants of a country. This section focuses on the institutional factors of a nation's trajectory. The most prominent scholars of the institutionalist school in economics include North (1990) and Williamson (1975, 1985), among others. However, China's rise posed many challenges to the existing body of thought with respect to institutions. Furthermore, Roland (2005) distinguishes different approaches to classifying institutions. First, a functional approach is described, 'which defines institutions by the needs of efficient contracting and investing' (Roland 2005: 6). However, the functional approach does not describe the processes by which change occurs and thus, is not suitable to understanding large-scale institutional change as a transition is. Second, a macro systematic approach can be chosen which classifies existing institutions into specific categories such as economic and social. Another distinction can be made between predatory and development institutions (Evans 1989; Acemoglu et al. 2002). With respect to this, the former relates to a minority determining the fate of the majority, while developing institutions relate to 'providing a "helping hand" to private agents, providing public goods like education, infrastructure, and incentives to invest' (Roland 2005: 8). The latter was particularly important at the beginning of China's reform period, which is addressed in detail in the historical background section as well as in the section on transitions of the institutional dimension. In addition to the above, historical institutionalism plays a particular important role in this book. 'Historical institutionalists see institutions as the legacy of concrete historical processes' (Thelen 1999: 382). This entails questions such as sequencing and timing as various different institutional arrangements emerge at different times with specific historical configurations. It is put forward that 'institutions continue to evolve in response to changing environmental conditions and ongoing political manoeuvring but in ways that are constrained by past trajectories' (Thelen 1999: 387). This is applicable, for instance, to the devaluation of the Chinese currency in August 2015. The event was constrained by the past experience of China with respect to currency movements, namely the events unfolding in 2005. In general, historical institutionalism plays an important factor with respect to defining the institutional factors laid out above and below.

To address the question of institutions and vulnerability, I will start by describing different forms of liberalisation. First, China has to be regarded as a transition economy. Although the country's transformation was highly successful over the preceding decades, its transition is far from complete and continuously poses new challenges to the Chinese leadership as well as to the global community. Second, capital flow volatility and the connection to financial crises will be examined in detail. In this respect, it is inevitable to touch upon topics such as capital controls. Third, financial repression and the impact of this on China's growth trajectory will be laid out. The speedy catch-up process of the country came at a cost for the local population, which had to be accepted given the country's ultimate goal of development. In addition, topics such as the pace of liberalisation, as well as sequencing of reforms will be addressed. In the next sub-section, I will analyse China's foreign exchange rate regime and its influence on the country's strengths and weaknesses. The currency regime is closely linked to the previously described parts of liberalisation. The development of the offshore market and its influence on China will be examined as well as the country's unique approach towards internationalising the renminbi, which includes targeted liberalisation, policy experimentation, and institutional hybridisation (McNally and Gruin 2017: 16). In the subsequent section, the influence of international financial institutions on China is described. This has to be seen in relation to the country's history. The influence of the IMF became particularly important with respect to the SDR inclusion in 2015, which will also be examined in detail. Further variables of the institutional section include governance and the rule of law, state-owned enterprise reforms, as well as technology and productivity. All the above-mentioned determinants make for the institutional section of the analytical framework, which will then be applied to China's troubles in the second half of 2015 and 2016 in the case study.

a) Liberalisation

Liberalisation and institutions are inevitably linked. Often liberalisation is termed premature when the institutional set-up of a country is not yet to deal with the challenges global markets entail. The researcher Roland Paris (2004) therefore brought forward the concept of Institutionalisation Before Liberalisation (IBL), in which he advocates the build-up of inclusive economic institutions before opening a country to the outside world. He says that research needs to consider the severe short-term costs of premature liberalisation with respect to social unrest, as well as lost income, although liberalisation can lead to a more sustainable long-term path (Paris 2004: 179). The costs mainly result from the dismantling of historic misallocations of resources, which significantly slows down the economy (Popov 2000: 9-11). Therefore, building-up inclusive institutions can serve as a mitigation strategy to dampen the short-term negative repercussions of opening. In fact, the radical approach towards liberalisation has severe costs, specifically in social terms. Liberalisation without an adequate system in place to dampen the negative repercussions results in a transformation of the economy with losers as shown in the historical background section (Roland 2000). The mitigation of the short-term negative effects includes establishing the rules of the game by constraining the volatile forces of liberalisation and thus, guaranteeing some degree of fairness. The market can lead to an improvement in the allocation of resources. However, on its own, the market might be insufficient to let a large part of the population profit from its establishment (Paris 2004: 199). To better understand the topic of liberalisation, economic transitions, capital flow volatility, and controls, as well as financial repression, interest rate liberalisation, and capital, market development must be analysed.

i) Liberalisation – Economic Transition and Price Liberalisation

Institutions belong to the most important determinants of a trajectory of a country. Liberalisation, which relates to the free movement of monetary flows, variable interest rates as well as the institutional set-up that govern economic performance, are analysed in this and the subsequent sections. As shown in the historical background part, many historic crisis episodes are related to these drivers. Transition economies in particular are prone to institutional fragilities as the transformation process itself must be regarded as large-scale institutional change (Roland 2000). The shift from plan to market includes topics such as price liberalisation, which can have disastrous consequences when there is no adequate system in place.

Given China's continued shift from plan to market, the country's approach towards development must be viewed in terms of transition. The basis for China's economy is a Soviet-style industrialisation, as laid out in detail in the historical background section. Reforms were adopted cautiously over the course of its transition. This gradual and incremental approach towards transformation contributed to the successful trajectory of China (Yueh 2013: 23-24). By doing so, the market was incrementally introduced to certain sectors of the administered nation. However, this happened without the significant shift in ownership from the government to the private sector as was performed in other transition economies. China's approach towards transformation can be characterised by local experimentation as well as institutional innovations (Qian and Xu 1993; Fan 1994). In contrast to other transitions, China's shift from plan to market started in the countryside. The successful establishment of township and village enterprises (TVEs) provided new impetus for the economy. The creation of TVEs helped industrialise the rural economy, which could then be further expanded through creating new jobs for abundant labour. Furthermore, the household responsibility system incentivised the rural population to produce more than production targets because any surplus could later be sold at market prices at the margin, as famously termed by Byrd (1991). The dissolution of the communal ownership structure entailed significant improvements in productivity in the rural economy and output picked up in the early 1980s (Riskin 1987). The successful reforms in the countryside gave the Chinese government the necessary backing to continue on the reform path. The introduction of incentives in rural areas spurred a wage reform in the sate-owned enterprise sector together with increased autonomy (Yueh 2004). Economic development and stability were the two main goals of the Chinese government. If one of these were violated, the reform impetus would have slowed down significantly. However, the dual-track reform process specifically was what made this combination a success. This partial liberalisation strategy allowed China to still make use of the means of the planned economy for the purpose of securing the necessary production for the state while at the same time introducing the market to the economy (Murphy et al. 1992). China also allowed for new experimentations in certain areas, which could either be expanded or reduced. This initially did not affect the entire economy, rather only certain sectors and areas (Qian and Xu 1993). Thus, China's transformation was characterised by the combination of market-orientated incentives with the means of the planned economy (Yueh 2013: 23-24), which distinguishes the country from other transition economies and is examined in detail below.

China proclaimed the socialist market economy in 1992 as explained in the historical background section. Given the disastrous output falls in some of the former communist countries, China had become a role model for economic transitions (Chen et al. 1992; Gelb et al. 1993). The incremental approach to reforming the economy was adopted by China in 1978 because a majority of the Chinese leadership preferred this approach to the more radical big bang method. In addition, the Chinese economic situation at the end of the 1970s was simply too good to opt for a more radical transformation of the economy. 'China registered 7.8% national income growth in 1977 and 12.3% in 1978 before the reform started in 1979' (Fan 1994: 101). Thus, most of the Chinese people had not fully lost trust in the old institutions as happened in other transition economies. 'Consequently, China has proceeded through a lengthy path of readjusting reform objectives, from "a planned economy with some market adjustment", to "a combination of plan and market", and now to "a socialist market economy"' (Fan 1994: 103). The rural household system, which formed the basis for the successful transformation of the Chinese economy on the countryside, was initially not supported by the Chinese leadership. As laid out in the historical background section, peasants nevertheless adopted this new institution and the government accepted it at a later stage. This resulted in the partial liberalisation of the rural economy and in the establishment of township and village enterprises, which further spurred the successful trajectory (Naughton 2007). One key determinant of transformation is how to deal with the old system. The manner in which China transitioned, allowed for the combination of the planned economy with the introduction of market-orientated incentives. This in turn allowed the country to circumvent the disastrous declines in output as experienced in other countries. Indeed, it distinguished China from other transition economies that it's state sector was in a relatively good shape as the transformation started. Moreover, the reforms in rural areas as well as the liberalisation of private enterprises led to fast enough growth to make up for the increased subsidies to the state sector (Fan 1994: 106). Given the above, the Chinese government always kept the power to control the speed and the path of reforms. The incremental approach did not endanger the existing system. Stability of the system was and remains key for China.

The dual-track system was first applied to the price reform and subsequently to all economic transactions. The reform of the ownership structure was among the most important cornerstones. 'China's rapid economic growth can be attributed mainly to the dynamic development of the "new track non-state sector", which consists of private and semi-private enterprises, community-owned rural industrial enterprises, foreign joint-ventures and individual businesses' (Fan 1994: 108). The benefit of the dual-track system is the honouring of the previous contracts. Various benefits provided by the old institutions could be kept in place, which significantly decreased the potential for social unrest. This stands in stark contrast to the transition experience in Central and Eastern Europe, as well as in parts of the former Soviet Union. Moreover, in case the old system stops expanding, the country would simply grow out of the old track (Naughton 1996), which reduced any significant resistance to the changes.

One of the most important differences between China and transitions in Central and Eastern Europe and in the former Soviet Union is the significant output fall that happened at the beginning of the reform period in the latter regions. The biggest decrease in GDP was observed in the year the liberalisation took place: Poland in 1990, Czech Republic and Slovakia in 1991, Russia in 1992 and the subsequent default at the end of the decade, Ukraine in 1994 (Roland and Verdier 1997: 1). Roland and Verdier (1997) show in their research that output falls due to the failure of corporations to renew capital and due to a significant decrease in investment. This helps explain why liberalisation entails an economic contraction as could be observed in the above-mentioned regions. In addition, the scholars show that big bang liberalisation is not preferable to a gradual liberalisation in the form China chose with the means of the dual-track system (Byrd 1987; McMillan and Naughton 1992). The latter was a unique Chinese innovation, which helped the country to avoid the significant decline in output as was recorded in other transition countries. The dual-track system allowed for liberalisation of prices at the margin; however, enterprises had to keep-up existing production and fulfil quotas at the non-liberalised prices. The stability of the Chinese system made this possible as the Chinese government could still make use of the system of the planned economy while introducing new innovations. Nonetheless, this was not possible in other transition countries since trust was completely eroded in the ruling elites and the former communist institutions. Roland and Verdier (1997: 4) show 'that a case can be made for Chinese style gradual liberalization in circumstances where some form of state control is maintained at the beginning of the liberalization period. Indeed, such gradual liberalization may avoid the output disruption and temporary fall in investment generated by big bang policy'. One special feature of the Chinese dual-track system was that most prices were liberalised at the margin over time. Companies could only trade excess production at the new price system, which allowed for the cautious establishment of a market system. This introduces information revealing characteristics of a market economy while maintaining the means of the planned economy. An incremental approach significantly smoothes economic volatility and thus, does not entail the negative repercussions the big bang approach brought with it (Roland and Verdier 1997: 13). Furthermore, Svejnar (2007) points out that in order to avoid an initial sharp decline in output, the old system must be maintained rather than changing the political and economic system in one go. The latter resulted in instability and many Central and Eastern European countries, as well as the Soviet Union had to move quickly. Another point that distinguishes China's transformation from other transition economies is in terms of privatisation. Svejnar (2007: 19) notes that on a country level the fastest growing transition economy were those which were among the slowest to privatise.

Moreover, Kornai (2014) points to further growth drivers, which particularly distinguished China. First, China continued to suppress household consumption in the reform period, which is known as financial repression. This process is described in detail in the subsequent section. Second, the share of investment to GDP was disproportionally high, which was in line with the country's high savings rate. The utilisation of national income purely focused on the development of the nation. 'There is no Western country where the public would have born with such a constraint on its share in the growth of production' (Kornai 2014: 3). In addition, state-ownership continued to be the predominant form in the economy. As laid out in the historical background section, growth can be split into two phases, namely in an extensive and an intensive phase. The former refers to growth driven by increases in the factors of production and the latter mainly refers to improvements in efficiency (Kornai 2014: 4). This is laid out in detail in separate sections of this book. Furthermore, Berglof and Bolton (2001) analyse the effects of the transition on the financial system and vice versa in their research. The researchers argue that the financial sector has played only a minor role in the reorientation of transition economies, 'and in some cases financial liberalization may have undermined real sector development' (Berglof and Bolton 2001: 2). This is examined in detail in the section on financial repression. In general, the financial sector only played a passive role in the planned economy. Banking institutions in communist countries evolved from a single institution, namely the mono-bank. In these systems, the level of credit was kept high to foster production, which was desired by the economic planners. The reforms brought the split between the mono-bank and commercial banking activities. The majority of the newly created banking institutions remained in state-ownership, which allowed for the postponement of difficult reforms, which in itself could have triggered a crisis. This was termed a 'too many to fail' situation by Mitchell (1998). With its gradual approach towards liberalisation China could avoid such a situation.

The Chinese dual-track approach changed in 1993 when the central government reasserted itself. The second phase of transition certainly permitted losers to appear. The material-balance planning system was completely abolished in the second phase of China's transformation, as laid out in detail in the historical background section. In contrast to the decentralisation in the first phase, the Chinese government consolidated fiscal revenues in the second phase, which led to a certain recentralisation. This was necessary in order to build a tax base, which should have made up for the losses in revenue from the shift from plan to market (Naughton 2007: 101). The shift in China's transition strategy made the country's transformation less distinctive. However, the focus on stability as well as on development remains one of the primary goals of the Chinese government. Deng Xiaoping noted that 'development is the only hard truth' (Naughton 2007: 108). The Chinese trajectory, as laid out in detail in the historical background section, clearly shapes the country's identity today. Despite the successful track record of China's transformation, success is not guaranteed in the future. The country's government has to further advance the transition process, while at the same time cushioning the effects of changes such as a rising level of inequality or economic uncertainty. The Chinese transition is far from complete and liberalisation remains a critical issue, which is part of the country's transformation. As Yueh (2013) noted, China is transitioning and developing at the same time, which continues to pose enormous challenges to the country as is laid out in detail in the case study. The Chinese success story of the last forty years can be partially attributed to the country's distinct approach towards transition. The gradual transformation helped to avoid the significant distortions other transition economies experienced during the shift from plan to market. However, due to China's incremental approach, the country is not yet finished with respect to its economic transformation, which poses a significant vulnerability. As laid out in the section on monetary policy, liberalisation of prices is one indicator with respect to China's transition. The underpricing of certain factor inputs forms part of a repressive system and the dissolution of price controls can temporarily contribute to uncertainty and to a financial crisis. In the case study, I assess the impact of this variable on the events of 2015 and 2016 from an early warning perspective.

ii) Liberalisation – Capital Flows and Capital Controls

Historic crisis episodes were often related to speedy liberalisation in light of weak governance and institutions. The liberalisation of the capital account can entail significant negative effects in terms of capital flow volatility. The market alone might not be sufficient to constrain the volatile forces of these flows. As is shown in the section 'Crises in Perspective', China was able to survive past episodes of crisis, for instance the Asian financial crisis of the 1990s, because of strong capital controls. The 1980s and 1990s were particularly prone to financial crises, which coincides with excessive liberalisation (Krugman 1998). 'When there is a single accident on a highway, one suspects that the driver's attention may have lapsed. But when there are dozens of accidents at the same bend in the same highway, one needs to re-examine the design of the road' (Stiglitz 2000: 1075). With his examination, Stiglitz (2000) builds a case against full liberalisation and for intervention to regulate short-term capital flows. In contrast, foreign direct investment has compelling attributes as it has the potential for improvement in the local human capital base as well as technology transfers. In this respect, China encouraged foreign direct investment over the preceding decades, while at the same time keeping a tight grip on portfolio flows. Furthermore, restrictions on short-term capital flows do not necessarily curtail long-term investment, as was shown by China over many decades. Also, Malaysia, which imposed restrictions on capital outflows, and Chile, which curtailed capital inflows, had not negatively influenced long-term investment due to the imposition of these restrictions. The aim of these intervening measures was to equate private and social costs (Stiglitz 2000: 1080; 1083), which would provide additional stability to a country.

Concerns have been raised about capital controls as restrictions on flows is against the notion of openness. However, there is a significant distinction between current and capital account convertibility. On the one hand, current account convertibility is one of the goals of the IMF. On the other hand, capital account convertibility is by far more critical due to the volatile nature of these flows. 'The instability associated with short-term capital movements results in there being a marked discrepancy between private and social returns and risks. The capital flows impose a huge negative externality' (Stiglitz 2000: 1081). With respect to this, capital controls are a measure to dampen this destructive volatility. 'As suggested by the Fund after the global financial crisis, countries may adopt temporary capital control measures when there are abnormal fluctuations in the international markets, or there are balance of payments problems' (IMF 2015). Indeed, capital controls are among the principal means to mitigate the negative effects of liberalisation in the short-term as shown by Paris (2004) and as is laid out in detail below.

Favourable views towards liberalisation came up with the idea of sequencing of reforms, which focused on the order of export and import related as well as capital account liberalisation (McKinnon 1973). Furthermore, Edwards (1999) was among the starkest critics of capital controls as these would be circumvented via illicit means. In this respect, Garber (1998) put forward that one mean of capital flight is the over-invoicing of imports and under-invoicing of exports. Thus, the question of liberalisation and capital controls is also connected to building a sound legal and regulatory framework. Calvo (1998) stresses that poorly regulated banks are the main culprits for increasing the risk of financial crises. This view is supported by Kaminsky and Reinhart (1999) among others. Eichengreen and Kawai (2014: 10) note on the pace and sequencing of liberalisation: 'Domestic financial market liberalization – introducing market-determined interest rates, deregulating scope of financial businesses and market entry, [...] – should be the first prerequisite. Supervision and regulation of domestic financial firms and markets should then be strengthened considerably in advance of capital account liberalization'.

The IMF commented on the matter of capital flows and controls as follows in its World Economic Outlook publication in October 2007:

'The influx of large capital inflows has induced policymakers to adopt a variety of measures to prevent overheating and real currency appreciation, and reduce the economy's vulnerability to a sharp reversal of the capital inflows. A key policy decision for countries facing large capital inflows is to determine to what extent they can resist pressures for the currency to appreciate by intervening in the foreign exchange market' (IMF 2007: 111). As a matter of fact, the main arguments for liberalisation are questionable if a country itself has a high savings rate and generates decent growth. The absorption of additional capital inflows leads to significant challenges for a nation and can lead to an unsustainable increase in asset prices (Stiglitz 2000: 1077) and instability in general. The importance of stability is underlined because economic growth tends to be sluggish several years after a financial crisis (Caprio 1997). In addition, instability often entails distributional consequences for crisis-inflicted countries. Most of all, liberalisation is associated with the increased occurrence of financial crises. Demirgüç-Kunt and Detragiache (1998) as well as Easterly et al. (1999) among others have confirmed this. Stiglitz (2000) notes that while there is no attractive case for liberalisation, there is a compelling case against it. The argument that capital account liberalisation provides greater stability through diversification benefits does not hold, which is because of the flows being procyclical, and thus exacerbating any state of the economy. Indeed, it is well known that capital flows are cyclical (Kaminsky et al. 2004) and that it is per se questionable to assume that capital flows from advanced countries to the developing world as postulated by the neoclassical growth paradigm. Specifically, Lucas (1990) analysed this phenomenon. Moreover, capital account liberalisation makes a country more prone to changing circumstances outside of a national sphere. Changes in perceptions of the international financial community towards risk can have severe consequences. In addition, 'on the negative side, the openness to capital flight makes countries especially sensitive, e.g., to corporate or capital tax rates or to changes in interest rates. Thus, openness may impose costly constraints on the ability of government to pursue legitimate objectives' (Stiglitz 2000: 1079-1080) and must be carefully planned.

As mentioned above, a higher degree of capital account opening leads to greater influence of international factors. In line with this, Reinhart and Reinhart (2008) put forward that global factors such as the international level of interest rates or economic performance in developed countries have an influence on capital flow cycles. These "bonanzas", as the researchers put it, are not beneficial to most countries as inflows are connected with a higher probability of financial crisis, for instance currency crashes. In addition, capital inflows tend to coincide with procyclical policy, which aggravates the problems caused when the tide turns. Also, the inflows tend to induce an appreciation of the exchange rate, which contributes to a fundamental vulnerability of a country as Reinhart and Reinhart (2008: 1) point out. This is examined in detail in the respective section. The researchers further point out that these bonanzas have become more frequent given the global lifting of capital account controls. The usual mistake by emerging markets is to treat these flows as permanent. As Calvo (1998) powerfully presented, the opposite holds true. He terms this "sudden stops", which refers to the reversal in flows and tends to coincide with a certain pattern on the left-hand side of the balance-of-payments, namely the flow volatility results in a V-shaped pattern in the evolution of the current account. In line with this, Reinhart and Reinhart (2008: 4) show that also other economic aggregates depict certain patterns due to these bonanzas. Among others, real GDP growth tends to be higher during times of inflows and asset prices get lifted. Additionally, the exchange rate appreciates as an effect of this. At some point this becomes unsustainable, which leads to the sudden stop problem. This was empirically shown by Calvo, Izquierdo, and Mejia (2004). Furthermore, the examination of Goldfajn and Valdes (1999) puts forward compelling evidence that in the large majority of cases, the unwinding of the prior appreciation of the real exchange rate happens through a swift nominal devaluation, often termed a currency crash, instead than through a more sluggish adjustment in the price level (Reinhart and Reinhart 2008: 42).

Capital account openness is assessed by the degree of restrictions on capital in- and outflows for transactions performed by locals as well as foreign investors. Over the previous decades, as laid out in the historical background section, many emerging markets reduced capital controls significantly. Only a few countries, foremost China, have kept relatively high barriers to monetary flows (Hooley 2013; Stiglitz 2000). The entity, which overlooks capital account transactions and controls in China, is the State Administration of Foreign Exchange (SAFE), which is a sub-institution of the PBoC. The SAFE was headed by Yi Gang from 2009 to 2015 and is guided by Pan Gongsheng since 2016. During this time, China increasingly opened its capital account (Prasad 2017: 37-38). However, Reinhart and Reinhart (1998: 93) cautioned that, 'Surges in capital inflows may distort relative prices, exacerbate weakness in a nation's financial sector, and feed asset-price bubbles'.

What are capital controls and how are they measured with respect to China? Capital controls foremost refer to legal requirements on monetary flows, which encompass simple registration procedures but also severe restrictions on transactions (Prasad 2017: 37-38). A capital control is if, for instance, a country denies foreign investors access to its bond market. One way to measure capital account openness is with the help of the IMF's Annual Report on Exchange Arrangements and Exchange Restrictions (AREAER). This data set provides insights on which categories of flows restrictions are applied (Chinn and Ito 2008). This is very much related to formal controls on flows, which does not necessarily reflect the reality on the ground. Another measure of capital account openness is the sum of a nation's external assets and liabilities as a percentage of output, which is generally known as the international investment position (Feenstra and Taylor 2014: 597; Ma and Zhou 2009). With respect to China, it can be observed that the country's assets and liabilities sharply rose in the last decade and amounted to USD 6.2 trillion in external assets and USD 4.6 trillion in external liabilities. Relative to GDP, China's external position is approximately 100 percent and thus, the country only lags more advanced economies like the United States, the United Kingdom or Japan (Prasad 2017: 40-41). What are the determinants of China's external assets and liabilities? FDI makes up for the largest part of the country's external liabilities with approximately 62 percent of the total in 2015. Portfolio equity and debt liabilities account for 13 and 25 percent respectively. This is a reflection of the country's strategy over the preceding decades. FDI is regarded by the Chinese government as being the most favourable type of monetary flow. An example of foreign direct investment would be if a foreign investor takes over a controlling stake in a Chinese company. FDI was welcomed by the Chinese government because it aimed for technological spillovers from external to domestic companies. 'Restrictions of its exchange rate and capital account while seeking technology transfers from FDI mean that several metrics are needed to calibrate the influence of opening on growth' (Yueh 2013: 3). China only allowed foreign enterprises to operate in the country if they worked together with domestic firms. To achieve the country's goal of catching up, the Chinese government incentivised FDI by cutting red tape as well as bureaucracy and also reducing the income tax rate of companies that are financed via FDI instead of domestic funds from 33 percent to 15 percent. This led to the so-called round-tripping problem, which refers to Chinese entrepreneurs moving funds to Hong Kong, then repatriate the capital as FDI and thus profit from the income tax advantage. In contrast to FDI, the Chinese government was always wary of portfolio flows as these were regarded as sources of instability. Many historical crisis episodes were related to severe capital flow volatility as shown in the section 'Crises in Perspective'. Given these experiences, the Chinese government tried to curtail foreign borrowing by domestic corporations. With respect to China's external asset position, FX reserves accounted for approximately 55 percent of the total in 2015. Outward FDI made up about 18 percent of foreign assets. In addition, outward portfolio debt and equity investments accounted for the remaining 27 percent of the total (Prasad 2017: 41-44).

As mentioned above, China's strategy welcomed FDI and historically tried to curtail portfolio flows. However, more recently China tries to attract the latter via various means. In this respect, the qualified foreign institutional investor (QFII) scheme, the renminbi, qualified foreign institutional investor (RQFII) scheme, the qualified domestic institutional investor (QDII) scheme, as well as the qualified domestic individual investor scheme (QDII2) have to be mentioned. First, the QFII scheme allows foreign investors to buy onshore renminbi and invest in locally listed stocks. The quotas are available to foreign fund managers or insurance firms among others. The programme was expanded in 2008 by increasing the quotas available to foreign institutions as well as raising the maximum quotas for individual investors. Nonetheless, the Chinese government still influences the allocation of the funds as it does not want the bulk of inflows to be invested into cash and bonds. In 2016, China took further liberalising steps with respect to capital inflows. The Chinese leadership declared that the local corporate bond market would be opened for the QFII scheme with hardly any restrictions. Additionally, the lock-up period was eliminated and thus investors could repatriate their funds after a three-months holding period. Thus, China made significant steps to facilitate capital inflows by foreign institutional investors (Lardy and Douglass 2011: 10-12; Sharma 2015 quoted in Prasad 2017). This is examined in detail in the case study. Second, the RQFII scheme was established in 2011. This programme refers to foreign investors using offshore renminbi directly to invest onshore in China. To do this, a license from the CSRC is needed and quotas have to be purchased from the SAFE. Initially, the programme was limited to subsidiaries of Chinese financial institutions based in Hong Kong. However, the scheme has gradually expanded since 2014. Both the QFII and the RQFII scheme refer to capital inflows. Third and fourth, the QDII and QDII2 scheme are related to Chinese financial institutions and individuals investing in equity and bond securities outside the country. The QDII2 programme was established initially in six cities and allowed Chinese locals with at least RMB 1 million in assets to directly purchase foreign securities. However, this is still currently capped at a maximum purchase limit of USD 50'000 (Lardy and Douglass 2011: 10-12; Prasad 2017: 47-56), which gets renewed every year. Reinhart and Reinhart (1998) and Laban and Larrain (1994) show that a response to increasing capital inflows is the lifting of restrictions in capital outflows. Locals are allowed to hold foreign assets and consequently outflows increase to such an extent that net flows turn negative for a developing country, which results in a performance drag for the nation. This also holds true for China since locals may seek to diversify their holdings of assets in case of the lifting of capital account restrictions (Bayoumi and Ohnsorge 2013), which could pose a systemic vulnerability for the country.

The former head of the PBoC, Zhou Xiaochuan, stated with respect to capital controls that, 'It is worth noting that the concept of capital account convertibility has changed since the global financial crisis. The capital account convertibility China is seeking to achieve is not based on the traditional concept of being fully or freely convertible. Instead, drawing lessons from the global financial crisis, China will adopt a concept of managed convertibility. After achieving RMB capital account convertibility, China will continue to manage capital account transactions, but in a largely transformed manner, including by using macroprudential measures to limit risks from cross-border capital flows and to maintain the stable value of the currency and a safe financial environment' (IMF 2015). This statement was made right before the troubles in China started, which is examined in detail in the case study. Zhou Xiaochuan continued to elaborate on China's capital account management practices. In particular, external debt financing would be closely watched by the PBoC because balance sheet mismatches significantly contributed to global crisis episodes in the past. Moreover, in case portfolio flows present a risk to financial stability of China, the country would pose restrictions on these. Thus, the Chinese government is waiting for windows of opportunity for reforms before pressing ahead with their ambitions. Given China's gradual approach towards liberalisation, the speed of reforms can be characterised as secondary for the Chinese leadership (Prasad 2017). Even though China's aim was to selectively as well as cautiously dismantle capital controls, capital flow volatility became a problem in 2015 and 2016.

iii) Liberalisation – Interest Rates, the Banking Sector and Capital Market Development

With respect to China's economic transition, the financial system is lagging behind the rest of the economy. Indeed, said industry is among the most protected in the country given the strong involvement of the Chinese state as well as the protection from foreign competition. In China, financing is dominated by local state-owned banks. However, given China's accession to the WTO in 2001, increased competition in the financial sector gradually became a reality (Yueh 2013: 21).

Steps towards a more open financial sector have since been taken by the Chinese government. However, capital market development also poses significant challenges to the country. As mentioned, China's transition is an on-going process. Given the incremental approach towards transformation parts of the economy have not been opened yet and China's financial sector is still among the heaviest controlled (Naughton 2007: 449) and the continued institutional transition poses a vulnerability factor for the country.

In general, financial development can be split into financial deepening and financial broadening. With respect to the former, the ratio of financial assets to GDP serves as a decent indicator. Financial deepening refers to the amount of savings that has been used for investment with the help of financial institutions. The accumulation of wealth in a society is one reason for financial deepening. The bank's primary purpose in this respect is the mobilisation of savings for investment. In contrast, financial broadening is related to a higher number of financial institutions, as well as a greater variety of instruments. This is the case as capital markets develop and stock and bond investments become more prominent. Financial deepening goes in line with the development of institutional investors such as pension funds, insurance companies or mutual funds. Thus, deepening financial markets are related to a higher reliance on capital markets instead of banks. Both financial deepening and broadening are associated with the growth rate of an economy. Financial intermediation facilitates the allocation of resources, as well as bridges the gap between short-term liquidity needs of savers and long-term commitments of funds to productive projects in an economy. In addition, an effective financial system also provides for governance functions; this is touched upon in a later part of this book. Given the importance of the financial system for an economy, there are multiple channels for 'revealing and responding to economic shocks' (Naughton 2007: 450). Consequently, this is an important variable in the case study on China.

In a planned economy, the financial sector plays a purely passive role since the allocation of resources is done by the state. Therefore, long-term funds for investment projects via financial intermediation and capital markets in general only play a minor role. Given China's shift from plan to market, the country started to build all the institutions necessary for a modern financial environment (Caprio and Levine 1994). As described in the policy section, the central bank guides monetary policy and today's financial system in China includes a variety of commercial banking groups as well as government policy banks among others. Stock exchanges in Shanghai and Shenzen were established in 1992 and the Chinese financial system has since generally become deeper over the last decades. Nonetheless, the current system can be described as "narrow" since the industry is still largely shielded from excessive competition (Naughton 2007: 451). The financial deepening in China stands in stark contrast to the experience of other transition economies. As described in the respective section, the liberalisation of prices led to a severe collapse in output in Central and Eastern Europe, as well as in the former Soviet Union (Wu 2005). This was accompanied by a wipe out of domestic savings via inflation. China decided for a more careful approach towards transformation. The country shielded savings in banks from any inflationary pressure resulting from the reallocation of resources. Supplementary interest in the magnitude of the increase in CPI was provided to household saving deposits, which led to the deepening of the Chinese financial system. This approach helped to stabilise economic growth in the first decades of the transition. However, a banking system with excess cash came at a cost for China. Petty projects by government officials became common and the entire state-owned enterprise system became fully reliant on the domestic banking system. Loss-making companies with good government connections were kept afloat with the help of beneficial bank funding (Naughton 2007: 452-453). These misallocations and the interconnectedness between all sectors posed a systemic vulnerability for China. In the 1990s, Chinese policymakers started to address these issues. Nevertheless, the transformation is far from complete. The development of capital markets is one means in this respect, which has effects on the degree of financial repression as argued by Boyreau-Debray and Wei (2005) and is examined below.

The foundation of China's banking system dates back to the planned economy. As Yueh (2013: 307) notes 'at the start of the reform period, China's banking and financial system under central planning was essentially an arm of the state'. This changed with the shift from plan to market in China. The Big Four state-owned banks, commercial banking groups, city banks, rural credit cooperatives and policy banks formed the basis for the evolving system. The Big Four were developed out of a mono-bank at the time of the fully planned economy, which were the Industrial and Commercial Bank of China (ICBC), The Agricultural Bank of China (ABC), The China Construction Bank (CCB) and The Bank of China (BOC). It goes without saying that all four banks are still carrying the burden of the old system. Credit on demand to state-owned enterprises was the common practice and vested interests still play an important role in decision-making today. Banking reforms in 1994 and 1998 tried to address part of these issues. In 1997, the national credit plan through which the Chinese government allocated funding in the economy was abolished (Naughton 2007: 454-456). Even though the reform era in China allowed for new forms of ownership, the country's financial system is still dominated by these four entities. Shen et al. (2009) estimate that in 2009 about 60 percent of all credit was issued by state-owned banks. In contrast to the Big Four, the joint-stock commercial banks (JSCBs), which were established between 1986 and 2001, represented new entrants to the system and are thus free from any legacy problems. Their amount of bad loans is not as significant because lending decisions can be made on a commercial basis due to these banks not being entirely government owned. The commercial banks are partially listed on local stock exchanges, which allows for public ownership and scrutiny, although mostly in the form of minority holdings. The third category of banks, which forms the basis of China's financial system, are city banks which are mostly urban credit cooperatives. On the countryside, rural credit cooperatives served the needs of the rural population. The successes of TVEs, as described in the historical background section, were partly based on these institutions. At the end of the 1990s, these banks ran into severe difficulties due to intensified competition and a more difficult economic picture (Naughton 2007: 456-459). The NPL problems in the aftermath of the Asian financial crisis are described in detail in the historical background section. In addition, due to the shift from plan to market, three policy banks were established in China in order to act as government institutions facilitating state projects. These banks were the China Development Bank, the Export-Import Bank, and the Agricultural Development Bank (Naughton 2007: 457). This is the fifth category of banks in China. The Big Four are the heart of the financial system (Walter and Howie 2011).

Given China's gradual approach towards transition, the development of capital markets before the lessening of the grip on the banking sector is key. Local governments played a crucial role for the establishment of the first local exchanges, namely in Shanghai and in Shenzen (Green 2004). These two local entities invested significant resources in the development of capital market institutions in the 1980s. It was only in 1991 that the central government formally approved of these endeavours, which led to a steady, but volatile rise in China's capital market activities. The shortcomings of this development repeatedly led to severe and prolonged market declines. These declines were largely independent from economic activity (Naughton 2007: 468). Zhu Rongji gave the go ahead to the development of capital markets, as these were meant to reform the state-owned enterprise sector. 'In 1993, 100 SOEs were selected to experiment with corporatization or transformation into shareholding companies under a new Company Law' (Yueh 2013: 93). Gruin (2013: 10) points to the importance of China's experimental approach in terms of development, which is further elaborated on in the policy as well as historical background section. In contrast to the privatisation experience in other transition economies, the partial floating of state-owned enterprises in China can be classified as a relative success. Minority shareholders provide an additional source of monitoring and improved information dissemination. In addition, capital markets can help raise funding for corporations. In the initial phase of the capital market development over 90 percent of floated companies were state-owned enterprises. The government always retained a majority stake in the listed companies. Those shares retained by the state or related institutions were simply not allowed to circulate (Naughton 2007: 468-471). In addition, the shares, which can circulate, are split in different segments. A-shares, for instance, are denominated in local currency, while H-shares are listed by Chinese corporations in Hong Kong and thus are denominated in the offshore renminbi (Prasad 2017: 43). The difference between the onshore and offshore market is examined in detail both in the section on the FX regime and in the case study.

Even though the banking system in China remains among the most protected sectors, some of the larger banks had to be recapitalised, restructured, and partially listed by the Chinese government. The appointment of independent members to the board has led to significant improvements in governance. The newly created China Banking Regulatory Commission (CBRC) serves as a supervisory agency, which is examined in detail in the section on governance. By most indicators the performance of Chinese banks has improved given the changes in the system. However, there is one area in which the financial system in China did not make much progress. The People's Bank of China (PBoC) and thus, ultimately the State Council, still engages in financial repression. Generally, the term financial repression was first used by McKinnon (1973), who used it in connection with government regulated interest rates as well as relatively high reserve requirement ratios for banks and the mandatory allocation of credit to mostly state-sponsored entities. Lardy (2008) examines exactly who the primary beneficiaries of this are. It can be deduced that the government accrues over half of the benefits. At a first glance, Chinese banks seem to be the primary beneficiary of financial repression. However, the benefits granted to banks by the PBoC in the form of cheap deposits, are partially taken back via the PBoC's sterilisation measures. The WTO membership of China in 2001 resulted in significant productivity gains for the country at the time when the RMB was pegged against the US dollar, which depreciated in the early 2000s. Hence, the PBoC significantly intervened in the FX market, which led to the accumulation of hard currency reserves. In addition to sterilising the increase of the local money supply as a result of the exchange rate policy, the Chinese central bank issued large amounts of central bank bills and significantly hiked the reserve requirement ratio (DeRosa 2009: 36-37). As these bonds were issued at depressed local interest rate levels, this can be regarded as an additional tax to the banking system. The nominal yield on the bonds diverged significantly from the amount of interest the financial institutions would have received in a fully liberalised economy. These measures served the Chinese government policies of keeping an undervalued exchange rate. Financial repression is also one reason why household income as a percentage of output has decreased according to Lardy (2008), which has made the goal of the government of rebalancing the economy difficult to achieve. This works because capital markets in China are still relatively underdeveloped and subsequently do not yet provide a suitable alternative to bank deposits. In addition, significant price volatility in Chinese equity markets represents another deterrent for long-term investors. Nonetheless, when equity prices start to increase a flood of money is pouring into local stocks leading to significant increases of valuation multiples. In addition, parts of the local population prefer to invest in real estate as a result of financial repression and the missing alternatives to invest their money (Lardy 2008). Thus, financial repression has both benefits and drawbacks for China. Gruin (2013) argues in his paper 'Asset or Liability? The Role of the Financial System in the Political Economy of China's Rebalancing' that financial repression was one way the government shifted resources towards investment and export sectors. At the same time, this helped China provide stability, which underlined the country's successful growth trajectory. Financial repression in China serves the purpose for raising cheap investment for government-led programmes. The PBoC, which is under the control of the State Council, supports this. As Gruin (2013: 7) notes the ultimate costs of this strategy accrues to the Chinese households, but it seems to be an acceptable cost. As long as the overall system develops well, individual destinies do not matter that much. Financial repression serves the goals of China well as all measures are judged given their effects on growth. In addition, it provides the government with another means of stability in the system. This is linked to the Chinese exchange rate policy, which is examined in detail in a separate section.

Research has not come to a definite conclusion on financial repression. Scholars argue that repressive systems result in a loss of efficiency but enable the local government to better handle market failures and financial risks. Proponents of the notion that the negative effects to growth dominate are McKinnon (1973), as well as Shaw (1973). In contrast, Stiglitz (1994) and Hellmann et al. (1997) point out the increased risk of financial distortions given market liberalisation. In China, the reform period started at the end of the 1970s but despite significant progress in many areas, the Chinese financial system remains repressive. 'Heavily regulated interest rates, state-influenced credit allocation, frequently adjusted reserve requirement' make up for the repressive system (Huang and Wang 2011: 834). Most of these measures were established around the inflection point of Mao's death in order to achieve higher economic growth rates while keeping financial risks in check. Credit-allocation directed by the state ensured that priority sectors received the necessary funds in order to develop in the initial years of the reform period. In addition, the depressed deposit rates should spur growth rates in investment at the cost of local savers. This is laid out in detail in the historical background section. Li (2001) points to the positive effects to growth of financial repression in the initial years of the reform period, but also underlines that in the long-term financial repression leads to dismal economic performance. This is supported by Lardy (2008). Additionally, Roubini and Sala-i-Martin (1992) laid out the theoretical connection as well as the negative empirical relation between financial repression and long-term economic performance.

In contrast to the aforementioned point, the financial crises of the 1980s and 1990s supported the view that excessive liberalisation leads to significant financial, economic, and political distortions. This is described in detail in the section 'Crises in Perspective'. The historic crisis episodes stand in stark contrast to the trajectory of China. Ito (2006) notes that the Chinese approach towards liberalisation has historically been on the cautious side and has lagged behind many other economies. Therefore, Huang and Wang (2011: 834) pose the following question: 'Does this asymmetric liberalization approach, especially its emphasis on financial restraints or gradual financial liberalization, provide a more appropriate model for developing countries embarking on economic reforms?' Huang and Wang (2011) construct a liberalisation index to examine the effects of financial repression. This index is constructed via matrix decomposition and includes the real deposit rate, the share of interest rates with are subject to government control, capital account control by assessing the restrictions for certain categories, reserve requirements, the percentage of government-owned banks in total bank loans, the state's credit allocation influence, and the share of the government sector in all loans outstanding. The researchers show that prudent measures with respect to liberalisation contributed positively to China's growth during the reform period. Moreover, Fry (1997) explains that certain prerequisites have to be met before a country should engage in financial liberalisation given historical crisis episodes. Prudent regulatory requirements and the supervision of capital markets are among these prerequisites. In case a country does not have adequate governance in place, liberalisation should be postponed. Many emerging markets, including China, do not yet fulfil these standards and thus, focused government intervention could be preferable to market liberalisation (Stiglitz 1994; Hellmann et al. 2000). China has always been on the prudent side in terms of liberalisation. Due to this, the country was able to avoid significant volatility during past crises.

b) FX Regime – Internationalisation, the Onshore/ Offshore Market and the FX Basket

Regarding the exchange rate, it can be distinguished between a fixed and a floating regime and indeed, both regimes as well as mixtures of these two are quite common. This is particularly important as fluctuations in the exchange rate can entail severe costs for the real economy. An own currency for a country is often related to the issue of sovereignty. In contrast to the latter, the Eurozone for instance is a currency union using a common currency, which comes with shared responsibilities for all member states (Feenstra and Taylor 2014: 424-427). Similar to this, stands the theory of an optimal financial area (OFA) from Jones and Underhill (2014). The researchers create certain criteria for an institutional framework that incorporates the malaise of capital and consequently helps a country to reduce the degree of institutional fragility, which is elaborated on in detail in the case study. Generally, the exchange rate regime is chosen by the government and is a crucial institution of a country. A fixed or pegged exchange rate regime is defined by very limited fluctuations of the local currency against a base currency, mostly the US dollar. This can only be feasible if the government intervenes in the exchange rate market. In contrast, a flexible or floating exchange rate regime is characterised by few government interventions in the market and thus, the local currency can fluctuate freely. As a rule of thumb, the distinction between narrow and wide fluctuations in the exchange rate is about +/- 1 to 2 percent for the fixed exchange rate while freely floating currency has no limits. The mixture between the two regimes is called a "managed float" or "dirty float" and allows for wider fluctuations but still depicts heavy interventions by the government in the foreign exchange market (Feenstra and Taylor 2014: 443-445). In order to fix an exchange rate against a base currency, a country must regularly intervene in the foreign exchange market by either buying or selling FX reserves, or by introducing capital controls. It must be said that by the means of intervention, many developing country's local currencies become overvalued at some point and thus, the monetary base contracts in the very country upholding the fixed exchange rate regime. Nevertheless, in case of a partial floating exchange rate, by intervening in the foreign exchange market the objectives for the central bank are mostly the accumulation of foreign exchange reserves, the provision of FX to the market, to supress excessive volatility and to correct a perceived misvaluation in the local currency. The problem with the exchange rate regime and potential interventions is that the latter institution must deal with capital flow volatility. Capital inflows can lead to an overvaluation of the exchange rate and vice versa (DeRosa 2009: 124-125), which hints to the problem of the monetary trilemma that is discussed further below in detail.

A managed floating exchange rate regime is one in which the local central bank intervenes in the FX market in order to influence the exchange rate. This has to be distinguished from a clean float in which the local institutions make no attempt to influence the value of the foreign exchange rate. Fixed exchange rates were quite common between the mid-1920s and 1931 as well as between 1945 and 1973. Today, many developing countries peg or manage their exchange rates against the US dollar or sometimes also against a basket of different currencies (Krugman et al. 2015: 528-529). An approach towards a country's exchange rate regime is very important due to a number of reasons. For instance, the intervention in the FX market by the central bank leads to changes in the money supply. To avoid this, sterilisation could be applied. Sterilisation refers to 'equal foreign and domestic asset transactions in opposite directions to nullify the impact of their foreign exchange operations on the domestic money supply' (Krugman et al. 2015: 532). This is that either open market operations or changes in the reserve requirements are aimed to neutralise these changes in the money supply caused by the intervention. Therefore, the latter may allow the central bank to keep the desired exchange rate regime while at the same time performing its tasks regarding monetary policy goals (DeRosa 2009: 129). Thus, under a fixed or managed floating exchange rate regime, the central bank accumulates or depletes foreign exchange rate reserves and removes the effects on domestic money supply by dealing in local and foreign assets. However, a country might decide on altering the value of its foreign exchange rate due to various reasons. For instance, devaluation has effects on the local unemployment rate, on the current account balance, on the amount of foreign exchange reserves held by the central bank, but also on the local price level among others (Krugman et al. 2015: 540). This book focuses in particular on foreign exchange rate crises.

An issue closely related to the FX regime of a country is the so-called monetary trilemma or impossible trinity. As a matter of fact, a country can only achieve two factors out of the following three: a pegged exchange rate, free capital mobility, and autonomous monetary policy (McNally and Gruin 2017: 5). Every country faces this crucial trade off. The discussion ranges whether systemic factors dominate, and China's future trajectory can be deducted from the evolution of other regions or whether the idiosyncrasies of the country dominate the future path of China. Eichengreen and Kawai (2014: 4) note in this respect that 'the PRC is not like other countries. This makes it important to ask, critically, how much can be learned about the prospects and pitfalls of RMB internationalisation from the experience of other countries. In particular, the PRC has a much more extensively controlled capital account of the balance of payments, and a more heavily controlled financial system and economy generally, than any other country that has previously aspired to elevate its national unit to international currency status'. These institutional determinants are examined in detail in this part of the conceptual section. In spite of above-mentioned trilemma, the country seeks for new ways to circumvent the trade-off as it desires for exchange rate stability as well as for a more autonomous monetary policy and openness at the same time. The foreign exchange rate buffer, accumulated by China over the preceding decades, helps the country to partially achieve its goals (Rey 2015). Nevertheless, for China it is crucial to keep in place distinct measures of exchange rate controls. This allows the country to experiment with reforms while always having the option to stop the process should unintended consequences arise (McNally and Gruin 2017: 9). This was termed by Bowles and Wang (2013: 21) as 'internationalization without full convertibility'.

As laid out in the historical background section, every historic crisis episode has led to a questioning of the liberalisation paradigm. Free capital flows, as well as deregulation contributed to past periods of stress. Hence, a common scheme for analysing financial crisis can be deducted. The exchange rate regime plays a crucial role in this respect as should be clear by examining the monetary trilemma. Nonetheless, China's trajectory is quite distinct from other emerging markets. 'China's capacity and willingness to forge its own path in managing capital mobility and the exchange rate already commenced in the early 1990s' (McNally and Gruin 2017: 12). This is laid out in detail in the section 'China's Economic Empowerment' and should contribute to the understanding of the state China finds itself in today. The control of its exchange rate as well as financial repression and the curtailment of capital mobility contributed to China's economic trajectory. The management of the country's exchange rate regime helped spur exports, which, together with investment, fostered China's economic rise over the preceding decades. As McNally and Gruin (2017: 22) note the current international monetary system is not a purely liberal one. Particularly in emerging markets, the free floating of exchange rates remains a myth, which was described by Calvo and Reinhart (2002). State-guidance is still the predominant form of how economic and financial institutions are managed. Manipulation regarding the FX regime includes the accumulation and depletion of FX reserves to target the currency level as well as restrictions to the free flow of capital. Given historical crisis episodes, the aforementioned certainly gained legitimacy. However, not only emerging markets intervene in capital markets. Quantitative management of the money supply as well as the low-interest policy pursued by major central banks have implications on exchange rates globally (McNally and Gruin 2017: 22), which becomes more relevant as China is opening.

China has always regarded the stability of its exchange rate as a virtue. As laid out in the historical background section, the country opted-out to devalue its currency at the time of the Asian financial crisis. While other Asian currencies collapsed under the pressure of the crisis, the Chinese currency remained stable against the US dollar. The PBoC decided for a non-devaluation strategy, which provided great stability to the region since any weakness in the renminbi would have been immediately transmitted into currency weakness of the neighbouring Asian countries. In the overall interest of the crisis inflicted countries China maintained its exchange rate regime. This was done despite huge pressure and came at a price for the country. However, China's decision to not alter its exchange rate helped to restore stability (Prasad 2017: 74-76). In 2001, China became a member of the WTO, which is described in detail in the section on international institutions. The subsequent increases in productivity should have led to an appreciation of the RMB. However, due to the peg to the US dollar, the Chinese currency depreciated in real-effective terms. This trend was corrected with the change in the FX regime in 2005 (Lardy 2012: 101). Before this change in the exchange rate regime, the Asian central banks generally focused on tracking the US dollar, which is described in detail by McKinnon and Schnabl (2004) as well as by McKinnon (2005) and has become known as soft pegging to the dollar regime. Calvo and Reinhart (2002) described the reliance of emerging markets to the US dollar as fear of floating.

Regarding China, the country's exchange rate regime has changed substantially over the past decades. In 1994, the unification of the various exchange rates led to a single currency. 'The Chinese government devalued the official exchange rate so it matched the swap market rate and then unified the two exchange rates. From 1994 onward, the value of the RMB was pegged to the U.S. dollar' (Prasad 2017: 79). In 1996, the yuan became fully convertible with respect to current account transactions, which formed the basis for the WTO accession of China in 2001. The Chinese currency remained pegged against the US dollar until July 2005, when the country announced that it would implement a floating FX regime going forward, which led to a gradual appreciation trend of the currency over the subsequent years (Lardy 2012: 101). It was announced that the RMB would be managed against a basket of currencies. However, in practice the dollar remained the benchmark for the altered peg (Prasad 2017: 79). Nonetheless, this led to the increasing influence of the RMB on other Asian currencies (Shu et al. 2007). China routinely widened its trading band, namely from 0.3 percent to 0.5 percent in May 2007 and to 1 percent in April 2010. The most recent widening of the trading band was performed in March 2014, when the Chinese leadership increased the trading range of yuan around the daily reference rate to 2 percent (Shu et al. 2014: 3). Due to the alteration of the exchange rate regime, the RMB appreciated about 25 percent relative to the US dollar from June 2005 to June 2014 (Prasad 2017: 83). However, the RMB weakened slightly by 0.8 percent relative to the US dollar from July 2014 to July 2015. This was due to the general strength of the US dollar as well as the dismal performance of China's external statistics as is laid out in the section on the country's fundamentals.

Furthermore, Shu et al. (2014) point out that the rise of the offshore renminbi market suggests that the internationalisation of the yuan is succeeding. This is in line with the increasing weight of China in the international economy. The influence of the Chinese currency was increased due to two developments in recent years, namely the increased exchange rate flexibility and the more frequent external use of the Chinese currency. McNally and Gruin (2017: 16) note on the development of the offshore market that 'the strategy shaping RMB internationalization has so far reproduced crucial elements of the

Sino-capitalist logic. Targeted liberalization, policy experimentation, and institutional hybridization have been widely employed, such as with the building of offshore RMB markets, and only made possible by the strategic collaboration of Chinese state actors with international financial centers, institutions, and networks'. He and McCauley (2010) show that the emergence of an offshore market goes hand in hand with the more frequent use of the currency outside of the home country. The onshore and the offshore market are virtually the same, however, the separation of the markets can lead to price discrepancies. Different players might react to events differently and arbitrage conditions do not hold in the short-term due to capital flow restrictions among others. With respect to RMB internationalisation, the Chinese leadership actively encouraged the use of the yuan outside Mainland China since July 2009. The gradual changes to certain capital account restrictions contributed to the events unfolding in the second half of 2015 and 2016. Cross-border settlement of yuan transactions has become a major source of liquidity, which was introduced in 2009. In addition, the Chinese Central Bank set-up bilateral swap agreements with the goal of encouraging the international use of the renminbi (Shu et al. 2014: 3). Moreover, with respect to the offshore market the spot fixing for the offshore renminbi was introduced in Hong Kong in June 2011 by the Treasury Markets Association (TMA), which is an institution closely connected to the Hong Kong Monetary Authority (HKMA) (Minikin and Lau 2012: 102). Furthermore, the fixing for the offshore renminbi interest rate benchmark (CNH HIBOR) was introduced in June 2013. With respect to the onshore market, the CNY exchange rate remains highly regulated. Spot transactions make up for the majority of the transactions with FX forwards being hardly used yet. The daily fixing of the yuan is announced every day at 9.30 am by the China Foreign Exchange Trade System (CFETS) in Shanghai, which is also called the reference rate or central parity (Prasad 2017: 80; Shu et al. 2014: 4). The change of the fixing regime led to increased uncertainty in August 2015 and the subsequent months, which is examined in detail in the case study. Despite the emergence of a more active CNY market, relative to the China's economic position in the world any FX transactions remain minor. With respect to the offshore market, spot transactions have become more frequent since the establishment of cross-border yuan trade settlement in August 2010. This has led to the more frequent use of FX derivatives in the offshore market. The offshore market is freely accessible for investors and hedgers outside of China. Liquidity, measured as the bid-ask spread, remains better onshore than offshore (Shu et al. 2014: 5), however, this is expected to convergence over time.

For the purpose of this case study, the onshore RMB will be referred to as CNY and the offshore RMB as CNH, which is general market convention. Hong Kong is the preeminent offshore centre for renminbi trading, but other centres are also evolving. Clearing banks were designated by the Chinese government in Taipei in 2012, in Singapore in 2013 as well as in Frankfurt and London in 2014. The rise of these offshore hubs is one key element of the internationalisation strategy of the renminbi (Gruin 2017). The development of the offshore market in Hong Kong started in 2003 as the Chinese government allowed for individuals to make use of the yuan for personal transactions. Hong Kong banks could provide loans as well as deposits in CNH to local residents and certain foreign business entities within tight limits (Gagnon and Troutman 2014). In general, the internationalisation of the RMB was pursued cautiously and gradually. This allowed for an experimental approach towards the promotion of the global use of the RMB without losing control of the process (Prasad 2017: 103). In addition, these banks could make a limited offer of CNH deposits to Mainland Chinese who could purchase these with CNY. In 2007, some Chinese institutions were granted the permission to issue bonds denominated in CNH in Hong Kong, which became known as the dim sum bond market. This is the biggest RMB bond market outside Mainland China. In 2009 as well as 2010, all restrictions with respect to CNH transactions were eliminated for Hong Kong as well as foreign institutions. In 2011, mainland trade companies were allowed to settle all transactions related to imports and exports in CNH. Today, the transactions between CNH and other foreign currencies have become fully liberalised. However, trading between CNY and other currencies is still heavily regulated (Gagnon and Troutman 2014: 2; Minikin and Lau 2012). Thus, the two markets are closely connected due to the use of the same currency, but still different rules apply to each segment. With respect to FX pricing, Gagnon and Troutman (2014: 5) note that 'the most important driver of expectations of future changes in the value of CNH is views about China's policy toward the value of CNY'. Capital transactions are subject to tight restrictions between Mainland China and the outside world. Therefore, the value of CNY and CNH can diverge as much as 1 or 2 percent in times of stress. Arbitrage, which could lead to the closing of this gap, is mainly related to trade settlement (Gagnon and Troutman 2014: 7). The elimination of differences in the exchange rate, as well as in onshore-offshore interest rates, would require a greater degree of liberalisation of the capital account. This will be examined in the respective sections. Another means of promoting the use of the RMB was the establishment of bilateral trading arrangements between the yuan and currencies of certain trading partners. This should have reduced transaction costs as well as helped to bypass the US dollar. For instance, an exchange for Russian rubles and the RMB was established in Shanghai, which was supported by a bilateral agreement between the two governments to establish local currency settlement in June 2011. The same year, China and Japan signed a similar agreement, which, in principle, could have been transformative for the Asian financial landscape. Nonetheless, other factors also played a role in this respect, which prevented the agreement from taking off (Prasad 2017: 112-113). Closely related to the internationalisation of the RMB is the status as a reserve currency. In this respect, the IMF's artificial currency unit, which is known as Special Drawing Rights (SDR), plays an important role. Since 2001, the value of the SDR has been determined by a basket consisting of four reserve currencies, namely the dollar, the euro, the Japanese yen, and the pound sterling. The inclusion of the RMB in this basket was a significant step in terms of perceptions as this grants China the official recognition of one of the largest supranational institutions (Prasad 2017: 120). This event is examined in detail in the case study.

c) The International Monetary System

Although states are still the principal actors on a global basis, international institutions play a crucial role in facilitating cross-border exchanges. Foremost, the International Monetary Fund (IMF), the World Bank

(WB), and the World Trade Organisation (WTO) are important in this respect.

i) International Financial Institutions

To start with, the protectionist period after World War I led to the Great Depression and ultimately, culminated in World War II. At the end of the Second World War, the dominating powers met in Bretton Woods in 1944 and discussed the international system. At this conference, the International Monetary Fund and the International Bank for Reconstruction and Development, which later became the World Bank (WB), were set up. In 1947, the GATT, the third famous international institution governing trade, was established. Under the GATT, the negotiations named the rounds based on which city the discussions took place. At the end of the Uruguay Round, the GATT was transformed into an extended institution, namely the WTO at the beginning of 1995. The WTO aims at lowering trade frictions, although tariffs are allowed under specific conditions. The key provisions of the international institutional trade arrangement are the "most favoured nation" clause, which requires equal treatment of member states with respect to trade barriers (Feenstra and Taylor 2014: 234-236). With respect to global governance, the dominant role of the United States has to be pointed out over the preceding decades. The US led several rounds of GATT negotiations and encouraged the formation of the European Economic Community. In addition, the establishment of the IMF's Special Drawing Rights as a suitable alternative to a dollar-dominated world was fostered by the United States. The SDR inclusion of the RMB in 2015 plays a particularly important role in the case study. In addition, the US supported the World Bank in its ambition to extend lending to developing countries. However, the Bretton Woods system also became unsustainable at the same time. Unilaterally, the United States ended the monetary system, as the US government could not pursue expansionary policy at the same time as keeping the currency peg. Therefore, the gold window was closed in 1971 which effectively meant abandoning the dollar peg to gold. The OPEC oil shocks in the 1970s further led to global distortions (Drezner 2015: 144-145). Many countries switched to floating exchange rates in the aftermath of the Bretton Woods system, which entailed the negative effects of higher FX volatility. The G7 forum was created as an attempt to manage these distortions. Moreover, the International Monetary Fund decided to focus its attention on developing countries affected by balance-of-payment crises (Drezner 2015: 146) and thus played a crucial role in past crisis episodes as laid out in the historical background section.

With the collapse of the Soviet Union, economic diplomacy changed substantially. Central and Eastern Europe abandoned communism in 1989 and the Soviet Union dissolved into various independent states in 1991. Before then, most communist countries did not participate in the international institutional system. Many things changed since this inflection point. Global interdependence makes it necessary to consider preferences of emerging powers. Barriers to international trade were reduced and subsequently, the promotion of more flexible exchange rate systems, as well as capital flow liberalisation, was put forward (Bayne 2016: 16). In this respect, a study by Böhmer et al. (2016) stresses the relationship between globalisation and economic growth. The rise of emerging markets over the previous decades coincides with the increased share of global exports of these countries. With respect to clothing, office materials, computers, and communication, emerging markets have overtaken the developed world. In general, the rise of these countries is mainly due to the success of China. For instance, in electronics China makes up for more than 50 percent of market share of all countries (Böhmer et al. 2016: 25-27). The growth of exports of China particularly increased sharply after the accession of the country in the WTO in 2001. This is a sign of the importance of international institutions with respect to the trajectory of a country as the institutional set-up significantly influences a country's strengths and weaknesses.

The negative side of globalisation included the fact that financial crises have become more frequent and contagious and poor countries have been left behind. In the 1990s, the advanced countries suffered from a slowdown in growth, leading the United States to advocate policies such as trade liberalisation, deregulation, conservative economic policies, and privatisations (Drezner 2015: 146). With respect to international institutions, Ngaire Woods (2003) attributes significant influence on decision-making to the United States, particularly with respect to the distribution of loans as well as to staff trainings. In addition, in light of widening trade deficits the congressional pressure on the US government to address China's currency policy increased in the mid-2000s (Drezner 2015: 147). As a matter of fact, the IMF and the World Bank are still regarded as extensions of US power and thus mistrust towards these institutions from the side of emerging markets is severe. As Pickford and Subacchi (2015: 4) note this is despite the softening of the Washington Consensus.

International institutions are still dominated by the United States, although the influence of emerging powers such as China is increasing. The establishment of the G20 forum to coordinate economic policymaking partly reflects the increasing importance of emerging markets. However, the slow pace of the reforms is undeniable. Therefore, 'the large emerging markets have responded by establishing new institutions and China promoted the use of the renminbi in a multi-currency international monetary system' (Pickford and Subacchi 2015: 1). Thus, the dominance of the United States in the international system is waning and a greater dispersion of power is visible, but also a higher level of integration. Turmoil in capital markets and economic recessions on a global scale are symptoms of this interconnectedness. Indeed, China is becoming fast a crucial part of the international system (Pickford and Subacchi 2015: 2; Krugman et al. 2015: 608-609). For instance, the great financial crisis of 2008 was a US centric crash, which had global spillover effects. Only extensive fiscal stimulus packages made a recovery possible and avoided a prolonged downturn as happened in the Great Depression. China was among the first countries to leave the state of crisis as is laid out in the section 'Crises in Perspective'. While the country projected stability on a global basis over the preceding decades, China itself became a source of global uncertainty in 2015 and 2016.This is examined in detail in the case study of this book.

ii) Further Institutions

With respect to the G20, the original G7 forum was expanded in 1999 with the inclusion of eleven developing countries. In addition, the G20 forum was elevated to include the heads of states in 2008. This date is mostly referred to as the origination of this rather informal institution (Wade 2013: 6). The re-emergence of the G20 forum was one response to the global financial crisis. The April 2009 G20 summit helped establish a series of measures to tackle the turmoil. Coordinated stimulus programmes on an unprecedented scale led to the avoidance of a prolonged depression and ultimately stabilised capital markets (Pickford and Subacchi 2015: 3). During the great financial crisis, the G20 countries decided that the forum they had created was explicitly meant for international economic cooperation. 'For example, the G20 has served as a useful mechanism to defuse tensions concerning China's undervalued currency. In response to congressional pressure for more robust action, in April 2010 Treasury secretary, Timothy Geithner, cited the G20 meetings as, "the best avenue for advancing U.S. interests" on China's manipulation of its exchange rate. In June of that year, President Barack Obama sent a letter to his G20 colleagues stressing the importance of "market-determined exchange rates." Three days after the president's letter was sent, the People's Republic of China announced that it would "enhance the RMB exchange rate flexibility." For the next two years, the renminbi nominally appreciated at a rate of 5 percent a year – more so if one factors in the differences in national inflation rates' (Drezner 2012: 10). In addition, another important event took place at the 2010 G20 summit in Toronto. Before that point, there existed a rough consensus among states that stimulus should help to reduce the negative repercussions of the global financial crisis. It has to be mentioned that those countries, which pursued Keynesian economic policy, were first to leave the state of crisis, foremost China and the United States. However, during this summit, a group of countries had other ideas that ultimately contributed to the European debt crisis of 2011 and 2012 (Drezner 2012: 2), which was another crisis with spillover effects to emerging markets. The current global institutional set-up is not without its critics. In particular, the G20 forum has been in focus of high-profile complaints.

For instance, the Norwegian foreign minister noted on the G20 that this is, 'one of the greatest setbacks since World War II' (Spiegel 2010 quoted in Vestergaard and Wade 2012: 258). In particular, the selection of the member countries of the G20 forum lacks any legitimacy. Furthermore, 'the selection of the 19 states included in the G20 membership in 1999 was made by the G7, and specifically by Timothy Geithner, then the US Under Secretary of the Treasury for International Affairs (with Lawrence Summers as his boss) and Geithner's counterpart at the German Finance Ministry, Caio Koch-Weser. In a series of transatlantic telephone calls Geithner and Koch-Weser went through the list of countries saying, Canada in, Spain out, South Africa in, Nigeria and Egypt out, and so on. They came up with an "in" group which covered a high enough proportion of world output, trade, and population for them to judge it 'representatively', sent the names to other G7 finance ministries, and after a few more iterations, sent out invitations to the first meeting went out' (Vestergaard and Wade 2012: 260). Therefore, the composition of the G20 forum was not based on any specific selection criteria hence making the legitimacy of the forum highly questionable.

iii) Voting Systems

Given China's rise, international institutions voting quotas came under review. For instance, between 2008 and 2010, the World Bank Group changed its voting system in favour of emerging countries, as is examined below in more detail. Moreover, the policies of international institutions also shifted in favour of less advanced economies. The IMF admitted the importance of capital controls in tackling both economic and financial instability in light of capital outflows (Drezner 2012: 11). This represents a break with the past, as shown in the section 'Crises in Perspective'. Nonetheless, the more formal institutional bodies face severe critic, foremost with respect to their voting mechanisms. Emerging markets are not represented adequately in these institutions given their relative gains in economic clout. The IMF and World Bank tried to address some of these issues. However, the improvements for some developing and emerging market countries were marginal relative to the improvements in economic wellbeing over the previous decades (Vestergaard and Wade 2012).

Furthermore, China's economic resilience during the great financial crisis of 2008 has only underlined its demand for increased voting power in international institutions. The country will shape the current set-up according to its own preferences, which might differ substantially from that of the current hegemon, the United States. A rising power challenging the status quo has historically led to disruptions of the system. This stands in stark contrast to China's peaceful rise over the preceding decades. 'The preferences of the emerging powers in respect of global governance are a crucial starting point: if they do not diverge substantially from the current institutional and normative status quo, then the potential for conflict and bargaining deadlock is diminished' (Kahler 2013: 712). Moreover, capabilities form an equal part of this equation, which are a function of economic weight. A failure to do so results in a lack of legitimacy of the current institutional set-up, as argued above, and in emerging markets investing in their own framework, which further undermines the current system.

As noted by Rodrik (2011: 713), most successful developing economies and emerging markets have not followed a market-orientated policy mix. Indeed, these countries have instead pursued an export-driven development strategy within a neo-mercantilist framework. China's rise makes it demand a greater voting power in the international institutions as well as more representation of Chinese citizens in top-management positions. Given some concessions, emerging powers were willing to commit more resources to the existing institutional set-up instead of investing in their own. It goes without saying that China remains sceptical about strengthening the grip of these institutions on the nation's economy. This has to be viewed in light of the country's history as laid out in detail in the section 'China's Economic Empowerment'. The resistance from the side of emerging economies led to various failures in G20 negotiation rounds. China is a status quo power and thus, the country's criticism of certain institutions 'appeared to aim at a strengthened multilateral system, not an overthrow of that system' (Kahler 2013: 714). Kahler (2013: 714-715) notes that an increased role for the renminbi in the international system has to be met by certain preconditions, which are discussed in detail in the corresponding section as well as in the case study. Changes in these variables are partly responsible for the turmoil China faced in 2015 and 2016 and stand in stark contrast to the strategy the country pursued over the previous decades.

As China started to engage with global institutions, the country became a more outspoken critic of the current practices. This is very much related to the capabilities of the country. With respect to economics, market size is one primary contributor to a country's capabilities and does provide a certain advantage in negotiations. In more detail, bargaining advantage is often related to the capability of a country to open or close a certain market (Barton et al. 2006: 10-11). With respect to China, flourishing internal markets, as well as its export-orientation is the basis for the nation's success (Kahler 2013: 719). A national currency, which is used as a medium for exchange instead of other hard currencies, provides for further influence, but also constrains a nation. Credibility in a country's monetary policy is one cornerstone of a functioning local currency system. One lever China has in negotiations with incumbent nations is its huge amount of FX reserves, which serve as a buffer for the country for financial shocks and help China manage its exchange rate (Lardy 2012). The sharp increase of China's foreign exchange reserves is a sign of the country's currency policy as well as its development strategy. Instead of letting the local currency appreciate, the nation built up a significant amount of FX reserves. In addition, by keeping the local currency at an undervalued level, the country further fostered its export strategy (Kahler 2013: 720; Krugman et al. 2015: 721). This has empowered China's influence. However, limiting factors with respect to the countries engagement with international institutions include domestic political factors. For instance, poverty and inequality are determinants which limit China's willingness to deal with international recommendations. This is laid out in detail in the historical background section.

As discussed above, emerging countries were allocated a larger share of voting quotas. However, these adjustments were minor in relation to the increase in economic clout of emerging countries over the previous decades (Vestergaard and Wade 2013: 153). In addition, the incumbent states also tried to reduce the outside options of emerging countries, which would increase future negotiation power of these countries. Indeed, their current strategy aims at co-opting emerging countries in existing clubs, which puts into question the viability of specific South-South institutions. Indeed, engaging in competitive regional arrangements undermined certain agreements. This is particularly relevant with respect to China and Japan. This counterbalancing resulted in an only minor increase of influence of emerging countries in the current global institutional set-up, which aimed at making the system more legitimate (Kahler 2013: 725-726). In 2010, the then-president of World Bank, Robert Zoellick, noted that the emergence of new powers needed a reform of the voting quota system of the institution (Zoellick 2010). Indeed, the institution performed a voice reform in 2010. However, the change in the voting system was more modest than appears on the surface. The so-called voice reform of international institutions happened in two steps. First, the initial idea of a voice reform emerged at the United Nations International Conference in Monterrey in 2002 and the main points included debt relief, development aid, as well as tackling corruption. Nevertheless, the conference also addressed the notion of enhancing the voice of developing countries. Second, an actual change in the quotas got established at the end of the decade. 'They reached agreement on voting power reallocation based on a quota framework in which quota votes are determined by three factors: economic weight as measured by GDP (weighted 75%); past and future contributions to IDA (20%); and "contributions to development", a measure of a country's history of Bank borrowing (5%). This seemed to be in accordance with the principle that voting power should "in large measure reflect" countries' relative economic weight' (Vestergaard and Wade 2013: 155). As mentioned above, the voice reform of 2008-2010, however, did not bring the hoped-for improvements for developing countries (Pickford and Subacchi 2015: 3). Regarding the quota framework, China decided to forgo some of its allocated voting power. The country gave up nearly half of its allocation according to economic weight. This was done in favour of DTC countries, which otherwise would have gained very little. Therefore, China's allocated voting power differs the most from its actual economic weight (Vestergaard and Wade 2013: 158-

159), which represents a positive contribution of the country to the international system. Moreover, the IMF governance reforms only took effect as of 2015, even though these had been previously agreed upon in 2010. As the reforms did not go far enough, China strived to establish institutions on its own. One example of the previous is the Asian International Infrastructure Bank. As a matter of fact, the United States tried to prevent other countries from joining these institutions established outside the traditional Bretton Woods system (Bayne 2016: 28) and include them instead in the existing system.

d) Institutions, Governance and the Rule of Law

The institutional dimension is key to assessing a country's strengths and weaknesses. Rodrik (2004: 131) notes that 'the quality of institutions trumps everything else'. According to Acemoglu (2004: 2), institutions are a key determinant of economic prosperity. As a matter of fact, the institutional dimension explains the cross-country differences in prosperity. The researchers first explain the limitations of econometric analysis with respect to institutions and a country's performance and subsequently, proceed by using a nation's history to proof the latter. Standard explanations as to why a huge difference in economic prosperity exists between countries usually focus on physical and human capital accumulation, as well as technological differences. However, the question should be why some countries have ample savings to invest in their future and why new technologies are adopted in some nations while others slide backwards (Acemoglu 2004: 7-8)?

Economic institutions include property rights or contract enforcement for instance. By analysing the trajectories of North and South Korea it is shown by academic research that the driving factors in the performance are institutions. In terms of the latter example, it is made clear that there is no empirical link between geography and industrialisation and moreover, cultural differences cannot explain the diverging trajectories of North and South Korea (Acemoglu 2004: 21, 31, 39). This is in line with Rodrik et al. (2004). In addition, it can be said that good institutions are those, which 'encourage investment in physical, human capital, and in technology, and bad institutions in the opposite' (Acemoglu 2004: 35). Another example of the lack of causal influence the culture of countries has on its trajectory can be seen with the examples of China, Hong Kong, Singapore, and Taiwan (Acemoglu 2004: 43). China, for instance, relied in the first decades after WWII on state planning as well as on communist political institutions, while Hong Kong, Singapore and Taiwan adapted capitalist traits. China only experienced the same prosperity the latter three countries had after Mao's death and the change in China's institutional set-up (Naughton 2007). This is shown in detail in the historical background section.

Economic growth and institutions are inevitably linked. Rodrik (2000) notes that, 'the question is no longer whether institutions matter, but which institutions matter and how to develop them'. Indeed, an improvement in the quality of institutions leads to a substantial spurt in economic growth. One crucial aspect with respect to institutions is governance. Governance can be defined as 'the traditions and institutions by which authority in a country is exercised' (Kaufmann et al. 1999: 1). Building legal and social institutions for governance is crucial for a functioning society (Park 2006: 100). Governance depicts a positive correlation with the income of a country. However, it has to be mentioned that economies can grow without a suitable governance system. The question is only how long this growth can be sustained and as shown in this book, whether a lack of governance has to be regarded as increased vulnerability of a country (The World Bank Group 2017: 138). To reduce short-term rent-seeking behaviour by actors, checks and balances could be introduced. For instance, horizontal political constraints as identified by veto power from independent observers or alignment across different government offices lead to less disagreement with respect to foreign direct investment (Jensen et al. 2012). In addition, Wright (2008) shows that the establishment of good legislative bodies, even in case of authoritarian regimes, can increase the cost of expropriation of investments significantly. Moreover, Laffont and Martimort (1999) show that with respect to regulators the division of power can hinder collusive capture through the reduction of the monopoly on information. In fact, the review of the regulators themselves by other government offices can prevent regulators from making decisions that are against public interest. One mechanism of vertical accountability would be media coverage. The latter can be an alternative for information gathering for instance (The World Bank Group 2017: 150). Whether and how these factors are applicable to China is laid out below.

China does not fit well into most studies with respect to institutions and growth because the country has been governed by the CCP since the establishment of the PRC. In general, governance and the rule of law are weak, since independent judiciary is rare in China. This, in light of the country's incredible growth rates, has been termed the "China paradox", which refers to the country's rise despite a well-developed set of institutions (Yao and Yueh 2009). Thus, the application of the existing theoretical knowledge to China is quite complex since governance and law support the trajectory of a country (La Porta et al. 1997, 1998; Acemoglu et al. 2005). However, China is generally left out of these studies, which put forward a causal relationship between these factors and growth. Allen et al. (2005) measure China against the rule of law and conclude that the country is a paradox in the sense that a weak legal system coincides with strong economic growth. China managed to rise steeply, particularly relative to other emerging market countries. In contrast to the study by Allen et al. (2005), Hasan et al. (2009) deduced a significant relationship between legal institutions, financial deepening as well as political pluralism and economic performance. The idea behind political pluralism is that authoritarian regimes can successfully direct capital accumulation as well as resource allocation, in the early stages of development, but face problems later. This is related to the distinction between extensive and intensive growth, which is described in detail in the section 'Crises in Perspective'. The researchers analyse data from 31 provinces between 1986 and 2002 and note that 'higher growth rates are found, holding constant a set of standard economic variables, in those regions with more rule of law, more property rights awareness and protections, more active capital markets and a more open political environment' (Hasan et al. 2009: 168-169). In addition, the researchers put forward that China followed quite a distinct path without democratisation, only incremental liberalisation as well as very limited privatisation. The country's tremendous rise in the last few decades poses a puzzle to scholars due to the nation's undeveloped legal system. The country's transformation from plan to market created the need for completely new institutions. In contrast to the Western Big Bang approach that many Central and Eastern European countries and the Soviet Union followed, China decided to address this issue in a gradual manner. This fundamental difference in transforming the nation's system is the reason for many of the different outcomes we can see over the last decades.

Given the above, China has to be regarded as an exception to the standard Coasian economic model due to China's rise despite high transaction costs and an inefficient allocation of resources (Coase 1937). Indeed, Clarke (2003b: 92-93) states that an economic system can go a long way in the absence of formal property rights. Therefore, the researcher notes that his "Rights Hypothesis" could be wrong in terms of the strong focus on the institutionalisation of rights and governance. Understanding the trajectory of China can contribute significant added value in this respect. As a matter of fact, it might be more important for an economic system to have predictability than the formalisation of the rule of law or governance principals. This is in line with the variation of this dimension along the chosen path of transition. Failure to distinguish between predictability and rights leads to a false view on the matter. In fact, Clarke (2003b: 97) puts forward that 'one must look at all the government agencies that adjust relations between parties and have the power to order the transfer of resources from one party to another'.

China's trajectory has to be understood in light of its gradual transition from plan to market as is laid out in the historical background section. This has resulted 'in a partially reformed economy within a communal property state' (Yueh 2013: 19). The country's incremental approach towards transformation has resulted in a poor set of property rights, as well as high transaction costs. Despite this, China's rise has been steady as well as steep. Indeed, the underdeveloped legal system forms part of this paradox of China's trajectory. The country only acknowledged the existence of private property rights in 2004 through the inclusion of these rights in the nation's constitution. Yet, China's unique trajectory proved the country right, as is laid out in the historical background section. The household responsibility system played a crucial role in this respect. As McNally and Gruin (2017: 16) note institutional hybridization contributed significantly to China's successful trajectory. In contrast to the literature on the connection between governance and the rule of law, Greif (1993) and Clarke (2003a) stress the importance of informal institutions with respect to ownership rights. The literature on social capital and networks, known as guanxi, is extensive. Nonetheless, there are clear limits to such informal institutions and the lack of well-established legal system in light of China's strong economic development is daunting (Cull and Xu 2005). As laid out above, institutions are one of the key determinants of a country's trajectory (Acemoglu et al. 2005). In the case of China, however, the country's development took place in the absence of good governance and a well-established set of laws. 'It raises the questions as to how China was able to instil economic incentives in the absence of private property rights and how an imperfect legal system could protect against expropriation that would normally limit investment and other private economic activities' (Yueh 2013: 32).

Studies postulate the relationship between property rights and economic rights with the former being a precondition for the latter. Less developed property rights are related to lower investment and growth in general (Claessens and Laeven 2003). In particular, the success of economic transformations via the big bang approach relies on the security of property rights given the uncertainty of a rapidly changing environment (Cull and Xu 2005: 119). However, McMillan and Woodruff (2002) put forward that in transition economies, in which a gradual approach is chosen, the importance of property rights relative to external financing is negligible. Only as the transformation advances, the importance of market-supporting institutions increases. Cull and Xu (2005: 120) note on this that 'China, a country whose transition to a market economy has been more gradual than those in Europe and the former Soviet Union. Lacking a big bang, uncertainties regarding the security of property rights could be less severe, and China thus offers a potentially interesting contrast to most other transitional economies'.

This set of questions is addressed in the section 'China's Economic Empowerment' and are generally related to the unique approach towards transition the country chose. Nonetheless, the question remains whether the current system or the steep growth rates are sustainable? Ultimately, governance and a consistent set of rules have to be established to support the rising private sector in China. So far, most of the investment decisions have been made by the state. The Chinese government has been regarded as a development state giving a helping hand to the private sector, but also prioritising certain sectors and trends (Roland 2005: 8). The establishment of a coherent governance structure and a well-developed rule of law will pose significant challenges to the country. Nonetheless, the absence of these factors in the country's growth history contributes to the China paradox (Jefferson and Rawski 2002). The connection between these determinants and economic performance have been well documented by empirical research, for instance by Rodrik et al. (2005). As described above, Acemoglu et al. (2005) put forward two types of market-supporting institutions, namely property rights as well as contracting institutions. However, for China, these factors only play a minor role in light of the country's steep rise since the reform era started at the end of the 1970s (Cull and Xu 2005). Measures such as the World Bank's Worldwide Governance Indicators or the Heritage Foundation's Index of Economic Freedoms suggest that China has a rather underdeveloped legal system and government. Hitherto, China's rise has been steady and steep. Nonetheless, China's economic performance picked-up significantly with the accession of the country to the WTO in 2001, which introduced a new set of international standards and rules to the Chinese system. Clarke (2003b) associates this event with the increase in transparency in the country.

In addition, part of the answer to the China paradox can be found in the country's approach towards transition as mentioned above. The gradual shift from plan to market allowed for time for experimentation, which forms a cornerstone of the country's transformation (McNally and Gruin 2017: 16). This also meant that 'markets were not always established by laws at the outset but developed over time with experimentation of various market mechanisms, such as the "dual-track" pricing system and the export-orientated Special Economic Zones (SEZs)' (Yueh 2013: 39). Given this particular focus on export- and state-led investment driven development, these areas were prioritised to the development of governance system and a consistent set of laws. In other words, although governance and well-established laws have so far played a minor role in China's trajectory since the beginning of the reform era, the increasing openness of the country to global determinants and the planned alteration of the Chinese growth model make these variables more important factors going forward.

e) The State-owned Enterprise Sector

China´s progress since the start of the reform era at the end of the 1970s has been enormous. The institutional change is at the heart when shifting from plan to market. The government-owned industry was crucial to the planned economy. This stands in stark contrast to a market economy where competitive market forces all participants to be more efficient. The dismantling of the planned economy led to the deprivation of SOEs´ high surplus earnings, which ultimately accrued to the state. This is also the reason why privatisation hardly played any role during the early years of the reform era. However, new entrants to certain sectors were encouraged which led to a realignment of the ownership mix in China over time (Naughton 2007: 297-298). While this entailed significant changes for the Chinese economy, there has also been continuity as large state-owned enterprises still play a significant role in China.

The SOE complex was expanded during the Maoist era, as laid out in detail in the historical background section. The SOEs did not only serve as work unit but also provided welfare as well as health services among others to the Chinese workers. In addition, there were few incentives or alignments of interests during said period. This changed in the reform era through the emergence of township and village enterprises. ´By 1996, then, China had developed a kind of tripod industrial structure, in which state, collective, and private (domestic and foreign) firms each produced about one-third of total output´ (Naughton 2007: 301). The Company Law of 1993 led to significant changes in terms of reforming

SOEs as it provided a legal setting for corporatizing SOEs. This could be used for the means of privatisation at some point as shares could be simply sold to the Chinese people and triggered a new wave of institutional change (Lin and Zhu 2001). Historically, the continuation of state involvement was necessary to preserve stability, particularly via providing employment in government-owned enterprises, as the Chinese leadership advanced with its reform agenda. ′Following from the corporatization policy of 1992 (share issue privatization) and 1993 (restructuring into limited liability companies or LLCs and joint stock companies), the zhuada fanxiao (′save the large, let go of the small′) policy was enacted in 1994, which effectively privatized the small- and medium-sized SOEs′ (Yueh 2013: 308). Lin and Zhu (2001) argue that the Chinese government′s approach towards state-owned enterprises changed in 1993. From the start of the reforms to 1993, the focus was on the delegation of decision-making autonomy to companies. In the early 1990s, the focus shifted towards ownership restructuring. This aimed at turning the government-owned enterprises into shareholding entities due to the fact that the performance of state-owned enterprises deteriorated in light of rising competition from the private sector. ′SOEs have been touted by CCP leaders as the leading force of China′s socialist development. Despite the abandonment of central planning and greater allowance for private economic activities since 1992, the ideological concern about the erosion of public ownership (hence socialism) has continued to cast a shadow over the extent to which reform can proceed′ (Lin and Zhu 2001: 312). Furthermore, the researchers note that China′s socialist market economy builds its fundament on a diverse set of ownership. Thus, the goal of the corporatisation of state-owned enterprises included making the Chinese government the holder of the majority stake of these companies, particularly of the larger companies. Nonetheless, more enterprises were restructured, which led to more workers being laid off. These changes led to severe troubles, in particular given the rise of debt for the SOE sector at the turn of the millennium (Holz 2003). This is described in the section ′China′s Economic Empowerment′. The emergence of a private sector in China led to a decline in profits in the state-owned enterprise sector, which in turn entailed a shortfall in revenues for the Chinese government. This, in return, led to the government distributing less money to certain sectors and thus SOEs turned to the banking sector for funding (Naughton 2007), which makes for part of the troubles China faced in 2015 and 2016.

In contrast to a market economy, an enterprise in the Maoist era has to be regarded as a social unit with various functions, which became known as danwei. These firms did not operate by the same rules that they would have in a competitive environment. Related to this is the term soft budget constraint, which was coined by Kornai (1979, 1980). This term is connected to a loss-making enterprise continuing to receive financing as well as to a tendency of these companies for unlimited demand of funds for investment purposes. With respect to the reform process, there have been two approaches to addressing this issue as described in detail in the sections on economic transitions. Many Central and Eastern European countries and the Soviet Union chose a rapid path towards transformation and privatisation. This resulted in a speedy conversion of ownership, however, at a huge cost in the form of transformational recessions. In contrast, China chose a gradual approach with hardly any changes to the state sector in the initial reform years, which helped the country to forgo some of the output losses experienced by other transition economies. China ´sought to make use of hierarchical relationship in which enterprises were embedded, remaking incentives and organization, while simultaneously creating "dual-track" market prices´ (Naughton 2007: 310). In the course of time, incentives were introduced to the Chinese state-owned system, mostly via profit contracting, which meant that companies were allowed to keep excess surpluses almost entirely. ´By liberating one "track" of the dual-track system, there was scope for these institutionally defined rights to foster a profit incentive to SOEs and state-owned banks which helped boost output again without creating private property rights in the ownership of these enterprises and banks´ (Yueh 2013: 26). In the mid-1990s, the soft budget constrained was stopped as reformers significantly hardened their stance towards state-owned enterprises. The tax reform of 1994 and the banking reform of 1995 contributed to this (Naughton 2007).

Sun and Tong (2003) point out that China decided on the corporatisation of its state-owned enterprises after prior reforms could not stop the decline in profitability of SOEs. This helped to partially privatise government-owned firms. Since the early 1990s this was the primary means of reforming Chinese enterprises, which allowed the government to retain a substantial stake in the firms. As the institutional innovation of the contract responsibility system could not make-up for the deficiencies of the soft budget constraint, the transformation of SOEs into shareholding companies represented an alternative. This helped introduce incentives without the Chinese government losing control over these firms. In the 1990s, further reforms of the SOE sector were conducted, known as gaizhi. These laid the foundations for later privatisations of SMEs. Privatisation in China only happened gradually over four decades of market-orientated reforms. Only in the 2000s, for instance, the Property Law of 2007 granted equal protection for private and public property (Yueh 2013: 34).

It is important to mention that the corporatisation of companies is different from privatising these enterprises. The latter refers to a change in ownership, while the former is connected to the creation of tradable shares. Furthermore, incorporated firms benefit from legal protection, such as limited liability and facilitated acquisition of funds (Himmelberg et al. 1999). Restructuring state-owned enterprises as corporations has been used as a method of privatisation in many countries. In the case of China, the initial attempt to incentivise managers to increase output was only partially successful (Hay et al. 1994). The Chinese government decided not to embark on mass privatisations and thus the above-described path represented a suitable alternative. However, the disadvantage of this strategy was the dismal performance of SOEs. Chen and Feng (2000) analysed data from 29 provinces in China from 1978 to 1989 and concluded that the SOEs reduce growth in the respective areas while the presence of private or semi-private firms leads to increased economic performance. Additionally, Biggeri (2003) found that output is negatively influenced by SOEs according to the data sample of Chinese provinces from 1986 to 2001. The percentage of government-led firms is regarded as an indication for the progress regarding the transformation from a planned to market-orientated economy.

By the 1990s, the dissolution of the "iron rice bowl", as laid out in the historical background section, led to greater labour market flexibility in China (Yueh 2004). The large restructurings during the gaizhi led to a significant reduction in the labour force in the SOE sector. By the mid-2000s, SOEs made up for less than one quarter of all urban employment. During this time, the non-state sector sharply rose and is now the preeminent employer in China. This includes private companies, privatised state-owned firms, as well as collectives (Yueh 2013: 65). The state-owned enterprise sector was a crucial part for the Chinese government in terms of raising revenues (Bai et al. 2000). A shock approach towards transitioning would have limited the Chinese states capabilities significantly. China´s gradual transformation allowed the country to incrementally change existing institutions, but not to engage in full-blown privatisation or marketization of the Chinese economy. Nonetheless, the state-owned enterprise sector continues to be a crucial part of China. ´The market is increasingly shaped by laws and policies from which state-owned firms are granted exemptions while continuing to benefit from policies such as financial repression in which the rules governing credit favour state firms over others´ (Yueh 2013: 301). The researcher continues by noting that the stability of the Chinese system largely depends on the transformation of the state and thus, the state-owned enterprise sector is a key variable of the analytical framework and will be applied to China´s troubles in the second half of 2015 and 2016 in the case study.

As is laid out both above and in the historical background section, China´s unique approach towards transition allowed the country to forgo any transformational recession and FX crisis as took place in Central and Eastern Europe as well as in the former Soviet Union. The incremental approach towards reforming China´s state-owned enterprise sector formed a key part of the country´s approach. Still, China´s transition is not yet complete and rapid reforms could lead to destabilising effects for the whole economy. The visible hand of the state guides the reform agenda and China is well advised not to deviate from its incremental approach towards transition from a stability perspective. Indeed, maintaining stability is still a priority for the Chinese government. The influence of the state-owned enterprise sector on the dependent variable – the currency debasement of the Chinese yuan, which took place in August 2015, together with the revision and the subsequent alterations in the exchange rate regime as well as the entailed capital flow volatility – is examined in detail in the case study. The link between the state-owned enterprise sector and currency crises can be multiple. First of all, SOEs have a direct influence on the growth trajectory of China, which is among the key explanatory variables for currency crises in early warning systems. Furthermore, the behaviour of state-owned banks can contribute significantly to a country's vulnerabilities.

f) Technology and Productivity

Improvements in technology lead to higher output given the input factors, mainly capital, and labour. An economy grows over time due to population growth or by taking output per worker due to improvements in technology. In developed countries, technological progress is mainly related to research and development (R&D). Increasing the spending on R&D raises the likelihood of an expanded set of products and thus, the profitability of firms. The outcome of spending on research and development are ideas and the success of R&D depends on the fertility of research as well as on its appropriability. Patents are usually used to protect new ideas coming out of R&D. Most developing countries tend to be users rather than producers of technology. These developing countries usually import new technology from developed countries and then adopt it, which then leads to productivity growth within the countries. Thus, the process of technological growth in developed and developing countries is fundamentally different (Blanchard and Johnson 2013: 249-260). Therefore, patent protection is generally weaker in the developed world. However, as countries are catching up, these topics become ever more important as is shown in the case of China below (Yueh 2013). Technological growth is generally measured by a method developed by Robert Solow as described in the section on fundamentals. The method reveals that most growth in developed countries comes from technological progress, as the latter is roughly equal to the increase in output per worker (Solow 1957). This is referred to as "balanced growth" since growth is not derived from an unusually speedy accumulation of capital. Thus, there are two ways in which developing countries can catch up to more advanced countries. First, the lower level of capital of developing countries relative to the developed world can lead to a catch-up via faster capital accumulation. Second, the lower level of technological progress also offers advantages of backwardness by adopting new foreign technologies and thus, driving higher growth rates (Blanchard and Johnson 2013: 261). How does this apply to China's growth trajectory? Empirical research shows that from the end of the 1970s to approximately the mid-1990s, China's growth in output per worker was driven by technological progress (World Bank 1997). As of the mid-1990s, growth was more due to an unusual speedy accumulation of capital (Zheng and Hu 2006; Zheng et al. 2009). Therefore, both factors explain the high development of China in comparison to other countries. Inevitably, the rate of capital accumulation will decline in China and Blanchard and Johnson (2013: 262) estimate that China will grow at a more sustainable pace of about 6 percent in the future given an extrapolation of the technological growth rate as well as a small increase in the growth rate of employment in China.

Continuous improvement in technology-driven productivity is required if a country is to sustain its successful trajectory. One way to analyse China´s technological capabilities is to examine R&D, the human resource base, and institutions as well as incentives (Cliff 1998; Liu and White 2001). The effort regarding technology and the human capital base contribute to the build-up of know-how, while technology and incentives refer to application of the aforementioned determinants in production. The split between the generation and the application of know-how is important since both significantly contribute to output. Most developing countries face a significant technology gap because new technology comes foremost from advanced countries. Therefore, the adoption of existing technologies is as important for developing countries as investing in research and development. However, most countries have significant difficulties using these advantages of backwardness resulting in a hampered catch-up process. Due to the awareness of the limitations of domestic technology development, many developing countries welcome foreign direct investment as a means to generating technological spillovers. Particularly China embraced the opportunities of gradually advancing its technological capabilities via FDI. Nonetheless, the identification and adaption of foreign technologies might require a country to invest itself in R&D. In addition, a country′s spending on R&D usually increases with its development. For instance, as Taiwan and South Korea approached middle-income status in the early 1980s, both countries increased the R&D per GDP ratio above 1 percent. Should a country reach a more advanced stage of development, this ratio is usually pushed above 2 percent (Naughton 2007: 350-352). Therefore, for many developing countries the Solow residual only plays a minor role in economic analysis. However, there are disagreements with the notion that a Solow residual of zero does imply no technological progress. This is due to different forms of development as developing countries adopt new foreign technologies rather than provide for R&D themselves and thus the technological progress is derived from imported technologies. Joseph Schumpeter related technological progress to the concept of creative destruction. However, empirically many transition economies focused too much on the destruction part and too little on the creation part. China continued pursuing its goal of allowing new entries of firm while at the same time keeping state-owned enterprises afloat and was thus able to grow out of the plan rather than demolish the whole edifice. Indeed, for developing countries, imitation rather than investing in innovation is a crucial point for a country's development agenda (Blanchard and Johnson 2013: 281-284) and only as the development proceeds the latter becomes more important.

As described in the historical background section, China pursued a high-technology industrialisation strategy during the Maoist period. Available resources were mobilised and reallocated for the development of military technology. This was mainly done in elite research institutions such as in the Chinese Academy of Science (CAS). The country was able to recognise certain successes in this sector such as the development of an atomic bomb or intercontinental missiles (Feigenbaum 1999). This came at a huge cost for the local population. During the 1950s, China adopted the model of the Soviet Union, foremost of key institutions that incentivised the development and adoption of technologies. The split with the Soviet Union in the early 1960s led to the complete inward orientation of China. Technological autarky was the main goal of the country during this decade. Reverse engineering and replication of foreign technologies aimed to help China close the technological gap with more advanced nations. While the country was able to achieve certain success in the military sector during the Maoist period, the transferring of technology to the civilian sector did not work mainly due to high security barriers. In addition, there were no incentives to commercialise existing innovations, which would have helped the distribution of technologies and supported growth. Therefore, this was one area to focus on after Mao´s death in 1976. During the reform era, China first tried to keep its outlays on technology high, foremost via purchases of foreign technology, which should have helped the country to emerge from isolation. However, due to the reforms and the subsequent restructuring of the SOE sector, the Chinese government lacked the resources for the continuous high spending on technology. Thus, the previous strategy had to be altered. ´China today steers technology imports toward "soft" technology licensing and away from the expensive purchase of "hard" assets that embody technology´ (Naughton 2007: 357).

Technology import continues to be a cornerstone of China´s catch-up. The country also grants privileged access to its market in return for access to foreign technology. In addition, China has increased the funding of its own research & development projects. Research institutions were incentivised to diffuse technologies into other areas than the military sector, which should support China´s growth rates (Naughton 2007). Nonetheless, FDI is one of the predominant sources of technology since 1992. Huwart and Verdier (2013: 62) note on this subject that 'since 1996, R&D investments have grown fastest in China thanks to investments by foreign MNEs. The Xi'an innovation area, which would eventually cover 90 km2, featured a technology park that housed thousands of companies. The Chinese space programme was developed here. Several major MNEs that crucially relied on R&D, including Japan's NEC and

Germany's Siemens, now develop some of their own products there. Meanwhile, US telecom manufacturer, Motorola, and database software giant, Oracle, have established R&D centres in Beijing. The Franco-American Alcatel-Lucent group now has an important research centre in Shanghai'. Regarding China´s human resource base, the country´s factor endowment dictates abundant labour, but with relatively low level of education. In addition, the top Chinese students do their PhD outside of China and only a minor fraction plans to return to their home country after they finished their studies. However, even when the PhDs do not return to China, they can play a crucial role in building a worldwide network of research and innovation from which China can benefit (Zweig 2005). It goes without saying that both R&D investments, as well as human capital investments have significant positive effects on China (Hu et al. 2005; Fisher-Vanden and Jefferson 2005). In addition, the abandonment of the ideological baggage in the 1990s led to realignment of incentives in the development of technologies. Spillovers via foreign invested firms were embraced by China, which was most visible in the relaxation of approvals for FDI. The promotion of technology intensive industries is among the primary goals of the Chinese leadership. Tax breaks and subsidised credit should facilitate this (Naughton 2007: 367).

The importance of innovation was recognised by the Chinese government in 1985 with the establishment of a patent law (Yueh 2013). In addition, the accession of China to the WTO in 2001 led to stricter intellectual property rights (IPR). Indeed, Chinese companies gradually adapted to the new environment and patent application increased significantly (Hu and Jefferson 2009). However, FDI, as mentioned above, continues to be one of the most important cornerstones of China´s technological catch-up. The theoretical underpinnings for FDI leading to positive spillover effects were observed by Gylfason (1999) among others. These technological transfers either occur through licensing agreements or direct transfers or via learning and imitating foreign technologies. In addition, competition also induces productivity improving effects. In the 1980s and 1990s, China´s opening, as well as the increased level of FDI, significantly contributed to the country´s growth trajectory (Chen et al. 1995; Wei 1993). In contrast, Woo (1995) and Rodrik (1999) question the positive spillover effects of FDI on local economies, which do not hold for China, as shown above and below. With respect to R&D, Lai et al. (2006) note that domestic R&D in China has positive growth effects. In addition, by using provincial data, the researchers show that a province´s capacity to absorb foreign technology depends on the local human resource basis as well as on the degree of openness. Kuo and Yang (2008) show that both R&D and technology imports significantly matter for provincial economic performance. Some of the first people who noted the positive spillover effects of international knowledge on endogenous economic growth were Grossman and Helpman (1991). Indeed, China is the first destination for FDI among developing countries. `Its FDI policy is geared at developing joint venture and attracting technology to improve productivity of domestic firms; evidenced by the Special Economic Zones (SEZs)´ (Yueh 2013: 154). However, China's catch-up process is far from complete, as is evident through GDP per capita differentials.

g) Remarks

The expanded analytical framework, consisting of a fundamental, policy-induced and institutional dimension, should encourage higher attention to the multiple forms of vulnerability to financial crises. The events, which took place in China in 2015 and 2016, do not receive appropriate attention from an early warning system perspective. With the unified framework I would like to demonstrate that policy efforts of China should aim at addressing underlying vulnerabilities. In this section of the analytical framework, I focus on institutional weaknesses and strengths of a country. Topics such as the exchange rate regime, capital flows and controls, financial repression, international institutions, governance and the rule of law, SOEs as well as technology and productivity are covered. These different forms of institutional factors should not be seen as competing concepts, but rather as different forms of vulnerability, which are related to each other. For instance, the analytical framework allows for multiple vulnerabilities to be present simultaneously. Financial repression reinforces capital outflows in case of the liberalisation of the capital account, which has an effect on the foreign exchange rate and can lead to increased economic and capital market volatility. Indeed, I demonstrate the different factors in order to understand and explain financial crises to a higher degree. Not all variables have the same influence most of the time. Instead, it depends on the variation as well as on the general exposure of the factor to the dependent variable how the influence of the factor varies over time. This is examined in detail in the case study.

As mentioned above, good institutions are not only associated with a higher level of income but also with less output volatility. The latter point also explains the difficulty in predicting economic activity in developing countries. The poor quality of institutions in developing countries makes them susceptible to all types of crises and thus, institutional weaknesses reflect key vulnerabilities. The determinants of the institutional part of the analytical section get applied to China's troubles in the second half of 2015 and 2016 in the case study. China is a complex case with respect to institutional fragilities because on the surface, it seems like a counterexample of the findings of many institutional economists. I show that the success story of China was supported by a distinct set of institutions.

2.D) FX Crises and Early Warning Systems

The global pegged exchange rate system ended with the Bretton Woods system and has seen numerous changes since then. The shift from pegged to floating exchange rates and the partial reversal of this by some countries, new financial instruments and the success of global capital markets have contributed to international capital being a non-neglible factor in vulnerability analysis. This was seen in the number of foreign exchange rate crises experienced with the rise of the international financial system. Speculative attacks regularly hit both developed and emerging markets (Leblang 2002: 69). Thus, there is a need to find the driving factors of potential currency distortions in order to create a priori that can help policymakers to better understand the situation.

'While a burgeoning literature focuses on the economic determinants of speculative behaviour' (Leblang 2002: 69), hardly any attention has been paid to other determinants of currency crises. It has to be acknowledged that currency speculators form their expectations with respect to FX movements not only from economic determinants but also from policy and institutional factors. Indeed, the literature on economic variables and FX crises is voluminous (e.g. Frankel and Rose 1996). However, in this literature, policy-uncertainty and institutional factors often do not get appropriate attention.

Economic fundamentals and foreign exchange crises have been well researched. Nonetheless, we are not aware how and when policy and institutions influence FX crises. To close this informational gap is of both theoretical as well as empirical importance. From a theoretical perspective, it makes little sense to observe economic variables in isolation from policy and institutional variables, as it is acknowledged that these dimensions influence the likelihood of an FX crisis. From an empirical side, the difficulty of explaining FX crises with economic variables alone justifies explicitly taking policy and institutional variables into account (Leblang and Satyanath 2006: 245).

If policymakers want to keep a fixed exchange rate, sufficient foreign exchange reserves, as well as the willingness to defend a peg, must be present. In case the peg is abandoned, a spike in FX volatility, as well as a decline in international trade and investment, and a loss in output can be observed (Leblang 2003: 533). Among the explanations for currency crises are poor economic fundamentals (e.g. Krugman 1979) or alterations in expectations (e.g. Obstfeld 1996). Nevertheless, not all speculative attacks on currencies result in an FX crisis. As a matter of fact, very little is known about the conditions leading to increased foreign exchange distortions. However, attacks on foreign exchange rate regimes are not unusual. Nonetheless, only less than half of the attacks on foreign exchange lead to an alteration in the FX regime. The decision whether to uphold a currency peg or let it go is not an easy one. Defending a pegged currency requires fiscal and monetary policy to adjust with the consequence that economic performance contracts. 'Borrowing reserves can increase public sector debt (and increase the debt service requirements); raising interest rates may result in an economic contraction and aggravate the fiscal situation by reducing tax revenue; and implementing restrictions on capital mobility will damage international investment' (Leblang 2003: 534). However, deciding to not defend a currency peg also entails significant costs for an economy. Higher exchange rate volatility and inflation, as well as lower consumption and investment, are just some examples of the failure to defend a currency peg (Eichengreen and Rose 2001). Current models of FX distortions mainly focus on economic variables. Yet, policy and institutional variables, that influence the ability as well as the willingness of policymakers to respond to a potential FX crisis, are often forgotten (Leblang 2003: 534). The benefits of a fixed exchange rate regime include the stability the currency provides for trade and financial transactions. Additionally, the currency can serve to uphold anti-inflationary discipline. The failure to defend a peg amounts approximately to the cost of one year of economic growth (Eichengreen and Rose 2001). Political costs from letting an exchange rate go include less political support from holders of mobile capital (e.g. Frieden 1991) and the loss of political credibility, as the promise to uphold the exchange rate peg was unfulfilled.

Economists have been studying the determinants of FX crises for the last four decades. The first-generation models of exchange rate crises emerged from the global debt crisis of the 1980s. These models primarily focused on deteriorating fundamentals. After countries got into exchange rate troubles in the 1990s, the second-generation models were developed in order to explain speculative attacks on currency pegs, where government policy was not inconsistent with the peg and economic fundamentals were sound (Leblang 2002: 72). In these models, currency crises are the consequence of self-fulfilling beliefs. The anticipation of an FX distortion leads actors to convert domestic assets into foreign currency in order to avoid the effects of the potential devaluation. 'First- and second-generation models neglect or overly simplify the role of policymakers and […] institutions' (Leblang 2002: 72). If there is uncertainty about the future course of the local exchange rate, it begs the question, "What information do currency hedgers and speculators use?" Their behaviour is influenced by economic, policy, and institutional factors. A great amount of literature already exists regarding the latter two factors. However, these sources were hardly used in early warning system analysis. After the Asian financial crisis of the 1990s, the IMF policymakers and academics developed a third generation of currency crises models, which focused on 'moral hazard faced by international lending institutions, the composition of external debt, and capital controls' (Leblang 2002: 80).

The first-generation models of currency crises include Krugman (1979) and Flood and Garber (1984). 'The notion of these models is that macro-economic variables are used as signals to spot potential exchange rate devaluations. This led to the development of the signalling approach of Kaminsky et al. (1998) and Kaminsky and Reinhart (1999). The first-generation models argue that excessive credit creation results in an overvaluation of the local exchange rate, inflation, and large external imbalances (e.g. Blanco and Garber 1986, Calvo 1995). With respect to the latter, an overvalued exchange rate (e.g. Kaminsky et al. 1997), foreign debt (e.g. Frankel and Rose 1996), vulnerabilities in the banking sector (e.g. Demirguc-Kunt and Detragiache 1997), and external imbalances (e.g. Dooley 2000) all play an important role. This research mainly focuses on economic fundamentals as determinants of crises. 'The state of economic fundamentals is captured through a number of variables that indicate the economy's internal and external vulnerability: the ratio of foreign exchange reserves to base money, an indicator of real exchange rate overvaluation and the rate of domestic credit growth; the level of U.S. interest rates; the ratio of external debt service to GDP; and a measure of contagion' (Leblang 2003: 538). In contrast to the first-generation crisis models, the relationship between bad fundamentals and FX distortions is loosened in second-generation models (Van den Berg 2011: 7). In second-generation models, the costs and benefits of a devaluation are considered by the government. Expectations affect these considerations and thus, an FX debasement may be self-fulfilling. More recent research points to market failure and distortions in capital market, as potential reasons for an FX crisis (Berg et al. 2004: 35). Leblang (2002: 82) shows that, 'the variables identified by first- and second-generation models are statistically significant and in the expected direction. Increasing an already overvalued real exchange rate, providing larger amounts of funding to the private sector (the indicator of banking crises), expanding domestic credit, and higher foreign interest rates all tend to make the probability of a speculative attack more likely'.

The country's ability to defend a peg depends on a variety of factors, namely the amount of FX reserves, interest rates, capital controls, and policy decisiveness. With respect to foreign exchange reserves, first-generation models suggest that speculative attacks should be deterred by a large pile of foreign exchange reserves. In contrast to this, second generation models suggest that attacks can happen when FX reserves cross some "red line" (Leblang 2003: 540). Regarding interest rates, a higher level makes the defence of a currency peg more likely. This should deter locals from converting their savings into foreign currency as well as speculators from betting against the local exchange rate. Furthermore, capital controls are additional means to defend an exchange rate peg. In the worst case, capital controls result in additional time for policymakers to bring domestic matters to order. In the best case, capital controls in themselves already deter speculation against the local exchange rate. In addition, 'the degree to which policymakers can react to a crisis is constrained both by existing institutional structures and by the extent to which different veto points are controlled by members of different parties' (Leblang 2003: 541).

In general, emerging markets experienced a number of terrible financial crises over the last decades, resulting in dire consequences in economic, social as well as political terms. 'As a result, international financial institutions have developed Early Warning System (EWS) models, with the aim of identifying economic weaknesses and vulnerabilities among emerging markets and ultimately anticipating such events' (Bussiere and Fratzscher 2002: 5). Among the institutions building an early warning model approach is the IMF, with influential papers from Kaminsky et al. (1998), as well as Berg and Pattillo (1999a,b). The US Federal Reserve (Kamin et al. 2001) and the Bundesbank (Schnatz

1998), as well as various private sector institutions, also developed early warning systems to identify financial crisis, mainly FX distortions, well in advance. Early warning system models can help detect underlying economic weaknesses, as well as vulnerabilities and thus, policymakers can reduce the risks of currency distortions. 'From a policy perspective, developing Early Warning System (EWS) models that help to reliably anticipate financial crises could become an even more important tool for policy-makers in the future. Many financial crises over the past few decades had devasting social, economic and political consequences. Developing reliable EWS models, therefore, can be of substantial value by allowing policy-makers to obtain clear signals of when and how to take pre-emptive measures in order to mitigate or even prevent financial turmoil' (Bussiere and Fratzscher 2002: 39). In addition, 'there is little evidence that "market views," or analysts' views, as expressed in spreads, ratings and surveys are reliable crisis predictors, important as they may be in determining market access' (Berg et al. 2004: 10).

Both the global emerging market crises of the 1980s, as well as the Asian financial crisis of the 1990s led to an increased interest in early warning system model research. These two crises took the international community by surprise and consequently, an increased focus was put on finding indicators of a country's vulnerabilities and methods to handle these weaknesses. Since 1999, the IMF has systematically applied early warning system models as part of an increased forward-looking vulnerability examination. However, as Berg et al. (2004) stress, an assessment of a country's vulnerabilities creates the need for considering all qualitative and quantitative information.

In order to set up an early warning system, what exactly constitutes an FX crisis must first be defined. 'There is no clear rule on the definition of a large depreciation. However, a depreciation is only likely to be disrupting if it is substantially larger than most other depreciations. Therefore, depreciation is typically considered large when it exceeds its mean by more than two or three standard deviations' (Van den Berg 2011: 2). In contrast to looking at standard deviations to spot FX distortions, I use the percentiles of the time series as a non-parametric means to spot significant depreciations. 'This effort is especially called for in the latter realm given the variety of definitions of currency crises that are prevalent in the literature, and the fact that these definitions share the feature that they are fairly arbitrarily chosen by scholars of crises, rather than generated directly from the data' (Leblang and Satyanath 2006: 260).

EWS models are used to econometrically predict currency crises. Only in the aftermath of the global debt crisis of the 1980s and the Mexican tequila crisis in 1994 and 1995 did literature aim at finding indicators for predicting currency crises emerge. However, the unanticipated Asian financial crisis of the 1990s provided the impetus for new research regarding these harmful events and thus, the basis for monitoring vulnerabilities that lead to financial crises (Berg et al. 2004: 35). To start with, the theoretical models of currency crises have to be reviewed in order to draw up a list of indicators that can be used as predictors. These mainly focus on fundamentals.

Until now, most research focused purely on economic distortions to spot currency crises. Among these researchers is Schnatz (1998), who showed that distorted macroeconomic conditions were already present before the currency distortions happened. 'In the past the distress in the foreign exchange markets in many emerging markets should be rather attributable to macroeconomic flaws than random products of unpredictable speculators' (Schnatz 1998). In the 1980s, 1990s, and the early 2000s, currencies of some emerging markets were attacked by speculators, which resulted in significant devaluations. The consequences of these attacks included the lack of access to international capital markets by the affected countries, as well as issues with the local banking sector and the imported inflation from the plunge in the value of the domestic currency. Further disadvantages of a devaluation included squeezes in demand as a result of these factors (Schnatz 1998). Rather than simply analyse the trajectory of historic crises, some seek to develop a predictive early warning analysis. Kaminsky and Reinhart (1999) divide macroeconomic variables into three categories, namely variables from the financial sector, external sector, and the real sector. In my categorisation, I use variables from the external and the real sector and I split the data from the financial sector into variables related to policy, such as monetary and fiscal policy, and variables related to fundamental vulnerability, such as the build-up of debt in China.

Two types of early warning system models exist, namely the KLR model proposed by Kaminsky, Lizondo, and Reinhart (1998) as well as Kaminsky and Reinhart (1999) and probit/ logit models, which were pioneered by Berg and Pattillo (1999b) as well as by Kumar et al. (2003). Most of the models used in practice are variations of these two early warning systems. For instance, the International Monetary Fund uses three models: (1) A signalling approach which is in line with the KLR model that monitors economic variables that deviate from its usual behaviour. (2) The Developing Country Studies Division (DCSD) model, which uses macroeconomic factors in a probit model. (3) The Policy Development and Review (PDR) model, which is the DCSD model extended by mainly corporate debt ratios. In my case study, I will build on these models and extend the dimensionality, which should help to spot crises in advance.

Part 3:
Historical Background Section

3. A) Crises in Perspective

a) Introductory Note

First of all, it has to be determined what events the analysis should warn of. For instance, early warning models focus primarily on external events, in particular on capital account crises (Ghosh et al. 2009: 36). As most financial crises are accompanied by an adjustment of the local exchange rate and this even precedes other types of crises, in this book the event which the vulnerability analysis warns of is a currency crash or to put it differently a foreign exchange crisis. Indeed, this section should also help the reader to understand that to analyse financial crises mostly fundamentals, namely economic variables (please refer to the conceptual section for further details) are used in the literature on early warning systems. This limitation in the conceptualisation of vulnerability to a financial crisis can be attributed to a disciplinary attachment, which leads to a myopic view on the matter. As Ghosh et al. (2009: 37) put it, 'The unique and diverse nature of crises inherently limits the ability of statistical tools to extract information that may be useful for identifying the next crisis or take full account of country-specific factors'. Therefore, in this book, the different concepts of vulnerability to financial crises are demonstrated not only with the help of a logit model, but also qualitatively with the examination of over five hundred research reports.

Scholars have already identified this indicated gap in the field. For instance, Goldstein et al. (2000) attribute the limitation of economic indicators to predict financial crises to the importance of political drivers for outcomes. Furthermore, Reinhart's comment on Drazen (2000) explicitly points to the lack of political and institutional factors taken into account in analysing financial crises and Reinhart and Rogoff (2009) notice in their review of early warning systems that the literature on early warnings is still lacking many crisis episodes as well as primarily looking at economic indicators to predict crises. The limitation of the debate on vulnerability and financial crises has led to a short-sighted view on the topic. In this section, I will show that many of the discussions of historic crisis episodes have focused on economic variables. In general, the conceptualisation of vulnerability is key as the definition of the concept already frames the answer to the fundamental question how to predict and prevent financial crises. Yet, scholars have failed to build a unified framework from an early warning analysis perspective. Conceptual favouritism leads to the disregard of different forms of vulnerability and therefore, also entails the failure to build a sophisticated understanding of outcomes.

Historical crisis episodes are reviewed to show the bias on economic variables as well as to set the scene for the application of the analytical framework in the case study. The 'Global Crisis of the 1980s', 'the Asian Financial Crisis of the 1990s' and 'the Great Financial Crisis of 2008' are reviewed. By speaking of historical crises one cornerstone in the academic literature is the book 'This time is different: Eight centuries of financial folly.' by Reinhart and Rogoff (2009). However, one important aspect of speaking about crises is neglected in their research, namely crises related to transitions from plan to market. These transitions historically led to a loss in GDP and to severe currency distortions as could be observed with the RUB devaluation in 1998. Therefore, I will add one section explaining what is meant by transition and give examples of successes and failures related to the transformations of former communist countries. To conclude this chapter, a review of the early warning literature will be given, which bases their insights mainly on these crisis episodes, and in this sub-section the conceptual bias as defining vulnerability as fundamental weakness viewed through an economic lens will become clear and the limitations of this will be pointed out.

b) Definition of Crisis

It is vital to first point out the definition of crisis as well as certain common characteristics (Reinhart and Rogoff 2009: 3). Given research by Ghosh and Ghosh (2003), Ghosh et al. (2008) and by Chamon et al. (2012) a crisis is defined as an underlying vulnerability in addition to a specific crisis trigger. The triggering event is endogenous to the underlying vulnerability (Chamon et al. 2012: 3). This shows that the key to predicting as well as preventing crises is to address the underlying vulnerabilities. In fact, a vulnerability may persist for a certain time period before a trigger creates a crisis event, which is laid out in more detail in the conceptual section. While the exact event or the threshold level which an underlying variable has to cross to trigger a crisis are difficult to evaluate, the identification of vulnerabilities is key to predicting and preventing emerging market crises (Chamon et al. 2012: 3).

Furthermore, it must be defined what kind of events these vulnerabilities warn of. Chamon et al. (2012: 1) show that even though not merely one type of crisis exists, the variety of different forms depict characteristic similarities, foremost a collapse of the local exchange rate. In fact, FX adjustments often precede other forms of financial crises. In this respect, Reinhart (2002) found that, for example, in 84 percent of observed cases an FX crisis occurred before a debt crisis. Therefore, I focus on FX crises in this book. With respect to currency crashes, Chamon et al. (2012: 3) point out that scholars have found it difficult to develop a unified framework. The first type of models, foremost from Krugman (1979) and Flood and Graber (1981), focus on the role of macroeconomic imbalances in the dissolvement of a currency peg. Furthermore, Obstfeld (1986) explained currency crises via speculative attacks given self-fulfilling expectations. In addition, the third-generation models emerged from the Asian financial crisis. Aghion et al. (2001) focus on balance sheet effects with respect to unhedged foreign currency liabilities. Given the different models in academic literature a more unified framework is needed to explain and understand emerging market crises, which is addressed in the conceptual section.

Regarding currency crises, Frankel and Rose (1996) were among the first to define these events, namely a currency crash is defined as an adjustment of the local exchange rate in excess of 25 percent per annum. These crashes are often accompanied by an increase in local interest rates as well as a downturn in economic indicators. In contrast, Reinhart and Rogoff (2009: 6) use a depreciation rate versus the US dollar of 15 percent per annum to define a currency crash. In this book, however, I take an additional step, which circumvents this generalisation of an FX crisis by taking into account individual circumstances of a country and its exchange rate. Therefore, I define a currency crash relative to the exchange rate's own history versus the US dollar or to put it differently, a foreign exchange crisis is related to an abnormal weakening in the local exchange rate given the time series statistical properties. This allows for a more flexible approach towards spotting crises, which takes into account individual circumstances and properties of countries and their asset price dynamics. Moreover, every definition of a financial crisis has to consider empirical breaks, which are persistent changes in the properties of a time series. Sharma (2016) shows that such a break occurred in the early 2000s, which is a crucial point regarding the predictability of emerging market crises. Indeed, by conditioning the predictability analysis on a specific time horizon, the problem of dynamic changes in the underlying variables is circumvented.

Thus, given the definition of an FX crisis, two events with respect to China are noteworthy within the defined time horizon, namely the end of the nominal exchange rate peg of the renminbi versus the US dollar in 2005 as well as the FX volatility in the second half of 2015 and its aftermath. The former event resulted in a 2.1 percent appreciation of the renminbi versus the US dollar and therefore, this must not be included in the empirical analysis (Lardy 2012: 101). Hence, only the 1.9 percent depreciation of the yuan versus the US dollar in August 2015 and its aftermath should be analysed in detail, as I will do in this case study. The reader might find it surprising that the financial crisis of 2008 did not cause a currency crisis in China. In fact, the Chinese leadership repegged the renminbi to the US dollar during this period until 2010 (Lardy 2012: 104). Other emerging markets experienced an extreme level of exchange rate volatility during that period. However, investors in the Chinese currency were relatively safe and therefore, the global financial crisis does not fit the definition of an FX crisis in China and thus, will not be treated in detail in the case study. Given the above, the importance of the events of the second half of 2015 and 2016 should be clear. I chose this case study due to its extreme value on the dependent variable. The percentiles of the daily movements in the USD/CNY exchange rate show why the currency debasement of the yuan from August 2015 is a rather unique event. I deliberately chose the events unfolding in China in the second half of 2015 and 2016 because of its extreme characteristics given time series analysis and its wider implications for domestic capital market reforms and China's unfinished transformation.

c) Historical Crisis Episodes

The historical background section sets the scene and builds the foundation for the subsequent application of the analytical framework to the case study. By obtaining a thorough understanding of historic financial crises and the drivers discussed in the literature, it will be possible to comprehend the current body of knowledge. Understanding what has to be done is derived from understanding what has not been done yet. I will discuss the 'Global Crisis of the 1980s', 'the Asian Financial Crisis of the 1990s', 'Transition Economies' and 'the Great Financial Crisis of 2008' in this part of the historical background section. The lessons learnt will serve as one angle to understand China's struggle in the second half of 2015 and 2016.

i) The Global Crisis of the 1980s

The boom in commodity prices in the 1970s helped commodity export regions, in particular Latin America, to generate enormous profits at a time when global growth was flourishing. Relatively high rates of inflation in developed countries led to low real interest rates sparking capital flows towards the emerging world. In addition, the recent state of low default rates in Latin America was extrapolated indefinitely into the future by investors. However, the build-up of obligations by developing countries did not end well as increasingly higher interest rates in the developed world in the early 1980s as well as a collapse in commodity prices led to defaults ranging from Mexico in 1982 to, subsequently, Argentina, Brazil and many other developing countries. These incidences coincided with a collapse in global demand and a vicious spiral was triggered (Reinhart and Rogoff 2009: 18). The entailed currency adjustments in Latin America in the early 1980s were the reason for the development of the balance-of-payment (BoP) crisis literature as described above, most notably Krugman (1979) and Flood and Graber (1981), and subsequently, also Obstfeld (1986), who explains currency crashes via self-fulfilling expectations and herding in capital markets (Kaminsky and Reinhart 1999: 473). A more detailed look at the lessons learnt is laid out in the early warning section.

The Latin American crisis started in the middle of 1982 when Mexico declared that it could no longer service its debt. Only a couple of months later, sixteen Latin American countries faced serious troubles, among them Argentina, Brazil and Venezuela in addition to Mexico. The latter four countries made up the majority amount of the outstanding debt (FDIC 1997: 191). In fact, a rapid expansion of US banking in addition to significant increases in the oil price had led to an increase in global capital flows in the 1970s. However, these factors also spurred inflation in the US in addition to deteriorating balance-of-payment dynamics for developing countries. At the end of the 1970s, another significant increase in the oil price led the US Federal Reserve under Paul Volcker to sharply increase interest rates (Woods 2014: 247). The US dollar appreciated significantly in the early 1980s which further contributed to the debt burden for developing countries as their loans were mainly denominated in foreign currency, namely in US dollar. In addition, most of the loans to developing nations were linked to variable rates, which were regularly repriced. This repricing represented a significant vulnerability for borrowing countries due to the variations in the variable rate, mostly LIBOR. Moreover, capital flight from these nations also increased as the real exchange rate overvaluation took its toll (FDIC 1997: 192-199). The sharp increase in US interest rates led to a global slowdown, significantly dampening demand and leading to a sell-off in commodity prices. The latter in addition to the stronger US dollar made debt servicing for the developing world, in particular Latin American countries nearly impossible (Velloso and Bustillo 2013: 21). The period from 1983 to 1989 was mainly dominated by attempts to resolve the Latin American crisis. However, it was only at the end of the 1980s under the US treasury secretary Nicholas Brady that the situation could be resolved. The new attempt included a reduction in the outstanding debt amount as well as a restructuring of the developing countries' liabilities. This debt relief was successful and ultimately, the Latin American countries were able to recover after this disastrous decade (FDIC 1997: 209; Velloso and Bustillo 2013: 28-31), which gave rise to a new strand of literature.

The events of the 1980s raised the question why the Asian countries continued to rise in this decade while the Latin American countries experienced what is being referred to as a lost decade. In general, in the three decades before this period developing countries progressed substantially (Woods 2014: 247). The emerging nations were well aware that the development of their labour force and that the provision of the industrial and technical infrastructure was needed in order to catch-up with developed countries. Indeed, by the 1970s many of the developing countries were able to compete in certain sectors with more advanced countries (Singh 1994: 1-2). Why was the rise interrupted in Latin America while Asia managed to continue its successful path in the 1980s? In particular, China rose at an incredible pace during this decade while other former communist nations such as the Central and Eastern European countries and Russia recorded substantial losses in output (Maddison 2007b: 172-173), which will be examined in a later chapter in more detail. In fact, China's transition and continued economic rise poses the strongest contrast to the sharp contraction in economic growth in the aforementioned regions. The main research on why Asia continued to rise in the 1980s and Latin America suffered a severe blow to its development efforts include Balassa (1984), Maddison (1985) and Sachs (1985) among others. These researchers argue that internal causes were mainly responsible for this lost decade in Latin America as these countries tended to borrow heavily in the preceding decade. The funds were squandered instead of invested in the development of local industry and in addition, the Latin American countries did not open themselves to foreign competition, which would have automatically led to a more efficient allocation of resources. Import substitution was the wrong way to go, the researchers argue. Moreover, their external balances, most visible in their exchange rates, were mismanaged, ultimately leading to capital flight (Singh 1994: 3-4). Apart from this line of argument, other observers stressed the importance of debt accumulation in these countries, which was not in the developing world's control and ultimately, led to the collapse of Latin America when Paul Volcker raised interest rates significantly. This sharp increase in US interest rates led to a severe downturn in global economic growth with various negative repercussions for developing countries, in particular Latin America (FDIC 1997: 192-199; Velloso and Bustillo 2013: 21). Four channels must be taken into account to derive a coherent picture of the situation in the early 1980s, namely a demand shock to exports, a decline in commodity prices, higher interest rates curtailing output and making debt unsustainable, as well as a shock related to capital supply. In particular, the last channel hit developing countries the hardest after Mexico announced the unsustainability of its debt in 1982. Mexico had extrapolated the good global conditions of the 1970s indefinitely into the future and thus borrowed heavily to invest in the extractive industry at the peak of the price boom. As the price bubble deflated many of the Mexican projects became unsustainable at the same time as the balance-of-payments deteriorated (Sachs 1985: 563; Singh 1994: 7-9). Given the Mexican default, international lenders tried to reduce their risk exposure to the developing world by shortening the maturity structure of their loans at the same time as pulling out money of Latin America. The high interest rate environment represented an unsustainable burden for the budgets of Latin American countries given the drag via variable interest rate adjustments (Sachs 1985: 527). The institutions in Latin America were not able to cushion and absorb these shocks and an absence of exchange rate controls in Latin America, in contrast to Asia, led to the free flow of capital out of this region reinforcing the vicious cycle (Diaz-Alejandro 1984: 336). In fact, Latin America and Asia shared many similar features in their borrowing and investment activities. However, 'the main reason why the Korean program eventually succeeded while the Brazilian and Mexican ones did not was the far more severe foreign exchange constraint to which the latter two countries were subject' (Singh 1994: 13). The crucial difference between the regions was that Latin America was more open to the global economy than Asia, foremost with respect to currency convertibility. Financial openness was far greater in Latin America than in Asia, whose countries tended to uphold strict exchange rate controls. India and China, which were still very much closed to the global economy, as well as South Korea, which rose on an export-orientated development strategy, could survive the crisis of the 1980s in a much better shape than the Latin American countries (Singh 1994: 10-14). The aforementioned provides little support towards the Balassa-Sachs hypothesis as was argued by Hughes and Singh (1991). The researchers deduce from their analysis that the Latin American countries were derailed due to their susceptibility to the external shock given their vulnerabilities due to a greater financial integration with the global economy, their high level of foreign FX denominated debt as well as their balance-of-payment dynamics, which represent the main differences to the success of the Asian countries.

To conclude, it holds across history that the memory of investors is generally short. Already in the 1990s capital flows returned to Latin America, not via bank loans this time, but rather via publicly issued bonds which led to a false perception of security by investors as bonds were considered more difficult to renegotiate than loans. Moreover, a wave of democratisation in Latin America further appealed to Western investors. Again, as the tide turned, Mexico collapsed in 1994, Argentina, Brazil and Uruguay faced severe financial distress in the end of the 1990s and the early 2000s (Reinhart and Rogoff 2009: 19). In between, the Asian countries were affected by a vicious currency crisis, which is examined next.

ii) The Asian Financial Crisis of the 1990s

In 1997, the emerging Asian countries became affected by an exchange rate crisis. A notable exception was China, which was better able to withstand the Asian financial crisis due to fewer vulnerabilities as the country made adjustments earlier on in this decade. The reasons for the Asian financial crisis range from financial-sector weaknesses over external-sector problems to contagion among others. However, the situation before the crisis evolved could be described as quite sound. 'The macroeconomic fundamentals in Asia by conventional definition looked strong – low inflation, fiscal balance or surplus, strong private savings, high rates of capital formation, strong export performance, ample foreign direct investment, stable currencies, large foreign exchange reserves, modest debt-to-GDP ratios. And, not least, the region had achieved a dramatic improvement in standards of living for a significant portion of the population' (Lissakers 1999: 3). Indeed, the countries were so successful in the years before the crisis started that they were often referred to as East Asian miracle. Government fostered education as well as the development of local industry contributed significantly to the success story over the preceding years. Export-led growth at the same time as the reluctant lifting of import restrictions served as a growth model for these countries. The overall economic prosperity also entailed a higher degree of social inclusiveness in these countries (Stiglitz 2002: 90-92) and thus, these countries could indeed be described as successful.

Although the macroeconomic picture generally painted a bright future for the emerging Asian economies, some indicators warranted a more cautious view. For instance, Thailand suffered from a real estate bubble and its current account had been deteriorating at a significant pace. The declining export performance gave first indications that an exchange rate adjustment would become necessary (Lissakers 1999: 4). In general, from 1990 to early 1997 most of the Southeast Asian currencies appreciated significantly in real terms. The first consequences of these FX misalignments were visible in a declining performance of exports in 1996 and increasing current account deficits (Glick 1999: 36). The loss in competitiveness also stemmed from the sharp appreciation of the US dollar in the preceding years. The Asian currencies were fixed against the US dollar and thus, appreciated significantly in effective terms leading to the loss in competitiveness (Glick 1999: 37). In addition, a non-negligible amount of foreign currency short-term obligations represented a significant vulnerability, which was partly incentivised through the pegged exchange rates. Moreover, what many observers underestimated was the high amount of leverage on financial and corporate balance sheets, which ultimately should represent a contingent liability for the governments (Lissakers 1999: 5). Thus, most of the weaknesses stemmed from the financial and capital account side of the balance-of-payments. Short-term flows are susceptible to shocks in confidence and when the tide turns the weaknesses of the system become visible. Given the events unfolding during the Asian financial crisis, it is very legitimate to ask what role the degree of openness played in this trajectory. In contrast to other Asian economies, Malaysia introduced capital controls to decrease its vulnerability on the external side. These measures proved to be successful (Moskow 1999: 13-14), which is touched upon below.

The Asian financial crisis as of 1997 was a currency crisis. The fixed exchange rate systems, which the Asian countries had pursued, posed a significant vulnerability. To defend the pegs the countries had to use their foreign exchange reserves as well as hike interest rates significantly, which further contributed to the downward trend in the real economies (Reinhart and Rogoff 2009: 18-19). Ultimately the countries had to let go their exchange rates. The contraction in the real economy led to reduced imports and the devaluation made exports more competitive which as a result picked-up again over time and thus, contributed to the recovery at a later stage (Goldstein 1998: 26-27). A problem in a currency crisis is contagion. The crisis started in Thailand, but quickly affected other Asian economies. What were the reasons for this? One reason for contagion is reflected in the "wake-up call" hypothesis. Other Asian economies depicted vulnerabilities like Thailand's and thus, the probability of a crisis taking place in these countries increased significanty with the events unfolding in Thailand (Eichengreen and Rose 1999). Another channel through which the crisis spread to other Asian economies was competitive devaluations; in order for other Asian economies not to see their competitive position deteriorate they had to follow suit any devaluation performed by one of its neighbours (Goldstein 1996, 17). In contrast to its smaller neighbours, China was not forced to devalue its currency although the country had the option to do so. The Chinese FX devaluation of 1994 left the country in a less strained position during the second half of the 1990s. Nevertheless, China experienced a significant real exchange rate appreciation during the Asian financial crisis of 1997 and 1998. The country contributed considerably to global stability by not engaging in a competitive cycle of devaluations (Goldstein 1998: 20).

The Asian financial crisis of 1997 and 1998 led to the involvement of the International Monetary Fund. The IMF prescribed a tightening of the affected countries' monetary policy in order to stabilise the currency after significant devaluations and to contract imports to influence the balance-of-payment dynamics favourably. In addition, fiscal policies had to be contractive as well, thus further adding to the downturn in the real economy. Many external observers posed the question whether the conditionality of the IMF assistance did go too far? One key reform area that the IMF targeted was the banking sector. Closures of the most badly affected banks were enforced. The credit contraction generally led to severe strains in said sector. However, bailing out large institutions always raises the question of moral hazard and of an equitable sharing of the burden of the effects of the crisis (Goldstein 1998: 33-44). Given the sharp declines in output, the IMF had to accommodate and adjust some of its programme's conditionality to reduce the burden (Lissakers 1999: 7) as some observers had asked for (Stiglitz 2002: 89).

What were the lessons to be learned from the Asian financial crisis of 1997 and 1998? The supervisory framework governing some of the Asian economy's financial sector needed to be significantly reviewed. In case of weak institutions, hidden weaknesses in the balance sheets of the financial sector are only discovered when the tide turns (Glick 1999: 38). A boom of credit and the concentration of these funds in certain sectors such as real estate are often followed by busts. Moreover, the debt burden of these countries needs to be monitored carefully, not only the level but also changes in the level as well as the composition of the debt (Goldstein 1998: 65-67). External account imbalances also play an important role in this respect. When a pegged currency leads to an overvaluation of the real exchange rate and the trade balance keeps on deteriorating, a country is in significant troubles. As the exchange rate inevitably has to be let go, unless severe capital controls are introduced, the currency tends to overshoot in these times of stress (Glick 1999: 36-37). The latter certainly adds to an environment of political instability (Akerlof et al. 1993). Thus, keeping the situation in control and holding up the credibility of a country's institutions is of utmost importance in these circumstances. One final word with respect to the debt dynamics: If debt is denominated in foreign currency, a weaker local currency adds to the debt burden. Also, it does not matter whether the debt was accumulated on private or public balance sheets. The distinction between private and public liabilities is not clear-cut in a crisis, as private liabilities are often only contingent liabilities for a country (Goldstein 1998: 65-67). Given the debt dynamics in Asian economies, some useful indicators to monitor the situation are the ratio of short-term foreign borrowing to official foreign exchange reserves. It must be pointed out that a ratio in excess of a 100 percent is not in itself an indication for a crisis as long as investors are confident and roll over the debt. However, it clearly points towards vulnerability. Another ratio that could be used is the ratio of M2 to foreign currency reserves (Glick 1999: 43), which could signal an increased level of vulnerability.

Furthermore, Stiglitz (2002) points to the faults of capital account liberalisation. 'Excessively rapid financial and capital market liberalisation was probably the single most important cause of the crisis, though mistaken policies on the part of the countries themselves played a role as well' (Stiglitz 2002: 89-90). Even the IMF changed its position on capital controls in its note from February 2010. 'A key conclusion is that, if [...], then use of capital controls – in addition to both prudential and macroeconomic policy – is justified' (Chamon et al. 2010). For financial market participants, capital account liberalisation in developing countries simply represents market access irrespective of whether additional capital is needed in these countries. The pro-cyclical nature of capital flows, however, makes those flows a dangerous undertaking. Investor sentiment, rational or irrational, can additionally exaggerate any trends in the flows, which can be completely independent of the real economic conditions (Stiglitz 2002: 100). Keynes referred to this in his book 'The General Theory of Employment, Interest and Money' (1935) as animal spirits. Therefore, capital flows can contribute to the build-up of bubbles and when they burst its effects tend to drag down the real economy as well (Stiglitz 2002: 101). Indeed, empirical evidence of financial liberalisation, booming credit growth, the build-up of asset price bubbles and the subsequent collapse has been plentiful since the 1970s (Bisignano

1999: 93). The damaging effects of capital flow reversals should be seen as a warning sign for premature liberalisation.

Compared to other East Asian countries, Malaysia decided to stem capital outflows with the help of capital controls which were to reduce the volatility of flows significantly over time. Indeed, Malaysia was able to limit the downturn and the turnaround was achieved faster with less economic and political strain than in other Asian countries. The impediments Malaysia introduced reduced capital outflows significantly and thus not only decreased financial but also economic volatility. Additionally, Malaysia could still freely decide on its interest rate policy and did not have to hike interest rates significantly unlike in other countries (Stiglitz 2002: 93). The aforementioned capital controls imposed by Malaysia helped to keep the exchange rate under control. The measures were not meant to be permanent but rather to limit the short-term strains of the crisis. In fact, the introduction of capital controls was supported by Krugman (1998a) as he put forward, 'Currency controls are risky, stopgap measure, but some gaps desperately need to be stopped'.

Edison and Reinhart (2001: 533) point out that the sale of hard currency reserves as well as raising interest rates sharply are among the most common means to try to stabilise a country's FX rate. However, the costs of these interventions in terms of increasing the economic strain at already difficult times are severe. Initially, a country starts to intervene in the foreign exchange market by selling hard currency reserves against local currency to artificially increase demand and to dampen short-term volatility spikes. Nevertheless, as the pressure continues and the market witnesses the depletion of currency reserves – even huge piles of reserves are, ultimately, too little of a buffer – a country has to consider its remaining options. Interest rate hikes can lead to a worsening of the situation as the higher interest rates lead to expectations and eventually to the realisation of weaker economic data and thus alternatives should be considered by the affected country (Edison and Reinhart 2001: 536). In fact, the introduction of an exit tax helped Malaysia to go through the crisis in a better shape than other East Asian countries (Edison and

Reinhart 2001: 539). These restrictions were lifted as the situation in East Asia relaxed. The case of Malaysia was a success story how to handle a crisis (Stiglitz 2002: 124). Nonetheless, it has to be mentioned that the response depends on the particularities of the situation.

Apart from Malaysia, China also followed its own policies and performed significantly better than other Asian countries (Stiglitz 2002: 125, Goldstein 1998: 30). China resisted devaluing its currency during the years when the crisis ravaged Asia. The devaluation of the Chinese currency in 1994 led to a safer position of the country in the second half of the 1990s. In addition, China depicted a current account surplus in said period which stood in stark contrast to the deteriorating balance-of-payment dynamics in other Asian economies. As there were hardly any portfolio flows due to a lack of convertibility of the Chinese BoPs' accounts, this made the country less susceptible to sudden changes in sentiment and left the country safe from any kinds of speculative attacks on its currency. In addition, China had no significant debt burden during that time. Even though the country was in a better position than the other Asian economies, China felt the spillover effect also in lower domestic growth and thus intervened using stimulus packages (Goldstein 1998: 30-31), which entailed some distortions for the Chinese economy as well. However, these were manageable as is shown in the section 'China's Economic Empowerment'.

iii) Transition Economies

As the transitions for most communist countries started, policies such as price liberalisation, balanced fiscal and tight monetary policy as well as privatisation of government owned companies were the prevailing doctrine. What was not expected was the sharp decline in output that accompanied these changes. In addition, crime increased significantly and privatisation often led to a squandering of national assets. The lessons that can be drawn from this experience are that without adequate institutions, these policies entail significant drawbacks for a country. Thus, the question shifts how the institutional transformation can be performed in an adequate manner (Roland 2000: XVIII – XIX). The institutional dimension is key; the benefits accrued due to liberalisation can be only harvested in case of strong institutional capabilities of a country (Popov 2000: 36-38). Indeed, transformation faces the 'problem of the drunken man who had lost his key in front of the doorstep but was searching under the streetlight because it was the only place where there was light' (Roland 2000: 13).

The problem with the transition of economies from plan to market was that hardly any knowledge was available as the transformation started in these countries. Thus, different streams of advice emerged at the beginning. For instance, Jeffrey Sachs became well known for pushing the big bang approach towards transformation. His view was supported by Åslund (1991), Berg and Sachs (1992), Murphy, Shleifer, and Vishny (1992) or Woo (1994) among others. On the other side, proponents of a more gradualist approach towards transition with a sequencing of reforms were Dewatripont and Roland (1995), McMillan and Naughton (1992), Aghion and Blanchard (1994), Litwack and Qian (1998) as well as Wei (1993). Furthermore, there were proponents such as Jonas Kornai, who proposed a combination of the two approaches towards transition (Roland 2000: 1). How do these different approaches towards a country's transformation differ? While gradualism focuses on the sequencing of reforms, the shock therapy proponents would like to adjust the system in one go and accept a short period of declining output as a consequence of their changes. However, nobody expected the sharp, disastrous declines in output experienced in the countries which went for the big bang approach (Popov 2000: 2). The recessions can be explained by the dissolution of the distortions built-up during the communist period of these countries, particularly in the industrial structure as well as with respect to trade. The mainstream view of transition economics is anchored on the supply-side, thus being mainly a structural adjustment process. Former communist countries have to cut back on their reliance on heavy industry. In particular, military spending has to be cut. This reallocation of resources is the main reason for the temporary decline in output. In contrast to this, the Keynesian view focuses on the demand side. Liberalising policies lead to an overshooting of certain economic and financial variables and drive a sharp decline in demand causing recessions (Popov 2000: 9-11). Thus, according to Roland (2000: 11), the main goals of the transformation were the stabilisation of the economic environment prevailing in the communist countries, a more efficient allocation of resources via the introduction of a flexible price system as well as a competitive market, the provision of incentives as well as better governance for companies, privatisations as well as the fostering of new companies entering the market and the build-up of adequate institutions. With respect to the latter, in particular political and institutional stability, the protection of private property rights as well as the prevention of predatory rent-seeking was emphasised. In fact, the transition process from plan to market has to be regarded as a process of large-scale institutional change (Dewatripont and Roland 1995). Kornai (2006: 210) describes the transition from plan to market as follows, 'The characteristic institutions of capitalism – private property, hired labour, market-type buying and selling, a credit system, and a legal system protecting the sanctity of private property and contracts – evolved in various countries at various speeds. Institutional transformation has been inseparably associated with such profound processes as urbanisation, industrialisation and commercialisation. All the above compromise what is known as the capitalist economy'.

With respect to the different performance of countries since the start of the transition, Popov (2000) shows that the divergence in the paths can be explained by the different conditions at the start of the transformation, the stage of the development, certain reform attempts pre-transition, as well as patterns in trade. In addition, institutional characteristics and inflation dynamics are important factors throughout the transition process. Popov (2000: 1) clearly stresses the importance of the institutional characteristics of a country and shows that the speed of the transition process gets too much attention in the literature, in particular in comparison to the institutional set-up of the transition economies. Moreover, the constraints of the process include the severe uncertainty surrounding the transition process, the complementariness and interactions between the reforms as well as certain political constraints. As there were hardly any experiences with economic transitions, the uncertainty of the outcomes with respect to the newly introduced changes was high. The main controversies related to the role of the government in the new system as well as to how to deal with the sharp decline in output in the transition economies. In addition, the transformation process had to be understood as a learning process in which experimentation played a significant role. China's open approach towards experimentation certainly provided the country with good guidance (Roland 2000: 12-13). In contrast, other approaches severely failed. 'In most FSU and Balkan countries the collapse of the institutions is observable in the dramatic increase of the share of the shadow economy; in the decline of the government revenues as a proportion of GDP; in the inability of the state to deliver basic public goods and appropriate regulatory framework; in the accumulation of tax, trade, wage and bank arrears; in the demonetisation, "dollarisation" and "barterisation" of the economy, as measured by high and growing money velocity, and in the decline of bank financing as a proportion of GDP; in poor enforcement of property rights, bankruptcies, contracts and law and order in general; in increased crime rates; etc.' (Popov 2000: 28).

Moreover, in contrast to China, the transformation of the former Soviet Union was a disaster. One of the attempts to reform the planned economy of the Soviet Union took already place in the 1950s as Khrushchev tried to delegate more power downstream, namely to local governments. However, this attempt to reform the Soviet Union resulted in chaos and increased regional fragmentation made the system close to unmanageable; thus, the Soviet leader was removed from power in 1964. Khrushchev was succeeded by Kosygin who tried to increase autonomy for enterprises. However, the lack of market mechanism and prices as information for resource allocation also led to the failure of the latter reform. Why did the Soviet Union first exhibit fast growth rates which then declined steadily through time regardless of any reform efforts? The initial decades were dominated by so-called extensive growth, i.e. growth deduced from an increase in input factors. Albeit, as resources became scarcer, the high information costs and low efficiency of the system led to a steady decline in the Soviet Union's growth rates. In the later decades of the Soviet Union, attempts were made to increase efficiency and advance its technological progress. However, the central planning system itself was so flawed that any attempts for renewal failed (Wu 2005: 21-22). In the final years of the Soviet Union, Gorbachev tried to fundamentally transform the system. Nevertheless, the ruling elites had lost so much credibility over the preceding decades that control over the situation was lost, leading to social unrest and the ultimate collapse of the Soviet Union (Wu 2005: 24). The disintegration of the Soviet Union was certainly another blowback to the transition. The breakup was an unforeseen consequence of the transformation process (Roland 2000: 4). Moreover, the biggest surprise was the double-digit decline in output in the transition economies as well as that the transformation entailed severe drawbacks such as the rise of organised crime and the failure of the privatisations. With respect to the latter, the performance of the newly privatised companies was sometimes even worse than before. Neither the privatisation via vouchers such as in the Czech Republic nor the mass privatisation in the case of Russia can be classified as particularly successful (Roland 2000: 3-4). One lesson from the latter is that many Central and Eastern European countries as well as Russia had an excessive focus on reforming the state-owned enterprise system instead of fostering competition by allowing new forms of entry. Thus, too much focus was on the destruction than on the creation side (Roland 2000: 7). Maddison (2007b: 172-173) asked the question 'Why China did better than Russia in moving towards a market economy?'. China's growth trajectory since 1978 has generally been steeper than in any other country. However, the diverging paths between China and Russia are particularly striking. There are many reasons for this difference in the growth trajectories. For instance, after 1978 China's reform efforts focused on the agricultural sector while Russia mostly ignored that sector during its transition. China's township and village enterprises created opportunities for the rural population to engage in the initial phase of a more capitalist society. This step was virtually impossible for Russia as Stalin had eliminated any rural reform ambitions in the 1920s. Moreover, the Soviet Union disintegrated in various nation states at the end of its communist period; China remained unified. Another reason why China fared far better than Russia was its advantage of backwardness at the beginning of the transition period (Gerschenkron 1962, 1964; Lin 2012: 12-17). The country's income and productivity level by far lagged those of other emerging markets. Indeed, Popov (2000: 26) finds that for a country's trajectory specific factors such as the benefits of backwardness and the level of aggregate distortions play a significant role. Ever since 1949, the Chinese leadership has had a strong focus on macroeconomic stability, e.g. on keeping inflation down. This desire for prudence emerged from China's history, in particular from the experience of the Nationalist rule and the hyperinflation ravaging China in that period. Furthermore, China did not engage in privatisations, while Russia was pursuing a shock therapy by trying to privatise the state-led industry as fast as possible (Maddison 2007b: 172-173). This form of transition entailed severe social and economic costs for Russia with the foremost 'undesirable results such as economic recession, rampant organised crime, social instability, and embezzlement of state assets' (Wu 2005: 29). Further differences between China and Russia were the rebalancing of the Chinese economy with a focus on its factor endowment. Labour-intensive industries were particularly fostered and light goods for exports were brought into focus of the Chinese leadership. A depressed level of its currency as well as cheap factor inputs made China's goods competitive in the world market and led to an unprecedented boom in exports over the coming decades. Russia, due to its commodity curse, never focused on the development of light industry for exports. In addition, the Chinese birth control system led to a decline in the dependency ratio spurring the Chinese economy (Maddison 2007b: 172-173), which, however, will pose a drag on the economy in the decades to come.

iv) The Global Financial Crisis of 2008

The promotion of global interdependencies has been a US strategic objective since 1945, which had enormous consequences for cross-border flows. In fact, the collapse of the Bretton Woods System in 1971 marked the starting point of a continuous reduction in capital controls globally, which, on the one hand, contributed positively to global growth, but, on the other hand, made many economies simultaneously more vulnerable to shocks. The freedom in capital flows came along with an increased number of financial miseries since the 1970s. In the

1980s, the Latin American debt crises emitted global shock waves and in the 1990s, it was the Asian financial crisis of 1997 and 1998 that had global repercussions (Pauly 2008: 198-199). In theory, financial markets should serve the real economies and not endanger the whole system. However, the social destruction caused by collapses in the financial system is significant. Clearly, the idea of increased interdependencies leading to a more secure world has worked with respect to wars but not with respect to financial crises. (Pauly 2008: 200-202). In particular, emerging markets were severely hit by past crisis episodes. In developed countries, a period known as the Great Moderation had brought a significant reduction in macroeconomic volatility with decent GDP growth. These decades of prosperity led many economists to belief that any downturn could be avoided, although risks due to the build-up in imbalances had been pointed out by some observers (Berg 2011: 5) but were rarely heard.

In 2001, the burst of the dot-com bubble in the US and the terrorist attacks of 9/11 contributed to a slowdown in the US economy. The US central bank reacted to the economic downturn by lowering the policy rate from 6.5 percent to 1 percent between 2000 and 2003. The low interest rate environment led to a significant pick-up in lending and consumption. A looser regulatory environment resulted in imprudent lending in addition to the aforementioned factors. Overall inflation picked up, which led the US Federal Reserve to increase short-term interest rates from 1 percent to 5.25 percent between 2004 and 2006 (Sun and Fu 2012: 4-6). The environment of increasing interest rates caused a slowdown in the previously rising real estate prices, which had been fuelled from the years of low interest rates. Housing prices topped and changes in prices turned negative in 2007, ultimately resulting in the subprime mortgage crisis. Thus, the financial crisis was preceded by a boom in housing prices as well as exuberant capital markets (Reinhart and Rogoff 2009: 20). Various financial institutions faced severe distress in the US due to the burst of the real estate bubble and bankruptcies became inevitable. Bank runs and withdrawals of assets from financial institutions occurred at the same time as collapsing prices set in motion a vicious spiral. One link of the tightly connected chain had caught fire and this fire spread quickly across the globe. In 2008, Bear Stearns was sold to JP Morgan Chase, Lehman Brothers went bankrupt and the closure of Washington Mutual left a dark mark on US history. Stock indices experienced the worst losses since the Depression in the 1930s and capital was withdrawn from emerging markets at a staggering pace and poured into alleged riskless assets (Sun and Fu 2012: 4-6), which led to a vicious cycle.

Reasons for the global financial crisis were various. One frequently mentioned factor was the imbalance in savings and consumption between developing and developed nations. Accumulated savings from China and oil exporters had to be invested and mostly flowed into developed country assets, foremost US treasury bonds (Berg 2011: 9). This artificially depressed yields and credit spreads and led to excessive risk taking and a mispricing of risk in general. The difference in preferences for consumption and savings was especially big in the case of the United States and China. The development model of many rising emerging markets resulted in emerging nations serving as the manufacturers of the global economy. The free-trade system and the relatively unrestricted flow of capital before the crisis led to cheap goods being produced in developing countries and exported, for instance, to the United States which subsequently became ever more indebted. In fact, the US has been running a current account deficit with the world since 1982 and only the dominant role of the US dollar has prevented the edifice from collapsing so far. Ever since the breakdown of the Bretton Woods system, the US dollar had played a crucial role in the system of goods and capital flows and, as a result, increased the indebtedness of the United States (Pauly 2008: 204). Thus, emerging markets, foremost China, accumulated ever more savings most visibly in the form of foreign exchange reserves and invested the reserves again in assets in developed nations; however, this in turn led to a further build-up of debt in the United States and fuelled asset price bubbles (Sun and Fu 2012: 6-7). Given the above, it should be mentioned that the crisis of 2007 was not a balance-of-payment crisis but that the burst of an asset bubble, namely in the US real estate sector, as well as the sharp contraction in the credit market triggered the severe economic downturn (Berg 2011: 11), which is examined in more detail in the early warning section.

With respect to monetary policy, the low interest rate environment in the US certainly contributed to the build-up in imbalances from the early 2000s. In general, the decade can be characterised by increasing globalisation and consequently lower trade barriers as well as the shift of former planned economies to the market, which entailed a support of global growth at the cost of building-up weaknesses. The most significant sign of the expansionary monetary policy pursued by the US during the 2000s was visible in the negative real federal funds rate between 2001 and 2005 which pushed asset prices increasingly higher (Berg 2011: 6-7). Thus, one reason for the global financial crisis in 2007 was the low interest rate environment prevailing in the early 2000s. Alan Greenspan was the key policy-maker supporting the aggressive cuts in the US policy rate, which triggered the easy-credit environment and part of the flows that resulted in the asset price bubbles (Bordo and Jeanne 2002). Too much optimism regarding the ever-increasing house prices also contributed to the crisis. The peaking of real estate prices in 2006, in line with the higher interest rate environment after the bottom of the policy rate cycle had been reached in 2003, led to the burst of the bubble in 2007 and to the vicious spirals in 2008 and 2009 (Sun and Fu 2012: 7-8). In general, price bubbles are not new with the most famous historical evidence being the Dutch tulip mania of 1636. Moreover, the railroad bubble in the United Kingdom in the 1840s and the US dot-com bubble are other well-known empirical evidences of said phenomenon. As often in history, speculation led to exuberant asset price increases which proved to be unsustainable at some point. One area that describes these phenomena well is behavioural economics which deals with the human psychology behind certain events. Investors often over-extrapolate price trends indefinitely into the future and thus contribute to the build-up of price bubbles. Herd mentality plays a crucial role with respect to this (Beachy 2012: 8-10; Brunnermeier and Schnabel 2014: 1, 30-53). Moreover, credit growth and price bubbles are often linked. 'This correlation between credit booms and price bubbles has been seen numerous times in history, since increased borrowing tends to foster increased demand for the asset in question (i.e. tulips, stocks, or houses), enabling the self-perpetuating rise in price' (Beachy 2012: 10). Given the build-up of a bubble, what causes a bubble to burst? The bubble started to deflate as supply of housing simply overtook the demand as new construction had been spurred over the preceding years due to the significant rise in prices (Beachy 2012: 13), which led to the disastrous events of 2008 and 2009.

Deregulation had been the norm in the decades before the global financial crisis. The economic stimulus in the early 2000s came on top of this liberalisation trend and resulted in market participants foregoing prudent practices. Oversight and supervision played an ever-smaller role in the system and financial institutions were allowed to reduce their capital provisions significantly which added to the vulnerability of the whole economic edifice. In addition, the deregulation resulted in increased financial innovation and the passing on of risks to various stakeholders. Securitisation certainly played a role in the prelude to the drama that evolved as of 2007 (Sun and Fu 2012: 8-9). Due to weak financial regulation, imprudent lending had been granted to borrowers with low credit ratings. As the real estate bubble started to deflate, a vicious spiral was triggered (Reinhart and Rogoff 2008: 339-342). Fannie Mae and Freddie Mac, two large institutional lenders, had to be taken over by the US government as a consequence of severe losses due to these subprime mortgages. As Lehman Brothers defaulted in September 2008, the crisis became systemic with global repercussions. The significant downturn in capital markets only stabilised between the first and the second quarter of 2009. Due to the collapse of global trade the US centric crisis spread to emerging markets (Berg 2011: 2-3). Indeed, the lack of supervision and adequate structure were not only visible in the domestic US sphere but also in international financial institutions (Sun and Fu 2012: 9). In addition, the weak financial regulatory framework allowed for a build-up in excessive leverage. Short-term benefits at the expense of prudent loan standards were sought after. This was exacerbated due to obscure financial securitisation. The sharp spike in correlations in an economic downturn showed the true nature of this securitisation and a high degree of risk concentration became visible, albeit too late to prevent the disaster to unfold (Berg 2011: 12). Moreover, the high degree of leverage in the US economy made it susceptible to shocks. A shock can trigger a downward spiral which is hard to escape without an automatic circuit breaker (Berg 2011: 15). 'It is possible to summarise the microeconomic factors behind the crisis as specific market failures related to excessive risk-taking due to weak regulation and government guarantees which were not priced correctly, uninsured short-term funding in the shadow banking system, externalities from failures of individual firms related to opacity in the financial system [...]' (Berg 2011: 16). This represents one reason for the global financial crisis of 2008.

On the macroeconomic side, the inclination to consume over investment led to an accumulation of debt. This scheme was attractive as long as asset prices continued to rise, but investors were punished severely as the crisis hit the stage. In contrast to developed countries, China has been suffering from different types of imbalances, mainly resulting from its development model. Differences in income between rural and urban areas are still large and consumption remains a negligible factor in China. Moreover, the global financial crisis entailed significant spill over effects from the US to China due to the sharp contraction in external demand, which hints to the country's dependence on exports (Sun and Fu 2012: 9). Furthermore, the deterioration in the financial conditions in the US also entailed severe costs for emerging markets. In particular, countries with weaknesses regarding external liabilities as well as currency overvaluations and excessive real estate prices were susceptible to the spillover from the US crisis (Berg 2011: 17). Research by Lane and Milesi-Ferretti (2010) points to the link between credit growth and the deficit in the current accounts of emerging markets as well as the decline in real output. In general, it can be said that the impact of the crisis was felt more sharply in countries that relied strongly on demand from developed countries and which had larger exposure to foreign banks (Berg 2011: 20). The downward spiral increased risk premia globally as investors faced an asymmetric information problem; nobody knew the degree of imprudence that was applied to financial practices before the crisis hit in 2007 (Berg 2011: 17). As the tide turned, real and perceived weaknesses entailed the increase in risk premia.

To counter the negative effects of the financial crisis, the US Federal Reserve cut interest rates sharply and the US engaged in fiscal stimulus, which was one of the lessons drawn from the depression of the 1930s (Reis 2010: 153). 'Keynesianism's central message – expansive fiscal policy when resource utilisation falls – is still valid' (Berg 2011: 27). Moreover, quantitative easing should help to relax the distressed financial conditions faced by many market participants (Krishnamurthy and Vissing-Jorgensen 2011). The usual transmission mechanism of monetary policy is the interest rate channel, the credit channel as well as the exchange rate channel. First, lower interest rates encourage consumption and thus, stimulate the economy. Asset prices should be more valuable today with lower interest rates and thus, this should stabilise the vicious cycle related to leverage and collateral. Second, lower interest rates also reduce credit spreads and thus, the risk-taking capability of an economy. Third, the exchange rate should weaken which helps the balance-of-payment dynamics of a country. The latter three channels work exactly in the other direction in case of interest rate hikes. Given the aforementioned, lower interest rates are vital to break-out of the self-reinforcing spirals described before (Berg 2011: 29-30). Indeed, 'If the central bank "leans against the wind" and acts symmetrically both in the upward and downward phases it can encourage more responsible behaviour on the part of investors and reduce the risk of future crises' (Berg 2011: 34). This holds across developed and emerging countries.

d) Early Warning Systems and Historic Crisis Episodes

The goal is to analyse the determinants of financial crises, in particular of currency crises, to better understand them and deduct implications for predicting and preventing these events. Empirical analysis of crises is one element of early warning systems mainly capturing economic and financial factors. The underlying vulnerabilities of EWS are, for instance, asset price bubbles or balance sheet mismatches (Ghosh et al. 2009). From these variables, the likelihood of a certain type of crisis is deducted. However, this significantly depends on the definition of crisis as well as on the forecast horizon. Nevertheless, most early warning systems do focus on currency crises (IMF 2002: 48-49). In general, there are two main approaches how to assess early warning indicators. The first is the signals methodology, also known as threshold approach. The second methodology is a logit or probit model. Those methodologies are used to assess indicators that are supposed to represent a vulnerability of a country and thus, give indications of weaknesses well ahead of a crisis (Goldstein et al. 2000: 15). After selecting the variables, it is common to examine which variable best explains the outcome in-sample, which is often termed a horse race. However, this approach entails certain disadvantages. Variables that have weak explanatory power, for instance, may have an impact on more significant predictors and thus, still could be vital. In addition, a horse race is prone to overfitting, which leads to a poor out-of-sample predictive power of the model (Chamon et al. 2012: 11) and thus, renders the exercise questionable.

The IMF for instance, on the one hand, uses the Developing Country Studies Division (DCSD) model with five explanatory variables, namely the real exchange rate, current account, FX reserves, exports as well as short-term debt to FX reserves. The model is calibrated with the help of a multivariate panel probit regression. The probabilities derived from the probit model are converted into a binary crisis indicator (IMF 2002: 50). On the other hand, the IMF also uses the KLR Crisis Signals model (Kaminsky et al. 1998) which looks at an extended set of variables, namely the ratio of FX reserves to M2, credit growth, differences in the money multiplier, real interest rate among others. The model applies a threshold approach with the threshold being expressed as an optimised percentile (IMF 2002: 50). This threshold or signals approach is also applied by Reinhart and Rogoff (2009). The researchers review the early warning literature in their book 'This Time is Different' and analyse which indicators accurately predicted certain crises. In fact, the literature on early warning signals is still quite incomplete, leaving out many crisis episodes as well as primarily looking at economic indicators to predict crises. Thus, this represents a gap in the literature (Reinhart and Rogoff 2009: 279). In general, with respect to predicting financial crises, the best indicator is deviations from trend in the real exchange rate. Apart from this variable, changes in real housing prices as well as indicators related to the external balances of a country such as short-term capital inflows to GDP and the ratio of the current account to investment serve as decent indicators for banking crises. Variation in stock prices is also a good indicator for currency crises. With respect to this, exports and the ratio of M2 to international reserves are good predictors as well (Reinhart and Rogoff 2009: 280). In line with the above, Chamon et al. (2012: 12) find that vulnerabilities related to the external sector have the best predictive power among fundamentals. An overvaluation of the real exchange rate as well as a deteriorating debt-to-export ratio were the most significant indicators in their analysis.

Regarding the Latin American crisis of the 1980s, an overvaluation of the exchange rate, dismal performance of the external sector, financial liberalisation and debt unsustainability in light of higher interest rates were the key vulnerabilities according to the literature overview previously given. With respect to the currency adjustments in light of the Asian financial crisis, Goldstein et al. (2000: 96) find the best monthly indicators to be an appreciation of the real exchange rate relative to the trend in the local currency, a slump in equity prices, a decline in exports as well as a high ratio of M2 to hard currency reserves. Regarding annual indicators, the current account deficit relative to output and investment is the best indicator for FX crises. The indicators usually give a signal about 10 to 18 months ahead of the event. Among those indicators, which do not work at all, are notably credit ratings. Research has found that the actual rating is decoupled from a sovereign's probability of default. In fact, credit ratings are lagging financial crises (Goldstein et al. 2000: 49-50). Moreover, Goldstein et al. (2000: 17-18) point out two important limitations of current economic vulnerability analyses. First, the previous does not capture the political dimension of crises. Second, as most early warning indicator analyses focus on past crises, China is not at all subject to these analyses, which also represents a gap in the literature.

With respect to crises in transition economies, in particular the research from Brüggemann and Linne (2002) gives important hints regarding important drivers of outcome. The researchers find the most important variables to be an overvalued exchange rate, weak exports as well as declining FX reserves. This is in line with other crisis episodes. Regarding the global financial crisis of 2008, Reinhart and Rogoff (2008) analyse the communalities between the recent global financial crisis and previous crises and find that a number of indicators also signalled a warning with respect to the crisis of 2007. In particular, capital flow statistics as well as balance-of-payment dynamics in general are useful predictors for financial crisis. Other similarities include the significant increase in real estate as well as equity prices in the years before the crisis. In addition, an increase in public debt is a universal indicator for upcoming economic distortions (Reinhart and Rogoff 2008: 339-342). Thus, 'while each financial crisis no doubt is distinct, they also share striking similarities in the run-up of asset prices, in debt accumulation, in growth patterns, and in current account deficits. The majority of historical crises are preceded by financial liberalisation' (Reinhart and Rogoff 2008: 342). The same is true for the financial crisis of 2007 in which a de facto liberalisation preceded the crisis. The lax regulation of the financial industry contributed to the growth prior to the crisis at a significant cost of greater vulnerability (Reinhart and Rogoff 2008: 342), which ultimately added to the evolution of the crisis.

To sum up, in this section it was laid out that the primary focus of scholars so far has been on economic variables. However, I believe that this is insufficient in explaining financial crises. As demonstrated in the conceptual section, two additional dimensions are key to understanding the trajectory of emerging markets. Indeed, the limitations of pure economic analyses with respect to financial crises were identified as a gap in the literature by various scholars. As mentioned above, Reinhart and Rogoff (2009) speak of the incompleteness of the early warning literature with respect to historical crisis episodes and criticise the conceptual favouritism of analysing crises primarily via an economic lens.

Albeit important, fundamentals only provide a fragmented picture of financial crises and thus, lead to a limited understanding of outcomes. Therefore, I expanded on the conventional method of analysis in the conceptual section by adding one dimension regarding policy-induced weaknesses and one category with respect to institutional vulnerabilities. I apply an expanded analytical framework to China as the country represents an excellent example due to its steep rise since the 1980s as well as its troubles in the second half of 2015 and 2016. In comparison to other emerging markets, China's rise did not get derailed by past crisis episodes. Indeed, I will point to the unique events China went through since the empirical break of emerging markets in the early 2000s. The historical review of past crisis episodes helps to draw lessons for China and to see the troubles from one specific angle of analysis, namely via economic variables. The expanded conceptualisation of vulnerability will provide for additional insights surrounding the events which ocurred in China in 2015 and 2016. Indeed, by taking into account policy-induced and institutional vulnerabilities a more sophisticated understanding of outcomes and how China is constrained and enabled to determine its fate, can be laid out as shown in the case study.

3.B) China's Economic Empowerment

a) Introduction

The former World Bank Chief Economist, Justin Lin, starts his book 'Demystifying the Chinese Economy' with the phrase 'Sustained economic development relies on continual technological innovation and structural transformation' (Lin 2012: xiii). This gives indeed a first indication of the framework, which is applied to the analysis of China's rise as well as the country's recent struggles. Fundamentals are often used as the dominant lens for analyses. However, technological progress and how the factors of production are used is a key driver of outcomes. Policy is the third area of focus when it comes to analysing a country's success. In my conceptual work, all three dimensions are used to increase the predictability of outcomes and give recommendations as to what a country can do to mitigate the risk of derailing events. I will subsequently apply the analytical framework to China in the case study. However, to do this, it is inevitable to first review China's historical background to better understand current circumstances.

History plays a significant role how vulnerabilities are viewed and addressed. The framework for engaging with current issues is often defined within the historical context. Indeed, China's memory of past events determines the country's strategy today (Gong 2001: 53). China's history defines its present and therefore, gives it an identity and channels the country's view of current strengths and weaknesses (Gong 2001: 45). In particular, the country's historic humiliations by more advanced nations have made it more sensitive regarding topics such as economic growth or the opening of its economy to the outside world. In China's history, the government was threatened by foreign invasions and external imposed policies were often seen as curtailment of China's sovereignty. In fact, these historical events have driven today's perceptions. The history of a country must be understood to comprehend its approach towards fundamental, policy-induced and institutional vulnerabilities.

b) Historical Background: Pre-1949

i) The Traditional Economy

In 1300, China was the dominant world economy and only by 1500, Western Europe could catch up and overtake China in terms of per capita income as well as with respect to technological progress. The initial supremacy of China was fostered by its bureaucratic governance structure backed by Confucian ideology. While the Chinese bureaucracy supported stability and a slow but steady expansion for centuries, it ultimately prevented the development of a commercial and industrial class at a time when the rest of the world was progressing in those areas (Maddison 2007b: 157-160). In fact, China's bureaucracy prevented the country from adopting the scientific advancements made during the industrial revolution in Europe (Lin 2012: xiv) and thus, accelerated the country's relative and absolute decline within said period.

The traditional economy of China was foremost made up of the agricultural sector as 90% of the population lived outside urban areas. Agriculture was driven by manual labour and applied certain technologies to enhance the output. Those technologies consisted of different kind of seeds, fertiliser and irrigation techniques. The latter helped the rural population to control the water supply of their fields and thus, improved the other two input factors: crops and fertiliser. The agricultural output was generated by human labour input, which stands in stark contrast to Europe's approach in this area, which included the use of animals in farming as well. In addition, the human diet also marks a distinguishing factor as the Chinese population had hardly any access to meat. Nevertheless, the farming and the application of said technology sufficed to support population growth throughout decades (Naughton 2007: 34-36), in particular due to the expansion of rice cultivation in the area south of the Yangtze (Maddison 2007b: 160). Indeed, China accounted for approximately one third of the world population in 1820 and, as living standards remained stable during this period, also for around one third of global output at that time (Maddison 2007a: 44; Maddison 2007b: 175-177). China's economy was supported by the institutional set-up of the period which included the use of paper money, the establishment of formal organisations as well as occasional capitalist attributes such as share issuances, written contracts and institutions to hold up the rule of law; additionally, trade networks, a banking system and markets for agricultural products as well as for land and human labour were competitive. Social mobility also contributed positively to the rise of China till the early 1800s (Naughton 2007: 34-36). China's ambitions resulted in a certain degree of globalisation as tea exports became a major economic activity after 1880. However, the traditional institutions of China at some point were no longer able to compete with exports from Japan and India as standardisation and high-quality standards became the norm in the early twentieth century. The structure of the predominant agricultural economy in China was mainly based on small-scale households and thus, individual land ownership rather than collectivism determined the trajectory of the traditional economy of China (Lieberthal 1995: 14). In fact, it was the notion of household-based economy, which is one legacy of the traditional economy, fostered by Deng Xiaoping in the transition period. However, the structure of small-scale producers at that time could not hold up with global competition and thus, Chinese exports were pushed out of world markets. The institutional set-up did not prove sufficiently sophisticated to compete on a global basis. The fragmentation of production made capital accumulation in China nearly impossible at some point (Naughton 2007: 37) and thus, the country lost ground relative to nations with a more sophisticated set-up.

The institutional backwardness became visible not only in the loss of market share of exports, but in the domestic sphere as well. Additionally, the rapid increase in population resulted in pressure on the resource allocation. China's factor endowment with abundant labour but limited land for agricultural cultivation confined the economy given the institutional set-up during the nineteenth century. The marginal decline in output per additional input given technology eventually made the strains of the rapid population growth visible. The Qing dynasty was facing its final decades as the capacity for renewal was non-existent. In the end, the institutional constraints, in particular in the agricultural sector after the end of the Qing dynasty, resulted in a catastrophic famine in the face of a severe drought in 1928-1931 which cost millions of lives (Naughton 2007: 38-39). The set-up of fragmented small-scale farms was not able to deal with contemporary challenges.

Given the institutional weakness in the nineteenth century, internal unrest shackled the leading elite of China with the Taiping Rebellion (1851-64) as well as the Boxer Rebellion of the 1890's disrupting local order at the same time as external pressure resulted in a further retrenchment of the country's capabilities. China saw a reversal of its fortunes with various challenges to the local elites emerging due to the country's fundamental, political and institutional weaknesses, which ultimately led to the end of the Qing dynasty in 1912 (Fairbank and Goldman 2006: 235). The perceived humiliation experienced by China in this period still influences current views and is described below.

ii) External Pressure and Humiliation

The understanding of China's current trajectory is closely connected to the country's history. In particular, China's frustration resulting from its backsliding and the humiliation induced by rising competitors in the nineteenth and early twentieth century contributes significantly to modern politics (Lin 2012: 57). Such Chinese sentiments had their origin in those decades of humiliation.

In the eighteenth century, China exported various goods to the world and thus, exhibited a trade surplus, which supported the country's economy. Britain, the dominant European power at that time, responded by looking for ways to compensate for the trade imbalance and discovered opium as a commodity that was in high demand in China. However, the Chinese government tried to restrict the flow of opium into its country, which led to the Opium War with the European power in 1839. The loss of the war meant that Britain gained effective control of Hong Kong and the first Treaty Ports under foreign control were established in China as per the Treaty of Nanjing in 1842 (Spence 1990: 128-132, 158). In the following decades, China was dragged into more wars with foreign contestants, which were all lost and resulted in conceding control of Chinese territory to foreign powers as well as repatriation payments. These treaties forced China to adopt a low tariff system and between 1842 and 1917 more than 90 Treaty Ports were opened. The latter system remained in place until 1943 (Maddison 2007b: 165). In Asia, Japan became the dominant power after the country won the Sino-Japanese war in 1895. The Meiji Restoration led to Japan's adoption of Western technologies. This catch-up process was also driven by a humiliating event in Japan's history induced by the American navy in the mid-nineteenth century. The subsequent introduction of a constitutional monarchy and a harsh modernisation programme encompassing schooling, banking, the military, land reform among others led to the modernisation of Japan known as the Meiji Restoration (Lin 2012:58-59), which institutional change led to Japan's rise and aggressions against the country's neighbours.

At the beginning of the nineteenth century, the systems in China and Japan depicted very similar traits. Japan was ruled by the Tokugawa family and the country's system was still a feudal one. That state was disturbed with US warships entering the Edo Bay in 1853 and effectively requesting preferential trade agreements from Japan. Similar events happened in China when hostilities related to the trade of opium were lost against the British and thus, China had to accept asymmetric treaties with the Western power (Acemoglu and Robinson 2013: 118-120). In both countries, China as well as Japan, the systems could be characterised as absolutist. However, in China no real opposition could be formed in the nineteenth century due to the extent of the absolutist rule. In contrast, in Japan the incident with the US triggered a wave of reforms, which ultimately would become known as aforementioned Meiji Restoration (Fairbank and Goldman 2006: 220-221). The reforms in Japan in the later decades of that century were indeed fundamental. The Tokugawa family had side-lined the Japanese emperor ever since they took over power in 1603 until the end of its rule in 1868 with the beginning of the Meiji Restoration. Emperor Meiji was restored to power and in the subsequent decades, extensive changes to the institutional system were implemented. Feudalism was abolished, the system of taxation was centralised, restrictions on mobility were lifted, property rights were institutionalised and the industrialisation was pushed forward by the ruling government. In Asia, Japan was the first country to adopt a constitution in 1890 (Acemoglu and Robinson 2013: 294-298). While China and Japan's military vulnerability was exploited by Western powers in the mid-nineteenth century, the trajectories of both countries went into completely different directions in the subsequent decades. The entrenched bureaucratic system in China made it virtually impossible to overthrow the ruling elites and thus, the absolutist system continued until its eventual downfall in 1912 (Fairbank and Goldman 2006: 235). Due to the far-reaching reforms in Japan, the build-up of an inclusive system that encompassed the whole of the society, the country rose to unprecedented power while China continued to suffer from humiliation until 1949 (Acemoglu and Robinson 2013: 296-298), which marked the start of a period of inward orientation.

After the Sino-Japanese war, Japan became a major investor in China as the Treaty of Shimonoseki, which ended the fighting, forced China to accept foreign direct investment (Naughton 2007: 41-42). Due to this, foreign investment increased significantly in China which led to an expansion in modern sectors such as banking, commercial and industrial activities as well as an extension of the railway system. At the same time, Japan gained access to the Korean peninsula and China had to cede Taiwan in 1895 (Maddison 2007b: 166). Thus, Japan's institutional changes, in particular the land reform and a programme of state-led industrialisation accompanying technological innovations as well as investments in human capital, spurred Japan's rise and aggressions to become the predominant power in Asia. In addition, the aforementioned Boxer Rebellion of the 1890s which was driven by anti-foreign sentiment led to further weakening of the Qing government (Fairbank and Goldman 2006: 230). This culminated in the occupation of Beijing by eight foreign powers in 1901 and the signing of the Boxer Protocol. The end of the Qing period in 1912 was the consequence of the challenges arising due to the various constraints, or to put it differently due to the fundamental, policy-induced and institutional weaknesses the nation faced. In addition to the internal discontent, the weaknesses were exploited by foreign powers resulting in decades of humiliation for China. Its sovereignty was severely confined by foreign imposed policies (Naughton 2007: 41-42). While China made up for approximately one third of the world economy in 1820, the relative rise of other nations caused China's position in the world to shrink to a mere 9 percent of global GDP by 1913 (Maddison 1998 in Naughton 2007: 42-43). In fact, from the early nineteenth century onwards China's output declined in absolute terms while other parts of the world progressed at a significant speed (Maddison 2007b: 157), which led to the relative decline of China.

iii) China's Failure to Adopt

China failed to emulate the technological progress of the West until the middle of the twentieth century mainly due to its institutional set-up which had helped to unify and govern the country over the preceding centuries. 'Ideology, mind-set, and education system of the bureaucracy led to a reluctant adoption of Western technological progress' (Maddison 2007b: 164). In this context, the question "What determines a country's growth trajectory?" should be asked. It must be answered first, before a more detailed look can be taken at the decades of China's backsliding. One approach to assess a country's growth potential is by looking at the factors of production (Blanchard and Johnson 2013: 265-266). Capital, labour and natural resources are the classical inputs which when increased also spur output. Natural resources are dependent on the area in which a country is located; labour is restricted by the speed of population growth; and thus, capital tends to be the variable most focus is put on. In the latter part of the twentieth century, China's growth trajectory was indeed primarily driven by saving and investment decisions. Apart from these input variables, there is a variable related to technology, productivity and institutions. In this book, this component is mostly covered in the institutional section, but all three terms can be used interchangeable. As capital depicts decreasing marginal returns per unit of input, the institutional dimension is the key area to focus on. In fact, it is this area that determines a country's long-term growth trajectory (Lin 2012: 10-11). In general, technological innovation can be split into product and process innovation. The former is usually related to research and development (R&D), which is either pursued locally or imported from abroad. For developing countries to profit from their state of backwardness, they must import technology from developed countries as investing in R&D often proves to be too costly. Imitation is therefore the primary source of progress (Blanchard and Johnson 2013: 281). This is frequently done by either copying more advanced technologies or buying patents, which is faster and cheaper than investing in R&D locally and thus, can improve a country's growth trajectory significantly. Consequently, a country can profit from its stage of backwardness, which is often assessed by looking at GDP per capita differentials, by adopting new technologies from more advanced countries (Lin 2012: 12-17). Whether this adoption is feasible or not depends crucially on a country's institutions; the failure of this system is what led to the decline of China in the late nineteenth and early twentieth century.

What does a failure of the institutional set-up mean in the case of China? The failure to adopt the advancements of the Industrial Revolution of the mid-eighteenth century was mainly because of the civil service system in China, which had served the country well for decades, but which proved incapable of fostering an adoption process, which would have prevented China's decline (Maddison 2007b: 157-160). The backsliding of China is often termed the Needham puzzle. Explanations for China's decline until the early twentieth century vary from cultural factors to a lack of national competition and insufficient demand for new technologies. Can this reasoning describe why China failed to adopt the technological innovations of the Industrial Revolution such as the steam engine, mechanisations in the textile industry or the increased use of iron and steel? This has been highly contested and thus, Justin Lin takes a step back before advancing a new hypothesis. As described above, technology or institutions improve the allocation of the factors of production and thus, contribute significantly to a country's long-term growth trajectory. Lin describes the Chinese bureaucratic system of that time as hostile to scientific advancements as the civil service entry exams discouraged mathematical and scientific skills. These were not needed to govern and keep China unified and thus, had been neglected in the civil servant examinations of China (Lin 2012: 32-48). China's bureaucratic system and civil servant examination dates to the Sui Dynasty and was extended by establishing the Four Books and Five Classics of Confucianism as the core of its examination. This institutional set-up had an enormous influence on the country's incentive structure and thus, its trajectory (Lin 2012: 49-51). When experience became an ever-smaller factor and scientific experiments turned into the primary source of technological progress, China lost ground to the European countries. The lack of a conveyed mathematical and scientific skillset due to the institutional set-up was therefore one significant driver of the country's backsliding. The early European capitalist system served the development and dissemination of technology better than the Chinese system. Thus, the answer to the Needham puzzle according to Justin Lin lies in China's entrenched institutions (Lin 2012: 32-48). The incentive structure in Europe due to basic capitalist traits fostered the factors which ultimately led to the Industrial Revolution. In China, in contrast, the collapse of the Qing government in 1912 was driven by the inability of the ruling elite to introduce effective reforms, which would have made up for the country's deficiencies. The attachment to privileges and status ultimately led to the downfall of the bureaucratic elite (Maddison 2007b: 167), as these vulnerabilities were not addressed.

iv) Early Industrialisation

The end of the Qing government led to nearly two decades of internal strife which was characterised by a civil war. It was only in 1927 that the Nationalist movement (Kuomintang) could unify the country and ruled China until the Japanese aggression continued in 1937. The period of Nationalist Party rule is known as Nanjing decade and, indeed, led to some of the cornerstones for improved long-term economic growth such as investments in education and agricultural innovations (Naughton 2007: 43) as well as a currency reform in 1935 (Maddison 2007b: 166). While the traditional economy was predominantly an agricultural economy, a period of industrialisation began in the early twentieth century. Two different streams of industrialisation can be distinguished, namely the 'Treaty Port Industrialization' and the 'Manchurian Industrialization' (Naughton 2007: 43) with both having significant influence on China's trajectory.

While the loss of the Opium War led to a period of humiliation in the eye of China, it also encompassed the start of the modern era with the Treaty Ports serving as areas of cultural exchange and technological transfer (Fairbank and Goldman 2006: 200). However, these areas were under foreign control and thus, companies were mainly started and directed by foreigners who competed in local and global markets. Nevertheless, the Nanjing decade resulted in the emergence of Chinese capitalists who learnt to survive in a competitive environment. Positive spill over effects in the Treaty Port areas ultimately led to the emergence of a modern, local industry. Skills were acquired rapidly and the improved policy environment as well as institutional set-up in the Nationalist period led to the beginning of the industrialisation in China (Naughton 2007: 44). As a matter of fact, these Treaty Ports served as examples for the establishment of special economic zones (SEZs) in the transition period after 1978 and fostered China's experimental approach towards opening-up the country's economy (Naughton 2007: 52). In contrast, the 'Manchurian Industrialization' focused on Japan's strategic goals and thus, fostered heavy industry as well as the development of a railroad network for the extractive industry (Fairbank and Goldman 2006: 241).

The exploitation of natural resources, especially coal and iron ore deposits, was carried out by the occupants of the Manchuria. However, there was little transfer of skills and hardly any technological transfer took place in this stream of industrialisation as Japan mainly imported equipment and key parts of factories from Japan with key roles being held by Japanese (Naughton 2007: 44-45). In contrast to Taiwan and Korea, which served as food producers and belonged to the closer circle of the Japanese empire, the Manchuria served Japan's strategic goals through the extraction of resources and as supplier for semi-processed goods. Nevertheless, by the end of the Japanese aggression due to the collapse of the empire, the Manchuria was the basis of China's industry (Naughton 2007: 48) and thus, also in the initial focus of the CCP's development strategy.

v) World War II and the Aftermath

The Manchuria was occupied in various stages. First, part of it was occupied when Japan won a war against Russia in 1905. Second, a further part of the region was given to Japan after World War I. This was another humiliating event for China as the country fought as an ally of the Triple Entente and instead of rewarding the country, Japan was allocated the former German territory (Lin 2012: 61-62; Spence 1990: 388). This humiliation by Western powers triggered the establishment of the so-called May Fourth Movement in China (Lieberthal 1995: 29-31), which was effectively divided in one part demanding the westernisation of China and another advocating communism. The latter was generally on the rise with the October Revolution of 1917 in Russia that marked the beginning of Marxism-Leninism. In contrast to the humiliation experienced by China from the West, communist Russia immediately saw an ally in China and withdrew most of the unequal treaties it had previously established with the country. With the rise of the Soviet Union in the subsequent decades, the communist model became ever more appealing for China. In 1921, the Chinese Communist Party was founded which initially emulated the Marxist-Leninist model of initiating uprisings in the city to induce a communist revolution in China. However, these uprisings failed as major factories were under foreign ownership and thus, the revolts were immediately suppressed by foreign military, foremost by the Japanese (Lin 2012: 61-66). With respect to Japan, to institutionalise its footprint the country formed a puppet state in 1931 and thereby, effectively extended its reach all over the Manchuria from which the empire resumed its war of aggression against China in 1937. While Japan represented a common enemy, the situation of war also led to the rise of the Communists relative to the Nationalists as the former gained legitimacy by fighting the Japanese aggression (Naughton 2007: 47). In a broader context, the chapter of the Japanese aggression after 1937 was a continuation of the humiliation of China by foreign powers in the eye of the Chinese (Naughton 2007: 50), which would affect Chinese policies for the decades to come.

During World War II, the Nationalist government of China was forced to retreat further into the country. The war led to an increase of interventionist policies and the Kuomintang Party established a National Resource Commission (NRC) to facilitate the extraction as well the allocation of resources. This institution made itself a good reputation by running factories effectively and staying away from overly corrupt practices. By the end of the war, the Japanese-built companies had been taken over by the Nationalist government of China leading to a large majority of the industrial capacity being controlled by the Kuomintang movement in 1945. This state-run complex formed the basis for the Maoist era after the civil war in 1949 (Fairbank and Goldman 2006: 357-358). In fact, with the establishment of the NRC, the Nationalist government had laid the basis for the planned economy in the Maoist period. Many of the bureaucrats that worked for the Kuomintang government even stayed on in the newly created state ruled by the Chinese Communist Party. Consequently, the People's Republic of China did not have to start from scratch. By not directly engaging in mass expropriations and nationalisations of factories in the initial years, the Communist Party was able to uphold a broad-based support of its leadership after the civil war (Naughton 2007: 49-51), which secured its initial success of rebuilding the country.

c) Historical Background: 1949-1978

In contrast to preceding governments, the Maoist leadership exercised a greater amount of control over the Chinese economy and society in general. The bureaucratic apparatus was held in tight grip by the CCP and the military hierarchy reached far into the civilian sphere. 1949 marked the end of the humiliation experienced by China from foreign powers. Nevertheless, for the decades to come the country's history greatly determined its new strategy of inward orientation (Gong 2001: 53). In the Maoist era, the growth performance of China picked-up significantly. This was achieved despite the country's lack of ties with the external world and hostilities between the West as well as between the neighbouring countries and China. Even with the Soviet Union, which greatly supported the initial steps of communist China, the relationship deteriorated significantly from the late 1950s (Fairbank and Goldman 2006: 379) and thus, China primarily acted on its own account until 1971 as the country was not a member of the United Nations and suffered from a trade embargo by the United States from 1950 to 1971. With respect to data, the Chinese Maoist era is unreliable as there were severe statistical blackout periods in the 1960s and 1970s. In general, the Chinese statistical system was based on the Soviet model, which makes it difficult to compare to Western data from that period. Adjusted statistical data from Maddison (2007a: 62), however, show that China's GDP per capita grew at 2.3 percent between 1952 and 1978 and at 6.6 percent between 1978 and 2003. This stands in stark contrast to the pre-socialist growth rates which were slightly negative with -0.1 percent on a yearly basis between 1913 and 1952. Other Asian economies also exhibited a significant pick-up in growth during the period from 1952 to 1978. While China grew at 2.3 percent per annum, GDP per capita in Hong Kong and Taiwan grew at 5.4 and 6.6 percent respectively. In contrast, India only grew at 1.7 percent during the same period (Maddison 2007a: 62), which marked one of the lowest growth rates in the region.

The significant differentials in growth rates between 1952 and 1978 in Asia should lead one to the question some of the policies of Maoist

China. In particular, factor inputs were not efficiently used during this period. Labour markets were virtually inexistent and the household registration system restricted any forms of migration, which trapped workers in Chinese rural areas. Residents in those areas did not receive the same benefits as urban workers since they were often compensated in kind and the accumulated work points were only paid in cash on an annual basis (Maddison 2007a: 64). Therefore, the poor performance of the agricultural sector in the Maoist era can be partially attributed to bad policymaking and partially to the weakness of institutions built by the Communist government, which were aimed at repressing the agricultural sector to foster the development of heavy industry. This system primarily served the extraction of resources for the ends of the Maoist regime (Naughton 1995: 138). As Maddison (2007a: 69) put it, 'the poor performance of agriculture in the Maoist period was due to a government squeeze on peasant income by fiscal, price and procurement policies, constraints on rural-urban migration and the adverse effect of institutional change, as collective arrangements reduced efficiency and incentives'. However, within the urban industries a lack of incentives also led to a depressed level of productivity. Wages were low and jobs were given for a lifetime; thus, workers could hardly be incentivised to perform above target. In fact, total factor productivity (TFP) was negative between 1952 and 1978. Maddison (2007a: 68) estimates that productivity declined at an annual rate of -1.37 percent during that period. This stands in stark contrast to the rising total factor productivity in the period from 1978 to 2003, during which TFP was estimated to have increased by 2.95 percent per annum (Maddison 2007a: 65). The increase in productivity in the reform period can be attributed to the reversion of some of the policy failures during the Maoist period as well as an institutional remaking in general.

i) The People's Republic of China

The People's Republic of China was founded after the civil war in October 1949 and this marked an inflection point for China (Spence 1990: 515). The economy was reoriented towards a capital-intensive industry. By doing that China's factor endowment was completely neglected as labour-intensive sectors, which would fit to China's vast human labour force, were forgone (Lin 2012: 71-72) and factories producing chemicals as well as machinery and metals were preferred in the country's development plan. This is known as the Big Push industrialisation as the investment in heavy industry was maximised by the Chinese government through the means of the command economy. According to Rostow (1960) a nation's investment rate must be above 11 percent of its GDP for the country to migrate from a low-income to a middle-income economy. Indeed, the spur in investment due to the reorientation of the economy was always higher than this threshold in the Maoist era. Although the Chinese era of Maoism resulted in a significant increase in economic growth, policy uncertainty was enormous (Naughton 2007: 55-56). Success could foremost be realised in the military sphere as China was able to test an atomic bomb in the 1960s and launch a satellite in the 1970s (Lin 2012: 98), which was the result of the significant investment in the military sector.

In general, the catch-up process of developing countries is driven by a tilt towards investment. On average low-income countries invest about 20 percent of GDP. However, China nearly continuously exceeded that number due to its focus on heavy-industry development. In fact, the Maoist government was very successful in increasing the rate of investment. In the years before the revolution, gross non-residential investment expanded at an average rate of 7 percent, which was subsequently raised to 11 percent in the early 1950s, to 18 percent in the rest of the Maoist era and to 22 percent in the transition period towards a market-orientated economy (Maddison 2007a: 66). By doing this, China was transformed from an agricultural economy to an industrial nation. Gross capital formation, which consists of new, replacement and inventory investment, only decreased in the aftermath of the GLF. During the Maoist period, the Chinese economy was reoriented towards the extractive industry as well as materials factories. In fact, the Chinese government made all investment decisions as it was the primary accumulator of savings (Naughton 2007: 57-59) and this state should endure for the decades to follow.

To facilitate the industrial transition, the Chinese institutions had to be changed. Most notably, a distorted price system was introduced. Decades of financial repression had their origins in the initial phase of the Maoist era as the rebalancing of the economy towards capital-intensive industries became the pressing topic at that time. Not only interest rates were distorted, but also the exchange rate, which ultimately resulted in shortages in the economy (Lin 2012: 76-77). However, this served the strategic goals of China to become self-reliant to a very large extent and stands in stark contrast to Hong Kong and Taiwan, which went for an open, capitalist approach towards rebalancing their economies. In contrast to China, Hong Kong and Taiwan focused on the development of light industry and relied on market prices for the principal allocation of resources. Savings for investments were not only accumulated by the government, but significant contribution was made by the private sector. Although the factor endowments of Hong Kong and Taiwan are substantially different to China, openness was clearly of benefit for both economies as inputs could get procured at lower world market prices for their light industries and ultimately, exports provided for the necessary hard currency reserves to pay for foreign knowledge transfers (Naughton 2007: 57-59). Those benefits were made available to China, only after its transition to a more market-orientated economy began at the end of the 1970s.

ii) China's Development Strategy

The Big Push development strategy initially resulted in significant economic growth in China. The cornerstones of said industrialisation were taken over from the Soviet Union and topics such as ownership, production targets and state-led allocation of resources, a controlled price as well as a nomenklatura system formed the main properties of the Chinese command economy. The development of industries was fostered through the repression of prices of agricultural products. Procurement quotas were introduced and the government presided over a monopoly over vital agricultural goods (Lin 2012: 80-83). The depressed input prices resulted in a highly profitable industrial sector, which was government-owned and thus, savings were primarily accumulated by the state with the goal of further advancing the industrialisation strategy by any means. Output and supply plans were the basis for the command economy, although the Chinese economy was difficult to manage for the planners due to its sheer size. The financial sector only served the government's development strategy and thus, had a purely passive role and did not at all influence the allocation of resources. Nevertheless, the Chinese command economy was less centralised and relied to a lesser degree on planning than the Soviet Union (Naughton 2007: 60-62). However, ideology and the suppression of the civil society were significant during the Chinese Maoist era. Lieberthal (1995: 120) puts this as follows, 'considering his fondness for division and struggle, it is little wonder that Mao left a country exhausted by social conflict'.

In general, with respect to industrial policy during the Maoist era, the following can be said: Imports of machinery as well as of commodities were needed to increase investment in the industrial sector. To achieve this, other sectors such as agriculture were repressed to maximise the allocation of resources to strategic sectors. This also served military purposes. As a matter of fact, the Maoist government succeeded in this regard and China became one of the most industrialised countries globally. The industrialisation during the Maoist period can generally be split in two sub-periods, namely a more cautious approach between 1949 and 1957, which tolerated the coexistence with some capitalist traits, and the period as of 1958, which virtually extinguished private property with the Great Leap Forward (Maddison 2007a: 80-81). Moreover, the industrialisation of China became seriously endangered with the end of the Soviet support in 1960 which meant that many industrial projects remained unfinished (Fairbank and Goldman 2006: 379). Other difficult periods for China's industry included the Cultural Revolution as well as the so-called Third Front programme of the 1960s. The latter served military purposes as industrial infrastructure was constructed in remote inward regions without any connection to the rest of the economy, which substantially raised the costs of these projects. The failure of this programme became evident as it was foregone in favour of the development of coastal areas in the 1970s (Maddison 2007a: 83), which formed the basis for China's successful development after Mao's death.

The Chinese development strategy was primarily driven by Mao himself and the reliance on one person resulted in significant policy instability and thus, uncertainty. Mao's firm belief in communism and his personal fight against his opponents resulted in various political and economic twists and turns throughout said era. From an economic perspective, the initial decades of the PRC can be classified according to the government's investment cycles. Institutional changes and political shifts coincided with investment phases and can be classified as attempts to fundamentally change the nature of the Chinese economy and provide for leaps forward to an industrialised nation. Each of the investment phases was followed by consolidation and moderation before the next cycle started all over again. The division in investment cycles is one way to classify the different growth phases of China (Naughton 2007: 63-64), given the country's approach towards development.

iii) Cycles during the Maoist Period

In the early 1950s, China essentially benefited from significant support from the Soviet Union. The beginning of North Korea's aggression against South Korea in 1950 and the subsequent, involvement of China further pushed the country away from the West (Lieberthal 1995: 330-331). A boycott of Chinese goods drove China even closer to the Soviet Union. During the initial years of the Republic, economic prudence helped to contain the damage of the Chinese civil war by bringing inflation under control and the Korean armistice agreement in 1953 temporarily deescalated the situation at China's borders. During the initial phase of Maoism, a land reform changed the ownership structure, although private ownership was not yet curtailed significantly. In addition, the CCP was willing to work with skilled workers from the Nationalist period and thus, did not have to start from scratch. Consequently, the Chinese industry could be revived relatively quickly in the years after the civil war by taking advantage of the whole pool of the Chinese labour force and by continuing to repress the most radical communist ideas. The initial phase of the Big Push strategy also focused on investment in the North-eastern area of China where the Japanese occupation had built industrial operations to advance its own rise.

Significant Soviet assistance facilitated the transition (Naughton 2007: 64-65) and ultimately led to a fully planned economy.

Between 1953 and 1956, a further adoption of the Soviet style institutional system was established. The first five-year plan starting from 1953 was the distinguishing mark of this period (Lin 2012: 81). The degree of the speed of the changes and decentralisation were pressing issues. Heavy investment of the Soviet Union in China resulted in technological transfers as well as in significant industrial projects and thus, spurred economic growth. Cultural exchange via student exchanges also brought the two countries closer together. However, during the later phase of this period, more radical communist ideas got implemented; for instance, ownership rights got curtailed by introducing primarily public ownership, which was advanced by Mao's personal intervention and led to the establishment of cooperatives or collectives in the countryside, effectively abolishing the household system. Private ownership became virtually non-existent by 1956 which can be classified as the first fully communist year of China (Naughton 2007: 65-67). The issuance of internal passports virtually restricted any free mobility in China (Acemoglu and Robinson 2013: 420) and helped to institutionalise the system built by Mao.

A short period of moderation took place in 1956-57. After Stalin's death, Nikita Khrushchev denounced the policies of his predecessor in 1956 and announced that all socialist countries were free to choose a different path than the Soviet Union. The proclamation of the right to self-determination for socialist countries by the Soviet Union led to the emancipation of China in the subsequent years. Initially, this triggered a period of moderation as the significant changes of the early communist years were re-examined and partially deemed reckless. Consequently, a more open approach with respect to the Chinese economy was proclaimed by party leaders in 1957. The movement was termed "Hundred Flowers" as its ideas served as an alternative to the rigid command economy. Again, only Mao's personal intervention changed the course of history (Naughton 2007: 67-69). The latter resulted in the GLF from 1958 to 1960. The liberal Hundred Flowers Movement was targeted by Mao's initiatives as he planned a leap forward in his communist utopia distinct from the Soviet economic model. A further increase in the reallocation of resources from the agricultural towards the industrial sector should advance the Chinese economy at all costs.

iv) The Great Leap Forward

Between 1956 and 1957, all peasants had to join the Maoist institutions and the pooling of land extinguished private ownership. In fact, Mao advocated the extinction of any form of material incentives in the Chinese economy and blamed individualism as the cause for the Rightists opposition and failures of the past (Wu 2005: 44-45). 'Together with people's communes in the countryside, the decentralised planned economic system, created by delegating power to every lower level of local governments within the overall framework of a planned economy and resource allocation by administrative orders, laid the institutional foundation for the Great Leap Forward' (Wu 2005: 49). By 1958, rural institutions were further altered by the creation of communes which laid the basis for the GLF. The communes were many times bigger than the Soviet collectives both in terms of labour force as well as the size of land (Maddison 2007a: 72). One example of the frenzy of the time was that in 1958, Mao proclaimed that China had to catch up with the steel production of Britain within a very short period of time. To meet the unrealistic targets proclaimed by the Chinese leadership, workers had to use scrap metal from pots, pans and even ploughs. Consequently, the agricultural population traded their future for surviving the imminent present (Acemoglu and Robinson 2013: 420-421).

In fact, the administrative changes together with unrealistic targets by the planners led to widespread chaos instead of the hoped-for growth spurt. The breath-taking success of grain and steel output of this time were mostly exaggerated through inflated inputs due to skewed incentives. In 1958, the negative repercussions of the reforms were already visible. However, instead of reversing some of the disastrous innovations of the Great Leap Forward in 1959, it was decided to rather wait slightly longer and draw lessons from the experience. Again, Mao blamed the Rightist Movement for these failures and even intensified the institutional changes of that time (Wu 2005: 51). It was not until 1960 that the policy of 'readjustment, consolidation, reinforcement, and upgrading' was implemented under the command of Chen Yun (Wu 2005: 52) and by 1962 many of the institutional changes previously introduced had to be reversed (Maddison 2007a: 73-74). Nevertheless, it should take years for China to recover from above described period.

From 1961 to 1963, China had to adjust its policies. Investment in agriculture was increased significantly and workers were dispatched to the country side. Households were given more decision authority and incentives were reintroduced in the agricultural production system. A partial recentralisation of economic decision authority facilitated the shift in policy-making. In addition, Maoist China entered global markets and started to import grains for the first time. As the rift with the Soviet Union seemed to be permanent, aid could no longer be expected from its communist neighbour (Naughton 2007: 72-73). Thus, China refocused part of its investment towards the fertiliser and chemical industry to achieve higher agricultural yields. One key lesson taken from the downturn was that the size of the communes was too immense. Although China initially recorded an increase in productivity due to economies of scale as it formed collectives, the size of the communes dis-incentivised single households, in particular as the right to withdraw from the collectives was eliminated (Lin 2012: 89-91). The communes' sheer size had incentivised freeloaders to take advantage of more diligent workers. Similar events happened in the Soviet Union during the time of collectivisation. As long as farmers had a right to disengage from collectives, individuals were still incentivised to uphold a high quality of work and productivity remained fairly stable. In 1929, for instance, productivity also plummeted in the agricultural sector of the Soviet Union as rights of withdrawals from the collectives were abolished (Lin 2012: 95). It goes without saying that this period belonged to the darkest hours of the PRC. Nevertheless, the experience of the Great Leap Forward and further policy failures ultimately made more market-orientated reforms possible (Wu 2005: 53), foremost after Mao's death in 1976.

v) Further Policy Uncertainty

In China, the period between 1964 and 1966 already marked another period of retrenchment, which again can be attributed to spill over effects of foreign policy into the domestic sphere as the United States increased its interventionist involvement in Vietnam. This resulted in the construction of the so-called Third Front leading to an increase in investment directed inwards to facilitate China's strategic independence (Fairbank and Goldman 2006: 398). The construction of heavy industry was focused on the inner areas of China with every sub-region forming an independent supply structure. The inefficiencies of these policies were enormous as their sole purpose was to guarantee China's independence in case of war. Later, this wave of decentralisation was stopped (Wu 2005: 53-54) and generally, the increased investment came to a halt with the Cultural Revolution (Naughton 2007: 73-74), which foremost took place between 1966 and 1969, though some extend this period until Mao's death in 1976 (Fairbank and Goldman 2006: 383). Mao encouraged Chinese students, subsequently labelled Red Guards, to attack the Communist Party's entrenched cronies except from himself. On the one hand, this served to revive the revolutionary spirit and cleanse the bureaucratic structure while on the other hand, Mao tried to get rid of his opponents with the Cultural Revolution and weaken the opposition to his rule in general. Thus, the Cultural Revolution was inward looking (Naughton 2007: 73-75). With respect to foreign policy, the situation in Southeast Asia relaxed with the United States facing a disaster in Vietnam. However, the relationship with China's former ally, the Soviet Union, further deteriorated and it even came to military clashes (Fairbank and Goldman 2006: 397).

From 1971 to 1972, Mao proclaimed another leap forward. The People's Liberation Army (PLA) was used to resolve issues from the Cultural Revolution and thus, the military complex was gaining importance and building-up significant ties to the Chinese economy. In addition, China continued to pursue its strategic goal of autarky and self-reliance was regarded as a source of strength (Naughton 2007: 75-76). Nevertheless, every leap forward was followed by economic problems. Thus, the period from 1972 to 1976 started in the same way as the experience of previous cycles would have suggested. By the end of 1971, China faced food shortages as the push towards industrialisation resulted in insufficient agricultural investment and the absence of significant incentives also played a role in this trajectory. These economic constraints had spill over effects into the political sphere of China. In 1971, Lin Biao, one of the key military leaders of the Cultural Revolution, was replaced (Fairbank and Goldman 2006: 400-401) and a rapprochement between the United States and China took place in 1972 with the visit of President Nixon to China. With subsiding pressures on this front, Premier Zhou Enlai was able to lead China towards a more moderate economic path. Coastal regions instead of the Third Front saw an increase in investment as China approached the capitalist sphere. In 1974, Deng Xiaoping entered the stage again, however, only to be replaced in 1976. The aging Mao named the so-called Gang of Four to continue implementing his vision and resist any trends towards a more capitalist system. However, after the death of Mao, the Gang of Four was imprisoned and Hua Guofeng emerged as new leader (Naughton 2007: 76-78) - albeit only for a short period of time.

Deng Xiaoping, who was a successful general in the revolution, witnessed the effects of the policies of the GLF. This triggered the famous proclamation by the future leader of China that 'It does not matter whether the cat is white or black, as long as it catches mice' (Fairbank and Goldman 2006: 407), which advocated in favour of a more practical policy-making with the goal of increasing production to provide food to the Chinese population. Ultimately, the future Chinese leader was jailed by Mao in 1967 for the divergence in views over the evolvement of the Chinese system. Deng Xiaoping was only rehabilitated in 1974 by Zhou Enlai and as of 1975, initial progress was made in terms of education and the introduction of material incentives into the economy. After the death of Zhou Enlai, Deng did not rise to power, but rather Hua Guofeng was promoted by Mao. It was only the death of Mao in 1976 that tipped the balance in favour of the reformists in China (Acemoglu and Robinson 2013: 421-423). In fact, Deng Xiaoping was reinstated by Hua Guofeng in 1977 and was then able to follow his own agenda as of 1978 at the same time as criticising some of the Maoist policies and everybody who supported these (Fairbank and Goldman 2006: 407). At the end of 1978, the Third Plenum of the Eleventh Central Party Committee altered China's strategy fundamentally. Class struggle would no longer be the primary focus of the Party, but rather economic modernisation became the primary development strategy for China. The gradual reintroduction of incentives and the build-up of more inclusive institutions led to an unprecedented growth spurt in China over the subsequent decades (Acemoglu and Robinson 2013: 424-427), which stands in contrast to the volatility of the Maoist period.

To sum up, the failures and successes of the Maoist era from 1949 to the 1970s were driven by China's Big Push industrialisation strategy, which initially propelled economic growth, but regularly reached its limits. The years of significant policy uncertainty left many Chinese dissatisfied and thus, allowed the new leadership under Deng Xiaoping to introduce gradual, but significant market reforms. The legacies of China's Maoist era still play a substantial role for decision making in China. At the beginning, the new leadership could benefit from the ideas of the Hundred Flowers Movement. In addition, some of the failures of the Maoist period served as reminders for future decision-making (Naughton 2007: 78-82). The reorientation of China's industry towards its factor endowment away from heavy-industry ultimately led to the successes of the decades to come and propelled China to the most important emerging market of recent times.

d) The Transition Period between 1978 and 2008

While 1949 marked the establishment of the PRC, 1978 can be regarded as the year of the beginning of the People's Republic most significant change. Economic reforms, in particular the adoption of capitalist traits, marked the last quarter of the twentieth century. Changes came in waves and by the mid-1990s, the country had left its Maoist past and made significant steps towards a market-based economy. China's path since 1978 will be examined in detail below as well as in the case study.

The Maoist system was effectively re-evaluated in the 1980s. 'The planned economy is to organise the whole society into a huge single factory and to allocate resources by the administrative means of the central planning organ' (Wu 2005: 17). The cornerstones of the planned economy are that the main organs have complete information as well as information costs are rather limited. However, feedback loops are severely curtailed in a planned economy (Wu 2005: 17-18). The strongest points made by critics of communism are that transactions costs to obtain the necessary information in a planned economy are enormous. Moreover, interests are generally not aligned. The trade-off between following your own interests versus common interests severely distorts the planned economic system. Communism attempts to overcome the trade-off between individual and common interests with increased supervision. However, this again leads to substantial information costs. The lack of efficiency that the system itself is exposed to due to planning, supervising and implementing the planners' guidelines is enormous. Thus, resource allocation is highly inefficient in a command economy. This stands in stark contrast to market-orientated economies in which prices carry information about the relative scarcity of goods as well as services and market competition leads to a more or less efficient allocation of resources (Wu 2005: 19). To sum up, the advantage of the command economic system is that resources can be shifted according to guidelines by the administration with the severe drawbacks of high information costs as well as low efficiency of the system due to a lack of incentives (Wu 2005: 20), which eventually curtails the planned economy.

The success of the rural reforms early on in its transition process gave China confidence to continue on its path towards a more market-driven economy. In general, two phases of reforms can be distinguished in China's path towards the market. The first period lasted from 1978 to approximately 1993, during which China implemented a gradual, decentralised transition most notably marked by dual-track reforms. With this approach, China tried to make the transition process as smooth as possible without any significant economic distortions and without a single group of the population having to do the heavy lifting with respect to the dismantling of the planned economy. Ownership structures were transformed, competition was introduced in specific sectors and free market prices were partially introduced to serve as signalling devices. These reforms took place within the existing institutional set-up. In the second phase of China's transition, which started around 1993, the institutional framework was also changed significantly to support the market-orientated reforms. Especially, the state-sector was further reformed and additional reforms are still needed in this area. Moreover, governance issues persist and a functioning regulatory framework supporting the market-based economy is still in its making but its origins date back to the reforms initiated since 1993 (Naughton 2007: 85-86). A more detailed view on the country's current institutions will be given in the case study.

Since the transition towards a market-based economy started at the end of 1978, Chinese policy-makers never lost sight of the ultimate goal of their reforms, namely development which was assessed by the country's economic growth performance (Naughton 1996: 61). If the reforms had led to a collapse in output, the policies would have been considered a failure and a conservative body of thought would have become more important instead. In this respect, China took a courageous approach towards its transition which was very different from the path chosen by Central and Eastern Europe as well as by Yeltsin's Russia (Roland 2000: 3-4). These countries rather preferred a rapid implementation of the changes towards the market and wanted to leave their communist past behind as quickly as possible. As a result, trust was eroded in the communist institutions and thus, the edifice had to be re-built from scratch. In contrast to China, Central and Eastern transition economies as well as Russia experienced significant losses in output as the destructive forces of the market had been underestimated in the speedy liberalisation of their economies. The short-term costs of the transition policies, chosen by said regions, were significant and therefore, the so-called Big Bang approach had clear disadvantages (Naughton 2007: 86-87), foremost with respect to growth and social order.

China, however, chose a different path towards its transition. Having learnt from its history, China never lost sight of the stability of the nation and thus, changes were implemented more gradually (Roland 2000: XX). Indeed, the Maoist era had left many sectors of the economy inefficient but turning the whole system inside out at once was certainly not the aim of the Chinese leadership. Instead, an experimental approach was chosen (Naughton 1996: 158) which marked China's transition period as certain parts of the economy were opened first while keeping a tight grip on other sectors. This gave the nation the possibility to evaluate the effects of its policies on certain areas before broadening its reform efforts. For instance, in rural regions township and village enterprises were the first signs of a more capitalist society (Lin 2012: 168). These enterprises led to increased local investment and thus, improved growth; the success of these initial reforms further encouraged the Chinese leadership to continue on its chosen path. Furthermore, special economic zones served as prime examples of China's experimental approach towards opening and transforming its economy (Naughton 1996: 158). These zones allowed for the development of new industries, transfer of knowledge from the outside and a gradual liberalisation of the country without endangering the overall stability of the nation. New entrants were attracted to certain sectors step-by-step and over time the balance between plan and market shifted towards the latter. From about 1993, the institutional reforms have been more pronounced in China as the initial steps towards a market-driven economy had clearly been successful. Topics such as rules governing the level playing field or the introduction of a unified tax code have become more important during the second phase of the transition. The dual-track system, which marked the first period of transition, was replaced by a unification of prices at the market level (Naughton 2007: 86-88). In contrast to Central and Eastern Europe the transition process was remarkably smooth in China.

i) The Transition Period between 1978 and 1993

After Mao's death, Hua Guofeng became the new Chinese leader. He promised to uphold Mao's legacy at all costs, which became known as 'the two whatevers' in the literature (Lieberthal 1995: 124). Hua with the help of the military managed to contain the Gang of Four and arrested them within a month after Mao's death. In 1977, Deng Xiaoping was rehabilitated by Hua after he wrote him two letters promising him his support as well as admitting some of his wrongdoings. However, on returning to power, Deng immediately started to undermine the authority of Hua and moved his own protégées into power positions. One of them, Zhao Ziyang, was going to replace Hua and another, Hu Yaobang, was promoted to the party general secretary (Dreyer 2004: 114). In contrast to Hua upholding the legacy of Mao, Deng announced to 'seek truth from facts' which on the one hand should further weaken Hua and on the other side make a new start without Mao possible for China (Dreyer 2004: 107-110; Fairbank and Goldman 2006: 407). Many of the modernising changes Deng took up in the late 1970s had been previously introduced by Deng's mentor, Zhou Enlai, some of them publicly in 1975. Those reforms were taken up again by Deng and reintroduced in the Third Plenum of the Eleventh Central Committee of the Chinese Communist Party in late 1978. The original proposal envisioned to adopt the industry first, similar to other communist countries, and change in the structure of the agricultural sector was only envisaged as a second step. By 1979, some of the failures of reforming the state-led industry became visible and the order of priority changed to reforming the agricultural sector first by introducing material incentives (Dreyer 2004: 151-152). In 1979, the Chinese leadership did not stop farmers' strong preference to return to a household-based system and the Chinese reform success story could further evolve. Deng's pragmatic approach became known as 'feeling for the stones as one crosses the river' (Fairbank and Goldman 2006: 408). This shift in China's strategy in the end of the 1970s was described by Chen Yun, one of the major architects of the reform period in China, with a 'bird in a cage' analogy (Howell 2012: 272). The bird serves as a symbol for the Chinese economy and the cage for the Communist Party's control over economic activities. With the start of the reform period, China enlarged the bird's cage, which improved its health (Acemoglu and Robinson 2013: 438). However, this first and foremost relates to the economic sphere of the country.

At the end of 1978, the Third Plenum of the Eleventh Central Committee of the CCP initiated the first steps in the direction of a more market-orientated economy. Economic incentives were reintroduced and markets were partially liberated. In addition, it was made clear that the so-called "iron rice bowl" would be smashed, which meant no guaranteed job for a lifetime without adequate performance (Dreyer 2004: 111). Moreover, China needed to acquire new technologies and learn from the international community and thus, Deng introduced an opening of the country to foster trade as well as the import of foreign technologies. In addition, a birth control policy was introduced which later became known as one-child policy (Fairbank and Goldman 2006: 409). Those reforms that started in 1979 were labelled as China's turn towards capitalism by Western observers; however, this was strictly rejected by the Chinese leadership. China aimed for 'socialism with Chinese characteristics' as Deng Xiaoping put it (Dreyer 2004: 112). In addition, Mao's legacy was examined in detail in the years after his death. In an official verdict, 70 percent was regarded as positive and 30 percent as negative, which in fact allowed China to uphold Mao's legacy (Dreyer 2004: 114) and allowed the CCP to keep its face.

With respect to corporations, reforms started in 1976 with the attempt to introduce a system of enterprise autonomy similar to the one Yugoslavia had implemented. In a meeting in 1978, economic planning materials on the Yugoslavian economic system were even handed out. The first province that implemented this reform of enterprise autonomy was Sichuan Province (Naughton 1996: 99). Enterprise management was encouraged to increase output profitability. However, as Russia's reform under Kosygin in 1965, the system failed due to a lack of market prices to guide resource allocation and the complete absence of competitive market pressure (Wu 2005: 60). After the initial failures of the state-owned enterprise reform, Deng Xiaoping shifted the reform efforts to the agricultural sector. This was in stark contrast to the Soviet Union and Central and Eastern Europe, which mainly focused their reform efforts on the state-led industry. As such, China's approach towards transition significantly differed from those of other communist countries (Wu 2005: 63-64) and in fact, still determines the country's trajectory today.

At the Third Plenum, the realisation of the limits of the planned economy with respect to the agricultural production led to significant changes in rural areas (Lin 2012: 176). The Chinese leadership decided to hold the procurement targets stable or reduce them slightly while at the same time raising prices for agricultural products produced above the target levels. Said policies initially came at a cost and thus, the Chinese planners had to first cut back on other expensive projects and were even forced to import grains in the initial years of the reforms. However, the belief that these reforms would ultimately lead to increased output in the agricultural sector, which had been holding back the country for the previous decades due to the failed policies of the Maoist era, supported the leadership's ambition to transform the economy (Naughton 2007: 88-90). In addition, collectives were given increased decision-making authority and allowed to experiment with different systems. Ultimately, the collectives gravitated towards a system of contracting land to individual households, which partially re-established the household system of the pre-communist era (Lin 2012: 160). The key term of the initial period of transformation in the agricultural sector is certainly incentives. Farmers had to be incentivised to increase production outside the plan and the measures outlined above indeed led to an increase in production by 1983. With the greater decision-making authority of individual households and higher prices for goods produced above the procurement targets, grain production levels by farmers could be raised significantly by even reducing the days of input. The time freed up as a result was dedicated in the establishment of the aforementioned township and village enterprises, which can be described as factories established in the countryside; the TVEs quickly generated profit from the increased set of opportunities and virtually marked the beginning of market competition for some state-owned enterprises (Naughton 2007: 88-90) from the which the system profited as a whole.

Given the dual-track approach towards transformation, the disruptions to the economy and to social order were minimal. The reintroduction of the household system did not abolish the plan, but it introduced additional space for the market, which incentivised farmers to increase output. The initial success of the reforms on the countryside further encouraged reforms in other areas and indeed, by the mid-1990s, China had virtually reduced the importance of the plan in favour of the market to a minimum. The reform process of the 1980s was mostly driven by Zhao Ziyang, who served as China's premier from 1980 to 1987 and was a strong supporter of gradualism which led to the prevention of a Soviet style economic disaster due to the gradual dismantling of the Maoist institutions. This initial phase of the transformation is often labelled as reforms without losers (Naughton 2007: 90-91). In this respect, most notable is the dual-track system which allowed the plan and the market to coexist with a gradual tilt towards the market system. The continuation of the planning system upheld the stability of the system and gave confidence to reform in sub-sections of the economy. Lin (1992) as well as Wen (1993), both attribute the rise in productivity in the reform period since 1978 to the changes implemented in the agricultural sector.

Thus, what ultimately made a difference was China's dual-track system in the initial decades of the reform period. Production above the plan could be sold at market prices, which effectively opened a new institutional set-up for the non-state sector (Lieberthal 1995: 248). Goods and services as well as commodities were no longer only influenced by the plan, but also by market signals which were further fostered through the opening of China to the world. Consequently, the successes of China's reform period can be attributed to a large extent to the dual-track system (Wu 2005: 70). The researchers Lawrence Law, Qian Yingyi, and Gerard Roland (1997) advocated for liberalisation using a dual-track system in their paper 'Pareto-Improving Economic Reform through Dual-Track Liberalization'. In contrast to China, which focused its reforms on the rural areas and the development of non-state actors, Russia and Eastern Europe were determined to reform their state sector at a relatively fast pace. However, it proved difficult for the state sector to be reformed fundamentally while at the same time upholding all its vital functions. Hence, China's reform efforts had various advantages, foremost the establishment of a non-state sector, which contributed positively to the whole economy, and the introduction of competitive forces due to a partial opening, ultimately leading to an alignment of interests (Wu 2005: 71-72; Roland 2000: 7).

Only after the success of these reforms was confirmed, China engaged in a broadening of the country's reform efforts. The dual-track system was one of the most notable innovations of the first period of change as it virtually introduced the market to the economy by establishing a two-tier pricing. Thus, the system is not linked to a change in ownership structure, but to an accommodation of the provision of incentives through market prices. Above-plan products were traded at market prices and thus, both plan and market coexisted in the dual-track system. Moreover, China committed itself to keep the resource allocation via the plan fixed in absolute terms in 1984, which led to the gradual tilt of the economy towards the market over time. In fact, the economy was allowed to grow out of the plan by fixing the materials-allocation via the plan. Given the latter, Chinese enterprises faced market prices on the margin as described by Byrd (1991) and therefore, any increase in production would further push back the plan in favour of the market. In fact, the plan can be regarded as a form of tax to the enterprise or even a subsidy for some state-owned enterprises. However, any further production decision was based on a free price system and thus, led to a better allocation of resources and encouraged the capitalist-traits of the economy such as profit maximisation. In the initial stages of the transition, Chinese planners had to sign individual contracts with each company that specified their targets and as mentioned, this plan could be regarded as a kind of tax system as no official unified tax code existed yet in China (Naughton 2007: 91-94). Moreover, the monopoly of the Chinese state was relaxed and initial entries in certain industries were permitted, thus creating a certain degree of competition. Start-ups flourished as of 1979 as entry barriers to industries were reduced significantly, in particular with respect to the manufacturing sector. China's size alone offers plenty of opportunities for entrepreneurs. The incentives to sell goods above the plan at market prices greatly encouraged the entry of new competitors in former state-monopoly sectors. As of 1985, even all state-led enterprises were operating at market prices in a new legal framework as above-plan production became the norm. Moreover, transactions between state-led enterprises and market participants were also liberalised, which led to cooperatives seeking to profit from the new set of opportunities. Apart from the price deregulation, the state-sector management structure was also transformed with greater flexibility being granted to the individual management teams and an improvement in incentive structures. This approach was an alternative to the otherwise difficult process of privatisation. The gradual transition from the planned system to the goal of profit maximisation was managed successfully through the aforementioned reforms. Increased competition, a better incentive structure and better monitoring, all led to significant performance improvements in state-led enterprises. As privatisation was forgone in favour of improving performance, China's stability was also preserved as some of the social distortions that privatisations would have entailed were avoided (Naughton 2007: 94-95), which is another distinguishing mark of China's transition.

Furthermore, from the end of the 1970s, the establishment of SEZs in China served its experimental approach towards transformation while not endangering stability (Naughton 1996: 158). These zones were initially separated from the planned economy and thus, a more open approach could be pursued in these areas. In most cases these zones became export-oriented areas of economic growth, which at a later stage could lead to positive spill over effects to the rest of the Chinese economy in cases where the zone was successful. Certain areas of the Chinese economy could be easily separated from the rest of the command economy and thus, reforms could be effectively tested in these regions (Naughton 2007: 95-96). The first SEZs were established in 1980, namely Shenzhen (nearby Hong Kong), Zhuhai (close to Macao), Shantou in Kwangtung and Xiamen (close to Taiwan). In addition, China allowed greater foreign involvement in 14 coastal cities as of 1984. Foremost, the Yangtze area as well as Shanghai were included in the coastal development and Hainan was established as the fifth SEZ as of 1988. This refocus of the Chinese economy led to the increase of export volume by a factor of twenty-eight between 1978 and 2003 (Maddison 2007a: 85-86; Wu 2005: 66). In fact, the coastal areas significantly contributed to export growth with the introduction of imported new technology as well as capital. China's foreign trade increased continuously at an unprecedented pace ever since the establishment of these economic zones (Wu 2005: 66). On the other hand, the opening of China to the outside world would ultimately also positively influence domestic reforms. The competitive forces introduced to China via the establishment of these zones led to the rise of Chinese enterprises to international standards and also brought the domestic price structure of goods and services closer to global market prices. In 1984, Deng Xiaoping predicted this development in his speech 'Make a Success of Special Economic Zones and Open More Cities to the Outside World' (Wu 2005: 67-68) and indeed, these areas were primary drivers of China's market orientation.

To summarise, the first phase of China's transition towards a market-oriented economy can be characterised as highly successful. Market prices at the margin and increased competition both contributed positively to China's economy. The reintroduction of incentives was highly beneficial and led to an increase in output while at the same time decreasing inputs (Lin 2012: 178-179). The gradual deregulation of the economy meant that any major downturns could be avoided, which stood in stark contrast to the collapse experienced by Russia. The changes in the managerial incentive structure combined with increased monitoring improved the state-led enterprises' profitability significantly. The careful approach towards transformation pursued by the Chinese leadership in the first phase of the reorientation towards the market worked very well. The outcome of the reform efforts was certainly not clear ex ante, but China's experimental approach focused on particular parts of the country managed to contain failures to a large extent. Whether a reform was a success or failure was most often judged against the ultimate goal of China, namely economic development (Naughton 2007: 97-98) and in this respect, history proved China right.

ii) The Student Protests of 1989

In 1989, political troubles were triggered through a combination of events. Factors such as rising inflation, the corruption still prevailing in large parts of the economy, certain privileges for specific groups and, most of all, rising expectations that the future should be better than today, led to a tense climate and motivated students in particular to stage protests against these practices (Naughton 2007: 98-99). In

1986, student protests became more pronounced and their demands were backed by parts of the Chinese leadership such as Hu Yaobang who had his background in the Youth League. However, the support of the protests led to the dismissal of Hu, whose position was taken over by Zhao Ziyang. While the protests calmed temporarily, the economic troubles continued to rattle China's economy. A failed price reform in the late 1980s led to bank runs as well as panic buying by the population (Dreyer 2004: 121-123). In 1989, Hu Yaobang, who was a strong supporter of the student protests, died. In addition, the continuation of the economic and political uncertainty sparked new countrywide protests (Lieberthal 1995: 140). The ones to become best known were the student protests in Beijing. Those protests brought forward similar demands as in other communist countries, such as Poland's Solidarity movement. In China, the demonstrators asked for economic restraint by bringing inflation under control and reining in rampant corruption in addition to demands regarding individual freedoms and democracy. The protests also received international media coverage, for example from Voice of America. Nearer to China, the citizens of Hong Kong closely watched the events as the colony was due to be returned to China from Britain in 1997. Zhao Ziyang tried to mediate between the different groups, but eventually was sidelined. On June 4 1989, Tiananmen Square was cleared by the military. Footage of tanks rolling in the direction of unarmed students was circulated around the world and the incident meant a decisive step backward for the PRC's reform efforts. Eventually, Zhao Ziyang, who had tried to avoid the standoff, was replaced by Jiang Zemin (Dreyer 2004: 124-126). However, the reform process survived this interlude in China's history. The incident still overshadows part of the successes achieved in the first phase of reforms. It also highlights the problems a government faces when discontent and grievance surface and endanger stability (Naughton 2007: 98-99). The years following 1989 continued to be troublesome for China and it was only in 1992 when the reform course was confirmed by Deng Xiaoping's journey to some SEZs in south China (Dreyer 2004: 127). The Chinese leader had fostered the growth of these economic zones for a decade and the tour was a reaffirmation of the continuation of China's path towards a more market-oriented economy. Deng's pure focus on development bore fruits. At the 14th Communist Party Congress in October 1992, it was proclaimed that China's socialist economic structure was now supported by the market in all sectors (Naughton 2007: 99-100). The economic transformation stood in stark contrast to the political events of the time.

iii) The Transition Period between 1993 and the 2000s

In the second phase of China's transition to a market-based economy, the key economic policymaker was Zhu Rongji. In contrast to Zhao Ziyang, who focused on consensus-based decision making, Zhu personalised many decisions. The latter emerged as the key policymaker in mid-1993 and became premier in 1998, a position he held until he stepped down in 2003. Key attributes of the second phase of reforms were the unification of prices from the dual-track system to a pure market pricing, macroeconomic prudence and a certain degree of recentralisation. In the second phase, the institutional framework was strengthened to accommodate the market in contrast to the plan. Key regulatory and administrative changes were made in the financial sector with respect to the tax system as well as governance. The accession of China to the World Trade Organisation in 2001 was a major event in the international institutional sphere (Maddison 2007a: 85-86). In addition, the state-led enterprises were downsized, which resulted in a reform period with losers, in contrast to the first phase of the transition without significant losers (Naughton 2007: 100). Further features of the second phase of reforms included the complete abolishment of the material-balance planning system. However, in contrast to the decentralisation of decision making, which was driven by the policymakers' desire to introduce market-orientated changes, foremost incentives, into the Chinese economy, the second phase of the transformation saw a certain degree of recentralisation to consolidate fiscal revenues and build a tax base on which China could operate. The dismantling of the command economy inevitably led to a shift of savings from the government to the private sector. To rebuild part of the clout of the government, a tax base had to be formed. Through the recentralisation, China could escape a fiscal crisis in the early 1990s (Naughton 2007: 101) and continued its rise.

At the Fourteenth Party Congress in 1992 the establishment of a socialist market economy in China was declared (Dreyer 2004: 127). However, in 1993, economic woes resurfaced with inflation increasing and people afraid of losing their savings. Corporate defaults further spooked the economy. The troubles led to the dismissal of the head of the Chinese Central Bank and Zhu Rongji took up responsibilities. With the new Chinese strongman, a period of austerity began. The dismantling of state-led enterprises was also supported by more rigid credit policies and a slower rise in money supply as well as prices. Zhou Rongji received much of the positive credit for turning the situation around 'utilising both administrative and market-based measures such as restrictions on investment, tightening credit, establishing price controls and subsidies releasing grain reserves to ease local food shortages, and subsidising food shipments among provinces' (Dreyer 2004: 160-161). This lasted until the Asian financial crisis of 1997.

During the Asian financial crisis and its aftermath, Chinese official growth rates are widely believed to have been over-reported. Declining energy consumption, rising unemployment and excess capacity in the industrial sectors pointed to a sharper slowdown in China's growth rate than official statistics would indicate (Rawski 2001). In this period, China launched a significant fiscal stimulus package and Zhou Rongji responded to critics of the programme that 'the national economy would have collapsed without it' (Dreyer 2014: 163). Social unrest as well as an increased rate of corporate defaults further hit the economy. Discontent within the labour force was contained by the Chinese leadership at any cost. Media coverage was severely curtailed to avoid a wave of protests against the economic woes of the late 1990s. In addition, the rural population suffered from the crisis due to a decline in the prices of their products. Their incomes only briefly recovered before China entered the WTO in 2001, which by itself posed new challenges for the Chinese agricultural sector (Dreyer 2004: 163), but led China to years of rapid expansion via exports.

Due to China's response to the Asian financial crisis as well as the downturn in general, the amount of nonperforming loans the PRC was faced with was enormous. High levels of corruption and a lack of transparency exacerbated this. In fact, issues such as corruption remained widespread and cost the Chinese people a significant portion of their output growth. Corruption had cost on average 14.5 to 14.9 percent of output annually from 1995 to 2001 (Shaoguang et al. 2002). Due to the above, NPLs rose to about 30 percent in the crisis according to official statistics (Dreyer 2004: 163-165). In 1999, an increasing number of defaults forced the Chinese government to act and asset management companies (AMCs) were established to take the worst performing loans off the balance sheets of the most important banks (Li et al. 2016b: 2-3). However, the AMCs had troubles handling these loans and thus, many were converted into equity stakes with the ultimate effect of the Chinese government keeping afloat various companies (Lague 2002). All in all, however, this programme was a success. In addition, the monetary framework was significantly strengthened in the second phase of the transition, which reflected the general trend towards more sophisticated institutions in China. In the financial sector, the first step was made in 1983 with the establishment of the People's Bank of China (PBoC). However, it was not until an administrative reform in 1998 that the PBoC was set up in line with the US Federal Reserve Board and the mandate of the Chinese central bank was extended to effectively conduct monetary policy (Naughton 2007: 103-104), with the ultimate goal of sustaining a stable path of growth.

With respect to institutions, the introduction of the Company Law in 1993 helped to dismantle the state-led enterprise sector. Consequently, SOEs were reorganised as limited liability companies; even selective listings took place in the newly founded stock markets in the 1990s. Regulatory oversight was improved through various supervisory bodies. In addition, the fiscal reform of 1994 was a significant milestone in the transformation process. A value-added tax as well as other taxes were introduced to the system with the goal of rebuilding fiscal revenues for the state. Evidence of the success of the fiscal reform was visible in the strong performance of tax revenues over the subsequent years (Naughton 2007: 103-104). Another crucial breakthrough was reached at the 15th National Congress of the CCP in 1997. At this convention, the former Soviet system of large state-sector ownership was denounced and the coexistence of different forms of ownership and business models were reinforced. The doctrine of Jiang Zemin said, 'keeping public ownership as the mainstay of the economy and allowing diverse forms of ownership to develop side by side' (Wu 2005: 87). These reforms, although necessary in China's process of transitioning towards a market economy, entailed a group which had to bear the bulk of the burden, namely state-enterprise workers. Thus, the second period is also labelled as reforms with losers as one social group lost out. In fact, the second phase of China's transition more closely resembled that of other transition economies in Central and Eastern Europe as well as in the Former Soviet Union. Nowadays, international policymakers focus their attention on strengthening the institutional framework that governs the newly driven socialist market economies. Stability rests at its core and, indeed, the transition is not yet finished. China's transformation and its development in general could serve many economies as successful example (Naughton 2007: 106-107). A closer look at transition economies' trajectory is taken in the chapter on emerging market crises as well as in the case study.

iv) China's Isolation and Emergence

With respect to China's foreign policy, the communist revolution of the 1950s marked significant changes. Initially, China focused on trade with other communist countries, foremost the Soviet Union. Loans were provided by the Soviet Union to support the Chinese economy, which was agreed upon in the Stalin-Mao agreements in 1950. With these funds, the Chinese government financed the imports of capital equipment and commodities to foster the reorientation of the economy towards heavy industry (Maddison 2007a: 84). The Soviet Union was among one of the few allies China had in the 1950s as the country sent troops in support of North Korea, a step resulting in various trade embargoes, mainly from the United States. However, the relationship between China and Russia deteriorated in the late 1950s (Fairbank and Goldman 2006: 379). This resulted in the termination of Soviet loans as well as in the withdrawal of the technical support from the Soviet Union. The removal of the latter left many industrial projects unfinished and in fact, left China almost completely isolated from the rest of the world. Exports as well as imports dropped further as the ties with other communist countries became even more complicated. In addition, China had to repay aid that it had received from the Soviet Union and thus, it was left in a difficult situation during the 1960s. It was the new Chinese leadership in the mid-1970s which restored China's ties to the world and refocused China on becoming a trade champion. In 1971, China joined the United Nations, which was the first step out of the country's isolation. As of 1972, relations with the United States were normalised and China joined international financial institutions such as the International Monetary Fund and the World Bank in 1980. In addition, the country became a member of the Asian Development Bank in 1986 and in 1982, China entered the sphere of the General Agreement on Tariffs and Trade ultimately resulting in WTO membership in 2001 (Maddison 2007a: 85-86; Naughton 2007: 104). On the external side, the accession of China to the WTO in 2001 marked a significant point in the second period of transition. Foreign trade was reformed extensively as of 1993 and the special economic zones helped to set the necessary steps in the opening of China. More specifically, China implemented a unification of its exchange rate system in 1993 and current account convertibility was envisaged clearing the path to the WTO membership. The regulatory framework had to be strengthened significantly as a result of the WTO membership and China approached international standards with huge steps (Naughton 2007: 104) helping the country over the subsequent years.

With respect to external engagements, the new leadership in China took over a country with no foreign debt in 1978, but also with virtually no foreign direct investment. Even though the country embraced a new approach as of the end of the 1970s, Chinese borrowing remained relatively modest between 1979 and 2005. In total 147 billion US dollars were borrowed in that time span, most of it with a favourable maturity structure. This left the country relatively unexposed to sudden changes in investor confidence, although contagious spill over from other country's debt binges could never be fully excluded. As a matter of fact, 'the Peoples' Republic has never been in arrears on foreign debt'

(Maddison 2007a: 89). However, China defaulted twice on its external debt in 1921 and 1939 (Reinhart and Rogoff 2009: 94). Both defaults were related to the World Wars with the first occurring in the post-war depression (Young 1971) and the second default during World War II (Cheng 2003). In addition, China defaulted on its local currency debt in 1932. The decades before the establishment of the PRC were generally marked by severe currency distortions and capital flight (Reinhart and Rogoff 2009: 113), which stands in stark contrast to the decades after WWII.

In comparison to other regions, China's path towards the market and the accompanied partial liberalisation has been relatively calm. This was partially due to China's cautious macroeconomic policymaking since 1940, which was strongly driven by the country's historic experience. The loans taken out from the Soviet Union during the early period of the Maoist era were repaid in 1965. By 1978, China had virtually no foreign debt. Although local debt has been rising since the end of 1970s, the total amount remains rather modest today (Maddison 2007a: 89), in particular as China managed to build up significant foreign exchange reserves. In the early decades of the PRC, the Chinese Communist Party can be credited with two achievements. First, they brought down inflation rates significantly and second, they rebuilt war-torn China. The former issue was dealt with in various steps: Initially, the Chinese currency was revalued, which helped to contain the black-market in FX transactions. Indeed, the CCP introduced hard punishments for currency speculation and followed through on its threats. Various forms of regional currencies were also forbidden, making the yuan the primary currency of China. Moreover, the Chinese People's Bank introduced unit prices tied to a basket of commodities, which helped to preserve the value of deposits in real terms (Dreyer 2004: 142) and thus, contained inflation.

What helped China's trade boom was its FX policy. China's exchange rate had remained unchanged between 1957 and 1970 as trade was a negligible factor for China. Between 1970 and 1980, the exchange rate appreciated; however, between 1980 and 1995 a five-fold devaluation of the currency against the US dollar took place. From 1995 to 2005, the yuan remained fixed against the US dollar at a rate of 8.33 (Maddison

2007a: 85). The Chinese exchange rate policy helped to spur export growth. The currency was effectively prevented from appreciating during the latter part of the 1990s and the beginning of the 2000s as China continuously sold the yuan against the US dollar and bought US government securities with the proceeds. These assets were meant to preserve China's independence and serve as vital buffer in times of crisis. Since 2005, China decided on a new exchange rate policy letting the yuan gradually appreciate against the US dollar (Kim and Yamakawa 2005). This held true until the financial crisis of 2008.

e) The Financial Crisis of 2008, Prelude and Aftermath

2007 marked the beginning of a global financial crisis, which had its origin in subprime mortgages in the Unites States. The crisis did not remain contained and spill over effects soon affected the globe. Measures to tackle the mortgage crisis had negative effects on their own with indebtedness increasing at a staggering pace at the same time as growth remained sluggish. This drove many countries to the verge of bankruptcy and ultimately, resulted in the European debt crisis in the early 2010s. The contagion of the US subprime mortgage crisis showed the high degree of international connectedness and made a global response to the crisis inevitable. Emerging markets were also severely affected by the global shock waves. China, which due its sheer size, remains among the most important contributors to global growth did not remain unaffected by the global downturn either (Sun and Fu 2012: 3). In this section, China's response to the global financial crisis as well as its prelude and aftermath will be analysed in detail as China's response to the crisis led to a build-up in significant vulnerabilities.

i) The Effect of the Global Crisis on China

China's opening process over the last decades has exposed the country to a greater risk of a global contraction in demand. However, capital controls and a state-led financial sector meant that China's institutions managed to avoid some of the consequences like those experienced in the US in 2008. Unsurprisingly, China's export-driven growth model developed from 1978 onwards increased its vulnerability to global growth shocks and made negative spill over effects from the US originated crisis inevitable (Lardy 2012: 5). Hence, contracting global demand also led to slower growth in China. These effects were most visible in the decline in Chinese exports on a year-over-year basis at the end of 2008 and at the beginning of 2009. The southeast coastal eras of China suffered severely from the sharp decline in exports and factory closures were not uncommon. In addition, the stock market crashed in China, which can be partly attributed to the decline in the real economy and partly to herd behaviour (Beachy 2012: 8-10). Investment was reduced, inventories piled up and new production had to be postponed. Unsurprisingly, this contributed negatively to every aspect of the Chinese economy (Jing 2012; Nolan 2015: 18-20; Sun and Fu 2012: 10).

Apart from declining exports, the crisis became also apparent in depleting foreign exchange reserves in China. Part of these reserves were invested in risky asset prices, which had a negative mark-to-market effect on the buffer. Moreover, FX interventions by Chinese policymakers also contributed negatively to the foreign exchange reserves (Sun and Fu 2012: 10). Furthermore, Foreign Direct Investment (FDI) fell also sharply. The inflows dropped because of the global financial crisis in 2009, which is negative as technological progress mainly depends on this (Nolan 2015: 16). The World Investment Report of the UNCTAD recorded the first significant decline in FDI in thirty years in China. To sum-up, the balance of payment dynamics developed negatively in every aspect. As FDI is one key contributor to growth, for instance via technology transfers, China would be well advised to strengthen the regulatory framework governing these dynamics (Sun and Fu 2012: 10-11). The global financial crisis of 2007 generally changed the Chinese leadership's attitude towards development and brought to the forefront domestic consumption as a growth driver to reduce the dependence on external demand which led to the spillover effects into the Chinese sphere in 2008 and 2009.

ii) China's Response to the Challenges of 2008 and 2009

The Chinese leadership tackled the negative effects of the spillover of the US centric crisis by introducing various macroeconomic and industry measures. Foremost, a fiscal stimulus package was introduced with the aim to propel Chinese output. The policy was made up of 4 trillion yuan for the years 2009 and 2010 (Pang 2016: 2-3). The programme 'immediately ramped up expenditure on affordable housing, rural and other infrastructure (highways, railways, and airports), public health and education, the environment, and technical innovation' (Lardy 2012: 5). The stimulus package was financed in a number of ways, partly through bank lending and partly through bond issuance in the case of local government funding needs. If the export contraction had continued, the Chinese premier, Wen Jiabao, would have increased the stimulus package. In light of the downturn, the Chinese budget deficit was set at about 3 percent in 2009 (Sun and Fu 2012: 11-12). In addition to the fiscal stimulus, China implemented also a looser monetary policy. The country had followed suit the global trend of tighter monetary policy since 2003, which could now be partly reversed (Lardy 2012: 10). As of November 2008, the country cut its short-term interest rate to a historic low and additionally, reserve ratios for banks were lowered as well and commercial lending quotas were relaxed. Moreover, the grip on mortgage loans was reduced to stimulate the real estate market. Money supply and credit were propelled in the first quarters of 2009. All these measures aimed at stabilising domestic demand. On the external side, the appreciation of the yuan was stopped in order not to worsen the contraction in exports (Sun and Fu 2012: 12-13). In addition to the fiscal and monetary stimulus, the Chinese government tried to soften the negative effects on employment by allowing enterprises to delay contributions to the social security funds and allowing these companies to use unemployment funds to keep the level of employment in the company stable (Cai et al. 2010).

iii) China's Growth and the Global Recovery

Due to China's sheer size, the country is a vital contributor to global growth and thus, its recovery had global implications. As of mid-2009, the recovery of China became visible due to the country's various forms of stimulus. In fact, China suffered from labour shortage from the beginning of 2010, which is a sign of the sharp economic recovery due to the introduced measures (Cai eta l. 2010) as well as to the end of the Lewis development phase in China (Nolan 2015: 55). Domestic demand played a vital role in the country's recovery; China provided stability to the global community and was not a source of uncertainty at that point in time. After the global financial crisis, China's ambitions to become a global leader became even more visible. Factors such as insufficient supervision and a lack of governance, which significantly contributed to the crisis, had to be tackled in a coordinated manner on a global basis. Ironically, this was promoted by an emerging market which had to suffer from the spill over effects of the US originated meltdown and furthermore, has not at all been adequately represented in international financial institutions (Sun and Fu 2012: 14). Even though China stopped the appreciation of the yuan against the US dollar during the crisis to mitigate the drag on exports, it did not engage in a cycle of competitive devaluations as other emerging markets did and thus, truly contributed to global stability. China decided to reform its currency in July 2005 and the yuan appreciated significantly in the subsequent years until 2008 (Lardy 2012:101-106). After the crisis, the appreciation of the local exchange rate continued, which led to the build-up of a significant fundamental vulnerability.

What can be learnt from the economic downturn of 2008 is that no country remains unaffected in the face of global problems and thus, coordination has become ever more important in a globalised world. The opening of China over the last decades has propelled the country into a new sphere, but also significantly contributed to its vulnerability through its external sector. A sharp decline in export growth rates and falling foreign exchange reserves in China were the signs of the negative spillover effects of the global contraction of demand during the crisis (Sun and Fu 2012: 14-15). In addition, the response to the crisis entailed its own problems for China.

Apart from the distortions resulting from the response to the crisis, China still faces some of the long-term issues it had already experienced before the shock in global demand. In March 2007, Wen Jiabao said that 'China's economic growth is unsteady, imbalanced, uncoordinated, and unsustainable'. In 2011, Hu Jintao voiced similar concerns (Lardy 2012: 44). These issues are mainly connected to China's growth model and relate to imbalances in investment and consumption as well as the still partly decentralised structure of China with the central government bailing-out local governments from time to time (Sun and Fu 2012: 14-15). Indeed, China's fundamental, policy-induced and institutional weaknesses pose significant challenges to the Chinese leadership and will be examined in more detail in the case study.

3.C) China's Growth Model

The bleak years of global economic performance after the great financial crisis of 2008 and 2009 stand in stark contrast to the growth rates of China. This is partially related to the country's model of development. China's approach to development, which is generally referred to as the developmental state, was never about rejecting markets, but recognises that markets on its own can be rather instable (Bishop et al. 2018: 2). Liberals put forward that the allocation of resources should be purely done by the market according to the comparative advantages a country has, the notion of the developmental state claims that these comparative advantages are changeable. The example of China has shown how the economic catch-up process requires some state direction (Bishop et al. 2018: 2). The notion of a development state emerged in the early 1980s as a rival explanation to the neoclassical growth model in light of the significant growth rates depicted by the Four Little Tigers (Singapore, Hong Kong, Taiwan and South Korea). The developmental state challenges the neoclassical growth theory with respect to the role of the state in the economic trajectory of the East Asian countries (Howell 2006: 273).

The role of state was reassessed at the end of the Cold War and fast-track liberalisation led to financial crises in developing countries. By the mid-1990s, institutions such as the World Bank recognised the important role states have with respect to the development agenda of a country. In particular, the Four Little Tigers served as examples for the developmental state model. This led to an increased interest in effective states as well as good governance, which was reflected in the analyses of development processes. In practice, the developmental state model often meant authoritarian government as well as the repression of the civil society. Nonetheless, despite these challenges to the good governance agenda and those posed by globalisation, the concept of the developmental state continues to be among the most important in political economy. Among those scholars who develop the concept further are Adrian Leftwich and Gordon White with the latter adapting the concept of the developmental state to account for the market reforms in China.

The Cold War led to a sharply polarised discussion about the role of the state and the market in the economy. In this environment, the notion of the developmental state gained currency in the late 1970s and 1980s. Scholars such as Balassa et al. (1982) and Lal (1983) put forward that the success of the Four Little Tigers was due to unconstrained market forces. In contrast to this, Amsden (1989) and Wade (1988) stressed the vital role of the state in guiding the development agenda of these countries. In doing so, the scholars underlined the earlier findings of Chalmers Johnson (1982) on Japan, which pointed to the vital role of the state in economic development. To advance, first it has to be defined what is meant by a developmental state. It must be clearly distinguished from particular economic policies such as protectionist measures. Such state actions do not make up for the developmental state, which does build on historical, political as well as institutional foundations. The ideal-typical developmental state has various features. First of all, the political and economic elites strive for economic growth as well as transformation. These elites have the power as well as the authority and capacity to drive the development agenda. 'Often motivated by strong nationalist sentiments, such elites strive to modernize their countries, raise economic living standards and bridge the technological gap' (Howell 2006: 275). Second, a competent, authoritative state administration is another feature of the developmental state. 'Both the political and policy elite and state institutions in general are relatively autonomous from particular vested interests, allowing them to stand above the demands of specific social groups, whether defined by class, ethnicity or region, to shape policy for a broader, national interest' (Howell 2006: 276). Third, the civil society tends to be relatively weak in developmental states. Finally, developmental states are also measured by their outcomes as they promote rapid economic growth as well as general well-being (Howell 2006). Moreover, Wade (2018: 525) puts forward that the developmental state is based on an elite consensus, which is mainly built on the following points:

1. The priority is given to high and sustainable growth rates in order to catch up with more advanced nations.
2. A high level of investment to GDP is needed in order to go through the targeted industrial transformation.
3. The state is needed for coordination purposes, which leads to the promotion of certain sectors over others.
4. The state also tries to curb consumption in favour of investment in order to push forward the development of the country.
5. Export promotion is among the key areas of focus for the developmental state.

In the development theory of the 1950s and 1960s, the state played a significant role, as market failure was a prominent feature of underdeveloped economies. The neoclassical response to this view dates to the late 1960s and early 1970s. Three main arguments were brought forward by neoclassical economists. First, inefficient industries were created by the promotion of import-substitution. Second, rent seeking was created by substantial government intervention leading to the foregoing of productive activities in favour of the attraction of subsidies as well as protection. Third, the East Asian success story was based on an outward-orientated growth model. However, the neoclassical view only partially captures what happened in these decades. A different picture is given by the capitalist developmental state theory, which was first developed by Chalmers Johnson (1982). His model depicted certain features. For instance, economic development was defined in terms of growth. In addition, private property rights are upheld. Nonetheless, the market is guided 'with instruments formulated by a small-scale, elite economic bureaucracy, recruited from the best managerial talent available in the system' (Önis 1991: 111). Strategic industrial policy is among the most important features of the developmental state model.

In addition to the above, Robert Wade (1990) suggests a governed market theory of the East Asian industrialisation. This theory is rooted in Johnson's developmental state model, which says that the East Asian performance is based on high levels of investment in certain industries. Thus, the state in addition to the market is guiding the process of resource allocation, which results in different outcomes than predicted by the neoclassical model. Amsden (1992) puts forward South Korea as an example of the developmental state model. As a matter of fact, Korea can be regarded as a prime example of Wade's governed market theory. 'The government has performed a strategic role in taming domestic and international forces and harnessing them to national economic interests. [...] The state has heavily subsidized and directed a selected group of industries and subsequently exposed them to international competition' (Önis 1991: 112). Price distortions via state intervention were the primary means through which a greater level of investment was achieved. Hence, government interventions aimed at distorting relative prices in order to increase investment in relevant industries. However, the state also imposed significant performance requirements on the companies in return for its support. Additionally, restrictions on the capital account were enforced. Investors were exposed to capital controls, which limited the significant volatility of capital flows. Also, the financial system plays a crucial role in the developmental state model. Rent seeking was strictly prevented and thus, companies had to focus on the accumulation of capital to foster growth. In addition, 'massive imports of foreign licenses have been conceived of as the principal means of attaining technological independence. Direct foreign investment has played a comparatively limited role' (Önis 1991: 113). Last but not least, the government's fiscal policy primarily aimed at investing; long-term investment in education and human capital formation rank among the primary goals for the developmental state (Önis 1991).

According to Johnson (1982), another interesting feature of the developmental state model is the unusual division of labour between the executive, bureaucrats, and military. In fact, bureaucrats rule while politicians reign. 'The politicians provide the space for the bureaucrats to rule by holding off special interest claimants who might deflect the state from its main developmental priority and also legitimate and ratify the decisions taken by the bureaucrats' (Önis 1991: 115). In addition, the special incentives provided by the state, helped to grow local enterprises, but also made them dependent on the government to some extent. State elites engineered extremely tight networks in many East Asian economies as the authoritarian political structures made the focus on growth as the primary objective possible. In this respect, Cumings' contribution (1984) is particularly important as the historical origins of the East Asian industrialisation are taken into account. For instance, the extensive investment undertaken by the Japanese occupiers provided for an industrial and infrastructural base for subsequent industrial growth in Korea. Furthermore, Haggard (1990) points to the special role of trade and capital flows with respect to the East Asian success story. 'The strength of the East Asian states enabled them to direct and limit the impact of foreign capital in local economies' (Önis 1991: 117). This represents a stark contrast to the countries in Latin America, which were highly dependent on Western countries in terms of financing. Peter Evans (1995) demonstrates this in his comparative analysis. Also, Haggard (1990) shows another striking difference between the East Asian success story and the Latin American failures. In East Asia the government primarily focused on long-term investment and excluded labour from the political process, which stands in contrast to the Latin American countries.

'Three key elements of the developmental state are extremely difficult to emulate. They are the single-minded adherence to growth and competitiveness at the expense of other objectives, the unusual degree of bureaucratic autonomy and capacity, and the equally unique and unusual degree of public-private cooperation' (Önis 1991: 120). One issue with the developmental state is its long-term stability. Amsden (1992), for instance, draws attention to the tension between the bureaucratic autonomy and the public-private cooperation. Another factor is that the size of the bureaucratic apparatus is not linked to an effective market-augmenting form of government. As a matter of fact, very small bureaucratic structures as well as public sectors can have an effective influence on a country. In addition, small but powerful pilot agencies can provide guidance for the private sector to undertake risky, long-term projects (Önis 1991). Increasing productivity and profitability are among the primary aims of developmental states, which is in line with the long-term economic transformation. However, the size of the state is not crucial to this transformation. Indeed, rent-seeking activities are a characteristic of bloated states, which impedes state capacity. Three key features are associated with interventions of developmental states. First, direct ownership of the industrial value chain is not as important as building up economic infrastructure through research and education. Second, cooperative labour-management relations are one of the principal goals of the state. Third, 'the state undertakes a leading role in comparative advantage. The state is involved in creating the conditions for economic growth and industrial adaption, yet refrains from exercising direct control. A central feature underlying this process is that the state works with and often promotes the market. The market is employed as an instrument of industrial policy by exposing particular industries to international competitive pressures. Developmental states systematically manage the market as a means of long-term economic transformation' (Önis 1991: 124).

The ideas of a developmental state reach back a long way. For instance, Friedrich List put forward that 'less advanced nations' make use of the state in order to catch-up with more developed countries in order to… accomplish the economical development of the nation and to prepare it for admission into the universal society of the future' (List 1885: 175). Furthermore, he claimed that '… a perfectly developed manufacturing industry, an important mercantile marine and foreign trade on a really large scale, can only be attained by means of the interposition of the power of the State' (List 1885: 178). Moreover, Gerschenkron (1962, 1964) put forward that the state would need to have developmental functions in order for the economic catch-up to be effective.

The success of the East Asian economies can be credited to the existence of a strong developmental state. Fast economic growth, foremost in Japan, South Korea and Taiwan, was built on a strong, autonomous government which guided investment into strategic industrial sectors. This became known as the East Asian model of development. By the 1990s, the developmental state model had achieved high status and gained recognition from key institutions such as the World Bank. However, the Asian economic crisis of the 1990s represented a setback for the East Asian developmental states. Nonetheless, 'the crisis should not blind us to the lessons, such as they are, of the last 40 years of economic growth in East Asia'. Moreover, 'it is arguable that financial and economic liberalization, not excessive intervention, contributed to the crisis. Throughout the 1990s, several East Asian countries dismantled state controls over external borrowing and local lending, making themselves more vulnerable to the massive financial flows which precipitated the crisis' (Polidano 2001: 514-515). According to Brownbridge and Kirkpatrick (1999: 13), 'it would seem that the departure from the model, rather than its pursuit, may have been a major cause of the East Asian crisis'. The crisis has reopened the discussion on state intervention in the economy, not settled it. For instance, Malaysia reintroduced capital controls in 1998 to prevent the situation from spiralling out of control. Taiwan also followed suit (Polidano 2001: 515).

Gerschenkron (1962, 1964) developed the concept of advantages of economic backwardness. Economic growth was partly due to the catch-up process with more advanced nations. Imported knowledge and technology from abroad is the primary driver of economic growth in this respect. 'China, once closed off to the rest of the world, also came to recognize during the late 1970s the imperatives and advantages of catch-up development; China has since experienced near 10 percent annual economic growth' (Wong 2004: 350). The East Asian developmental state became under pressure through economic globalisation. The integration into the world economy made the East Asian states feel the pressure for convergence of economic policies. In addition, the economies became increasingly integrated into the global capitalist system. 'Japan in the mid-1980s, followed by Taiwan and South Korea during the 1990s, were both compelled by the United States and the global community in general to liberalize exchange rates. Financial markets were also gradually pried open by foreign investors and made more competitive' (Wong 2004: 354). Cerny (1997) puts forward that in light of global competition it becomes more difficult for a state to be developmental. 'Increasing involvement in global economic and political processes erodes the political autonomy and policy capacity of the developmental state. Cerny contends that with the spread of neo-liberalism in the 1980s, the classic competition state – namely, the developmental state – is giving way to a new orthodox state model – namely, the neo-liberal state' (Howell 2006: 277). A further challenge comes from the good governance agenda, which is particularly important for aid-dependent countries. This implicitly challenges the authoritarian government argument being an essential driver for growth in the catch-up process (Polidano 2001: 515).

Regardless of the above, 'it is true that in some places, such as China, the developmentally orientated state continues to focus on infrastructural and catch-up development, exemplifying the classical developmental state model' (Wong 2004: 357). Since the inception of the reform area, China's economy has grown at a remarkable rate. While economists tend to focus on the determinants of the growth rate, the underlying political economy played a vital role for this. 'The overriding economic policy objective was the achievement of rapid economic growth, and the policies that were adopted managed to do this. China became a developmental state' (Knight 2012: 3). At the end of the 1970s, there was a reordering of priorities from the political to the economic in China. The new leadership made economic growth the highest priority of the government agenda. There needed to be an improvement in living standards after the Maoist years, which should increase the Chinese Communist Party's legitimacy to rule the country. Failure to provide this new form of economic legitimacy would result in stagnation, political decline as well as social tensions. Moreover, the greater awareness of the West's wealth and the success of the East Asian Tigers led to the altered government agenda. Furthermore, the chaos of the Cultural Revolution had led to a weaker central planning system. As a result of the above-mentioned factors, the new leadership engaged in two reform programmes, an economic as well as a political. Thus, not only was economic growth the primary overarching goal of the state, but also political reforms should support this goal. Education qualifications, cadre training and an incentive system were introduced in order to professionalise the leadership system. 'Thus, the party and state bureaucrats including managers of state owned enterprises (SOEs) were moulded to meet CCP objectives, to which the achievement of rapid economic growth was central. China became a developmental state' (Knight 2012: 5).

Historically, there were different reasons for the establishment of the developmental state. For Japan, a series of crises led to the evolvement of the developmental state. For South Korea and Taiwan, it was the external threats from North Korea and China. 'In China's case, the developmental state arose from the need of the ruling party to restore and maintain the political legitimacy that it had lost' (Knight 2012: 5). Therefore, China embarked on a gradual economic reform, where policymakers could learn from experiments without incurring significant risks. Bolesta (2015) argues that China went through a dual process since 1978, namely a transformation from plan to market as well as a socio-economic development to achieve higher income. China's model combines the economic transition with the establishment of a developmental state. 'It does so by introducing economic nationalism as the paramount state ideology, by creating a central economic bureaucracy to guide reforms, by keeping planning as an important state instrument, and, foremost, by maintaining a strong and authoritarian state in charge of development' (Bolesta 2015: 107). China's model incorporates features of the developmental state as well as of post-socialist transformation. The background for these economic policies is nationalism as the state tries to shield the local economy from unwanted competition from foreign companies. Thus, the government is creating a cocoon for the local economy to mature before exposing it to global competition. Import-substitution industrialisation is followed by export-orientated industrialisation (Haggard 1990). 'The developmental state is a strong state that presides over developmental transformation. The economic system exhibits features of a free market and central planning at the same time' (Bolesta 2015: 112). This was shown by Johnson's work (1982) on the industrialisation of Japan, which was described as "plan rational". The developmental trajectory of a country has the highest priority and not necessarily social cohesion. The transition is governed by a development agency with its economic bureaucracy. Also, external conditions such as the threat of a violent conflict were a prominent feature of the developmental state model. 'In addition to guiding development trajectory, the post-socialist developmental state must also be responsible for post-socialist systemic transformation, namely economic liberalisation, market institutionalisation and microeconomic restructuring' (Bolesta 2015: 113).

China has gone through a transformation from a closed command economy to a market-based, open economic model. In that sense, China has become a post-socialist economy. Baek (2005: 487) puts forward that 'Chinese aspects of this developmental state include: the high rate of domestic savings, the huge infrastructure of heavy industry, the promotion of industrial policy, the legacy of central planning, labour-intensive industry accompanied by import-substitutive capital-intensive industry, a strong central government with huge bureaucracy, and corporatist control over the society'. The academic scholar claims that these features of the Chinese model fit into Wade's policy advice for the governed market and hence make China an imitator of the developmental state model. For Ping (2011) the Chinese model is based on socialist state directed market capitalism. Lee and Mathews (2010) put forward that China drew lessons from the developmental experiences of its successful neighbours, namely from Japan, Korea, Taiwan and Singapore. Wong (2004: 5) claims that 'though there are significant differences between the current path of China's development and that of Japan and South Korea, they should be seen as in different stages traveling along the same rout'. According to this literature, China can be called a post-socialist developmental state.

As the reforms started in China, the country immediately rejected the ideas of economic radicalism. A gradual path was an alternative. What makes for the Chinese developmental state? Among others, the reform selectivity plays a crucial role. In addition, the tight grip of the economy in certain sectors as well as certain barriers and investment limitations to establish a strong domestic base (Bolesta 2015: 117). 'Moreover, the reform focused on creating economic bureaucracy with an influential pilot agency to preside over economic modernisation. The powers of China's National Development and Reform Commission (NDRC) equal almost those of the Korean Economic Planning Board (EPB) and far exceed those of the Japanese Ministry of International Trade and Industry (MITI)' (Bolesta 2015: 118). Extensive planning capabilities were retained by China. Central planning was seen as the cornerstone for economic liberalisation. Thus, China did not give up extensive state interventionism. 'Instead, it has searched for new means and instruments of intervention and control in the new market conditions' (Bolesta 2015: 118). Also, politically China maintained a type of authoritarianism. In this case, China was closer to the Taiwanese and Korean examples than to the Japanese one. A strong and capable state was the main purpose for keeping an authoritarian state according to the view that authoritarianism is better suited than democracy for fast development (Howell 1998).

'Import-substitution industrialisation (ISI), in China's case a legacy of state-command economy, was supplemented by export-orientated industrialisation (EOI) in the post-socialist era, and subsequently tuned into the DS pattern of gradual change in the industrial targeting from labour-intensive to capital- and technology-intensive sectors' (Bolesta 2015: 120). As a matter of fact, exports fuel growth as domestic consumption is too weak initially to drive any growth spurt. Thus, China rapidly developed its R&D base and imported technology in order to be able to manufacture goods for the world market. The domestic development was guided by the Chinese state via certain means. This varied from directly targeting the industrial development to trade-related as well as financial system-related policies, which also included distorted market incentives. An undervalued yuan helped to make the country's exports more competitive globally. Also, the banking sector is not independent, but rather a tool for the Chinese state's developmental goals. 'China has been utilising indirect (rate manipulations, rebates and exemptions) and direct subsidies (direct payments) to targeted sectors and enterprises. Fiscal (tax) subsidies have also played an important role' (Bolesta 2015: 121). In addition to the above, the government started to create large state-owned enterprises in the 1990s, which were similar to the Korean chaebols and Japanese keiretsu. As described in the historical background section, this was part of the policy of keeping the large and letting the small go.

At the same time, China went through an extensive liberalisation process since the end of the 1970s; a market-based economy evolved. However, under the Hu-Wen administration this liberalisation process fell short of expectations and China only reluctantly fulfilled its obligations with respect to its WTO membership. The Xi administration's rhetoric can be regarded as a resumption of this liberalisation process and market-based reforms. Nonetheless, this is examined in more detail in the case study. 'At the same time, some of the current policies are explicitly aimed at broadening the support for the state and the state leader by means and tactics well versed within the historical developmental states' (Bolesta 2015: 124). 'The state has not abandoned intervention, as the summer 2015 cases of stock market and RMB exchange indicate. The government is believed to have spent over 150 billion USD in an attempt to stabilise shares of listed companies. Due to some alleged methodological changes, which resulted in the devaluation of the RMB in August 2015, the policy of Central Bank's continuous manipulation of the national currency's exchange rate resurfaced as a topic' (Bolesta 2015: 124).

Part 4:
Case Study

4. A) Qualitative Analysis of China's Vulnerabilities in the Second Half of 2015 and 2016

In 2015 and 2016, China's exchange rate was struck by unprecedented volatility, which does not get appropriate attention from an early warning perspective. Specifically, China's steep growth trajectory together with the country's successful exchange rate management since the nation's accession to the WTO in 2001 made these events rather unique. The aim is to analyse China's trajectory from an early warning perspective, particularly the events of 2015 and 2016. In other words, the unified analytical framework, consisting of a fundamental, policy-induced and institutional dimension, aims to better understand the troubles China faced during this period.

For this study, I used a unique and rich data source as the basis for reconstructing these events, namely over five hundred research reports from international banks, as well as research by supranational organisations and economic magazines such as "The Economist". Indeed, no single academic report can give a more detailed view on China's trajectory in these two years. What happened in China in 2015 and 2016 sent shockwaves of uncertainty around the world. To better understand these events, I apply the extended analytical framework. Fundamentals are key when it comes to explaining the troubles China faced in the second half of 2015 and 2016. However, focusing on this dimension alone can lead to a myopic view on the events. By expanding the conventional way of thinking by two additional categories of vulnerability, policy-induced and institutional vulnerabilities, I show that outcomes can be explained to a higher degree. My research creates awareness of the crucial drivers of outcomes by expanding the dimensions of analysis. By detaching the discussion on financial crises, particularly on currency crises, from fundamentals, I encourage stakeholders to see the multiple forms of vulnerability. My research helps to better understand the holistic picture of China's struggle and demonstrates that policy efforts of China should aim at addressing underlying vulnerabilities.

The dependent variable of my research is the currency debasement of the Chinese yuan, which took place in August 2015, together with the revision and the subsequent alterations in the exchange rate regime as well as the entailed capital flow volatility. Thus, the analysis focuses on FX distortions, which are defined in this book as being relative to the currency's own history rather than as a fixed percentage of currency weakness, as it is usually defined in research. To put it differently, a foreign exchange crisis is defined as an abnormal weakening vis-à-vis to the US dollar given the statistical properties of the times series. This allows for a flexible approach towards spotting crises, which takes into account idiosyncrasies of a country. Furthermore, empirical breaks must be considered and as previously shown, one such break occurred in the early 2000s. The conditioning of the time horizon helps to focus the attention on two events, which can be classified as abnormal exchange rate movements given the renminbi's own history. First, in 2005, China cancelled the peg of the yuan versus the US dollar, which led to a 2.1 percent appreciation of the local currency. Given the appreciation of the Chinese yuan, this event does not classify as an exchange rate crisis. The second event took place in August 2015, when the PBoC devalued the renminbi 1.9 percent against the US dollar. This event in particular was very unique given time series analysis.

The above-mentioned shocked global capital markets; policymakers did not anticipate the repercussions of the unfolding of the 2015 and 2016 events, which Keynes (1937: 13) put as follows, 'the idea of the future being different from the present is so repugnant to our conventional modes of thought and behavior that we, most of us, offer a great resistance to acting on it in practice'. The expanded analytical framework should help to clarify the vulnerabilities China faced in this period and thus, ultimately should help to prevent a repeat of these events. I will start out with the discussion of fundamentals, before presenting policy-induced and institutional vulnerabilities in detail.

a) China's Current Fundamental Vulnerabilities

I begin with discussing the key fundamentals that led to the increased susceptibility of China with respect to the FX distortions of 2015 and

2016. As noted in the conceptual section, the intervening properties of certain variables help to identify relevant mechanisms. Indeed, fundamentals play a key role in vulnerability analysis as shown with the conceptualisation of the idea of an early warning system as well as in the analysis of historic crisis episodes. In general, I split the section on fundamentals into one subsection on 'Growth and Fundamental Change' and another subsection on 'Balance-of-Payment Dynamics'. With respect to the latter, one of the key fundamentals, as shown in the conceptual section, is the real exchange rate, which can be used as a monthly indication for various types of crises. In addition, important annual indicators according to prior research by Goldstein et al. (2000: 11) are variables related to the current as well as to the capital and financial accounts. For instance, one annual indicator that accurately predicts currency crises is the current account balance as a percentage of investment. In fact, these fundamentals that were previously identified by academic literature were present in China in mid-2015 as the sharp decline in Chinese asset prices, as well as the turmoil surrounding the Chinese yuan, led to global economic uncertainty.

Prior to these events, the quasi peg of the renminbi to the US dollar entailed a significant real appreciation of the Chinese currency, which led to a loss of global competitiveness of Chinese exports and thus, to a declining export performance. The amount of both Chinese exports as well as imports dropped significantly, with the former being a consequence of the above-mentioned weaknesses, and the latter, a sign of the slowing economy. The Chinese government decided to counter these effects by granting more flexibility to the exchange rate against the US dollar. The yuan was announced to be managed against a basket of currencies because of these events (Bloomberg 2015b). As a matter of fact, the country had been suffering from a monetary dilemma (McNally and Gruin 2017), which was most visible in the form of fundamental vulnerabilities.

Regarding growth and debt dynamics, the build-up of leverage in China is another dangerous development. This debt is a consequence of the response to the global financial crisis of 2008, which had significant spill over effects to emerging markets. Governments were forced to intervene in the private sectors of their economies during the crisis, which then led to a significant build-up in debt. The economy had to be stabilised and restarted, thus making stimulus packages necessary. J.P. Morgan (2015b: 17) shows that that most of the debt is corporate liabilities and still exists in the form of bank loans. It is estimated that the latter accounts for about 85 percent of all outstanding liabilities and only the remaining amount is financed via capital markets. This should lead us to increasingly focus on the banking sectors of developing countries as a source of vulnerability. However, as most of the debt is denominated in local currency, a balance-of-payment crisis is not likely in China. Instead, this debt overhang could result in slower economic growth as the increased burden on these countries drains resources from other important areas (The Economist 2015a). To summarise, the largest percentage of the total debt of emerging market countries is on corporate balance sheets. These liabilities are mostly denominated in local currency as well as in the forms of loans. As a matter of fact, only 10 percent of the total outstanding liabilities are denominated in hard currency as opposed to local currency debt (J.P. Morgan 2015b: 1), which underlines the limited exposure of China with respect to currency mismatches.

As mentioned above, the increase in debt on corporate, as well as government balance sheets was a direct consequence of the spill over effects of the financial crisis of 2008. It is quite common among analysts to primarily focus on government debt as a source of vulnerability for countries. However, historic crises clearly showed that private debt must be regarded as a contingent liability for sovereigns and thus, must be equally considered as a weakness for a nation (Breslin 2014). Although a number of countries have already shifted private debt to the state's balance sheets, there are many other countries that have not gone yet through this process. In 2014 and 2015, emerging markets generally faced increased challenges with commodity prices slumping and economic growth decelerating (J.P. Morgan 2015b: 2-4). The Chinese state currently has no outstanding external debt since all its debt contracts are denominated in local currency and, as laid out in the historical background section 'China's Economic Empowerment', the PRC has never been in areas on its debt. Instead, Chinese leadership is exposed to significant weaknesses in the country's banking sector via the staggering amounts of loans provided to Chinese companies. Thus, China is facing significant problems with their government-owned and state-owned enterprises. The total debt of these entities together with debt fuelled asset price bubbles pose a non-negligible vulnerability for the Chinese economic system (Quah 2013: 18-21). In this respect, Reinhard and Rogoff (2009: xxv) note that a country and its institutions often misplace their confidence in the sustainability of the status quo via the build-up of debt. Indeed, the debt binge often overshadows an inefficient allocation of resources and is thus a sign of lower growth performance of a country.

i) Growth, Fundamental Change and the Build-up in Debt-to-GDP

In 2013, Goldman Sachs published a sequel to the famous paper on BRICs by Jim O'Neill (2001). Wilson and Purushothaman (2003: 1-2) estimated the emerging worlds growth trajectory until 2050 in the paper "Dreaming with BRICs: The Path to 2050". The vital conclusion of the report was that the countries developed institutions and avoided bad policies, which would hinder their growth trajectory. Indeed, none of the dimensions of the theoretical framework shown in the conceptual section exist on their own; rather all three of the dimensions are interconnected. Wilson and Purushothaman (2003: 6) admit that long-term projections suffer from a very high level of uncertainty. Such uncertainty could have been observed with the rise of the Soviet Union or the extrapolation of growth in Japan. Nevertheless, the researchers tried to specify the growth potential of developing countries to catch-up with advanced economies. Indeed, growth variables are among the key predictors in early warning systems. First, in terms of relative growth to advanced economies, developing countries could increase capital accumulation making up for the fact that they have less capital available than developed countries. Second, developing countries could adopt technologies from more advanced economies, which raises the growth rate of said countries (Blanchard and Johnson 2013: 218-221). By adopting advanced technology, productivity increases and thus, appreciating currencies can contribute to the catch-up process of developing countries. The research report identified the significant deviation of the emerging nation's currencies from their purchasing power parity. By increasing productivity, emerging country's currencies should converge with their PPP rates (Clark and MacDonald 1999; Krugman et al. 2015: 447). To better understand this concept, Wilson and Purushothaman (2003: 7) apply growth accounting to their analysis, which distinguishes between growth in employment, in capital stock and in total factor productivity, as shown in the conceptual section. The researchers identify the income gap of developing countries with advanced economies as a so-called advantage of backwardness. The higher the gap, the greater the potential to catch-up via higher capital accumulation and total factor productivity growth as laid out in the conceptual section.

The discussion below demonstrates that fundamentals remain among the key predictors in early warning systems. This is shown with the examination of China's troubles in 2015 and 2016. In addition, China is suffering from a credibility issue. Investors assumed that the country was trying to stabilise economic volatility, understating it's output numbers in boom phases while overstating output in economic declines, and in line with the previous, market participants assumed that China overstated its growth numbers in 2015. This became particularly relevant in 2015, when China's output was published at 7 percent in the first half of 2015, which market participants doubted due to different signals from high frequency indicators. Among those indicators are 'the Li Keqiang index, industrial production (IP), steel output and cement output', which largely mirror economic activity in the manufacturing sector (Chen et al. 2015b).

China is trying to shift the country's economy from the export-led growth model, which has helped the nation to prosper over the previous decades, to domestic demand as the crucial motor for growth. In fact, between 2007 and the second quarter of 2015, the Chinese economy experienced a structural shift. The secondary industry fell from about 47 percent to 42 percent and the tertiary industry rose from 43 percent to approximately 49 percent in the Chinese GDP. Investors often neglect this structural shift. Thus, China tried to rebalance its economy, 'from industry towards services on the supply side, and from investment to consumption on the demand side' (Abiad et al. 2016: 5). This approach should help make China's growth trajectory more sustainable through correcting historic imbalances entailed by the steep growth path over the previous decades. Employment should be fostered by increasing the share of services relative to manufacturing in the Chinese economy. This could help the country to cut back on its reliance on external demand (Abiad et al. 2016: 5). Since the service sector is increasingly becoming more important in China, it is crucial to use high-frequency indicators such as 'the non-manufacturing PMI, consumer confidence, retail sales, financial sector growth, auto sales, and floor space sold', in addition to the aforementioned variables (Chen et al. 2015b). However, despite this structural shift in the Chinese economy, the manufacturing sector remains key to the country's vulnerability as it determines the marginal growth rate. Thus, the disappointing numbers of high frequency manufacturing indicators represented a clear warning of the events to follow.

Indeed, growth in 2015 did not reach the country's target of 7 percent, but came in a touch lower at 6.9 percent, mainly due to the severe difficulties the country faced in the second half of said year. This significantly contributed to the currency debasement of Chinese yuan in August 2015, together with the revision and the subsequent alterations in the exchange rate regime as well as the entail capital flow volatility. Growth variables are among the key predictors for currency distortions. The growth rate in the manufacturing sector was especially disappointing, reaching only 0.9 percent in 2015, while the service sector depicted a respectable 11.7 percent nominal growth rate. For 2016, the Chinese growth target was lowered from 7 percent to 6.5 percent with the continuation of the reduction in overcapacity as a crucial goal. Moreover, the fiscal deficit was set higher for 2016 to stimulate the economy (Chen et al. 2016e: 1). In fact, the fiscal deficit was increased to 3.0 percent of GDP, M2 growth was targeted at 13 percent for 2016 and the inflation ceiling was left at 3 percent (Deng and Tao 2016). Chen et al. (2016e: 4) point out that the slowdown in the manufacturing sector was in line with the deceleration of fixed investment growth, in particular in manufacturing and real estate growth. The state-owned enterprise issue is crucial in this respect. The announced SOE reform in September 2015 might give some clues on the topic. In general, M&A should be the driver of the reform in contrast to outright destruction, which would have negative repercussions throughout the entire value chain (Chen et al. 2016e: 6; Li et al. 2016b: 11-12) and thus should be avoided.

The discussion above shows that on the fundamental side, growth disappointed in China in 2015, which contributed to the troubles the country faced in said period. As a response to the slowdown, Li et al. (2016a) show that China substantially increased the country's credit impulse. Total social financing (TSF) forms the basis of said credit impulse and there exists a statistical significant relationship between said metric and China's growth rate. A spike in credit provides a boost to investment and short-term output as shown in the conceptual section. Nonetheless, the sustainability of this growth over the medium-term is questionable, which contributes to the vulnerability of a country. Moreover, the actual impulse of credit is driven by the second derivative of the stock, namely by changes in credit growth. Proxies to the credit impulse, such as bank lending standards, also yielded good results with respect to short-term economic growth projections (Li et al. 2016a). However, in May 2016, China started to tighten credit standards. This sudden shift in policymaking was a result of an article published in the People's Daily. Subsequently, financial regulators tightened standards significantly. The aim was to contain leverage in the system by the Chinese government. Through this initiative, the new Macro Prudential Assessment (MPA) framework, which uses broad bank credit instead of bank loans for the assessment, became more important. Broad credit can be observed on the asset side of banks' balance sheets while broad money supply, M2, is depicted on the liability side. Moreover, as described above, total social financing can also be used as an indicator, which focuses on the financial activity provided by the financial to the non-financial sector (BoAML 2016: 34; Zhang and Zeng 2016b: 5). Indeed, the surge in credit is an early warning sign.

Even though an increase in total social financing offers higher near-term growth prospects, the indicator served well empirically as a predictor for slowdowns over the medium to long-term. The measures implemented by the Chinese government to tighten credit was perceived as a step towards containing this risk (Bisignano 1999: 93). Nevertheless, Zhang and Zeng (2016b) analysed what could be potential catalysts for an unwinding of the credit boom. The structural slowdown in China makes the country more vulnerable to said risk. One potential catalyst could be a credit event of a major company in China. However, given that the credit market in China is not yet fully liberalised, the likelihood of such an event is rather low. The government still serves as a lender of last resort via implicit or explicit guarantees. Thus, a credit event is unlikely to trigger a systemic crisis in China unless a change in policy is implemented (Zhang and Zeng 2016b: 7-8). This specific situation will be further examined in a later section.

Contrary to several statements listed above, Chang et al. (2016) argue in their research that China increased credit substantially in 2016 in order to stabilise the economy. As described above, the researchers show that TSF has not significantly picked-up and mention that China's leadership has said to reduce corporate leverage. Inevitably, the question 'How can credit expansion be measured in China?' arises. 'Defined by the PBoC to measure the domestic financial sector's (non-government) support to the real economy, the TSF statistics include bank loans, corporate bonds, three traditional shadow banking activities, as well as equity financing since its release in 2011' (Chang et al. 2016: 3). Per definition, total social financing does not include government bonds, nor does it include local government financing vehicle (LGFV) loans and bonds and does not consider China's external debt in the form of FDI or other foreign borrowings (Chang et al. 2016: 3; Chen et al. 2017: 14). As a matter of fact, Chang et al. (2016: 3) show that central and local government debt, as well as credit via off-balance sheet wealth management products (WMPs) have grown rapidly in the second half of 2016, although this growth is not visible in total social financing. By taking this information into account, the sharp rise in the Chinese credit-to-GDP ratio in 2016 can be explained, which represents a significant vulnerability to the country. However, given that China's debt is mostly denominated in local currency, an Asian financial crisis style disaster is rather unlikely (Sequeira and Tilton 2016: 1). 'The heavy state involvement, with the majority of loans coming from state-controlled banks to state-owned enterprises, the strengthening state control and sizeable state assets suggests that the Chinese government still has the capacity to manage the pace of NPL recognition and debt restructuring in the banking system' (Chang et al. 2016: 8). These factors can only be understood within the historical context. Nonetheless, the researchers point out that the speed of credit expansion in China is unsustainable. In addition, the connection between the government, state-owned enterprises, as well as the financial sector points to a systemic vulnerability as no independent circuit breaker seems to be available (Chang et al. 2016: 8), which would help to stabilise a situation of market stress.

Indeed, China's build-up in debt is unprecedented. The total debt-to-GDP ratio rose from 154 percent in 2008 to about 250 percent in 2015. The change in the debt level ranks in the 98th percentile of global debt binges since the 1960s. This does not even account for the rise in opaque lending in China. In comparison to other debt build-ups, two factors stand out. Firstly, China is a huge economy in GDP terms. Secondly, most of the country's debt is denominated in local currency, which reduces the risk of sudden stops in the provision of external financing (Sequeira and Tilton 2016: 1). Nevertheless, across historic samples, researchers have found that growth significantly slows down in countries with high amounts of debt (Bisignano 1999: 93; Reinhard and Rogoff 2009: xxv) and thus, this variable is one important predictor in early warning systems for currency distortions. Foremost, fixed investment slows and the decline in domestic demand leads to an easing of inflation. China's growth has been investment driven and thus any slowdown in this factor would have severe negative repercussions for the country. Additionally, the level of local interest rates is usually reduced to support domestic demand and make the debt binge more sustainable. It must be mentioned however, that throughout a country's development process a certain amount of build-up in leverage can be considered as normal. This process is known as financial deepening and goes along with rising per capita incomes. However, the magnitude of China's debt binge is so massive that it cannot be traced back to financial deepening (Sequeira and Tilton 2016: 3), which underlines the importance of this variable with respect to the analysis of vulnerabilities.

The global financial crisis played an important role for the recent increase in China's debt level. The stimulus needed to stabilise the Chinese economy resulted in a 28-percentage point increase in the total debt level in 2009. The 4trn renminbi stimulus package was needed to initiate an economic turnaround; this was possible due to China's strong fiscal balance. In addition, China lost a vital driver of growth, which led to a further increase in the country's debt-to-GDP ratio. China's opening to the world, due to the WTO entry in 2001, fostered an unprecedented export boom (Kim and Yamakawa 2005: 6-7). This export impulse contributed significantly to output growth in the early to mid-2000s as described in detail the section 'China's Economic Empowerment'. However, the financial crisis of 2008 led to a collapse in this growth driver in addition to the aforementioned build-up in debt (Sequeira and Tilton 2016: 4). Moreover, Sequeira and Tilton (2016: 9) mention that the peak of the debt boom could be related to demographics. In fact, the ratio of the working age population tends to peak right before the end of a debt boom (Nishimura 2012).

Research shows that China's total non-financial sector debt further increased from approximately 250 percent of GDP at the end of 2015 to 277 percent of GDP at the end of 2016. Overall, China's debt level rose by about 130 percent since the great financial crisis, which is an unprecedented build-up in leverage. This fundamental vulnerability was a consequence of the imperative by the Chinese leadership to hold-up the country's growth momentum at all costs. Indeed, one sign which indicates that the debt binge was becoming less sustainable is an increasing proportion of new credit that was used to cover servicing costs of outstanding liabilities (Chen et al. 2017: 12). Moreover, the financial liberalisation in China, which is touched upon in more detail in the institutional section, entailed a significant increase in shadow credit. 'This was facilitated by the gradual liberalization of interest rates and general financial market conditions, which saw the government tightens its control over bank lending even as it simultaneously relaxed rules and rates in the rest of China's financial system' (Chen et al. 2017: 13). How is the total non-financial sector debt split between the different sectors? Of the outstanding liabilities of 277 percent of GDP, government debt accounts for about 68 percent of GDP, household liabilities for approximately 45 percent, and corporate debt for approximately 164 percent of GDP. Inevitably, in order to adequately analyse the debt binge in China, a closer look at state-owned enterprises (SOEs) has to be taken. It is estimated that over 60 percent of the non-financial corporate debt or about a 100 percent of GDP is related to liabilities from SOEs (Chen et al. 2017: 15). These estimates are based on the following assumptions (Chen et al. 2017: 15):

1) Aggregate SOE debt amounted to about 75 percent of total non-financial corporate debt at the end of 2016. However, this number includes inter-company liabilities such as working capital items (i.e. account payables).

2) 55 to 60 percent of all outstanding loans at the end of 2014 were taken out by companies connected to the Chinese state.

In comparison to other emerging markets, the Chinese state has a relatively sustainable balance sheet. However, the inevitable question of "how high are the contingent liabilities?" arises. Before 2015, local governments in China were not allowed to issue debt themselves. However, provincial government financing vehicles were set-up to circumvent this regulation. During the great financial crisis, these vehicles helped to support the Chinese economy significantly via property and infrastructure projects (Chen et al. 2017: 17). To recognise and tackle the debt problem, China passed a new budget law in 2014, which allowed local governments to issue debt themselves with the existing debt being officially recognised by the Chinese central government. The recognition included a debt-swap into long-term bonds, which reduced the burden for provincial governments significantly. Nonetheless, given that these new rules also foresaw a tightening of funding for local governments, the increase of debt via hidden channels has continued so far. Chen et al. (2017: 17) put this as follows, 'Taking into account various channels of quasi-fiscal spending, including land sakes-financed spending and special construction bonds-related credit, we estimate that China's Augmented Fiscal Deficit (AFD) has exceeded 10% in recent years'. However, the researchers note that a systemic debt crisis in China is unlikely, even though many countries faced troubles at lower levels of debt-to-GDP, as demonstrated by Reinhard and Rogoff (2009: 24). The chance of a crash is even less likely given that over 90 percent of liabilities is domestic debt financed via local banks, which is mostly under government control. In addition, these liabilities are financed via deposits or quasi-deposits, which are more stable than wholesale funding (Chen et al. 2017: 18). However, the debt binge in China is likely to result in a misallocation of resources and thus depresses growth (Reinhard and Rogoff 2009: xxv). Hence, the above-mentioned factors allow China's credit cycle to be longer than many observers expect at the cost of building-up fundamental weaknesses.

Moreover, one side effect of China's stimulus driven growth is the build-up of asset bubbles, for instance in the real estate sector, which can represent a significant vulnerability to a country. Since the 1990's, the property boom in China has been driven by factors such as urbanisation (Acemoglu and Robinson 2013: 439). However, banks have reinforced this trend via certain credit channels, most notably mortgage lending, as well as credit to developers have been expanded rapidly. In addition, real assets such as real estate often secured lending to corporates and provincial governments and lesser attention was paid to whether the projects, for which the funds were meant to, would bring up the necessary cash flows to pay back the debt. Therefore, various channels link property prices to the debt level of the Chinese economy. In case of a vicious cycle, the burst of this asset price bubble would certainly reinforce these dynamics (Chen et al. 2017: 45). The property sector is one of the most important contributors to GDP in China as property investment makes up for about 23 percent of total fixed asset investment. A collapse in this sector would have spill over effects along the value chain (Chen et al. 2017: 47). The Chinese demographic shift in particular may put a strain on the real estate sector. This is partly offset from the hukou reform and urbanisation, which underlines the importance of slow-moving trend variables for early warning system analysis.

ii) Balance-of-Payment Dynamics, FX Reserves and FX Valuation

As shown in the conceptual section of this book, fundamental variables that have an important role in explaining currency distortions are the real exchange rate, FX reserves, exports and the current account in general. These variables yield a warning signal in case an unusual deviation from trend occurs and therefore, the indicators depend on their own history whether a warning signal is issued or not. FX valuation in the form of the real exchange rate is identified as the best indicator in this respect as laid out in the analytical section. Strong deviations from historic trends in this variable point to a misvaluation of the exchange rate, which tend to be related to capital in- and outflows. The latter is examined in detail in the institutional section of this book. I proceed by linking China's current account dynamics to the country's saving rate and subsequently, I describe the importance of changes in FX valuation and external statistics for the dependent variable, namely the currency debasement of the Chinese yuan, which took place in August 2015, together with the revision and the subsequent alterations in the exchange rate regime as well as the entailed capital flow volatility.

China's Saving Rate

Before the balance-of-payment dynamics are related to FX valuation and FX reserves, the question how demographics and other slow-moving variables influence the current account of China is answered. According to research, 'slow-moving trends in variables that affect the propensity to save, including the age structure, the level of education and the trend level of GDP, go a long way why some Asian countries have trended strongly towards surplus over the past 35 years' (Kim et al. 2016: 2). Based on these variables, a trend in the structural current account is created. Equilibrium current account definitions usually relate to a stable stock of foreign debt (Kim et al. 2016: 3). The factors that affect the current account most are age structure, education, and growth. The first effect refers to the fact that people between the age of 35 and 69 save the most money (prime savers). The second effect is related to the link between financial literacy and high saving rates. The third effect refers to the inverse relationship between the long-run trend growth and the current account via savings and investments (Abiad et al. 2016: 4; Kim et al. 2016: 6). One of the first individuals who connected a lower dependency ratio with a higher current account surplus were Coale and Hoover (1958). As the share of the young and the elderly falls in percentage of the total population, others are freed to save and spend more. In fact, the current account represents the gap between domestic savings and investments; the increase in savings spurs the current account surplus. Kim et al. (2016: 7) argue that the increase in the share of prime savers propels the current account towards surplus. For instance, China started the country's demographic transition in the 1970s and profited immensely over the preceding decades from this (Naughton 2007: 168), which benefits, however, have peaked now as is examined in detail in the policy section. With respect to education, a higher level of national education induces increased savings by the local population. The individual savings rate is strongly linked to financial literacy (Lusardi and Mitchell 2011). Moreover, the educational attainment may simply stand for other factors determining the saving rate of a country. In general, the increase in educational attainment has supported the Asian countries over the previous decades in building up a substantial current account surplus (Kim et al. 2016: 8-9). The last factor, which determines the structural current account balance, is the change in a country's long-term growth rate. In theory, due to the catch-up potential of developing countries, growth should be extensive and thus, capital should be attracted to these countries leading to a natural deficit in the current account balance (Kim et al. 2016: 9; Krugman et al. 2015).

From the information presented above, it should be clear that the external balance is inevitably linked to China's saving rate, which is globally among the highest. However, the effects of the one-child policy could lead to a decline in the national saving rate from about 46 percent in 2013 to 35 percent in 2020. This drop can potentially present severe consequences for the country. In general, the high saving rate helped China's development tremendously. Two methods on how to estimate a country's saving rate exist. The first method is by calculating the metric as the sum of the current account balance and gross capital formation. The second method is the derivation of the savings rate from the flow-of-funds statistics, which is described in the paper 'China's high saving rate: myth and reality' by Guonan Ma and Wang Yi (2010). The latter splits the saving rate into household, corporate, and government saving.

In general, China's saving rate is explained by the rise in the working age population up until 2010, through financial underdevelopment, which leads to cash hoarding as a prevention for uncertainty. In addition, China's transition led to a restructuring in pension systems and thus, to high household savings. Moreover, corporate earnings were boosted by China's rise over the previous decades and thus, high retained earnings also contribute to a high corporate saving rate (Chen et al. 2016d: 1). All these factors contributed to the country's high saving rate and consequently to China's strength in its external balance. However, in recent years China's saving rate started to decline. As mentioned above, reasons for this are the aging population in China as well as improvements in social safety nets. Moreover, corporate profitability declined in 2015, which can be another reason for this. Overcapacity, as well as overinvestment in sectors such as steel, cement or real estate, led to a declining return on investments (The Economist 2017f). This severely reduced corporate profitability in some sectors.

Nevertheless, the most striking factor for the recent decline in China's saving rate was the change in demographics. The country's working age population peaked in 2011 and has steadily decreased ever since (Chen et al. 2016d: 2-3). China's one-child policy led to a decline in the dependency ratio, which propelled the nation's growth over the last decades. However, the policy has now backfired. Rather than having a balanced ratio between the young and elderly, there is a drop in young individuals while the share of elderly people continues to increase. This will eventually lead to a reversal of the dependency ratio at some point. Given that China has already harvested all benefits of the fall in the dependency ratio, the projected aging will ultimately lead to a decline in the country's saving rate (The Economist 2017g) and thus, in China's current account surplus.

Indeed, the decline in the saving rate could be one severe risk China is facing over the upcoming decades. The drop in savings would coincide with a decline in investments as a percentage of GDP, which would curtail China's economic strategy. Thus, China must either borrow more from external sources to keep up the pace of output growth or improve overall efficiency in the country's economy (Chen et al. 2016d: 2-3). The latter will be further examined in the institutional dimension and the former would represent a fundamental vulnerability to China.

FX Valuation

Empirically, Asia followed a so-called center-periphery model with respect to exchange rates as part of the development agenda. This means that the Asian countries pegged their currencies against the center, namely the US dollar, and usually at a level below the fair value of the currencies in order to foster exports. This entailed monetary policy credibility due to the nominal anchor provided by the fixed exchange rate regimes, and additionally, the development of exports as primary source of the countries growth strategy (Kim and Yamakawa 2005: 4). The modern era of exchange rate flexibility began in the early 1970s with the breakdown of the Bretton Woods system. The Plaza Accord in the mid-1980s focused on another Asian giant, namely Japan. Consequently, the JPY appreciated significantly over the following decade, which meant the end of the rise of said country. The other Asian countries decided to remain their peg against the US dollar. However, the Asian financial crisis of the 1990s served as a reminder that a pegged currency can lead to significant risk of crisis in case of an overvaluation (Goldstein et al. 2000: 67). What is particularly important for a country is its real exchange rate, which is described in detail in the conceptual section. 'If the economy in question is buffeted by persistent shocks (e.g. terms of trade) or is undergoing deep-seated structural change (e.g. rapid productivity increases on the back of economic reforms), the underlying real exchange rate should adjust' (Kim and Yamakawa 2005: 5). Kim and Yamakawa (2005: 6) take four variables into account, which they argue matter for real exchange rates, namely productivity growth, terms of trade, capital flows, and government expenditure. Moreover, the FX reserve accumulation must be accounted for as a means for preventing exchange rate appreciation. The researchers analysed the period from 1995 to 2000 and 2001 to 2004, when China entered the WTO. It can be seen that in particular after the WTO accession, the country's labour productivity growth took off in absolute terms as well as relative to other Asian countries, which should have led to an appreciation of the renminbi. Regarding Chinese exports, two waves are identified: first, since the 1990s and second, since 2001. This shift in the Chinese economy clearly underlines the importance of export-driven development for the country's growth trajectory. Also, a pick-up in FDI can be recorded due to China's accession to the WTO. Upon entering the WTO, China became a low-cost production center for many foreign companies. This is also important for the catch-up in terms of the productivity gap, which goes back to the Balassa-Samuelson effect (Kim and Yamakawa 2005: 6-7; Sequeira and Tilton 2016: 4). The importance of the international institutionalisation will be further dissected in one of the subsequent sections.

Although initially predicted to increase in strength, the yuan weakened in real effective terms from 2001 to 2004 due to the peg of the Chinese currency against the US dollar (Lardy 2012: 103-104). The undervalued real exchange rate greatly benefited China's external balances at the cost of supressing domestic consumption (Kim and Yamakawa 2005: 8-9). This can be regarded as a subsidy to the tradable sector in China in that period. While it is said to be a tax on the non-tradable sector, this also supressed domestic consumption as import costs are higher than they should be. Therefore, in mid-2005, China changed its FX rate against the US dollar. The yuan was revalued at a 2.1 percent level higher and China announced that it would reference the local currency against a basket. However, what this meant exactly was unclear. Before the revaluation of the renminbi in 2005, the currency was managed quite strictly against the US dollar with the daily volatility not even coming close to the allowed band of +/- 0.3 percent (Kim and Yamakawa 2005: 14-15). The US dollar had served China for about 11 years as a nominal anchor before the change in FX management in 2005. China conducted a significant FX devaluation in 1994, however, given the closed capital and current accounts of China at that point, this was not seen as particularly important for global affairs (Kim and Yamakawa 2005: 24). In the 2000s, China's capital account was relatively closed, which allowed the Chinese to exert great control over capital flows. However, what ballooned China's growth was its openness on the trade account. Exports and imports as a percentage of GDP, which is one definition of openness, showed China as a world champion in trade (DeRosa 2009: 39).

In 2005, China ended the currency peg of the yuan versus the US dollar, which had been established in the mid-1990s. The real exchange rate was significantly undervalued at that point in time and thus, the period of gradual renminbi appreciation started with this revaluation. This was a consequence of the previous US dollar peg. In 2002, the US dollar started to depreciate, which also dragged down the RMB in real, trade-weighted terms. However, at that point in time, the recent WTO accession of China led to significant productivity gains and thus, should have entailed an appreciation of the yuan. This is the reason for the significant undervaluation of the RMB in 2005 (Arora et al. 2015). Since then, the PBoC has undertaken the following changes in the exchange rate band (Arora et al. 2015: 3):

- 2005 Jul: CNY depeg against USD, a band set at +/-0.3 percent in Jul 2005
- 2007 May: Band widening to +/-0.5 percent
- 2012 Apr: Band widening to +/-1 percent
- 2014 Mar: Band widening to +/- 2 percent
- 2015 Aug: USD/CNY fixed 1.9 percent higher

The local exchange rate appreciated nearly 40 percent from 2005 to 2014, which resulted in an overvaluation of the exchange rate and thus, in a deterioration of China's external statistics. The Chinese export driven growth model had come under pressure as exports became less competitive (Heilmann 2017: 220). Therefore, China decided to act. On

August 11th, 2015, the PBoC devalued the CNY against the USD by 1.9 percent by increasing the fixing from 6.1162 on August 10th, to 6.2298 on August 11th (Tao and Deng 2015). The PBoC labelled the currency move as a one-time adjustment. However, at that point, significant uncertainty surrounded this event, which relates to a lack of credibility and is touched upon in the policy section in more detail. The actions by the PBoC reflected an adjustment of the fixing towards the market as the yuan traded consistently, on average about 1.5 percent, above the fixing since June 2015. In addition to the exchange rate adjustment, the PBoC also adjusted the fixing mechanism per se as they announced that 'going forward daily fixing will align more closely with the closing spot rate on the previous day' (J.P. Morgan 2015a). Previously, the appreciation of the real effective exchange rate in China in 2015 had led to a severe deterioration in export performance. Moreover, at the beginning of August, an IMF report clearly stated the institution's discontent with the current fixing mechanism of the Chinese currency in light of a potential SDR inclusion (J.P. Morgan 2015a), which will be examined in more detail in the policy section.

China's FX Reserves

Apart from the overvaluation of the real exchange rate and the dismal performance of external statistics, FX reserves are a vital indicator regarding a country's fundamental vulnerabilities. In the second half of 2015, capital and currency markets in China faced severe dislocations and capital flowed out of the country at a staggering pace. In total, the country faced over USD 1trn in annualized outflows in the second half of 2015, which makes Chinese FX reserves of approximately USD 3trn appear quite small in comparison. Taking the significant outflows into consideration, the built up in FX reserves is not enough of a buffer (The Economist 2016c). Nevertheless, the FX reserves gave the government some time to counter the outflows. China fought the symptoms of its problems and not the causes in the sense of a weak political and institutional set-up (De Jonquieres 2013: 6). The introduced capital controls bought China some time to further invest in an effective institutional set-up.

In June 2016, the IMF published a new guidance with respect to a country's reserve adequacy, which takes into account some degree of capital flow management (Liu et al. 2016: 1). In the note, the IMF (2016b) first summarises traditional metrics such as import coverage, the ratio of reserves-to-short-term debt, and the ratio of reserves-to-broad money. As a rule of thumb, a minimum of three-month import coverage is usually recommended, a ratio of 100 percent cover of short-term debt is considered necessary, and a 20 percent ratio of FX reserves-to-M2 is considered as prudent (IMF 2016b: 23). A combination of these rules is used to come up with an estimate of FX reserve adequacy for a country. In general, the IMF admits the positive attributes of a sound FX reserve buffer since this buffer can significantly reduce the risk of a balance-of-payment crisis or a currency crash. To determine the right level of FX reserves for a country, one needs to understand the country's vulnerabilities. Reserves are an external liquidity buffer, which help a nation to maintain confidence in its currency as well as in the economy in general or to directly intervene in FX markets (IMF 2016b: 3-4). Thus, precautionary requirements to enable a country to manage an external shock significantly influence the needed level of FX reserves. In this respect, factors such as capital controls or the depth of capital markets play a significant role.

Indeed, capital controls tend to decrease the potential for capital outflows and thus, lower the required reserve level. Among others, Binici et al. (2010) and Saborowski et al. (2014) confirm this and therefore, the level of FX reserves must be conditional on the capital restrictions in place. The IMF (2016b: 15) even notes that this discussion must be forward-thinking in the sense that a country should accumulate additional FX reserves if liberalisation is expected in the near-term. To determine the degree of capital controls in place various measures are used by the IMF, such as Chinn-Ito (2008), Quinn (1997, 2003) and the IMF share. Thus, the adequate level of FX reserves for a country is determined given individual circumstances. One example of how the IMF calculates FX reserve adequacy for a country with capital controls would be as follows: 'Fixed Exchange Rate: ARA Metric = 10% × Exports + 5% × Broad Money + 30% × Short-term Debt + 20% × Other Liabilities' (IMF

2016a). In addition, the formula for reserve adequacy without controls has a higher weight on broad money as capital flight might be more severe: 'Fixed Exchange Rate: ARA Metric = 10% × Exports + 10% × Broad Money + 30% × Short-term Debt + 20% × Other Liabilities' (IMF 2016a).

China started out with relatively low international reserves in the early 2000s. In 2001, when China entered the WTO, the country depicted about USD 168bn in FX reserves. In the years following China's WTO membership, the country's FX reserves increased steadily. FDI inflows and the trade surplus led to a steady accumulation of reserves. In addition, the relative undervaluation of the RMB also helped the build-up of FX reserves. In 2007, China established a sovereign wealth fund (SWF), the China Investment Corporation (CIC), to manage the country's reserves. China further pushed the internationalisation of the yuan starting in 2009, and thus, the reserve continued to accumulate. In August 2014, China's FX reserves peaked at around USD 4trn (Liu et al. 2016: 3).

Due to the troubles China faced in 2015, FX reserves declined from close to USD 4trn in the end of 2014 to around USD 3trn in the end of 2016. Chen et al. (2017: 4) point out that 'At this level however, they are still 3.5x China's total non-RMB foreign debt, 6x its short-term external obligations, and can cover over 20 months of goods and services imports (minimum requirement is 3 months)'. The research further stresses that most of the FX reserves are liquid as an estimated 60 percent of these is invested in USD with USD 1.1trn directly invested in US treasury securities. In 2016, the IMF estimated the FX reserves needed by China to manage a currency attack effectively. The buffer needed depends on the degree of capital controls in place. With capital controls, the IMF estimated that China would need about USD 1.75trn, and without controls about USD 2.82trn in FX reserves to manage a currency attack. However, China is quite unlikely to deplete its currency reserves; the country would rather further tighten capital controls to get hold of such a situation (Chen et al. 2017: 4-5). This approach will be further discussed in the policy and institutional section.

To conclude, the importance of fundamentals is demonstrated in this section to better understand the currency distortions that happened in China in 2015 and 2016. This also shows that policy efforts of China should aim at addressing underlying vulnerabilities. In this respect, fundamental vulnerabilities remain key. However, in the next sections, I show that an expanded set of independent variables along the three dimensions leads to a better understanding of the dependent variable. A unified approach must be applied to better understand the events of 2015 and 2016, which has not yet been done from an early warning perspective. Thus, I proceed by analysing the currency debasement of the Chinese yuan, which took place in August 2015, together with the revision and the subsequent alterations in the exchange rate regime as well as the entailed capital flow volatility from a policy-induced weakness perspective.

b) The Policy Dimension

The initiation of the reform period in the 1980s had crucial influences on China. Chen Yun described the Chinese system with a bird in a cage metaphor as laid out in the section 'China's Economic Empowerment'. He compared the Chinese economy to a bird and the framework imposed by the Chinese Communist Party to a cage meant to ensure that the bird does not fly away (Acemoglu and Robinson 2013: 438). China made significant steps forward due to the reforms. Especially, the agricultural sector experienced crucial changes, also triggering waves of urbanisation, which spurred the increase in productivity as cities can be regarded as hubs of knowledge (Acemoglu and Robinson 2013: 439). Without a doubt, the Chinese state under the new leadership provided vital guidelines, i.e. development policies, for the Chinese economy to flourish, as laid out in the historical background section.

Accordingly, I first examine China's most important development policies related to the rise of China and to financial crises, namely policy experimentation, population control and urbanisation as well as poverty reduction and inequality. I then address monetary policy uncertainty as well as fiscal policy and the link to the previously discussed debt binge.

Ultimately, soft factors such as the demand for status and ideational determinants will be factored in and shown how this influences policy-induced uncertainty. These factors help to explain the dependent variable, namely the currency debasement of the Chinese yuan, which took place in August 2015, together with the revision and the subsequent alterations in the exchange rate regime as well as the entailed capital flow volatility. Indeed, I demonstrate the different factors of policy-induced vulnerability in order to understand the events of 2015 and 2016 to a higher degree.

i) Development Policies

Deng Xiaoping noted that 'development is the only hard truth' (Naughton 2007: 108). Among the most important of these development policies are policy experimentation, population control and urbanisation as well as the reduction in poverty and inequality. I laid out the concepts of these policies in the analytical section, which now get applied to China's trajectory in 2015 and 2016. Indeed, the events in said period do not receive appropriate attention from an early warning perspective analysis and with my research I aim to close this gap.

Policy Experimentation

Policy experimentation is a means to support institutional innovation as well as avoid steps in the dark. The trajectory of China suggests that experimentation can facilitate transformative change. Heilmann (2008b: 2) notes on this, that the focus 'on how existing, and initially deficient, institutions can be put to work, transformed, or replaced for economic and social development in an open-ended process of institutional innovation' is crucial. China's policy experimentation allowed its political economy to avoid systemic breakdown while at the same time master large-scale economic change. Mukand and Rodrik (2005) stress the unusual adaptive capacity of China's economic transition that was facilitated by policy experimentation.

In general, the internationalisation of the RMB can be regarded as a success story of policy experimentation. Now the question 'What went wrong in 2015 and 2016?' has to be asked. 'Policy experimentation is not equivalent to freewheeling trial and error or spontaneous policy diffusion. It is a purposeful and coordinated activity geared to producing novel policy options' (Heilmann 2008b: 3). In contrast to the development of the offshore market, which can be regarded as a coordinated institutional innovation, the currency debasement of the Chinese yuan, which took place in August 2015, together with the revision and the subsequent alterations in the exchange rate regime as well as the entailed capital flow volatility, resembled trial and error.

In this respect, the events of 2015 and 2016 can be hardly said to have followed the usual forms of experimentation and therefore, uncertainty was projected on a global basis. For instance, the establishment of the local stock exchanges was initially limited to certain areas. 'Most major reform initiatives in post-Mao China were prepared and tried out by means of experimental points before they were universalized in national regulations' (Heilmann 2008b: 7). This does not hold for the events of 2015 and 2016 with respect to the local exchange rate. The changes were introduced abruptly at a time when the stress in the FX market was already high due to the prior build-up of fundamental vulnerabilities.
Historically, experimentation helped to deal with uncertainty and ambiguity in the Chinese economy. By using decentralised experimentation, the central government minimised the risks as well as the costs in case of failure. Local reform efforts, which did not fulfil the political goals, never reached the national policy agenda (Heilmann 2008b). This stands in stark contrast to the troubles China faced in 2015 and 2016. In contrast to the implementation of reforms via experimentation on a local level, the currency distortions in August 2015 and the changes in the FX regime can be regarded as leaps in the dark.

Population Control and Urbanisation

During the time of Mao Zedong, the Chinese population increased significantly. This population growth contributed in turn to economic growth but did not significantly improve living standards. At the beginning of the reform era, at the end of the 1970s, the Chinese government therefore decided to introduce population control measures. These restrictions were globally quite controversial. In particular, the Chinese population on the countryside felt severely restricted in one of their most basic rights (Greenhalgh 2008; Heilmann 20117: 244). China's government stated that these measures prevented about 400 million births between the 1980s and the 2000s. However, this number has been contested due to the negligence of trends in population growth with the development of society (Feng et al. 2013). Not only did the country's population feel deprived of their future, the Chinese government did not foresee the negative effects of the policy on growth. A reduction in the working age population makes it difficult for the country to build-up a social security system. The fertility rate in China is one of the lowest in the entire world (The Economist 2013). Therefore, in the autumn of 2015, China decided that all Chinese couples should be allowed to have a second child. This change in policy could potentially add 1.1mn additional children per year in China according to Kurumlu et al. (2015). This decision had already been announced in the 3rd Plenum in November 2013, but the one-child policy only officially ceased to exist in the latter half of 2015. This new policy has led to a growth boost over the preceding decades since 1979 at the cost of the next generations.

The Economist (2017g) cited the philosopher Auguste Comtes 'Demography is destiny' in its article on China's demographics. More than thirty years after the introduction of China's one-child policy, the country reached one of the lowest fertility rates globally, a mere 1.2 percent. 'The fertility rate is the number of children an average woman can expect to bear during her lifetime. If it is less than 2.1 a population will shrink in the long run' (The Economist 2017g). If this trend continues, China will face a significant shortage of young workers to support the older generation.

As is laid out below, local governments must provide for public services themselves and thus, pension provisions are partly a matter of the provincial administrations. Thus, the burden each province carries depends on the respective demographics. In particular, a low fertility poses significant challenges for local administrations (The Economist 2017g). For instance, the Asian Development Bank (2016) analysed factors determining China's trajectory in the long run. First and foremost, demographic changes must be mentioned with respect to China. The international institution points out that the change in the working age population turned negative in 2012 and the share of population between 15 and 64 topped in 2014. This will pose a fundamental drag on growth, in contrast to the demographic bonus over the previous decades.

In addition, the change in demographics has an overall impact on a country's saving and investment patterns and thus, on its external balances as well. China's old-age dependency ratio is estimated to double within two decades, which will have negative effects on private savings and will increase public spending on social services. The change in demographics is a reflection of China's very low fertility rate. The reason for this dates back to the 1970s as China introduced the one-child policy. As mentioned above, this policy was recently abolished, but the fertility rate remains low (Abiad et al. 2016: 4). In addition, the reduced labour supply in China, due to decades of the one-child policy, will lead to rising labour costs and thus, reduced competitiveness in Chinese exports. This is known as the highly debated Lewis turning point, which when crossed, leads to a slower growth rate of the economy (Sharma 2012: 6) representing a significant vulnerability from an early warning perspective.

As a matter of fact, the demographic change China experienced in 2010 closely resembles what Japan went through in the early 1980s. Further similarities between Japan's experience and China's current state are excessive equity valuations, financial liberalisation as well as excessive leverage in the corporate sector, which are addressed in different parts of this book. Differences are China's global presence as well as urbanisation ratios and human capital among others (Baba et al. 2016: 1; Kim and Yamakawa 2005: 5). The vulnerabilities Japan faced in the 1990s led to a financial crisis and to two lost decades for the country. When a country faces a peak in its working age population, economic growth tends to lose momentum as the social burden increases and overcapacity becomes a severe issue.

With respect to China, in the decades after the country introduced the one-child policy, the nation profited from a demographic dividend. 'The per-person social burden for the working age population declines, the saving rate rises, and the economy can channel their savings into investments. As the proportion of elderly citizens rises, however, the social burden of caring for the elderly increases and eventually surpasses the positive effect of the decline in social burden due to the lower birth rate' (Baba et al. 2016: 3). Moreover, the peak in the demographic dividend seems to coincide with equity valuations. Both Japan and China experienced severe excesses in capital markets, which bursting of the bubbles dragged down both countries (Baba et al. 2016: 4). The excessive extrapolation of good times is one of the primary mistakes applied by financial analysts and investors alike.

Gong (2016) split a country's development into two stages. The idea for this approach is related to President Xi's term "new normal" of May 2014, which refers to China's growth rate, as well as to the term "middle-income trap" labelled by Gill et al. (2007). Keeping the notion of two stages of economic development in mind, Gong (2016) explains both phenomena with the help of the turning point literature (e.g. Lewis 1954). The researcher notes that urbanisation is one vital factor in the catch-up process of developing countries. This is related to the so-called Lewis Turning Point, which refers to the stage in a country's catch-up process when labour surplus is no longer available and thus, any further expansion will lead to wage increases (Gong 2016: 5). One notable difference between China and Japan is the urbanisation ratio. In his paper, 'Economic development with unlimited supplies of labor', Arthur Lewis (1954) explores the relationship between economic growth and urbanisation. Lewis showed the migration of parts of the rural population to urban centers spurs economic growth as this shift from the agricultural sector to the manufacturing and services industry goes along with increased value-added for the economy (Baba et al. 2016: 8-9). In China, urbanisation was restricted with the help of internal passports during the Maoist period; the country only benefited from this factor as of the end of the 1970s. When the catch-up process due to urbanisation is exhausted, any further growth must be related to technological progress or efficiency in general. This is known as total factor productivity. However, the way a country can catch up via technological progress is also transformed. First, a country can simply import foreign technology and profit from the advantages of backwardness. Imitation and adoption spur economic growth in this stage of the development. Second, at some point a country needs to invest in its own research & development capabilities, which is a more difficult way to progress. This led to the term middle-income trap (Gong 2016: 7) and is examined in more detail in the sections on fundamentals and institutions.

Poverty Reduction, Inequality and Stability

China depicts a fairly complex relationship between economic performance, inequality and poverty. The former has been the highest in urban areas of the coastal regions, while rural households in western and northern parts of China did not do particularly well. China grew at a tremendous rate over the last decades, but became more unequal, which should yield a warning signal. 'Within China an increasingly widespread perception holds that society is less equal than it used to be and less fair than it should be' (Naughton 2007: 209). Indeed, China's trajectory can be split into two different paths, namely one rural as well as one urban. The urban-rural gap is the most visible sign of inequality in the country. Due to the reforms on the countryside, real growth on the countryside exceeded the performance in urban areas. This lasted approximately until the mid-1980s, when the situation turned around. It has to be mentioned that the official data quality during this time is rather unreliable (Naughton 2007: 211). In general, economic growth leads to a reduction in the absolute level of poverty in a country. Official statistics paint a picture of a substantial reduction in poverty from the start of the reform era to 1985. Even though the speed of poverty reduction slowed down after the mid-1980s, the number of Chinese living below the poverty line gradually decreased. One caveat of the official Chinese statistics is that the local cut-off level – the poverty line – is set lower in China than globally. This is critical because there exists a very large number of people which have income very close to the Chinese poverty line and thus, the threshold level is a political critical mean for adjusting official statistics. People living close to the Chinese poverty line are very likely to suffer from malnutrition (Ravallion and Chen 2004). Ravallion and Chen (2004) adjust the official Chinese statistics for some of the biases and find that the total number of Chinese living in poverty is larger during the whole sample period. Still, poverty was alleviated to great extent in China. The initial sharp reduction in rural poverty can be deduced to the distribution of land to households at the beginning of the reform period, which meant that a floor for intra-village poverty was established. The reduction in poverty slowed down after the mid-1980s, which led to the establishment of the Leading Group for Poverty Reduction in 1986, which identified particularly poor areas in China designated for increased state-support. Park et al. (2002) found that this support raised economic performance significantly in the relevant provinces.

Since China opened up its markets for trade, it is the cities that have primarily benefited from the new source of growth (Naughton 2007: 212-216) pointing to the topic of inequality. In the Maoist era, China's society can be described as dualistic, but egalitarian. Income levels across the society were fairly equal within the respective sectors in rural and urban areas. The successful reforms in the rural regions at the end of the 1970s led to a higher level of equality in the mid-1980s than during the Maoist era. As a measure of income distribution, the Gini coefficient is often used, which can take a value between 0 and 1. At the lower bound of the range, the distribution is fairly equal, while the closer the measure approaches one the more unequal the society is. Since the mid-1980s, a steady rise in the Gini coefficient can be observed. Urban residents were favoured in terms of education and access to capital (Naughton 2007: 217-220). Today, China is among the most unequal societies given the Gini coefficient (Atkinson 2015: 22), which is an important issue for the Chinese leadership given their preference for stability in the social as well as in the financial and economic sphere. Thus, the Gini coefficient serves as one variable in the quantification of an early warning system in this book.

ii) Monetary Policy

China's investment and export driven growth was fostered at the cost of savers and thus, China is a prime example of financial repression (McKinnon 1973; Gruin 2013; Heep 2014). 'The central bank ensured that state-owned enterprises were able to receive financing at favourable rates by placing a ceiling on deposit rates and a floor on lending rates' (Heilmann 2017: 216). The spread between these two rates secured the profitability of the banks. However, as described in the institutional section, financial liberalisation led to the abolishment of the floor on lending rates in 2013 and the cancellation of the ceiling on deposit rates in 2015. These changes have far-reaching consequences for monetary policymaking. These consequences also extend to the CCP's grip on the economy as a whole, 'since the ability to steer policy is vested in the state-owned enterprises and financial institutions, which are tightly linked to the CCP and the government through their managerial staff and ownership rights' (Heilmann 2017: 217). The financial reforms sped up in 2015 (Heep 2015) and will be further touched upon in the institutional section as these are crucial determinants of the early warning analysis.

China's monetary policy framework has changed significantly over the last decades given liberalisation. However, certain unique traits of monetary policymaking remain in place, namely the crucial role of the Chinese government in allocating resources via the ownership of commercial banks, which must be understood within the country's history. Moreover, the People's Bank of China is still subordinated to the Chinese State Council in terms of decision-making. Furthermore, the PBoC's Monetary Policy Committee, which meets quarterly, only serves as a consultative body with no decision-authority (BoAML 2016: 30; Chen et al. 2017: 24). Thus, the objectives of the PBoC are more or less the same as the economic goals of the Chinese government, namely growth at a low rate of inflation as well as employment and stability in the country's external balances including the local exchange rate. The State Council decides on policy stances at the Central Economic Work Conference in December; however, policies may change during the year if necessary (BoAML 2016: 30-31; Heilmann 2017). This flexibility within a coherent framework is crucial for the country.

To achieve the annual targets of the Chinese government, which are announced every March at the National People's Congress (NPC) meeting, the PBoC targets broad monetary aggregates since 1998. M2 is the key macroeconomic indicator for the Chinese monetary policy, which is managed via the adjustment of base money with the help of a short-term interest rate corridor as well as various lending facilities. The M2 target is usually set as the real GDP growth rate plus CPI in addition to 2-3 percentage points for the monetisation process (BoAML 2016: 31). In addition, credit management supports this policy making primarily via benchmark deposit and lending rates as well as via different reserve requirement ratios (RRRs) and various other guidelines (Chen et al. 2017: 24-25). This fractional reserve banking system is set up to provide liquidity for banks, which should engage in lending for instance. The management of base money helps the PBoC to target broad monetary aggregates and thus to secure liquidity in the system. Due to the partial liberalisation, the PBoC included interbank rates, foremost the 7-day repo rate, in its base money supply adjustment procedures. This was initially done after the liquidity squeeze in the interbank market at the end of 2013 and the beginning of 2014 (Chen et al. 2017: 25-26). Indeed, the more active use of repos indicates that the PBoC is moving to the management of a short-term market interest rate. Moreover, the PBoC established a Macro Prudential Assessment framework, which helps the central bank in its credit management (BoAML 2016: 34). As of 2006, the PBoC has used adjustments in the RRR for sterilisation purposes given significant changes in FX reserves. However, this became less important as the Chinese central bank showed some reluctance to fully normalise RRRs due to the risk of capital outflows. Instead, the central bank used open market transactions (OMOs) such as repos in addition to various other liquidity-providing facilities in order to achieve its goals (Chen et al. 2017: 26).

Given the partial liberalisation of China's capital and financial accounts, the PBoC's framework had to adapt over recent years. Capital outflow pressure as well as the need for exchange rate management made an independent monetary policy impossible. 'If it wants to prevent the RMB from depreciating much without depleting its FX reserves, China will have to tolerate higher domestic interest rates. With tighter capital controls, China can insulate domestic rates from the impact of external factors to a large extent, but any impact cannot be entirely eliminated' (Chen et al. 2017: 27). Regarding monetary aggregates, M2 is the most important indicator, which is comprised of RMB cash and deposits of the private sector as well as institutions other than banks. At the end of 2016, China's M2-to-GDP ratio reached a level of 208 percent, making it one of the highest of major economies. M2 can be targeted by the central bank indirectly via base money and credit, which in return influences China's asset prices. Given financial liberalisation, M2 has become more inaccurate in measuring liquidity in the economy due to the emergence of wealth management products. This is also reflected in the country's divergence between M1 and M2. In China, M1 encompasses corporate and institution's demand deposits, which tends to pick-up in line with corporate profitability and spending. Therefore, a pick-up of M1 tends to coincide with a strong equity market performance in China. However, this relationship did not hold in 2015 and 2016 as WMPs gave a false picture of the situation (Chen et al. 2017: 31; Chang et al. 2016: 3). This underlines the importance of shadow financing activities.

Given China's vulnerabilities, particularly its high level of debt, liquidity management to prevent a Minsky moment is key (Chen et al. 2017: 32). Therefore, new regulations, necessary to make the system sustainable, must gradually be introduced. Indeed, China's vulnerabilities led authorities to tighten regulations significantly in 2016. 'This development ultimately heightened credit market sensitivity to tighter bank funding rules and market liquidity conditions, further exacerbating December's bond market correction' (Chen et al. 2017: 33). Thus, to counter the slowdown China faced in the aftermath of the great financial crisis, the country cut its benchmark lending rate by 165 basis points as well as eased real estate policies in 2015 and early 2016 (IMF 2017: 5). The IMF (2017: 5) estimates that the general government net borrowing increased by 23/4 percent of GDP between 2014 and 2016, which in turn helped the country to contain the troubles faced during this period.

Moreover, China addressed problems related to overcapacity in certain industrial sectors and restructured some ailing state-owned enterprises, which also contributed to the stabilisation of the situation (IMF 2017: 5). The above-mentioned measures worked that well that China had to tighten controls again in the second half of 2016 and the beginning of 2017.

iii) Fiscal Policy as well as Creditability Issues

Since the 1980s, China has tried to build a state taxation and budgetary system. In the planned economy, the Chinese state's financial power was derived from the profitability of the SOEs. Provincial governments sent the collected funds to the central government, which then made the decisions about as to how the funds would be spent. After the death of Mao, the reform of the state-owned enterprise sector led to less revenue for the Chinese central government (Wong and Bird 2008). This issue was partly addressed in the reform of the taxation system in 1994. However, crucial topics remain unresolved. Provincial governments in China are responsible for providing public services such as health care or road building. However, since the transfer payments from the Chinese central government were not sufficient to cover these expenses, the local governments had to raise funds themselves as laid out in the conceptual section.

To complicate things further, until 2014 these local governments were forbidden to officially get into debt, which led to hidden channels of fund raising. During the great financial crisis in particular, the local governments were requested to support the Chinese economy via spending programmes, which led to the heavy indebtedness of some provinces (Heilmann 2017: 107-108). The debt burden has become a serious issue in China as described in the section on fundamentals. 'At the same time, the lack of transparency in the use of extra-budgetary funding has opened the way for uncontrolled appropriations, corruption, and the accumulation of debt' (Heilmann 2017: 109), which should have issued a signal in any early warning system analysis.

A revised budget law tried to address these issues in 2014. During this year, China also went through a change in policy as the country experienced one of the first corporate defaults in the SOE sector, which trend continued in 2015 and 2016. Before these events, only insignificant corporate borrowers could go bankrupt and any of the larger corporations were one way or another saved by the state (The Economist 2015b). This shift in policy might be difficult to manage for China and thus, the trend should be closely watched and managed by China to avoid severer disruptions. Many transition economies faced severe downturns while going through such changes and therefore, history would suggest to closely monitor the reallocation of resources.

Another point that makes the situation more complex, as indicated above, is the trust deficit that China suffers from. China is suspected of deceiving certain stakeholders and observers in order to reach the country's objectives (Buzan and Cox 2013: 115). Since legitimacy is derived from economic growth, many official economic headline numbers are carefully monitored by the Chinese government. Fiscal deficits from provinces or purchasing manager indexes serve as excellent leading indicators for an economy and thus, can entice confidence or uncertainty in the market. For instance, in late 2015, the Markit's flash indicator, as well as the China Minxin purchasing manager index, suddenly were not published anymore. As both purchasing manager indexes previously indicated that the Chinese economy would head into a recession, the trust deficit with respect to China was further increased (Bloomberg 2015c). The high level of opacity and the lack of transparency in already uncertain times increased the doubt of capital markets exponentially (De Jonquieres 2013: 11). The unpredictability of China's policy leads observers to factor in a greater risk premium for many aspects related to China.

As Thomas Orlik (2012: 4) notes, 'Some things have stayed the same in the last 50 years, but a lot has changed'. The conflict of interest between reporting accurate numbers and career progress is still present today, as demonstrated by The Economist (2017a). Over the last decades, the 1998 controversy over China's output growth remains the most well-known example. Among others, Rawski (2001) criticised official Chinese data.

However, the Chinese government never admitted any wrongdoing. Ironically, during the statistical revisions in 2004, this data point was the only one that remained unchanged. Premier Zhu Rongji referred to this as a 'wind of embellishment and falsification' (Orlik 2012: 15). Another recent example was presented by an article published by The Economist (2017a). In its article, 'A big Chinese province admits faking its economic data', the economic magazine commented on the reliability problem of official statistics. The province Liaoning overreported its fiscal data from 2011 to 2014, with reporting revenues about 20 percent higher than incurred. As early as the 2000s, Li Keqiang, the current Chinese prime minister, said to the US ambassador that China's GDP figures are man-made and unreliable. Indeed, China is often accused of engaging in deception strategies, particularly regarding economic data. The province Liaoning was also accused of meddling with investment numbers when their fixed-asset investment dropped 63 percent from 2015 to 2016. This drop dragged down the overall investment rate of China and might have led to policymakers engaging in excessive stimulus. The drop in fixed-asset investment reported by the province Liaoning might simply be related to overreported numbers in the previous years (The Economist 2017a).

Another aspect of this data problem is that the National Bureau of Statistics (NBS) does not yet fully shift towards the service sector and smaller companies providing added value in their publications (Wu 2014). In addition, neither the NBS nor the local governments, which provide data, are independent from the influence of the Chinese government, which in turn causes people to not fully trust the supplied data. Career paths in the Chinese society crucially depend on whether growth targets are met. Powerful incentives to cover up shortfalls provide for significant problems in the statistical data set (Holz 2014) and thus be considered in the build-up of an early warning system.
Nowadays, the NBS does not rely solely on inputs from provincial governments, which has led to an improvement in the data quality, although China still has some way to go. The issue only can be resolved when 'the benefits of supplying credible data are greater than the costs of reporting an unwelcome reality' (Orlik 2012: 4). Nevertheless, given

this uncertainty, alternative indicators are often used to validate official statistics. One of these indicators is the Li Keqiang index, which takes into account measures such as electricity consumption, freight traffic and bank lending (Heilmann 2017: 199). However, many of the alternative economic assessments primarily focus on heavy industry, which is a problem due to the structural shift in the Chinese economy as explained in the previous section.

iv) Soft Factors that Generate Tangible Outcomes

The soft factors, which I apply to the dependent variable, namely the currency debasement of the Chinese yuan, which took place in August 2015, together with the revision and the subsequent alterations in the exchange rate regime as well as the entailed capital flow volatility, are legitimacy and status as well as ideational factors. For the soft determinates no quantification is derived; instead, these factors are analysed with the examination of over five hundred research reports.

Legitimacy and Status

Financial crises do not only lead to significant economic costs but also entail political dislocations. For instance, the Asian financial crisis of the 1990s and the counteracting measures led to social and political disorder in these countries. The austerity and the entailing reduction in food and fuel subsidies in Indonesia during difficult times led to significant disruptions. The liberalising policies prescribed by many advisors to the affected governments further aggravated the situation, particularly for those members of society who already felt victimized. The subsequent political and social unrest fuelled vicious spirals and undermined already battered investor confidence (Stiglitz 2002: 119). In fact, the social disorder resulting from crises is closely related to the legitimacy of a country's leadership, which should be monitored closely. How legitimate is a country's government if they cannot provide basic goods and services for the poor? Can leadership be legitimate if only the strong prosper? Quah (2013: 18-21) points out that a reduction in inequality is a vital step towards making a country's growth path sustainable and leads to a higher level of social justice. The researcher points out that an increased level of state-sponsored investment, in particular in rural areas in China, would result in a significant reduction in inequality, which in return would also support the Chinese leadership's legitimacy.

In fact, if the Chinese system faces severe disruptions, one of the first things, which would vanish, is the local population's perception of a superior state capitalist system in China (Sharma 2012: 6). Historically, the evaporation of a leadership's legitimacy has almost always been a step backward in a country's trajectory. Thus, Xi Jinping significantly tightened control of the Chinese leadership and tackled corruption via various campaigns as China's Gorbachev moment is not welcomed by the country's government (De Jonquieres 2014: 6). China's economic success is one of the principals the legitimacy of the country's elites is built on and stands in stark contrast to the failed transformation of the former Soviet Union. However, the past decades of double-digit growth rates have led to the extrapolation of the improvements achieved by Chinese citizens. This means that any subsequent economic downturn might make the debt burden unsustainable, which would in turn lead to social turmoil and the demand for a change in leadership. Therefore, the drive to safeguard the country's economic success is inherently related to the Chinese elite's survival. Performance-based legitimacy is the government's only justification for its grip on power (De Jonquieres 2014: 1-2). This explains the determination of the CCP in terms of achieving its development targets.

Indeed, the incredible economic success of China in the decades after Mao's death made the country the primary symbol of Jim O'Neill's acronym BRICs, as introduced in one of his research reports in 2001. The importance of China's positive economic development cannot be denied. The country is well aware of this fact as it could also be seen in Xi Jinping's trip to Shenzhen. This trip was the first one since the new leadership of the CCP took over and is reflective of Deng Xiaoping's journey to this SEZ. Xi Jinping is also convinced that the fundamental strength of China is inevitably connected to the country's economy. At the same time as engaging in economic reforms and further fostering China's economy, Xi Jinping also decided to hold a strong grip on political power (Breslin 2013b: 2). Nevertheless, it goes without saying that the Chinese government's legitimacy was tainted by the recent economic downturn, collapse of equity markets and the mini-devaluation of the Chinese yuan in mid-2015. The latter further reinforced the ambiguity of the situation and capital outflows out of China increased sharply in mid-2015 (The Economist 2016b).

An economic slowdown accompanied by a severe downturn in capital markets led to global ripple effects in the form of uncertainty in 2015. The devaluation of the yuan against the US dollar in August 2015 further contributed to the turmoil and sparked fears of competitive devaluations in Asia (Nurske 1944). The Chinese government was forced to intervene in local capital markets in order to stabilise the situation. A circuit breaker was needed to stop the asset prices from getting out of control (The Economist 2016c). China faced increased challenges from capital markets such as asset price bubbles or the build-up of debt. To counter this, Xi Jinping introduced a variety of reforms with the aim of stabilising and ultimately rebalancing the economy (De Jonquieres 2014: 1). These reforms included the increased opening of the capital account as well as the domestic financial sector and the reforms of state-led enterprises among others (De Jonquieres 2014: 4). The SDR inclusion by the IMF further enticed China to engage in pro-market reforms. Volume-wise, this inclusion was not significant. However, the global perception of the Chinese currency changed due to the SDR inclusion and enticed the Chinese leadership to give the market a greater say in the fixing of the onshore yuan. The SDR inclusion led China to embrace a more market friendly regime. In fact, the IMF helped China to escape from its past stigma and labelled the Chinese currency as freely convertible (The Economist 2015c). This must be seen in light of the historical background laid out in the previous section.

What exactly were the detailed events regarding the SDR inclusion? In October 2015, the IMF stated that the institution would support the SDR inclusion of the RMB with the decision being made at the end of

November the same year. The IMF labelled the Chinese currency as 'freely usable' as the initial doubts by the IMF staff had been addressed (Chen et al. 2015a). On 30 November 2015, the IMF decided to include the RMB as one of its reserve currencies. The weight of the yuan was determined at 10.92 percent in the basket, which should become effective as of October 2016. The RMB was included as the 5th currency in the basket, which allocates the highest weights to USD and EUR (Chang et al. 2015b). There were two criteria for including the RMB in the basket. First, the currency had to have been used for trade-related transactions, a criterion which the Chinese currency clearly fulfilled. Second, the respective currency had to be freely convertible. The fulfilment of this criterion was questionable. The decision by the IMF to include the RMB in the SDR basket was primarily politically driven, as the IMF wanted to pull China closer in its sphere (Barry Eichengreen quoted in Chang and Fernandez 2015: 2). The inclusion of the Chinese currency should have encouraged the country to be part of the Bretton Woods system instead of investing further in separate international institutions and represents a historical inflection point as China refused to engage with the IMF over many decades as laid out in the section 'Crises in Perspective'.

China had committed itself to opening its capital account and thus, to internationalise the RMB. 'RMB internationalisation is partly a vanity project, in that it matters more to the political elite and the financial sector than it does to the Chinese economy. However, it is also part of the larger process of rebalancing the Chinese economy away from state direction, since a more flexible exchange rate and a more open capital account are concomitants of both rebalancing and RMB internationalisation' (Barry Eichengreen quoted in Chang and Fernandez 2015: 2). The aforementioned is a sign of status being an important driver of outcomes. In the conceptual section, status is linked to concepts such as prestige, for instance, and in doing so, entices certain actions. As troubles hit China, the country had to monitor the trade-off between opening the country while partially reversing previous steps of liberalising the capital account in order to keep the situation under control. The above-mentioned example should demonstrate that even in case of materially adverse outcomes, status can prevail, and is thus a crucial driver of outcomes (Wohlforth and Kang 2009: 3-4). Hurrell (2009) summarises his thoughts on status as follows, 'status is centrally about the legal or political standing of a state as determined by its membership in some class, category, or grouping…a concern with the principles and criteria by which states were able to enter international society and be accepted as sovereign members of the society of states'. The SDR inclusion, as described above, entailed significant value for the Chinese leadership in the form of status. The membership in a selective group enticed China to take steps closer to a new economic system, which should have attracted proper attention from an early warning perspective analysis.

Ideational Factors

The Asian financial crisis of the 1990s has to be regarded as a formative experience for Chinese policymakers. The dangers of various vulnerabilities became visible as movements in exchange rates delegitimised as well as destabilised sovereign nations and their governments (Minkin and Lau 2013). In the aftermath of said crisis, China embarked upon a set of reforms concerning its financial system including the refurbishment of the Chinese Central Bank as well as state-owned banks. 'Given the rapid assaults on Asian currencies during the crisis, the critical threat to the stability of these nations' financial systems appeared to come from speculative capital flows, which were facilitated by currency convertibility on the capital account. Fixed exchange rate regimes always appeared vulnerable to attacks from international speculators' (Wright 2009: 20). The uncertainty of the different exchange rate regimes and their ultimate benefits and drawbacks in light of capital flow volatility made Chinese policymakers susceptible to the influence of ideational factors. Conditions of uncertainty can lead to ideas being more important than interests (Blyth 2002). Ideas in times of severe uncertainty provide a framework for understanding the nature of crisis. This was very much valid with respect to the exchange rate reforms in China in 2005 as well as for the events taking place in 2015 and 2016.

'These ideas were the shared causal beliefs concerning the power of speculative capital flows and the difficulty of sustaining fixed exchange rate regimes' (Wright 2009: 21-22). This was made possible by the consensus-driven politics of Hu Jintao and Wen Jiabao, which enabled the considerable influence of international norms regarding flexible exchange rates (Goldstein and Lardy 2008a). Short-term costs due to the change in the FX regime accrued to the Chinese banking system as well as to the export sector in 2005. Nonetheless, the formative experience of the Asian financial crisis as well as the international consensus regarding flexible exchange rates determined China's interests. 'Under conditions of considerable uncertainty regarding the effects of ending the yuan's peg to the dollar, the ideas that emerged from the formative experience of the Asian financial crisis played a critical role in influencing Chinese leaders' perceptions of the state's economic interests in the long term. Fixed exchange rate regimes were viewed as eventually unsustainable while flexible exchange rate regimes would permit Chinese leaders additional autonomy in monetary policy to manage the domestic effects of the new threat of capital inflows' (Wright 2009: 23). Both the formative experience of the Asian financial crisis, which played a crucial role in driving the outcome of the change in the FX regime in July 2005, and ideational factors driven by international financial institutions were vital components. 'The influence of global financial institutions operated at multiple levels, both by socializing China's central bankers into a worldview privileging monetary policy flexibility in a world of capital mobility and by creating incentives for China's high-level leadership to present China's economy as consistent with standard global economic practices rather than standing outside them' (Wright 2009: 11). These incentives include status or reputation as drivers of outcomes (Wohlforth and Kang 2009: 3).

This is also valid for the events of 2015 and 2016. In the absence of global norms, the Chinese exchange rate reform of 2015 would not have occurred. Nonetheless, the exchange rate reform likely slowed down China's capital account liberalisation as policymakers had to reimpose capital controls due to flow volatility. It must also be mentioned that China's engagement with the international system carried considerable risks for the domestic economy given the fragility of the financial institutions. Also, the formative experience of the global financial crisis played an important role in the decision to alter the exchange rate regime in August 2015. Fixed exchange rate regimes played a role in building up macroeconomic imbalances in 2008 and 2009 and therefore, ideas regarding a more flexible exchange rate were crucial with respect to the decision to alter the exchange rate regime. However, this is not equal to a more efficient exchange rate system as is clearly visible with the events which took place in China in 2015 and 2016.

To conclude, the troubles China faced in mid-2015 and 2016 are a materialisation of certain risks. 'We saw how the risk of capital flight can be heightened by policy missteps on the part of the Chinese authorities' (Barry Eichengreen quoted in Chang and Fernandez 2015: 3). China had not yet invested enough in checks and balances to keep any arbitrary actions by policymakers under control (Barry Eichengreen quoted in Chang and Fernandez 2015: 4), which leads us to the topic of institutions.

c) Institutional Weakness

Regarding the institutional dimension, China still has some way to go. The build-up of inclusive institutions together with the further strengthening of a coherent economic framework are necessary steps for China to safeguard a sustainable long-term growth trajectory. This leads us to the third dimension of the theoretical framework and the application to China during 2015 and 2016.

Acemoglu and Robinson (2013: 439) show that the build-up of inclusive institutions is a prerequisite for safeguarding the success of a country via the establishment of a consistent set of rules. The period of economic transition has fostered growth, but also led to widespread corruption. China needs to discourage any forms of predatory rent seeking at the same time as continuing its successful way of transition. This is only possible if the country manages to establish a set of rules that creates a level playing field for all members of that society and provides equal economic opportunities to a wide range of people. Only this can help the country to make its emergence more sustainable and reduce the externalities of its success story. Therefore, the institutional dimension should receive appropriate attention in a unified early warning system analysis, which helps to spot financial crises. Cox (2012: 375) hints at significant institutional weaknesses in the Chinese system that need to be tackled. Among these fragilities are most notably poor intellectual property rights and a high degree of inward orientation of Chinese companies. Due to the curtailments of the rights of the Chinese civil society, the system in China can be hardly described as fostering innovation or creativity, which has been a primary impediment of China's development. Effective institutions are the basis for the aforementioned and thus, institutionalisation should be one of the priorities for the Chinese government. The institutional dimension is key for safeguarding a sustainable trajectory of a country.

Regarding the liberalisation of a country's system, prior research has shown that an effective institutional system can significantly mitigate the negative effects of this. Paris (2004: 204) describes this notion as 'comprehensive economic liberalization should be delayed while the governmental and legal frameworks needed to regulate a market economy are being established'. As shown in the historical background section, premature liberalisation can have negative consequences (Goldstein 1998: 66) and thus, liberalisation is one key variable in the early warning system. Indeed, China engaged in financial liberalisation as Japan did in the 1980s. However, this liberalisation is a double-edged sword and led to the build-up of severe fragilities and imbalances. The relationship between crises and financial liberalisation was documented by Kaminsky and Reinhart (1998). In their research, they show that financial crises are quite likely to occur within a period of 5 years of liberalisation because excessive lending and bubbles in asset prices usually accompany this process. Furthermore, Claessens et al. (2014) point to the badly sequencing of deregulation and financial liberalisation as significant drivers for financial crises. To address these vulnerabilities, Jones and Underhill (2014) describe an institutional set-up, which allows for smooth financial integration. By using the theory of an optimal financial era (OFA), the researchers deduce an institutional framework, which decreases the malaise related to capital significantly and therefore, helps to contain the institutional weaknesses of a country.

Capital flow volatility is an underestimated side effect of liberalisation, which is frequently cited when thinking about the institutional set-up of a country (Stiglitz 2002: 100). The pro-cyclical nature of capital flows makes its management especially challenging. Such a feature is not desirable for a country as every economic state is reinforced by monetary flows. An economic downturn is reinforced by capital outflows and periods of growth are supported by inflows, sometimes to a degree that asset bubbles build-up. This feature of capital flows leads to a high level of correlation with the business cycle of a country (Reinhart and Rogoff 2009: 31). Reinhart and Rogoff (2009: 80-81) show that solvency problems of countries often follow high levels of capital inflows. The prior borrowing spree often turns out to have been imprudent, which leads to financial crisis. In addition, FX debasements often precede these events. Therefore, sequencing matters with respect to liberalisation. The build-up of effective institutions has to be given priority over the opening of a country's capital account.

Reinhart and Rogoff (2009: 30) relate a country's growth trajectory to 'institutions, corruption, and governance'. China needs a coherent and effective framework in order to mitigate the negative effects of opening the country and subsequently, to reduce any blowbacks from liberalisation. Inefficient resource allocation has to be tackled by China, but not at the cost of economic and political stability. 'Economic liberalization without attention to domestic stability [...] is likely to prevent successful economic and political adjustment', as Thomas Callaghy (1993: 165) noted. Therefore, the build-up of an inclusive institutional system is a prerequisite for China's future success. The Chinese leadership should see the previous from the perspective of stability (Gruin 2016: 26), which would help the CCP to manage uncertainty, not only domestically, but also on a global level.

I proceed by applying the factors of the institutional dimension, as laid out in the conceptual section, to China's troubles in the second half of 2015 and 2016. Thus, I demonstrate that the dependent variable – the currency debasement of the Chinese yuan, which took place in August 2015, together with the revision and the subsequent alterations in the exchange rate regime as well as the entailed capital flow volatility – can be better understood with the help of these variables. In more detail, liberalisation, factors related to China's FX regime, the international monetary system, governance and the rule of law, the SOE reform as well as technology and productivity play a role in the subsequent analysis. This helps stakeholders to better understand the holistic picture of China's unfinished transition and that efforts of China should aim at addressing underlying vulnerabilities.

i) Internationalisation of the RMB and Capital Account Liberalisation

The internationalisation of the RMB is inevitably linked to the build-up of the CNH offshore market, which was announced in 2003 and started in 2004 when foreign customers were allowed to buy RMB in Hong Kong (BoAML 2016: 40; Goldman Sachs Research 2013b). The "dim sum bond market", which is the name given to the offshore RMB bond market in Hong Kong, was established in 2007. However, the offshore market took a couple of years to take off. Between 2009 and 2010, the onshore trade transactions could be settled in CNH in Hong Kong, which significantly helped the internationalisation of the RMB. This spurred cross-border flows between onshore China and Hong Kong and eventually led to the build-up of CNH deposits by Chinese export companies dealing in global markets. Moreover, direct investment could be settled in the offshore renminbi in 2011. That same year, the RQFII was introduced. Under this scheme, foreign investors were allowed to make onshore equity and fixed income investments and pay for these investments with offshore RMB. The latter represented a step towards financial account liberalisation. In 2013, an offshore bond market was also established in Taiwan, which became to be known as the "Formosa bond market". In addition to the internationalisation of the RMB, various measures to safeguard the liquidity of the offshore market were also introduced. The CNH HIBOR, the interbank interest rate fixing, was introduced in 2013 (Goldman Sachs Research 2013b) and became an important device for liquidity management.

Even though an onshore and an offshore market exist, the Chinese RMB is one currency. However, capital controls hinder perfect arbitrage between the countries and thus, RMB spot rates may differ depending on the market conditions. In addition, there is also a spread between the onshore and offshore interest rates. Nonetheless, the offshore renminbi tends to trade quite closely to the CNY. However, in cases of heightened capital market volatility, the basis between USD/CNH and USD/CNY tends to widen. Market stress leads to higher demand for USD in the offshore market, which in turn leads USD/CNH to trade higher and, naturally, widens the basis (Barclays 2012: 15). For instance, in 2011, the offshore and the onshore renminbi market traded at a significant spread to each other for the first time. In this year, the flows between Mainland China and Hong Kong also significantly increased (Barclays 2012: 4). The onshore and offshore renminbi differ in how the currency trades are settled. USD/CNY non-deliverable forward (NDF) trades settle daily against the CFETS USD/CNY fixing and the USD/CNH forward trades are settled against the fixing of the Treasury Markets Association (TMA) (Barclays 2012: 17).

The aforementioned ultimately leads to the question with respect to China's progress regarding capital and financial account liberalisation. Capital controls have prevented onshore and offshore interest rates from converging in China. The country's regular widening of the FX band was an important step towards liberalisation. The Chinese government began to take this topic seriously as of 2013. So far, China has resisted pressure from Western stakeholders to liberalise the exchange rate and capital as well as financial accounts, which historically had significantly improved the country's resilience to shocks. The risks of higher capital flow volatility are significant, as shown in the analytical framework, and thus the sequencing of reforms is a vital topic for China (Goldman Sachs Research 2013a). With respect to liberalisation of the RMB bond market, China decided to further open the market to foreign investors in February 2015. As a result, bond investment quotas were abolished for qualified foreign institutional investors (Liu 2016). In order for institutional investors to get access to the onshore bond market, the custodians of the investors now needed to register their clients with the

PBoC. The liberalisation of the Chinese bond market applied to both QFII and RQFII investors (Liu 2016). The PBoC introduced the QFII in 2002, which allowed approved investors to buy onshore exchange-traded bonds. As access to the interbank bond market was granted via quotas, the scheme was significantly expanded in 2012. In contrast to QFII, RQFII relates to offshore RMB invested in China via quotas (BoAML 2016: 37). Both schemes are related to capital flow volatility and thus, are important in early warning system analysis.

'China approved the aim to "gradually achieve convertibility of the renminbi under capital accounts" in its Twelfth Five-Year Plan. The Third Plenum in November 2013 was effectively seen to have outlined a blueprint for foreign exchange reforms, giving the green light for a more rapid progress' (Kotecha and Pepper 2014: 2). In early 2014, the country's FX regulator, the State Administration of Foreign Exchange, underlined the goal of speeding-up reforms with respect to CNY convertibility. It is important to note that while China's economic integration since the 1980s has been remarkable, the country's financial integration has overall been a calculated and cautious move (Kotecha and Pepper 2014: 2), which can be termed as 'feeling for the stones as one crosses the river', as described in the historical background section. This cautiousness could be the reason why China has been so successful with respect to avoiding financial crises.

Empirical research by He et al. (2012) and by Sedik and Sun (2012) estimate that in case of a full capital and financial account liberalisation, the outflows from China would substantially increase due to risk diversification demands from locals. How can China's capital account openness be measured? One possibility would be by summing up China's external assets and liabilities. By looking at this measure relative to other nations, Kotecha and Pepper (2014: 3) conclude that China's capital controls are still very tight. Moreover, capital and financial account openness could also be measured by the Chinn-Ito index (Chinn and Ito 2008), which counts the number of transactions that are subject to any kind of restrictions. This also supports the conclusion by Kotecha and Pepper (2014) that China's financial openness is still relatively restricted. Given the above, an increased financial openness in China could potentially lead to significant capital outflows and thus, to a banking crisis in the country if not carefully managed. In addition, FX weakness would further aggravate the situation through various channels. These risks should not be underestimated.

In August 2015, China devalued its exchange rate. Regarding the new fixing mechanism, the PBoC stated that the market would have a greater say in determining the local exchange rate. Consequently, market makers had to submit their quotations of the previous day's closing price of USD/CNY. The new fixing was then based on this data. In fact, the fixing was composed of a weighted average of these submitted quotations, which was then determined by the China Foreign Exchange Trading System (CFETS), a PBoC's subordinate. However, the aforementioned does not mean that the band of +/-2 percent disappeared (Buiter et al. 2015: 2), but that the yuan trades closer to a managed float now.

The Chinese government's liberalisation increased market volatility. The collapse in the equity market and the severe stress in the foreign exchange system were obvious signs of the potential consequences of the sudden and rash introduction of liberalisation to a system. The institutional quotas for foreign investors opened a window for capital flows and the connection between onshore and offshore equity markets also meant increased volatility (Buiter et al. 2015: 3). The equity markets were in bubble territory due to the increased flows. From June 2014 to June 2015, equity markets rose more than 150 percent before ultimately collapsing. The Chinese government had to intervene in order to prevent the whole system from collapsing. IPOs were cancelled, trading was restricted, and credit was provided by the PBoC to purchase equities (Buiter et al. 2015: 3). The inevitable market volatility brought by liberalisation changed the Chinese government's stance on this. Indeed, the Chinese government should have drawn lessons from past crises, in particular from the Asian financial crisis of the 1990s, that liberalisation should be carefully pursued and sequencing is key. Especially cross-border financial liberalisation can entail negative effects in the form of the significant build-up of imbalances and subsequently, vulnerabilities

(Buiter et al. 2015: 4). Therefore, it is fair to ask why the Chinese government decided to go down this road?

Historical examples have shown that hot money flows such as 'portfolio and other investment plus E&Os' are susceptible to movements in capital market asset prices and to sentiment (Chang et al. 2015a: 3). In addition to these flows, China also has to deal with illicit ones. One source of these illegal flows was multiple transfers of FX deposits by individuals, which was partly restricted by the SAFE in the aftermath of the one-off devaluation. Cross-border arbitrage between USD/CNY and USD/CNH, as well as illicit current account transactions, are other determinants of illegal capital flows. Export under-invoicing as well as import over-invoicing are the most common means in this respect (Chang et al. 2015a: 4). To counter the risk of continued capital outflows, China started to introduce additional capital controls during the second half of 2015. Officially, capital can flow out of China through current account transactions. In addition, market-based channels for capital outflows include the qualified domestic institutional investor scheme, for instance. The sources of capital outflows are examined in more detail below.

ii) A New Basket Exchange Rate and the Beginning of 2016

In mid-December 2015, the China Foreign Exchange Trade System, a sub-institution of the Chinese central bank, announced the publication of a CFETS CNY index. This basket was comprised of the currencies of important trading partners of China. The 13 currencies were trade-weighted with USD and EUR receiving an initial weight of 0.2640 and 0.2139, respectively, in the basket. However, several currencies of China's trade partners such as the KRW, TWD and INR were not included in the basket. The currency index was rebased on December 31, 2014. Previously, capital markets had only focused on the bilateral exchange rate, i.e. USD/CNY. The PBoC tried to change this through the introduction of a basket-based exchange rate. The new focus on the trade-weighted exchange rate was also used as an explanation for the renewed weakness of the renminbi in late 2015. The success of the trade-weighted basket hinged on China's domestic economic and financial conditions and flow dynamics (Chen et al. 2015d). With a new focus on the basket, the PBoC could avoid CNY appreciation during a time of broad-based USD strength. This could reduce the necessity for excessive FX interventions in the market in the long run, so long as the renminbi does not significantly deviate from the NEER basket (Arora et al. 2015: 1). Moreover, the new FX regime is also set to tackle the build-up of fundamental vulnerabilities, namely an excessive REER overvaluation.

In mid-2015, the Chinese government also introduced a circuit breaker mechanism in the A-share market. This mechanism stopped share trading for 15 minutes when a loss of 5 percent on the day was recorded and closed the equity market when shares went down by 7 percent. The circuit breaker also should have helped contain vicious downward spirals. At the beginning of 2016, major Chinese stock exchanges hit the threshold and stopped trading. The Chinese equities performed poorly due to the weak manufacturing PMI release. In addition, the market did not positively regard the IPO reform and the potential increase in supply due to this reform (Chen et al. 2016a: 1). In fact, the sharp correction in the equity market at the beginning of 2016 led Chinese authorities to introduce new measures to prevent major institutional investors from dumping shares in the open market (Wang and Zhao 2016), which aimed at supporting Chinese capital markets.

In May 2016, a new basket rule for China's currency was introduced. The PBoC elaborated 'that it uses the 4:30pm close of the previous day and the change-on-day in three trade-weighted baskets for the next day fix' (Gu and Cavenagh 2016: 1). However, the aforementioned fixing mechanism did not explain the weakness in the TWI in 2016. Research assumes that the weakening bias of the Chinese TWI basket was driven by the general strength of the USD. The new rule can be laid out as follows according to Gu and Cavenagh (2016: 1): USD/CNY fixing on day T = (USD/CNY spot close at 4:30pm on day T-1) + beta * (change in level of three basket indices i.e. the CFETS trade weighted index, the BIS basket and the SDR basket on day T-1). Liu and Jin (2016d) assessed the PBoC's basket guidance with the help of a RMSE analysis. It is necessary to note that the Chinese government referred to a currency basket ever since the exchange rate adjustment in July 2005, when the country de-pegged the renminbi from the US dollar. In the beginning of 2016, the PBoC specified that its newly introduced exchange rate policy would specifically refer to baskets calculated by CFETS, SDR as well as BIS. However, more details were not provided. Therefore, Liu and Jin (2016d) econometrically analysed which basket was the most important in terms of determining the PBoC's daily fixing. In addition to the aforementioned three currency baskets, the DXY was used as a control variable for broad US dollar movements. The researchers apply an out-of-sample root mean square error (RMSE) selection criterion to determine which basket has the highest predictive power for the RMB currency fixings. In fact, Liu and Jin (2016d: 4) found that historically the CFETS index had the best out-of-sample explanatory power. However, during times of USD strength, the validity of the basket rule was questionable. In December 2016, China decided to extend the number of currencies in the CFETS basket. 11 new currencies were added, among these, the ZAR, KRW, TRY and MXN. The weighting methodology, based on international trade weights (Chang et al. 2016a), led to a closer alignment of the basket weights with China's trade statistics.

iii) Sources and Sizes of China's Capital Outflows and Capital Account Tightening

Li et al. (2016c) show that China's capital flow dynamics shifted significantly over the last two years. From the second quarter of 2014 onwards, capital flows turned negative in China. This was not a mirror of the current account surplus of China as the outflows happened at the same time as the PBOC sold FX reserves. To put it differently, the Chinese authorities had to sell FX reserves to prevent the renminbi from adjusting. The usual culprits for capital outflows are portfolio flows. However, in the case of China, authorities still strictly controlled this channel and thus, other determinants also have to be taken into account in an early warning system analysis.

In fact, the two biggest factors for flows were 'other investment' and 'net errors and omissions'. 'Other investment' reflects deposits and FX loans from Chinese enterprises, trade credit as well as the CNH balance. The first two factors relate to onshore sentiment and the last point to offshore sentiment. Still, these flows are relatively transparent for Chinese authorities (Li et al. 2016c: 2-3). 'Net errors and omissions' are more difficult to explain as in theory this item should be zero. Zeng and Zhang (2016a) contribute to the analysis of Chinese capital outflows by analysing current account transactions in more detail. The researchers admit that by looking at the right-hand side of the balance-of-payments one cannot directly identify the channels of capital outflows. In fact, misreporting of exports and imports explains most of Chinese capital outflows. This can be observed by looking at the data discrepancy between the China Custom's total goods imports and the SAFE's bank payment data. This discrepancy is related to FX sentiment and was caused by the relaxation of documentation requirements by Chinese authorities in 2011. The researchers argue that the Chinese authorities themselves needed some time to find out the channel of capital outflows, but that they now can target capital controls more effectively (Zeng and Zhang 2016a: 2-4). Due to substantial capital flight, China had to further tighten the country's capital controls in November 2016 because of the increased exchange rate pressure. Errors and omissions in the balance-of-payments increased sharply in this time period, which is a sign of increased capital flight (Liu and Jin 2016b: 1). This further stresses the importance of looking at both sides of the balance-of-payments in order to determine the channels of capital outflows.

At the beginning of December 2016, Chang et al. (2016c) commented on the significant decline in FX reserves in November 2016. Although part of the decline was attributed to a valuation effect, the changes in FX reserves were a sign of capital outflows. The depreciation of the CNY over the previous months coincided with a pick-up in outflows. The capital outflows were partly due to domestic reasons and partly due to an increase in US interest rates. Given the increase in outflows, the Chinese leadership decided to further tighten controls. Chang et al. (2016c) report the following measures: '1) banning mainland Chinese citizens from buying investment-related insurance products in Hong Kong; 2) imposing quotas on the equivalent value of bitcoins that can be sent abroad; and 3) strictly scrutinizing outward direct investments (ODIs) to curb large-scale capital flight via overseas M&A'. Moreover, the Bank of China limited FX purchases by their corporate customers in Shanghai (Chang et al. 2016c). For a more detailed overview of the implemented capital controls, please refer to Chang et al. (2016b: 6-7) and Liu and Jin (2016b: 3). Capital controls helped China to significantly reduce capital outflows and thus, de-escalate the situation (Chen et al. 2017: 6), which underlines the importance of the institutional dimension for preventing financial crisis.

iv) Further Notes on Financial Liberalisation

In 2013, the process of interest rate liberalisation sped up remarkably. The effective control of lending rates was abandoned in July 2013 and the deposit rate ceiling ceased to exist in October 2015. This helped bring lending rates closer to deposit rates. However, the primary beneficiary of this seemed to be state-owned enterprises as well as mortgage borrowers (Arora et al. 2015). With respect to the new monetary regime, the PBoC tries to build a market-based policy rate having in mind a further liberalisation of capital markets. Bank lending as well as deposit rates were two key areas in this respect. The deposit rate ceiling was lifted in October 2015, which decreased the importance of the 1y benchmark rates. In contrast, the PBoC tried to center its monetary policy around a short-term rate, namely the 7-day repo rate. In addition, a corridor was established around the short-term rate, which should have reduced interest rate volatility as well as have served as a liquidity guidance by the PBoC. The ceiling of the corridor was the standing lending facility (SLF) rate. In addition, the rate on excess reserves of banks served as floor (Chang et al. 2015c). China's monetary policy entered a new era with a stronger focus on market-based interest rate transmission. This should eventually replace the control of bank lending rates, which in turn should help to support the role of market-based interest rates as an allocation device. The monetary policy reform should reduce financial repression, increase the competition in the Chinese banking system, and give a higher weight of short-term interest rates at the expense of the 1y lending rate (Arora et al. 2015). This supplemented the introduced changes in the FX market.

The monetary regime in China includes interest rate as well as quantitative measures. In terms of interest rates, the PBoC gives more weight to the 7-day reverse repo rate to inject liquidity into the banking system (BoAML 2016: 31; Chen et al. 2017: 24-25). In terms of quantitative measures, reserve requirements remain a key tool as well as the PBoC lending facilities continue to help direct the market. In fact, the country initiated the gradual liberalisation of interest rates in the 1990s. However, the banking sector faced severe difficulties with an unsustainable level of NPLs due to the Asian financial crisis. Hence, the spread between deposit and lending rates was still upheld to ensure the profitability of banks. This financial repression led to deposit rates which were significantly lower than GDP growth in China and meant that the Chinese households paid for China's development policies over the last decades (Arora et al. 2015). While China tries to reduce the repression in the system by decreasing the spread between lending and deposit rates, short-term rates are not yet allowed to rise, which is at the core of the problem. The correct steps in liberalising the Chinese economy would require short-term rates to rise first. As can be seen by the troubles China faced in the second half of 2015 and 2016, without the correct sequencing the project of liberalisation is accompanied by excessive volatility, which forced the Chinese leadership to reverse part of this. The troubles the country faced in said time period are due to the country's unfinished transition from plan to market; financial distortions have hardly been touched yet.

v) The International Monetary System

Jim O'Neill (2001) significantly altered the perception of emerging markets in the paper 'Building Better Global Economic BRICs' by Goldman Sachs. In this research note, the international bank predicted the rise of Brazil, Russia, India and China, for which the acronym BRICs stands, over the next 10 years as well as these countries increased influence on global affairs. In particular, China was identified as an economic superpower, which was said to increase its influence exponentially. Competitive issues with respect to China's currency and the country's export dynamics were named to have global impact. In this respect, China's entry into the WTO in 2001 was identified as an inflection point, which raised China's potential GDP (Jim O'Neill 2001: 6). The opponent of the BRICs was said to be the Group of Seven (G7), which was formed in the aftermath of the breakdown of the Bretton Woods system in the early 1970s and got expanded to the Group of Twenty (G20). The G7 meetings served as informal get-togethers to discuss global policy issues and coordinate policy responses. FX management was regularly part of the discussion. For instance, the strengthening of the US dollar in 1995 can be identified as an outcome of the G7 forum. The research report concludes with the recommendation to give emerging markets a greater say in the global system. In addition, it is argued that the inclusion of China in established forums could have prevented the build-up of economic imbalances in Asia in the 1990s. Giving emerging markets a voice in the global system could significantly reduce the overall risk for crises (Jim O'Neill 2001: 8-11). Having said that, the IMF enticed China to implement more market friendly reforms with respect to the country's currency regime in 2015. This happened at a time when China was under immense pressure due to the realisation of fundamental vulnerabilities. The dismal performance of the country's external statistics and the collapse of the Chinese equity markets left the country vulnerable to further distortions. It was at that time that the potential for the SDR inclusion enticed China to give the market a greater say in the fixing of its local exchange rate, which resulted in increased FX volatility and subsequent alterations of the fixing regime as well as a spurt in capital outflows.

vi) Institutions, Governance and the Rule of Law

Viñals and Singh (2011: 7) demonstrate how China can further improve on its domestic institutional set-up in their IMF report 'Financial System Stability Assessment'. The report notes that the country faced significant vulnerabilities that needed to be addressed. Through the ever-increasing integration of China within its borders as well as globally, institutions are facing new challenges (Feenstra and Taylor 2014). Four risks were identified which need to be tackled through investing in China's institutional capabilities, namely the speedy credit expansion entailing negative effects on banks' balance sheets, off-balance sheet lending posing a significant risk to the system, the deflation of real estate prices calling into question the balance between collateral and liabilities and lastly, any imbalances resulting from the country's growth trajectory (Viñals and Singh 2011: 7). To solve these problems, China needs to engage in institutional reforms, particularly in terms of the country's capabilities regarding financial oversight (Paris 2004: 204). The IMF paper describes this as follows: 'The mandates of the supervisory agencies should focus on ensuring the safety and soundness of regulated institutions, risk management, and proper market conduct and avoid taking on the responsibility for promoting the development of specific economic sectors or for making decisions on how capital should be intermediated and allocated. Ensuring the operational autonomy of the central bank and financial supervisors is crucial' (Viñals and Singh 2011: 8). As shown in the historical background section on transition economies, a further build-up of institutional capabilities is needed before China should continue with its liberalisation strategy. 'Certain pre-conditions have to be made before broader acceleration of financial deepening, liberalization of interest rates, and finally, full liberalization of the capital account. Such pre-conditions include putting in place a well-functioning legal, regulatory, supervisory, and crisis management framework; improving corporate governance in banks; early absorption of the current liquidity overhang in the financial system; and greater reliance on market-orientated monetary policy instruments' (Viñals and Singh 2011: 10). China has tried to address some of these issues on various occasions.

In the 13th Five-Year Plan, particular emphasis was put on China's financial regulatory reform. The PBoC suggested that China should adopt 'dynamic adjustments in differentiated reserve requirements' and 'desirable loan management'. China ended up implementing both ideas in 2011, transforming the system into a Macro Prudential

Assessment (MPA) framework. Regarding the 'dynamic adjustments in differentiated reserve requirements', the PBoC used different RRRs for various types of banks depending on credit expansion as well as on capital adequacy ratios. Moreover, the MPA scheme put the focus from bank loans to a broader credit concept (Chen et al. 2016b). Underhill and Jones (2014) name a comprehensive MPA framework as one of the bricks for building an inclusive institutional set-up that prevents some of the malaise of capital.

vii) SOE Reforms

I describe different institutional factors in order to provide for a better understanding of the currency debasement of the Chinese yuan from August 2015, together with the revision and the subsequent alterations in the exchange rate regime as well as the entailed capital flow volatility. One such factor is SOE reforms in China, which is described in detail below.

Since the 1980s, the state-owned enterprise sector has been reformed significantly. Nonetheless, state-owned enterprises still contribute about 30 percent of total industrial output as well as investment in China (Li et al. 2016b: 1-2). Thus, SOEs play a significant role in the Chinese economy and should be considered in any analysis. The reallocation of resources from SOEs to the private sector has spurred China's growth over the preceding decades (Song and Hsieh 2015). In the late 1990s, the SOE reform somewhat progressed, however, a serve crisis struck said corporations during that time. About 40 percent of the state-owned enterprises lost money in the industrial sector. Leverage was excessive and overcapacity plagued the enterprises (Li et al. 2016b: 1-2). Given these challenges, the Chinese government started a 'Three Year Reform Plan' in 1998, which included the following measures: 1) Unprofitable, small SOEs were closed and larger SOEs were transformed into more profitable corporates under the "grasp the large and let the small go" strategy. 2) In 1999, a debt-to-equity programme helped to reduce the problem of excessive leverage and thus, also dealt with the NPL issue in the banking sector. Asset management companies were the primary vehicle through which the programme was implemented. 3) Inevitably, the restructuring of the SOE sector led to increased layoffs in the three years of the programme (Li et al. 2016b: 2-3). These three measures supported the performance of SOEs at the cost of certain layers of the population (Naughton 2007) and also mitigated issues in China's banking sector and thus for the whole economy and asset prices.

In total, about 600 SOEs participated in the programme in the early 2000s and about RMB 405 billion in loans were swapped into equity stakes. The key terms of the agreement between the SOEs and the asset management companies included the following: Within a period of ten years, restructured SOEs had to buy back their stakes from the AMCs, but the SOEs had to pay-out certain cash-flows to the AMCs until they bought back the stakes. In addition, local governments often guaranteed stock-market listings of SOEs as an exit option (Pang 2016: 4). To purchase the stakes in the SOEs, the AMCs issued bonds themselves and received additional financing from the PBoC as well as from the Ministry of Finance. In fact, the debt-to-equity scheme was labelled a success since the average corporate indebtedness measured as the debt-to-asset ratio decreased from about 70 percent to 50 percent (Pang 2016: 5). The scheme also helped to resolve the NPL problem in China's financial sector, which is described in the historical background section in more detail.

Today, SOEs are still an important player in the financial sector. In addition, in terms of strategic sectors, SOEs hold the dominant share of assets, for instance in petroleum or utility sectors. Furthermore, over 50 percent of outstanding bank loans are given to SOEs and about 90 percent of all outstanding bonds are issued by state-corporations. SOEs are one key lever for countercyclical policy for the Chinese government (Li et al. 2016b: 4). Due to the government ownership of SOEs, the enterprises served as a principal means for the Chinese government to support the economy in the great financial crisis. Preferential access to loans helped state-owned companies to support investments, but also led to a steep rise in leverage. Ultimately, the crisis response to the challenges of 2008 and 2009 led to the NPL problem the Chinese financial sector is facing today (Chen et al. 2017: 15). In general, the official NPL number is an underestimation of the actual numbers the sector must deal with. For instance, the official NPL number is about 2 percent for 2015, while international banks estimate the real NPL number to be closer to 10 percent (Li et al. 2016b: 6) and thus, addressing this problem is inevitable. However, it goes without saying that any further reforms of the SOE sector is a politically sensitive topic in China (Naughton 2007).

Reform dynamics must factor in the following points: 1) State-owned enterprises are the most fundamental economic institution in the current set-up. Due to ideological reasons, the SOE sector will continue to play an important role in China. Therefore, a full separation between the SOE sector and the Chinese government is highly unlikely. However, the government could allow for increased diversity in ownership as well as for more leeway in the corporate administrative systems. 2) As a matter of fact, SOE reforms include on the one hand the improvement of corporate efficiency and on the other hand, the aim of increasing the impact of said sector on the Chinese economy (for instance, via M&A). 3) Gradualism is still vital in China's reform efforts. Various stakeholders are included in the reform process and the execution of the reforms is equally important as the reforms themselves (Li et al. 2016b: 11-12). A gradualist approach should prevent the situation from spiralling out of control.

Pang (2016) compares China's previous debt-to-equity swap programme in the late 1990s with today's situation. China is facing a debt problem in the corporate sector as non-financial indebtedness rose from 98 percent of GDP in 2007 to a staggering 190 percent in 1H16. In the late 1990s, the debt-to-equity scheme helped to reduce corporate indebtedness significantly as well as resolved the NPL problem in the financial sector (Naughton 2007: 462). Today's scheme is similar to the previously applied swap programme (Pang 2016: 1). China responded to the financial crisis of 2008 with substantial stimulus, which amounted to RMB 4trn for social spending as well as infrastructure. However, the crisis response led to an excessive increase in corporate indebtedness in China, which in return increased defaults (The Economist 2015b). State-owned enterprises, which faced severe financial difficulties in 2016, included Dongbei Special Steel and Guangxi Nonferrous Metals for instance. Given the increase in defaults, China decided to tackle the corporate debt problem with a debt-to-equity scheme, which should also support the financial system (Pang 2016: 2-4). Currently, the government aims at reducing the leverage on corporate balance sheets. The enterprises in question are foremost state-owned companies. Today's scheme fulfils the IMF criteria for a successful programme, which are the following (Pang 2016: 7):

- Strict solvency and viability criteria for corporates;
- Sound corporate governance;
- Bank ownership of equity should be limited in scope and time;
- Conversion should be at fair value and losses recognised;
- Robust regulatory treatment of equity holders.

These criteria were laid out by the IMF by Daniel (2016) in 'Debt-Equity Conversations and NPL Securitization in China – Some Initial Considerations'. Given the current Chinese reform efforts, mergers and acquisitions might be the primary means through which China aims at dealing with the overcapacity problem. Excessive leverage and the NPL problems are targeted via debt-to-equity swaps as well as via securitisation. The success of these efforts depends on the details of the implementation (Li et al. 2016b: 14). However, it can be said that the SOE sector will continue to serve as a means for the Chinese government to influence the economy.

viii) Technology and Productivity

Wilson and Purushothaman (2003: 13) list the most important determinants of growth; factors such as economic stability, a sound institutional framework, openness, and investment in human capital are identified as being crucial for a country's growth trajectory. Macroeconomic stability refers mainly to keeping inflation rates stable and providing incentives for saving and investment decisions in a country. Openness with respect to trade and foreign direct investment has been an important source of technological progress and investments in human capital is often a prerequisite for countries to advance further. Institutions refer to the efficiency of a country, which is described in detail in the conceptual section as well as in this section. The Economist (2017h) points out that historical innovation in China has been mostly driven by imported technology. In fact, the Chinese government grants market access in exchange for more advanced technology. The Chinese government blocks access to strategic industries in the country and at the same time, finances take-overs abroad in the very same areas. In addition, some of the biggest foreign firms operating in China are targets of the country's anti-monopoly assaults (The Economist 2017h), which underlines the Chinese leadership's goals. In general, developed countries usually do not share their technologies with other countries. In fact, it is almost impossible for many developing countries to catch up with more advanced countries since the advanced countries tend to fence off their technological innovations (Naughton 2007: 351).

Apart from importing foreign technologies, China is increasingly engaging in R&D itself. 'The CPC Central Committee's Recommendation for the 13th Five-Year Plan on National Economic and Social Developments' included significant progress with respect to innovation (Chen et al. 2015c). The new strategy included the development of new sources of growth, for instance, the further fostering of new businesses and competition leading to a more effective resource allocation. In this respect, the Chinese government decided to remove price controls in various sectors such as electricity, energy and telecommunication. Furthermore, the scope of the development should be expanded by including a regional development strategy as well as the development of new industries related to technological advancements. In addition, innovation-driven progress via R&D should become a major source of development for China in terms of moving forward. This includes more secure intellectual property rights (Chen et al. 2015c), which would be a crucial progress with respect to addressing institutional weaknesses. Indeed, as pointed out in the conceptual section, China's trajectory has been influenced significantly by improvements in technology, which makes it one key factor from an early warning perspective. This is examined further with the help of a logit model in the quantitative part of the case study.

d) Remarks on the Qualitative Analysis

I applied the three dimensions of vulnerability to China in the second half of 2015 and 2016. Hence, I started out by analysing fundamentals which were identified by academic research as important drivers of past crisis episodes, foremost in the global crisis of the 1980s as well as in the Asian financial crisis of the 1990s. I then demonstrated that an overvalued currency, as observed via the real exchange rate, should be interpreted as a significant predictor for a currency crisis. Furthermore, I analysed the build-up of debt and argued that, although this factor should be watched closely, the high level of indebtedness is not per se a guarantee for a financial crisis without any significant currency and maturity mismatches. China's high indebtedness on the corporate side must be regarded as a contingent liability to the sovereign and indeed, the most visible effect of this debt binge will be a lower growth rate.

With respect to policy-induced volatility, I demonstrated the crucial importance of China's past development policies, such as population control and urbanisation. These can be used to identify turning points in a country's growth trajectory. Furthermore, monetary and fiscal policy is analysed in light of China's transition. The former mostly refers to the vital importance of financial repression in the country's economic trajectory; this changes as the development proceeds. The former is also linked to China's debt binge as well as to the problem of restructuring companies and the renewed policy of allowing state-owned enterprises to default on their debt. Moreover, policy-induced vulnerabilities are related to soft factors such as demand for status or legitimacy of a country's leadership as well as ideational determinants. As shown in the case study, status is a powerful driver of outcomes in material terms. The IMF inclusion of the Chinese renminbi in the SDR basket entailed significant value for the Chinese leadership and might have led to suboptimal decision-making.

This is connected to the final dimension of the vulnerability analysis, namely institutional weaknesses of China. If sequencing is not performed diligently and the institutional set-up is not ready to deal with the challenges posed by new policies and ideas, liberalisation can entail significant volatility for a country. Indeed, sometimes two steps forward should be followed by one step backward. China had to tighten capital controls in the observed period to stem outflows. This provided the country with time to invest in institutional capabilities. Financial sector reforms and improvements in the regulatory framework are crucial steps in this respect. Furthermore, I touched upon the most fundamental economic institution in China, namely state-owned enterprises, and the influences of SOEs on the country's weaknesses and strengths.

Given the analysis of the events that happened in China in the second half of 2015 and 2016, I recommend using the expanded conceptualisation to analyse a country's vulnerabilities. Albeit important, fundamentals only capture part of the picture. By expanding the tools and building a unified framework, an improved understanding of financial crises can be deducted. Indeed, evaluating emerging market vulnerabilities is invaluable to policymakers. The improved understanding derived from the expanded set of analytical concepts can provide a country's leaders with new perspectives to help guide their decisions on various options to mitigate a nation's vulnerabilities and thus, ultimately prevent financial crises. Essential lessons can be learnt from studying historical crisis episodes, expanding the analytical framework and applying this extended conceptualisation to China's troubles in the second half of 2015 and 2016.

China's double-digit growth rates over the last decades has fuelled their citizen's hopes that tomorrow will be better than today. President Xi Jinping touched upon this topic in his annual New Year's speech on December 31st, 2015, by promising to build a 'moderately prosperous society' (The Economist: 2016b). How the Chinese President's aspiration will exactly play out is yet to be seen. Certainly, by applying the expanded analytical framework, vital lessons can be learned which can help the country to avoid financial crisis and continue its path towards prosperity.

4.B) Quantitative Part of the Case Study

In this study, I deduce policy prescription for crisis prevention as well as management. I list the previously identified leading indicators for currency crises and show that an early warning system based on these indicators performs well. The indicators not only identify crises, but also help to anticipate states of stress. The analysis provides an empirical test of early warning indicators for currency crises in China. The goal is to enable officials and private market participants to assess vulnerability to FX distortions at an early stage. This should facilitate the undertaking of corrective actions that would hinder such financial crises from taking place. Interest in identifying early warning indicators to currency crises is motivated by two factors, namely the high costs inflicted by crises and the insufficiency of pure economic indicators to predict crises. With respect to the former, there is a rising recognition that currency crises can be very costly for countries. Furthermore, these crises can have spill over effects to other countries and increase the vulnerability of these nations to financial crises. Indeed, the costs of currency crises are significant in terms of lost output growth (Goldstein et al. 2000: 3). The IMF (1998) estimated that emerging markets incur about an 8 percent cumulative loss in real output during a substantial currency crisis. Furthermore, contagion is a major issue. Even after controlling for fundamentals, a currency crisis significantly increases a country's vulnerability to currency distortions elsewhere in the world (Eichengreen et al. 1996). Indeed, the costlier financial crises are, the higher is the return of a well-calibrated early warning system. Regarding the second point of interest, evidence that a pure focus on economic variables leads to a dismal performance in predicting financial crises should be taken more seriously. This is in line with research by Goldfajn and Valdés (1998), who stated that currency forecasts collected from survey data do not provide much help in warning of currency crises. In addition, the evidence suggests that in past crisis episodes such as the Asian financial crisis, economic variables were unable to anticipate the crisis (Goldstein et al. 2000: 6). One reason for this is that economic variables did not provide for the holistic picture of the situation. 'Thailand's commitments in the forward exchange market and South Korea's lending of international reserves to commercial banks meant that official figures on gross international reserves gave a misleading (i.e. overoptimistic) view of each country's net usable reserves' (Goldstein et al. 2000: 7).

In this section, I lay out the details of the approach to identifying currency crises from an early warning perspective. I use monthly data in order to analyse FX distortions, which allows us to learn more about the timing of the early warning system as well as on the persistence of the signals. Additionally, annual data is often only available with a substantial lag, which makes them unsuitable for a timely assessment with an early warning system, but useful for a retrospective analysis. Thus, I conclude that the advantages of monthly data outweigh any disadvantages. As a matter of fact, I was able to assemble monthly data for about two thirds of the indicators used in the early warning assessment; for the remaining third, I had to use the annual data points for the analysis.

Another element of the approach is that I include relatively broad sets of indicators in the early warning analysis. I based the decision, which indicators to include, on a review of broad and recurring themes in the literature on China as well as on financial crises. These themes encompass:

- Growth stories that stress the importance of factor accumulation for the trajectory of a country;
- External variables, which indicate that there is a need for a currency adjustment in order to improve an unsustainable balance;
- Balance sheet mismatches in relation to the build-up of unsustainable levels of debt;
- Policy-induced vulnerability;
- First- and second-generation models of vulnerability to currency crises;
- Premature financial liberalisation stories that aim at the perils of liberalisation given a weak institutional set-up,
- Factors which are specific to the transformation from plan to market;
- Interactions of various kinds of crises.

In operational terms, these different views of financial crises result in a list of indicators that span across three dimensions – fundamental, policy-induced, and institutional vulnerabilities. Once a set of variables identifying a currency crisis is found, I distinguish between the better performing categories among them and calculate the probability of a currency distortion. This is done with the help of a logit model in which the dependent variable is associated with a value of either one (if the period is classified as an exchange rate crisis) or zero (if no financial crisis takes place). The statistical significance reveals which dimensions are significant and which do not contribute to the identification of currency crises (Goldstein et al. 2000: 14-15).

Another guideline of my thinking is to employ out-of-sample tests to help assess the usefulness of the three dimensions in predicting FX crises. The in-sample power of a model may lead to a false sense of optimism about how well the leading indicators identify currency distortions. 'A good case in point is the experience of the 1970s with structural models of exchange rate determination for the major currencies. While these in-sample models fit well, subsequent research indicated that their out-of-sample performance was no better – and often worse – than that of "naive" models' (Goldstein et al. 2000: 17). In this respect, one of the cornerstones of academic literature is the paper by Meese and Rogoff (1983).

It is important to be aware of the limitations of this type of analysis. The quantitative leading indicator exercise does not generate information on why or how the three dimensions affect the probability of currency crises. This is assessed with the help of the examination of over five hundred research reports. Furthermore, the early warning analysis of financial crises is susceptible to the "Lucas critique", which points to the fact that if a reliable set of indicators were empirically identified, policymakers would be able to identify currency crises a priori and thus, behave differently, 'thereby transforming these variables into early warning indicators of corrective policy action rather than of financial crises' (Goldstein et al. 2000: 17). This feedback effect is not yet strong enough to impair the predictive power of the three dimensions, however, there is no guarantee that this feedback effect will not be stronger going forward.

Furthermore, the research regarding early warning systems is still in its infancy. As Goldstein et al. (2000: 18) note, 'too few "horse races" have been run to know which approaches work best'. Indeed, this approach towards modelling early warning systems shows promising signs of adding real value and that it is indeed useful as a first screen for gauging the different dimensions of vulnerability to currency crises over time.

a) The Events of 2015 and 2016

The exchange rate troubles China faced in 2015 and 2016 could have been triggered by a number of factors. These determinants are broadly split among the three independent categories, namely fundamental, policy-induced, and institutional factors. The first factor that I would like to examine is growth. Economic performance in China is on a structural downward trend. Growth targets were revised downward year-after-year. In 2014, real GDP was 7.3 percent, in 2015, 6.9 percent, in 2016, 6.7 percent. Only in 2017 did the real GDP growth recover to 6.9 percent. In comparison to China's troubles in this period, real growth in China realised at 9.4 percent in 2009. Given China's downward trend in real growth, higher frequency indicators have to be taken into account to get a clearer picture on the situation. One indicator that could be examined is the official manufacturing PMI. From this, we can see that the indicator was in contractionary territory in 2015 with an average level of 49.9. The economic indicator also hinted to a contraction at the beginning of 2016 before recovering at the end of said year. Another measure that pointed to a severe slowdown in 2015 was the Li Keqiang Index, which consists of three sub-indicators, namely outstanding bank loans, electricity production and rail freight volume. The indicator started to contract in 2014 and only recovered in 2016. The cumulative magnitude of the decline is comparable to the economic slowdown in China in 2008. Other factors that pointed to a slowdown in China were housing prices. The year-over-year changes in the "China 70 Cities Newly Built Residential Index" turned negative in the last quarter of 2014 and stayed negative until December 2015. The first and the second quarters of 2015 were particularly bad, with an average decline of -6.1 percent in the index. The last indicator of China's economic performance in said period is credit growth. By examining aggregate financing in China, we can see that after the peak in stimulus in 2013, credit growth declined substantially and even contracted in 2014 and 2015.

With respect to China's external statistics, a strong appreciation of the real effective exchange rate was observed in 2015. The year-over-year changes in the REER peaked in July 2015 at 14.7 percent. This overvaluation of the local exchange rate was one factor leading to the adjustment in the exchange rate in August 2015 as well as for the subsequent FX volatility the country faced. This coincided with a dismal performance of China's exports. Exports depicted a decline of -9.2 percent in July 2015 and of -15.2 percent and -28 percent in January and February 2016, respectively. This led to a necessary adjustment in the level of the exchange rate. China initially refused to adjust its exchange rate, which was in line with the historical experience during the Asian financial crisis. This was particularly visible in the FX reserves' decline. Year-over-year changes in FX reserves turned negative in 2015, peaked at a negative growth rate of -15.8 percent in February 2016, and only turned positive again in 2017. The initial decline in FX reserves was one indication that the Chinese exchange rate was overvalued. After the adjustment of the local exchange rate of August 2015, China tried to smooth exchange rate volatility by selling its hard currency reserves in order to ensure a gradual adjustment of the exchange rate mechanisms. This strategy partially succeeded but at the cost of a significant loss in hard currency reserves.

With respect to policy variables, the first factor I would like to examine is the Hong Kong Interbank CNY Reference Rate Overnight. This is the rate used to manage the exchange rate and reduce the speculation against the local exchange rate in the forward market in times of market stress. Four dates are worth mentioning. On January 12th, 2016, the rate surged to 65 percent, on September 19th, 2016, the rate rose to 25 percent, on January 6th,, 2017, the indicator topped at 60 percent, and on June 1st , 2017, the rate rose to 43.75 percent. A similar pattern can be observed in the 3M offshore implied yield. The first spike in the yield can be observed in August 2015, at the time of the devaluation, the second increase was recorded in January 2016, and the third spike in January 2017. The spikes coincided with reversals in the exchange rate's performance as higher rates predicted a positive performance of the local exchange rate going forward. The third variable, which depicted a similar pattern to the previously discussed two indicators are forward-forwards. I calculated the 3 to 6 months forward rate and it became visible that the forward-forwards peaked in January 2016, which was related to monetary policy expectations. The greater the gradient of the forward curve is, the higher are the forward-forwards. This increase coincided well with reversals in the performance of the local exchange rate.

The next policy indicator I would like to discuss is M2. Money supply reached a temporary low in the first half of 2015. This is in line with the aggregate financing number that showed a reduction in stimulus in the run-up to the events of 2015 and 2016. Similar to this, money supply has depicted a downward trend since 2013. This lag was also reflected in the real economy, as described above. A similar pattern can also be seen in the indicator M1, which bottomed in 2014. M1 only picked up again at the end of 2015, as the Chinese leadership started to react to the troubles the country faced in this period. The next indicator I would like to discuss is equity price performance. I use the Shanghai Shenzhen CSI 300 Index as a proxy for China's capital market performance and thus, also for revenues accruing to the Chinese government via the fiscal deficit. The index reached a temporary high in June 2015, with a year-over-year return of about 150 percent. This was right before the complete collapse of the Chinese equity markets. The index lost about 40 percent of its value over the subsequent months. The extreme volatility of the equity market coincided with China's FX troubles in said period, namely with the currency debasement of the Chinese yuan in August 2015, the change in the FX regime and the frequent revisions of this as well as the entailed capital outflows. The first wave of the sell-off started in June 2015 and lasted about 3 months until September 2015; the second wave commenced at the end of 2015 and lasted approximately until mid-2016.

This indicator depicted a great amount of variation and served well as a signal for the currency debasement of August 2015.

The next two indicators, namely the old dependency ratio as well as the Gini coefficient, depict a limited amount of variation. However, with respect to the former it can be seen that China is aging at an increasing speed. The indicator continuously picked up in speed since the mid-2000s, which points to China's problems with respect to demographics. Furthermore, the Gini coefficient is nearly constant in the years of China's troubles, which gives a hint that inequality is econometrically not related to the struggle China faced in 2015 and 2016.

Regarding institutional variables, I would like to discuss those indicators first which are linked to liberalisation. With respect to China's growth model, the lending to deposit spread slightly decreased in the run-up to the events of 2015 and 2016. However, this happened in a gradual manner, which points to the fact that the dissolution of China's growth model cannot be a reason for the country's troubles in said period. Another indicator of financial repression is the real interest rate. By visualising this indicator, it can be seen that the real interest rate depicted an unusual low level during said time period. Only in 2017, the rate increased slightly; however, it was still relatively low compared to China's real growth rate. This could have been one reason for the FX distortions China faced in 2015 and 2016. In order to examine this idea further, the yield differential with respect to the US has to be observed. Thus, the push and the pull factor can be examined together. Indeed, the yield differential decreased substantially in the first half of 2015. This further supports the idea that financial repression in the form of an overly low interest rate on an absolute basis as well as the interest rate level with the United States, was one of the reasons for China's struggle during said period.

In addition to the above, I examine indicators with respect to the FX regime. Due to the currency debasement of the Chinese yuan in August 2015 as well as the change in the FX regime and the subsequent alterations of this, the onshore-offshore spread markedly increased as well as the level of the FX volatility. At the time of the devaluation of the Chinese renminbi in August 2015, the onshore-offshore spread increased due to further speculation that other one-off events would follow. The spread remained elevated for about a month until it reached a new high in January 2016. The differential served well as an indication for temporary reversals in the exchange rate. These two events were accompanied by severe capital market stress in China, as described above. A similar pattern could also be seen with respect to FX volatility. Due to the events in August 2015, the FX volatility spiked significantly and reached its temporary high in February 2016. In contrast to the onshore-offshore spread, the FX volatility depicted another spike at the end of 2016 and beginning of 2017. This marked the reversal in the depreciation trend of the Chinese yuan.

With respect to state-owned enterprises, I use the difference between the number in offshore and onshore listed enterprises as an indicator regarding China's reform progress in this area. From this determinant, we can see that reform efforts with respect to listing companies onshore relative to the offshore market slowed down before the China's troubles started. It can also be seen that during both states of crisis, during the great financial crisis and during the troubles of 2015 and 2016, reforms picked up. Furthermore, I use the China Innovation Output Index (the number of patents granted per 10000 R&D personnel) as an indication for technology and productivity. We can see a decline in the index before the troubles of 2015 and 2016. Regarding the rule of law, we can observe a slight improvement of the indicator during the bespoken time period, which gives a hint that this indicator is econometrically not related to the FX debasement of 2015.

The feature of limited volatility of some of the above-mentioned indicators do not make them appropriate for econometric analysis. However, this does not mean that these indicators are not important over time. Hence, my case study includes a qualitative section as well.

b) Research Strategy

I begin by analysing the IMF's Core Early Warning System Models. First, the IMF makes use of the Developed Country Studies Division (DCSD) model, which applies five variables to predict exchange rate distortions. These variables are the real exchange rate, the current account, FX reserves, exports and short-term debt to reserves. In the analysis, I left out the current account as the main driver of the predictability of this variable is exports. In addition, I skipped the ratio of short-term debt to reserves in the analysis since FX reserves are used as a separate predictor for exchange rate crises and any debt issues should be captured by credit growth. Second, the Kaminsky, Lizondo, and Reinhart (KLR) model is used by the IMF, which uses the real exchange rate, the ratio of broad money to gross international reserves, output, credit growth, and equity prices among others. In the part on fundamentals of this book, I use PMIs as a leading indicator for output; credit growth is applied in order to monitor any debt burden to the economy. Moreover, Reinhard and Rogoff (2009) note in their review of early warning systems that housing prices serve as a good indicator for financial crises.

Apart from these mostly economic determinants, I include one dimension with respect to policy-induced uncertainty. The Hong Kong Interbank CNY Reference Rate Overnight as well as the offshore forward implied yield are used as proxies for China's policy experimentation with respect to the renminbi's internationalisation; the old-age dependency ratio is applied as a proxy for China's shift in demographics and the Gini coefficient for inequality. The country's monetary policy stance is assessed via forward-forwards and M2 growth and China's fiscal position is examined via the performance of equity prices. In contrast to these variables, no quantification is deducted for any soft factors used as explanatory variables in this book. Instead, these soft factors are solely examined with the help of over five hundred research reports, which serve to reconstruct the events in a great degree of detail.

In addition to policy-induced uncertainty, one dimension with respect to institutional vulnerability is used in the analytical framework. The lending to deposit spread, the spread between US and China interest rates as well as real interest rates are all determinants that serve as proxies for China's progress with respect to liberalisation. Furthermore, China's FX regime is taken account for by the option implied FX volatility, as well as by the onshore-offshore spread, which should make China's progress with respect to renminbi internationalisation clear. Further institutional factors are approximated by the difference between the number in offshore and onshore listed enterprises, the China Innovation Output Index, and by an index representing the rule of law in China.

A matrix decomposition is performed for each of the three dimensions, namely fundamental, policy and institutional variables. This results in various vectors that capture most of the variation of the explanatory variables per category of vulnerability. Subsequently, these vectors are used as input factors in the logit model, which allows me to show that fundamentals, although important, are not the sole drivers of outcome and hence, a unified framework consisting of fundamental, policy-induced and institutional weaknesses should be used in predicting currency debasements. Thus, the link between the dependent variable – the currency debasement of the Chinese yuan, which took place in August 2015, together with the revision and the subsequent alterations in the exchange rate regime, as well as the entailed capital flow volatility – and the explanatory set of dimensions is shown quantitatively with the help of a logit model as well as qualitatively with the examination of over five hundred research reports.

I proceed with the examination of the independent variables along the three dimensions. As laid out in the analytical section, these variables help to explain financial crisis. Subsequently, I will describe the quantitative methods applied in this case study in detail. I start out with principal component analysis, which helps reduce the matrix of independent variables per dimension to a few vectors. The first two principal components per dimension are subsequently used as input factors in the logit model with which I will show that not only fundamental vulnerability helps to explain currency crises in China.

c) Independent Variables

i) Fundamentals

As laid out in the analytical section of this book, I start the analysis with growth factors. One of the most important indicators to do this is the Purchasing Manager Index issued by the China Federation of Logistics and Purchasing and National Bureau of Statistics. This indicator covers one of the vital parts of China's economy, namely manufacturing, and can have significant market impact (Chen et al. 2016a: 1). In fact, it provides access to the views of business managers and thus, not influenced by local government officials. The time series is available monthly and hence, provides a view of the current moment of the Chinese economy. In China, the survey data started in 2005 with a panel of over 800 businesses; however, the exact decomposition of the survey data is not known. The methods of calculating the indicator is based on that of the U.S. Institute of Supply Management (ISM), where respondents are asked to comment on the following areas: production, new orders, new export orders, backlog of orders, stock of raw materials, purchasing of inputs, imports, input prices, inventories, employment, and supplier delivery times. The surveyed business managers are asked whether this month is better, the same, or worse than the previous month. The index is constructed in a way that a value of 50 means no change to the previous month. In contrast, a score above 50 means that the economy is expanding and below 50 that it is contracting. For instance, a score of 50 for production means there was no change in production from the last month to this month according to the survey. In order to come up with the overall score of the index, a weighted composite of the five most important subindexes is calculated: PMI = (New orders * 0.3) + (Production * 0.25) + (Employment * 0.2) + (Supplier delivery times * 0.15) + (Stock of raw materials * 0.1). The weights are almost identical to that of the U.S. ISM survey (Orlik 2012: 40-42). The headline figure of the CFLP PMI usually attracts most attention. A score above 50 means that the manufacturing sector is expanding and a score below 50 indicates a contraction of output. Historically, expansion is the normal state and thus, the key question is related to the variation in the indicator and not necessarily to the level. In 2008, 'the CFLP index pointed to negative growth from the beginning of the third quarter – among the first data points to identify the rocks ahead' (Orlik 2012: 42). In addition to the composite index, the CFLP subindexes provide for a detailed view on the Chinese manufacturing sector. The index of new orders is the best estimate of the near-term future of China's manufacturing sector and the index of new export orders is a gauge of the health of the Chinese export sector, for instance. To conclude, the CFLP is among the most important indicators for the health of the Chinese manufacturing sector. 'Currency markets also pay attention to the PMI data as an early indicator of the overall state of the Chinese economy' (Orlik 2012: 44).

Apart from the CFLP PMI, credit growth gives an important indication about the trajectory of the Chinese economy. One important aspect of this is that China has a bank-based economy. Although all major banks have been listed, the Chinese government itself holds a controlling interest in these (Naughton 2007). 'A dominant role for the banks in intermediating between lenders and borrowers, and a controlling hand for the government in the behaviour of the banking sector, gives Beijing a powerful tool that it can use to dictate the speed and direction of the economy' (Orlik 2012: 193). Indeed, during the great financial crisis, the Chinese leadership propped up the domestic economy with the help of CNY 17.4 trillion in new loans, which significantly helped the economy to recover (Breslin 2014). The new lending caused a spurt in investment, which resulted in growth rates above 8 percent during a period when the rest of the world suffered from the dire consequences of the global financial crisis of 2008. In 2011, the PBoC started to publish total social financing numbers, which include such items as off-balance sheet lending and capital raised via equity and bond offerings. This implicitly recognises the need to capture other items aside from bank loans, although the latter remain the dominant source of financing in the Chinese economy. As such it results in a broader picture of the credit conditions. Nonetheless, the first item the market focuses on is new loan data. This remains the main source of new credit in the Chinese economy (J.P. Morgan 2015b). The Chinese leadership uses new loans as one of the main levers to control the pace of the economy. 'Banks are

told how much they can lend over the course of the year, and regulators tighten and loosen the quota depending on the outlook' (Orlik 2012: 195). New loan data depicts strong seasonal patterns. In order to avoid this seasonality problem in the data, I use changes in the year-over-year growth rates in total social financing as an input for the principal component analysis.
One interesting feature, from a qualitative, not econometric perspective, is that total social financing includes foreign currency loans. The demand for foreign currency is closely linked to expectations of yuan appreciation or depreciation. 'If borrowers expect the yuan to appreciate, it makes sense to borrow a fistful of dollars, covert them into yuan, wait for the yuan to appreciate, convert a portion back into a few dollars again, repay the loan, and pocket the difference. High levels of foreign currency loans indicate that borrowers expect a period of strong yuan appreciation to come' (Orlik 2012: 198).

Another important indicator in the part on fundamentals is house price data. The housing market was liberalised at the end of the 1990s. Since then, prices have increased. Some were lucky and were allocated a house when ownership changed from public to private and some made a profit as they bought before prices soared. Given the rapid increase in housing prices, the dream of home ownership is out of reach for many Chinese. As a matter of fact, China's investment-driven growth model has made the real estate sector the biggest single domestic contributor to economic output. Investment in real estate makes up for about ten percent of GDP according to Orlik (2012: 75). The contribution rises even more when one counts the indirect contribution of building materials such as cement and steel. The Chinese real estate boom of the mid-2000s significantly contributed to output and the increase in iron ore prices. 'A real estate bust in the second half of 2008 was the domestic complement to the global financial crisis, […] crunching GDP growth to a 10-year low of 6.6% YoY in the first quarter of 2009' (Orlik 2012: 76). One important driver for the demand for Chinese real estate is the repressive system. Low returns on savings pushes Chinese investors into real estate and equity investments. Savers use the property market as a substitute for investment, which gives housing price data predictive power with respect to financial crises. At the beginning of 2011, a new system for collecting house price data was introduced in China. Since this point, data has been collected and published in a more detailed manner. For instance, data for the 70 cities is now split between commercial residential property and new residential property among others. The difference between the two categories is that new residential property includes social housing (Orlik 2012: 77-83). Given the above, it should be clear that real estate is a substantial driver of growth for the Chinese economy.

The next data I would like to elaborate on are FX reserves. As laid out in the conceptual section, FX reserves are a vital buffer against financial turmoil, particularly currency distortions (Pesenti and Tille 2000). The Chinese FX reserves have accumulated more or less automatically over time as the country pursued an export driven growth strategy during the time when the local exchange rate was pegged vis-à-vis the US dollar. Thus, the country used exchange rate policy to support its export strategy and consequently, built-up a pile of FX reserves. In light of China's current account surplus, the country had to regularly intervene in the FX market in order to prevent the currency from appreciating. 'The change in China's FX reserves maps closely to the change in China's current account surplus, and this is no accident' (Orlik 2012: 136). Only by accumulating the proceeds of the surplus was the country able to maintain its peg vis-à-vis the US dollar.

The IMF's Balance of Payment Manual can be used to calculate the value of FX reserves. However, the adoption of these standards by SAFE did not improve the transparency of the calculations. For instance, without knowing the exact composition of the FX reserves, it is not possible to validate the value of the reserves each month. Nonetheless, it is known that the largest part of the Chinese reserves consists of US Treasuries and other debt securities. That being said, FX reserve data provide vital clues on speculative capital flows. As laid out in the historical background section, capital outflows were one of the reasons for the disastrous outcome of the Asian financial crisis. Even though China still has some capital controls in place, illicit flows in and out of the country are a significant factor influencing the Chinese exchange rate.

FX reserves, as the residuum position of the balance of payments, give some hints on the direction of the flows (Orlik 2012: 136-141). Given the above, it should be clear that currency market participants closely watch FX reserve data.

Exports are a further indicator of significant importance to the FX market. China's rise as an export champion started with the country's accession to the World Trade Organisation (WTO) in 2001 (Naughton 2007). Over time, China has stepped up in the value chain and today is the world's largest exporter. China's exports include mobile phones as well as machinery manufactures. Exports make up for 1 in every 3 yuan of domestic output and the Chinese export sector serves as a gauge for global demand. China's entry into the WTO helped spur growth in the sector. However, the country's repressive system, foremost low cost of capital, labour, land, and energy, all helped keep prices for Chinese products very competitive. What is more, an undervalued yuan in the 2000s supported the relative advantage of China's export industry (Orlik 2012: 109-110). In theory, a country with a trade surplus should let its currency appreciate. However, the peg of the Chinese yuan to the US dollar resulted in an undervaluation of the renminbi and in the accumulation of a massive pile of FX reserves, as pointed out above. The focus of capital markets is on the year-on-year growth rate of exports. In the years of tremendous growth figures, double-digit growth rates in exports were the norm in China. Only in 2008, with the collapse of global demand, did exports decline and served as a leading indicator for the Chinese economy. Exports recovered somewhat due to the rebound in global demand; however, gone are the years of export growth between twenty and thirty percent. Nonetheless, Chinese exports are still a very good gauge on the valuation of the renminbi and on the health of the domestic economy (Orlik 2012: 112-120). As the headline export data is not corrected for seasonal variation, year-on-year growth rates have to be used as input for the econometric analysis.

The last variable of the fundamental framework is FX valuation. As pointed out above, the undervaluation of the renminbi helped to spur China's export-driven growth strategy in the 2000s. Instead of floating the yuan, the renminbi remained pegged at a rate of 8.27 to the US dollar between China's entry to the WTO in 2001 and July 2005. Improvements in productivity during this time should have led to an appreciation of the local currency. Thus, the undervaluation of the renminbi helped to build-up FX reserves and led to the subsequent appreciation trend between 2005 and 2008. At that point in time, a decrease in global demand led to the stop in the appreciation trend in the Chinese renminbi. However, the undervaluation was corrected due to the prior appreciation trend. This makes clear the importance of FX valuation for the evolution of the yuan. As Sharma (2016: 263) pointed out, an overvaluation of the local exchange rate can lead foreigners and locals to move capital out of a country and thus, curtails domestic growth. The concept of FX valuation is closely linked to the law of one price, which says that the same goods have to have the same price in the same currency, otherwise arbitrage may occur. This is linked to the purchasing power parity. A country would see no changes in valuation if it were not for deviations from the PPP (Krugman et al. 2015: 447). In practice, Goldstein et al. (2000) identified deviations from the trend in the real exchange rate as one of the best indicators for financial crises from an early warning point of view. Often, in high volatility regimes the market enforces an adjustment of the real exchange rate in order to adjust for an overvaluation. The indicator should yield a warning signal in case of an unusual deviation from its trend. As a matter of fact, these deviations are usually associated with excessive capital flows.

ii) Policy-induced Weaknesses

Apart from fundamental factors, I am adding one dimension with respect to policy-induced uncertainty. The first variable I would like to discuss is policy experimentation in terms of the yuan's internationalisation. The Hong Kong Interbank CNY Reference Rate Overnight and the forward implied yield serve here as an indication. As pointed out in the conceptual section, policy experimentation should help to facilitate institutional innovation; this is the case with China's local currency as well. China is a transition economy and therefore, the ultimate question relates to how to facilitate the shift from plan to market. Due to the country's incremental approach towards transformation, this is not yet complete. The process China is currently undergoing has to be considered as large-scale institutional change (Roland 2000). The question is how to facilitate the transformation process without triggering a financial crisis. The political economy of China depicts a substantial ability for creative solutions that help the country to forgo some of the crises other transition economies went through (Mukand and Rodrik 2002). Indeed, China's unique approach helps the country to overcome some of the impediments of the shift from plan to market that rattled other transition economies (North 2006). This is also valid in terms of the development of the Chinese offshore market, which helped facilitate the RMB internationalisation. McNally and Gruin (2017: 16) stress the vital importance of 'targeted liberalization, policy experimentation, and institutional hybridization'. Indeed, both the Hong Kong Interbank CNY Reference Rate Overnight and the forward implied yield serve the Chinese leadership as a means to facilitate the institutional transformation from a purely domestic to an international useable currency. Anytime the yuan experienced serve stress, the PBoC squeezed offshore yields in order to bring down the pressure in the exchange rate market. This can be classified as an experimental approach, as the offshore yields are used to manage the onshore exchange rate. In this respect, the Chinese leadership prevents excessive speculation on a one-off event in the local exchange rate and consequently, averts significant exchange rate distortions from occurring.

The next variable I would like to discuss, as part of the policy-induced framework, is the old-age dependency ratio. China is on the verge of a demographic shift that has substantial consequences for the domestic economy. Sharma (2016) notes that the downward trend in global economic growth can be partially attributed to the decreasing supply of labour. The full effect of this is not yet visible. Foremost in China, the implemented birth control measures have effects on the growth rate of the country. The replacement rate is about 2.1; anything below this number means that the Chinese population is declining. One side effect of this policy is the rise of the old-age dependency ratio. In China, the working-age population is shrinking due to the aging population.

Indeed, the Chinese one-child policy had negative repercussions for the whole system. Initially, China benefited from the so-called demographic dividend, as elaborated on in the conceptual section of this book. The decline in the dependency ratio since the end of the 1970s spurred economic growth. However, a pick-up in the dependency ratio represents a significant drag to the Chinese economy. This represents vulnerabilities, which should not be underestimated given that it creates a higher social burden and disadvantages due to a predominately old population. A lower dependency ratio allowed the country to save and invest more over the previous decades, which was reflected in China's current account and thus, in its currency. The appreciation pressure the yuan faced over the last decades can be partially attributed to the build-up of the current account surplus and thus, to this window of opportunity the country grabbed. This has now backfired in the form of a higher old-age dependency ratio, which coincided with a lower current account surplus of China. Part of its previous population control measures had to be reversed in order to stop the old-age dependency ratio from increasing. Whether this works is questionable. In the econometric analysis, I use the old-age dependency ratio published by the NBS as a proxy for this demographic shift in the economy, which contributed to the decline in the appreciation pressure of the Chinese yuan. The vulnerability is assessed with the help of principal component analysis, which output serves as the basis for the logit model.

Furthermore, inequality is assessed with the help of the Gini coefficient. As the IMF pointed out in 2012, higher levels of equality are associated with higher macroeconomic stability as well as more sustainable growth (Atkinson 2015: 12). The free market spirit of the last decades contributed to the rise of levels of inequality seen today. Markets on its own might not guarantee the best outcome for everyone. China shows a fairly complex link between inequality, poverty, and economic performance. The latter has been tremendous, foremost in urban areas, as well as in the coastal regions. China's growth was significant over the last decades; however, the society has recently grown more unequal. Indeed, the urban-rural gap makes inequality very visible. Initially, due to the reforms on the countryside, growth did outperform urban output. This turned around in the mid-1980s. One measure of income distribution is the Gini coefficient, which depicts a value between 0 and 1. The closer the reading is to 0, the more equally is a society and vice versa. Since the mid-1980s, the coefficient depicts a steady rise, as urban residents were favoured in many areas of the society. Today, China is among the least equal societies globally, according to the Gini coefficient (Atkinson 2015: 22). As a matter of fact, the growth in inequality undermines economic development as pointed out by Hardoon et al. (2016). Additionally, an OECD (2012) report notes that there is higher likelihood of financial crisis due to this.

The next variable I would like to discuss is monetary policy. I use forward-forwards and M2 as gauges for the monetary policy stance of China. Forward-forwards give a good indication on the markets pricing of future implied yields. This has been already touched upon in the section on policy experimentation and thus, I primarily focus on M2 in this part. This indicator needs explanation, as it slightly differs from the usual calculation of money supply. First of all, both households' time and demand deposits are included in M2. Furthermore, the data does not capture new developments in financial products. For instance, wealth management products are not classified as deposits and are therefore not included in M2. This exclusion reduces M2 as an indicator for money supply (Orlik 2012: 200-201). Nonetheless, M2 is the broadest measure for money supply and it is still used as an intermediate target for China's monetary policy. Often times, a target is announced for M2 at the annual government work conference. This should be interpreted only as a guideline for the overall government's thinking, as the actual number can differ significantly from the target. Thus, the ratio of M2 to GDP should be regarded as a measure for the overall state of China's monetary condition. With a higher ratio, more money is chasing output. With respect to the exchange rate, Krugman et al. (2015: 411) pointed out that money supply is among the most important factors determining a currency's trajectory. Changes in money supply have an influence on both channels affecting the exchange rate, namely on the interest rate component as well as on the expected changes in the exchange rate. Thus, in theory, this variable should be particularly relevant for the dependent variable, namely the currency debasement of the Chinese yuan, which took place in August 2015, together with the revision and the subsequent alterations in the exchange rate regime and the entailed capital flow volatility.

The last policy variable I would like to discuss is fiscal policy. As an indicator for this type of policy, I chose equity price performance. Given the various levels of government, the official fiscal number does not capture the policy stance of China and therefore, we have to come up with a proxy. Equity price performance covers the policy-induced area very well. With respect to fiscal policy, it was virtually forbidden for local governments to raise debt themselves until 2014. Under the Chinese fiscal law, these entities had very little leeway themselves and thus, were dependent on the share of taxes allocated by the central government to them. However, this was not sufficient to cover the spending by local governments and thus, the fiscal rule was circumvented by setting up investment companies, which then enabled the local governments to spend more when needed. This should make clear that the official fiscal number is a very bad gauge for the fiscal stance of China.

Most of this borrowing was indeed done unreported, as these vehicles were off budget. Equity prices in China, in contrast, capture the fiscal policy stance well. Monetary policy is not yet advanced enough to play a particular important role for the performance of equity markets. However, fiscal policy is one of the key levers for the Chinese leadership to control the speed of the Chinese economy and thus, also have an influence on the renminbi. A faster pace of economic output growth should attract foreign capital and should make it more attractive for locals to invest domestically rather than take their money abroad. In contrast, a lower economic performance should also coincide with a weaker currency, as domestic and foreign capital is repulled by a slower growth rate.

iii) Institutional Factors

Apart from fundamental and policy factors, one dimension of institutional determinants will be added to the vulnerability analysis. The first factor

I would like to discuss is liberalisation. As a proxy for the different forms of liberalisation, the lending to deposit spread, the US-China yield differential and real interest rates are chosen. Indeed, China's financial opening is lagging behind other parts of the economy, as laid out in the conceptual section of this book. The country's transformation is an ongoing process. Given the country's incremental approach with respect to transition, China's financial sector remains heavily controlled. The People's Bank of China and thus, the State Council, still consider financial repression as one of their key levers to controlling the country's economic model. Financial repression refers to government regulated interest rates. Whether or not liberalisation in terms of China's repressive system played a role in the troubles the country faced in 2015 and 2016 is examined with the help of the lending to deposit spread as well as with real interest rates.
In general, research has not been conclusive whether the benefits or drawbacks of a repressive system are more important. On the one hand, it is argued that financial repression results in a loss of efficiency. On the other hand, the repression enables governments to better handle financial risks. This discussion is laid out in detail in the analytical part of this book. In China, financial repression is a vital part of the country's growth model. The system was put in place as part of the export-driven system China benefits from.

Moreover, with the US-China yield differential the probability of capital flight is assessed. A narrower yield differential should make it more attractive for locals to invest capital abroad; capital outflows represents a significant risk for the Chinese currency. In contrast, a wide yield differential should entice foreigners to bring in capital, which should coincide with an appreciation trend of the local exchange rate.

Further factors relating to the FX regime include the onshore-offshore spread and FX volatility. The latter is a sign for the FX regime. In general, a managed floating system should depict a higher FX volatility than a fixed regime. The Chinese government chooses the regime and regular interventions in the exchange rate market are necessary in order to uphold the system. In case of a migration from a fixed system to a floating exchange rate regime, a pick-up in FX volatility should be observed. A fixed regime does not depict any volatility. Thus, the option implied volatility has to be interpreted as a risk premium for a currency devaluation. In line with this thought, the pick-up in the FX volatility at the time of a regime migration represents the realised risk of currency distortions. In contrast to this, China has always thought of stability in its exchange rate as a virtue. In its history, China often opted for a non-devaluation strategy as for instance during the time of the Asian financial crisis. This makes the events of 2015 and 2016 particularly interesting.

Regarding the onshore-offshore spread, in theory, the Chinese renminbi is one currency. However, capital transfer restrictions make perfect arbitrage impossible between the onshore and offshore currency. Every time there is stress in the foreign exchange market, the offshore yuan depreciates more than the onshore yuan. This is related to the fixing of the onshore renminbi. The Chinese government can better control the daily fixing of the onshore yuan due to the lack of internationalisation of this currency; it is only traded on a non-deliverable basis outside China and thus, the daily value greatly depends on the Chinese leadership. In contrast, the offshore renminbi is not fixed daily by the PBoC and thus, it is dependent on market supply and demand. Therefore, in times of stress, USD/CNH is pushed higher by the market, as pointed out in the conceptual section of this book.

The next variable I would like to discuss is governance and the rule of law. As laid out in the conceptual section, China is often left out in studies regarding institutions. Governance and the rule of law are rather weak in China and thus, the tremendous growth rates and the absence of crises are often labelled as the "China paradox". Indeed, the application of the existing academic literature on China is fairly complex. The country was even used as a counterexample of the existing literature with respect to institutions. This was in light of China's rise in absolute terms as well as relative to other emerging markets. To assess this and the connection between China's absence of crises and the country's recent troubles in 2015 and 2016, I take the World Bank's rule of law index into consideration. This should help figure out whether a strengthening or backsliding of the rights of the civil society has any effects on the dependent variable, namely the exchange rate distortions China faced in said period.

The country's rise over the previous decades poses a puzzle to academic researchers. However, in this respect, research which takes into account provincial data has shown that in those areas with better governance and rule of law the growth rates and thus, the avoidance of crises is more prominent. Therefore, on a provincial data level, the link between this factor and distortions exists. Whether it is also visible on an individual country basis is examined with the help of over five hundred research reports and quantitatively with a logit model. China is often named as a counterexample of the Coasian economic model due to high transaction costs but good economic growth numbers and the absence of financial crisis. Therefore, understanding the distortions of 2015 and 2016 from a perspective of governance and the rule of law can add significant value.

A further variable I would like to cover in the institutional section of this book is state-owned enterprises. China's gradual approach towards transition has left the SOE sector as a still-crucial part of the Chinese economy. Over time, the capital market reform in China helped advance the government-owned enterprise sector reform. State companies were first listed and then a partial change in ownership took place. Therefore, I use the difference between the number in offshore and onshore listed enterprises as a proxy for the progress of the SOE reform.

In contrast to Central and Eastern European countries as well as to the Soviet Union, China chose a gradual approach towards transforming its economy and thus, towards privatisation. The rapid transitions of the former regions came at a huge cost for the countries, namely transformational recessions coupled with currency devaluations. This speedy change in ownership resulted in the state being rapidly pushed back. In contrast to this experience, China's incremental approach towards transforming its economy left ownership restructuring initially untouched. Companies were listed only gradually on the stock exchange.

This allowed the country to forgo some of the faults which the countries in Central and Eastern Europe and the former Soviet Union experienced. Still, China's transformation is not completed yet due to its incremental approach and thus, whether or not the increased marketization of the Chinese economy contributed to the troubles of 2015 and 2016 has to be assessed. This is done with the help of the difference between the number in offshore and onshore listed enterprises.

The last variable of the institutional framework I would like to use in the logit model is technology and productivity. I use the China Innovation Output Index as an indicator for said category. In general, the rate of technological growth is measured with the help of the Solow model. This method shows that in developed countries the trajectory is coined by technology. For developing countries, this represents a vital category in which they can catch up with more advanced nations. As the catch-up process advances, the way in which development progresses also changes. First, a country only profits from imported technologies. Subsequently, spending on R&D increases. As China is advancing in huge steps, it is fair to say that R&D spending should make an ever-increasing portion of this variable. Also, as pointed out in the conceptual section, the adoption of foreign technologies might need a country to invest in R&D. Therefore, I use the China Innovation Output Index as an indication for China's ability to innovate.

Given the variables of the three dimensions, I proceed in the following way: First, I will perform a principal component analysis for each set of the independent variables. To do this, I start with a description of the statistical method. Second, I use the three 1st vectors of the principal component analysis as input variables in the logit model. In this respect, I am able to show that not only fundamentals, but also policy and institutional determinants play a role in foreign exchange distortions.

d) Principal Component Analysis and the Logit Model

The vectors of the principal component analysis are used as input variables in the logit model. In this model, the dependent variable will be a binary indicator. This indicator is related to China's exchange rate troubles in said period, namely the currency debasement of the Chinese yuan in August 2015, the change in the FX regime and the frequent revisions of this as well as the entailed capital outflows. The model helps calculate the probability of a state of crisis given the three dimensions, namely fundamental, policy-induced, and institutional vulnerabilities.

I start out with setting up a predictive model for the dependent variable, the FX distortion in China in 2015 and 2016. The input variables to this model are the three first and second principal components of the matrix factorisation performed with the help of PCA. The basic statistics for the predictive model – 6 months ahead of the events - are depicted below:

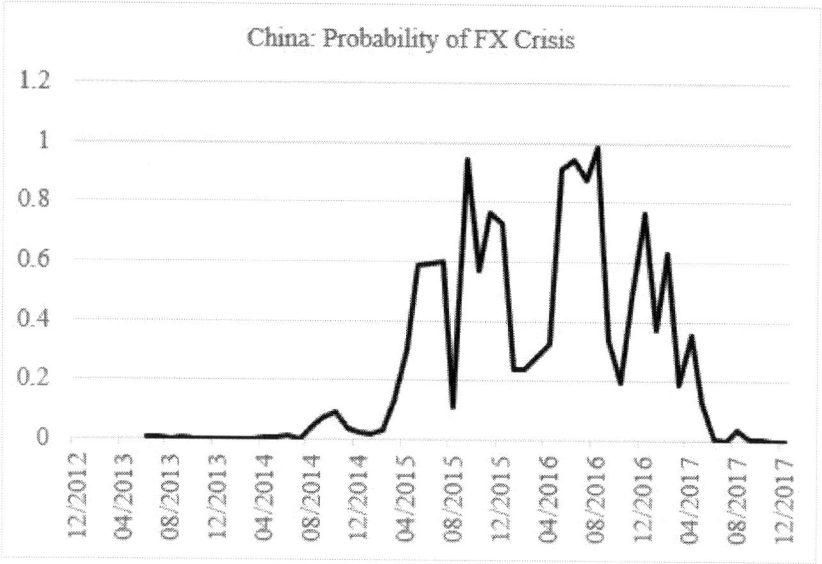

Inference Table

PCs	Estimates	Std err	t-stats
Constant	-12.52	5.97	-2.10
PC1 - Fund.	-0.15	0.07	-2.20
PC2 - Fund.	-0.08	0.05	-1.61
PC1 - Policy	0.06	0.00	84.75
PC2 - Policy	1.12	0.44	2.56
PC1 - Instit.	1.21	0.30	4.03
PC2 - Instit.	-1.15	0.76	-1.50

By running the model, it can be seen that all three dimensions are statistically significant as per the t-value. In particular, the policy dimension depicts a high level of statistical significance, which is related to the high variation in equity prices ahead of the events. The second principal components do not depict any significance except for the policy dimension. This hints to the fact that most of the variation is already captured by the first principal component.

To conclude, I laid out the details of the quantitative research strategy. First, I started with a general outline of the idea given the early warning literature. I based the decision of which indicators to include on a review of broad and recurring themes in the academic literature on China as well as on financial crises.

Part 5:
China in Constant Transition – The Aftermath and the Path Forward

An expanded conceptualisation of vulnerability to currency crises, which forms a unified framework, is applied to China's troubles in the second half of 2015 and 2016. A different conceptualisation of a country's strength and weaknesses provides a different response to the fundamental question of how to better understand and thus, predict currency distortions, particularly in regard to the change in the FX regime of the Chinese renminbi, which took place in August 2015. In general, this event does not get the attention it should.

In this book, I aim to create awareness of the different forms of vulnerability – fundamental, policy-induced, and institutional. Analysing each one helps to generate an improved understanding of key drivers of outcomes from an early warning perspective. The expanded approach provides a framework for integration with respect to the distinct, but interconnected, forms of fragilities that China faces. By obtaining a thorough understanding of the drivers of crises, it is possible to better comprehend the rise of China as well as the country's recent struggles. By developing a unified framework to analyse currency crises and apply this to China's troubles in the second half of 2015 and 2016, I help stakeholders to better understand the holistic picture of China's unfinished transition and demonstrate that efforts of China should aim at addressing underlying vulnerabilities. In the subsequent sub-sections, an overview of the lessons learnt and corrective actions that could be taken by policymakers in the future is given.

a) Fundamental Vulnerabilities

i) Reversion to the Mean

The growth of large emerging markets, particularly China, is one of the most important developments globally. Lawrence Summers noted on this subject that, 'the dramatic modernization of the Asian economies ranks alongside the Renaissance and the Industrial Revolution as one of the most important developments in economic history' (Summers quoted in Eichengreen et al. 2011). Double-digit growth in China during the decades of the reform era led to an unprecedented catch-up process for the country. Thus, emerging markets contribute the bulk of the share to global growth every year. Gerschenkron (1962, 1964) associated this with the advantage of backwardness. Instead of inventing new technologies, developing economies and emerging markets can import existing innovations from advanced countries. Productivity gains result from underemployed workers in the countryside who move to export-orientated manufacturing sectors closer to urban areas. A young population saves more than elderly people and thus, can finance an investment spree. All of these factors contributed to the catch-up process of emerging nations. However, this cannot last forever. Declining marginal returns per input factor make the need for new growth drivers. A large capital stock means higher depreciation rates, which requires even higher savings in order for growth not to slow down. A country's growth cannot solely rely on imported technology, but the growth model must be changed towards indigenous innovation. As laid out in this book, these issues are among the most important for developing economies and emerging markets, particularly for China today. Since China is the growth engine of the world, anything that affects the country has global repercussions. Eichengreen et al. (2011) comment on this issue, saying that, 'while China recovered faster than expected from the global crisis, its policymakers are grappling with how to sustain growth in the medium and long terms'. As noted in the introductory section of this book, many observers extrapolated China's growth rate into the future without considering the different stages a country goes through (Shambaugh 2014:39). Other examples of fast-growth episodes suggest that all growth miracles eventually slow down. The question remains, whether China will slow down significantly?

This is relevant from an early warning perspective as variables related to growth are among the key fundamental predictors. Historically, a growth decline of at least 2 percentage points happened at per capita incomes of approximately USD 17,000 in 2005 constant international prices, 'a level that China should achieve on or soon after 2015' (Eichengreen et al. 2011). However, more open economies tend to sustain high growth rates for longer, while rapidly aging societies slow down faster. This and more factors were discussed in this book and related to financial crisis, foremost currency distortions. Furthermore, Eichengreen et al. published a sequel of their analysis in 2013. 'In contrast to our earlier analysis which pointed to the existence of a single mode at which slowdowns occur in the neighborhood of $15,000-$16,000 2005 purchasing power parity dollars, new data point to two modes, one in the $10,000-$11,000 range and another at $15,000-$16,000' (Eichengreen et al. 2013). The conclusion of their analysis is that the growth decrease of middle-income countries happens in steps instead of a one-off deceleration. In addition, the researchers associate a higher degree of growth consistency with a higher level of secondary and tertiary education as well as with a higher share of high-technology exports in the trade balance of a country. This is consistent with the general notion laid out in this book. Extrapolation of historical growth episodes can lead to a wrong picture, as growth slowdowns are positively associated with earlier growth spurts suggesting the presence of mean reversion. Furthermore, Eichengreen et al. (2013) states that regime changes from autocracy to democracy are related with slowdowns, a concept which is elaborated on in more detail in the section on economic transitions from plan to market. Moreover, the researchers find that the likelihood of a slowdown peaks at USD 17,900, which is higher than in their previous work.

The term middle-income trap is related to a stage of stagnating per capita income given a previously rapid catch-up process relative to advanced nations (Glawe and Wagner 2017; Huang et al. 2017). How can countries avoid the middle-income trap? This is one key question for China given early warning analysis. Factor accumulation leads to a likely slowdown given diminishing marginal returns. Three predictions are put forward by modern growth theory regarding the potential slowdown: 'First, diversification will slow and then reverse, as countries become more specialized in production and employment; second, investment will become less important, and innovation should accelerate; third, education systems will shift from equipping workers with skills that allow them to adjust to new technologies to preparing to shape new products and processes. These would be the observable outcomes associated with a successful shift in strategy as countries progress through middle-income status.' (Gill and Kharas 2007: 17-18)

Whether or not China is able to manage this remains to be seen.

Due to the unprecedented rise of China, the economic centre of the world shifted towards Asia. However, Pritchett and Summers (2014) put forward that China will grow at a lower rate in the future than over the past decades. 'Abnormally rapid growth is rarely persistent. Indeed, regression to the mean is the empirically most salient feature of economic growth' (Pritchett and Summers 2014). Discontinuous drop-offs in economic performance in relation to financial crisis, foremost a currency adjustment, make up for a large part of the variation. Therefore, Chinese policymakers should factor in a wider range of outcomes with respect to economic performance in China. Apart from Japan, another growth story that was extrapolated indefinitely was that of the East Asian Dragons consisting of the four Asian Tigers, namely Hong Kong, South Korea, Singapore and Taiwan, as well as of Malaysia, Indonesia and Thailand. As laid out in the section 'Crises in Perspective', the macroeconomic performance of these nations was very sound before the financial crisis hit the countries and temporarily derailed their success story (Lissakers 1999: 3). Now there is China, which has grown at a significant speed over the past four decades. Compound interest as well as a substantial population helped China to become an economic powerhouse. However, past growth performance is no guarantee for future success. Indeed, 'the lack of persistence in country growth rates over medium- to long-run horizons implies current growth has very little predictive power for future growth' (Pritchett and Summers 2014). Errors in economic forecasting have come from the simple fact that growth rates should not be extrapolated indefinitely into the future because a country's different growth stages have to be considered (Shambaugh 2014: 39). In many developing countries, the trajectories are marked by discontinuities with frequent accelerations and decelerations of economic performance, which foremost relate to currency distortions. The crisis of 2008 should remind us that growth risks as well as fragility of the system are often vastly underestimated. In this respect, Pritchett and Summers (2014) show that 'rapidly growing countries are substantially more likely to suffer a downward discontinuity in growth than upward movement'. This low persistence has been statistically quite robust across decades according to the researchers. With respect to China, it is argued that the country does not have the high-quality institutions that lead to steady economic performance, which should be a concern from an early warning perspective. This was examined in detail in the institutional section of this book.

As Bai and Zhang (2017) note, China's economy is structurally slowing. The signs of this slowdown have been particularly visible for researchers since 2008. 'Though the government stimulus triggered a pullback from 2009's record low, this rebound proved to be short-lived: the growth rate slumped again in 2011. Between the years of 2011 and 2015, the annual growth rate for the PRC economy stood at a mere 7.84%' (Bai and Zhang 2017: 1). As pointed out in the conceptual section, neoclassical models suggest that growth is driven by labour, capital accumulation, as well as productivity. While the early decades of China's growth were driven by both productivity gains as well as capital, the former took a hit in the period after the great financial crisis of 2008 (Lardy 2012: 5; Sun and Fu 2012: 11-12). This coincided with a decrease in both labour as well as productivity rates. In their growth accounting analysis, the researchers find that economic opening had a crucial positive effect on efficiency as well as technology. This is in line with prior research and is described in detail in the institutional section of this book. In contrast to the aforementioned, the income level of a country has a negative effect on economic growth and vice versa, which is in line with the notion of benefits of economic backwardness. Moreover, the stock of inventory and productivity of a nation are significantly and negatively correlated. The same holds for the size of the government or the investment rate in relation to productivity. Nonetheless, the latter could be a simple effect of the specification of the growth accounting exercise. 'Lastly, we conclude that the diminishing late-mover advantage and the growth in investment rate are all major contributors to the decline in the PRC's productivity since the financial crisis' (Bai and Zhang 2017: 1-2). 'But how to describe the descent of an economy from high-speed growth? Chinese planners have seized on "L" as their letter of choice. The suggestion is that, after an initial lurch downward, growth will coast along a new plateau for years' (The Economist 2017b). This description of the growth trajectory of China is quite accurate as growth declined from the sphere of double-digit speed after 2010. In addition, output more closely reflected the horizontal base of the L from 2015 to 2017. This coincided with China's significant exchange rate troubles in said period. Some worry that what could derail China's path is the excessive amount of debt, financial fragility, and the property bubble (Li et al. 2017b; Hu and Peng 2016; Zhang and Zeng 2017b). However, the Chinese government is aware of the above-mentioned risks and is taking steps to counterbalance the situation. Controls on mortgages as well as on house purchases have helped to rein in the property bubble. Slower credit growth and controls on leverage should slow down the debt binge (The Economist 2017b). Nonetheless, these measures primarily focus on fundamentals.

ii) Risks

Li et al. (2017b) analyse the biggest risks for China's growth trajectory after the high volatility years of 2015 and 2016. Stability is a key priority for the country. Such risks stem from the credit boom as well as from the calibration of policy-measures. In addition to these domestic factors, very large risks loom from abroad. In general, 2015 and 2016 were challenging years for the country given the currency debasement of the Chinese yuan, which took place in August 2015, together with the revision and the subsequent alterations in the exchange rate regime as well as the entailed capital flow volatility. However, large policy stimulus helped to get through the stormy waters with respect to economic variables. 'Fiscal and regulatory easing, alongside continued rapid credit growth, underpinned strong growth in infrastructure spending and a rebound in cyclical sectors like property and motor vehicles. Real GDP growth came in on target' (Li et al. 2017b: 2). This reflects the continuous commitment of the Chinese Communist Party to high economic performance in this decade; an idea which was put forward by the previous administration and confirmed by many senior officials. In particular, 2017 represented an important year for China, in which hardly any financial and economic turbulence were tolerated thanks to the 19th Party Congress at the end of the year (Jin and Liu 2017e). In this respect, the so-called policy put played an important role, which refers to the commitment of the Chinese leadership to its development targets at all costs.

This has entailed a build-up in leverage, which on an absolute and relative basis has reached non-negligible levels. 'Sustained debt booms typically lead to slower growth, greater financial volatility, and heightened risk of a financial crisis. Looking at more than a century of historical data, [...] "a large domestic debt boom" last at least 7 years where the debt-to-GDP ratio increases by over 52pp – China's easily qualifies – is typically followed by a 2pp slowdown in growth and a heightened risk of financial crisis' (Li et al. 2017b: 4). Another way to see this issue is via the negative credit impulse (Milesi-Ferretti and Lane 2010). International tightening, external shocks, as well as a collapse under their own weight are some of the reasons for the stop in credit booms. In addition, a shift in domestic policy could also curtail the credit impulse, which would affect growth negatively. Chinese policymakers are well aware of this and have thus tried to postpone the slowdown given its potential consequences. However, at some point the stimulus has to be stopped, which leads to the second major risk identified, namely a major policy tightening. 'Historically, the growth target was a "policy put" that was out of the money – a reassurance that growth would not be allowed to drop too far' (Li et al. 2017b: 6). However, this has become a binding constraint on policy in China. 'To meet the GDP growth targets, credit growth has boomed [...] and a key driver of demand for that credit has been a large increase in the broadly-defined fiscal deficit' (Li et al. 2017b: 6). Indeed, as growth hit the target range in 2016, policymakers started the tightening cycle by increasing housing restrictions, regulating shadow banking activities, tightening monetary policy via hiking short-term interest rates and imposing capital outflow controls. Even if the intention is to gradually slow down the credit impulse, there is a risk of doing this too fast accidentally. For instance, the spike in repo rates in mid-2013 and the heightened equity volatility surrounding policy interventions, such as with the introduction of a circuit breaker in early 2016, can be classified as policy-induced uncertainty. In this respect, 'the biggest vulnerabilities to unintended tightening are probably in the less formal areas of off-balance sheet spending (on the fiscal side) and non-bank credit extension (on the monetary side)' (Li et al. 2017b: 8). In addition, to these two domestic risks identified, potential shocks from abroad were often named as risks for China's growth trajectory. As exports remain one cornerstone of the Chinese success story, demand outside the country also plays an important role for China. Therefore, the nation remains vulnerable to any global growth shocks or to increased protectionism, particularly from the side of the US.

In addition to the above, Hu and Peng (2016) analyse the debt situation in China and whether this represents a potential risk, which could lead to a currency adjustment. The researchers find certain unique features of this in China. The debt binge is foremost financed by domestic savings with external FX debt making up only a minor fraction of the total debt, namely about 3 percent. This makes a crisis similar to the Asian financial crisis quite unlikely. Moreover, although the country's debt-to-GDP ratio is continuously on the rise, its debt-to-asset ratio is declining. Indeed, both debt and assets are stock variables and thus, the comparison is better than in case of the debt-to-GDP ratio. The debt-to-asset ratio has declined over the last few years and is almost 10 percentage points lower than it was in the late 1990s for industrial enterprises. The same picture holds for the Chinese government, which has borrowed a lot due to build-up of capital such as infrastructure, factories, and to develop land. Thus, 'the key is not to lower the overall leverage, but the "bad" leverage, which doesn't create enough value to justify the funding costs' (Hu and Peng 2016). Another feature of the Chinese debt build-up is that corporate debt is excessively high. However, two thirds of the corporate debt is mainly owed by state-owned enterprises to state-owned banks and thus, the majority of the corporate debt is owed by one government entity to the other. Debt-to-equity swaps, for instance, are means to reshuffle debt within the system. This has significant implications for financial stability. Consequently, 'China could prevent a classic EM crisis, given its low foreign debt, high FX reserves and capital controls' (Hu and Peng 2016). In addition to the above, a Minsky moment, which refers to a fire sale of assets in a general panic, is relatively unlikely in China given that sticky bank deposits back most of the outstanding debt, not volatile wholesale funding. Indeed, a liquidity squeeze is the main reason for a banking crisis, not necessarily solvency problems. In the late 1990s, NPLs in China's banking system amounted to about 40 percent, but the Chinese banks still functioned due to liquidity inflows from depositors. Nonetheless, the debt build-up in China is a worrying development. 'China's high debt is just a reflection of the problem instead of the problem itself. On the surface, China's high debt is inevitable due to its high savings rate [...] and low equity financing. But, at a deeper level, a high savings rate is the outcome of a system we call "State capitalism", under which the state extracts resources from the private sector through three channels: financial repression, SOE monopoly and land controls' (Hu and Peng 2016). The three channels work as follows: 'the first one is land. The government monopolizes land supply, selling land for revenue and using land as collateral to borrow. Moreover, limited land supply also boosts home prices, forcing households to save more to buy properties. The second one is SOEs. SOEs monopolize the "Commanding Heights" in the economy such as energy, telecom, and utility, while leaving the downstream industries for market competition. In this way, SOEs could extract "rent" from the private sector' (Hu and Peng 2016). The third channel is financial repression, which is described in detail in another section of this book. All these channels serve to extract resources from the private sector and lead to an artificially high saving rate, which is partly exported via the country's current account surplus. The rest of the savings have to be deployed domestically, which lowers the marginal return to capital. Thus, the debt binge is most likely to result in lower growth for China.

With respect to real estate, Zhang and Zeng (2017b) note that the main reason for the property bubble is the loose monetary policy pursued by the Chinese central bank in order to prop up growth. The bubble has positive effects on China in the short-term due to the so-called wealth effect. However, this comes at increased macroeconomic risk going forward. Thus, a decline in real estate prices would have severe negative consequences for the Chinese economy with respect to the country's re-allocation towards consumption as well as growth in general. Furthermore, the wealth effect not only encourages higher consumption, but also leads to a lower current account surplus due to lower savings. Zhang and Zeng (2017b) give various reasons why the Chinese government tolerates the property price bubble. 'The property and construction sectors accounted for 33% and 15% of local government tax revenue growth between 2010 and 2015. They contributed 43% of local government tax revenue in 2015, compared to 11% from manufacturing [...]. Besides taxes, local governments heavily rely on land sales to finance infrastructure projects' (Zhang and Zeng 2017b: 1). In addition, a crucial factor according to researchers is that the government believes that they can avoid a severe drawdown in the real estate sector. Indeed, China does have a stronger control over property prices than other countries due to its relatively closed capital account, a high saving rate and a current account surplus. Nonetheless, empirically the deflation of most property bubbles was preceded by higher interest rates. The ultimate long-term drivers of real estate prices are demographics as well as urbanisation and indeed, both indicators are slowing for China. In December 2016, the Chinese president, Xi Jinping, noted that, 'properties are meant for residence, not for speculation'. Nonetheless, this caution did not last long, even though China depicted very favourable price development in January and February 2017. The Chinese government published its work plan for the whole year in March 2017, which put forward the reduction in inventory but not the tackling of the property bubble, meaning that the latter was not a policy priority for the Chinese government. With respect to Chinese data releases, the quality of the data is still a huge problem. The same also goes for real estate data. The Chinese leadership has tried to curtail any information from anyone aside from NBS. Indeed, 'the SouFun 100 city index, is somehow discontinued since the end of 2016' (Zhang and Zeng 2017b: 3). In China, the real estate sector has become far too important to let any uncertainty ripple markets, as the sector is the biggest among all. In addition to the above, vested interests such as from homeowners, central and local government as well as from corporates and the financial sector, lead to government inaction with respect to the bubble. Apart from the trends in population growth and urbanisation, which should slow down the price development automatically, higher interest rates could lead to the deflation of the bubble. 'Higher interest rate triggered by inflation,

Fed tightening, or RMB depreciation. Major property bubbles in other countries, such as Japan and the US, ended when interest rates went up. We do not believe the government would pop the property bubble on purpose, but the PBoC may be forced to hike rates to fight inflation, defend currency, and/or mitigate capital outflows' (Zhang and Zeng 2017b: 9). This is in line with the research of Li et al. (2017b), which also points to the importance of policy-induced volatility for economic variables.

iii) Further Facts

According to The World Bank Group (2017b), China's growth rate for 2016 gradually slowed down to 6.7 percent, which is marginally lower than the 6.9 percent growth rate in 2015. The service sector, which makes-up for approximately half of the Chinese economy, is now the growth driver of the economic performance. However, industrial production growth stabilised at a rate of 6 percent year-on-year after it slowed down significantly due to overcapacity. 'Accommodative policies continued to support economic activity, including multiple policy interest rate cuts in 2015 that were complemented by fiscal measures since mid-2015. Policy-supported infrastructure investment, has partly offset a decline in private investment. […] Accommodative monetary policy continued to fuel credit growth, led by a rapid expansion of lending to households' (The World Bank Group 2017b: 83). This coincided with housing prices in China reaching record levels in the end of 2016. FX reserves continued to fall in 2016, although not at the same pace as in 2015, which is in line with a slowdown in capital outflows. In 2016, the renminbi has depreciated about 7 percent vis-à-vis the US dollar and approximately 5 percent in trade-weighted terms. For the yuan the volatility remained high in 2016, although the currency remained about 40 percent above the level before the change in the exchange rate regime in 2005 measured in nominal trade-weighted terms (The World Bank Group 2017b: 84). The trajectory of the RMB was described in detail in the sub-section on the FX regime.

Jin and Liu (2017e) note on the Chinese GDP numbers that Chinese growth figures surprised to the upside in the fourth quarter of 2016 with a 6.8 percent YoY growth rate. This was mainly due to credit easing as well as a speedier service industry growth rate and was in line with China's growth target for 2016, namely with a range of 6.5 to 7 percent. In particular, the tertiary sector did well, while the manufacturing output stabilised. 'For 2016 as a whole, secondary and tertiary industries expanded at 6.1% and 7.8% respectively, growing at a slightly slower pace than previous year's 6.2% and 8.2%. Nonetheless, China's economic rebalancing has continued, this is confirmed by the rising GDP share of the service sector (nominal: 51.6% in 2016 versus 50.2% in 2015)' (Jin and Liu 2017e). With respect to the expenditure approach, it is shown that consumption made up for 64.6 percent of economic performance in 2016, while investment contributed to about 42.2 percent. In general, it was expected that 2017 is a more stable year due to the 19th Party Congress in the second half of the year. Also, with respect to the RMB, the authorities signalled their strong preference for stability. Jin and Liu (2017e) note on this that 'China's capital controls and ill-developed FX derivatives market suggest both a free-floating exchange rate and large one-off devaluation are out of the question'.

Regarding the 1Q growth of 2017, Jin and Liu (2017i) note that the output release was better than expected with a 6.9 percent growth rate. Domestic demand was a key driver of the quarterly GDP release with consumption contributing 77.2 percent of output versus 64.4 percent in 2016. High frequency data also pointed to economic stabilisation with industrial production surging to 7.6 percent in March 2017 due to manufacturing (Jin and Liu 2017i). Furthermore, Jin and Liu (2017c) report on the policy targets and priorities announced by Premier Li Keqiang in the government work report in March 2017. The main points, according to the researchers, were as follows: The real growth target for China was set at a rate of around 6.5 percent for 2017 with a higher-than-expected new jobs target. In comparison to the growth range of 6.5 to 7 percent in 2016, this target is slightly lower. The fiscal deficit continues to be targeted at 3 percent and M2 and total social financing are set at 12 percent respectively. Chan et al. (2017b) note on the macro targets for 2017 that the term "seek for better performance" reflects the ambitions of the Chinese leadership to ride the upswing triggered through stimulus. Nonetheless, stability remains one of the key goals of the government, with four areas of particular attention, namely distressed assets, bond market defaults, shadow banking as well as Internet finance.

Global trade recovered from the post financial crisis stagnation and emerging markets could benefit from this trend. This coincided with a recovery in investment as well as industrial activity globally. Indeed, global trade was fuelled by the recovering demand (Goldman Sachs 2017). Asia's exports reached a low in 2015 and 2016, but significantly rebounded in 2017. China, Hong Kong, and Taiwan are among those beneficiaries. 'Their large share of manufacturing exports and integral role in the region's production chain also position them relatively better as real domestic demand strengthens outside of the region' (Ahya et al. 2017). This was preceded by a prolonged period of weakness of exports in volume terms in Asia. For example, Japan did not register any growth from 2012 to 2016 compared to the average rate of 20 percent between 2003 and 2007. 'In the past two years, exports growth in the region had turned even weaker relative to the post-crisis average. In nominal dollar terms, export growth slipped into negative territory in 2015 and 2016, averaging only -6% a year, while in volume terms, CPB data shows that export growth in EM Asia dropped to just 1.2% a year over the same period' (Ahya et al. 2017: 2). The weakness in exports in the region can be attributed to various factors, namely to weaker domestic demand in developed countries in the aftermath of the great financial crisis and to the shock to the demand of commodity producers in 2015 and 2016. This trend revered in the second half of 2016 with the growth rate in export values recovering significantly in Asia. Due to the acceleration of growth in developed markets in 2017, the recovery in exports was in good shape. This is particularly important for China; from an early warning perspective, this meant lower fundamental risks for the country.

Chen et al. (2017c) analysed China's balance of payment dynamics with respect to capital outflows econometrically and found that fundamentals, growth and interest rate differentials, sentiment, and policy uncertainty are key all drivers for capital outflows. In addition, capital controls play a crucial role in containing outflows, which is visible in the regression as historic relationships over-predict outflows in late-2016. In March 2017, China's FX reserves continued to stabilise. For the second month in a row, FX reserves pointed to modest capital inflows after a long period of capital outflows, which started in 2015. A rebound in domestic activity as well as capital controls helped to ease the pressure on China's balance-of-payments. Sentiment improved, and policy-uncertainty is contained. These factors are taken into account by Chen et al. (2017c) when analysing the drivers of non-FDI capital flows. FDI is generally long-term in nature and is thus relatively stable at high frequency levels, which makes it unsuitable for the analysis. Non-FDI capital flows hardly exceeded US $50 billion between 2001 and 2007. The great financial crisis led to more volatility on the flow side with the situation improving in the aftermath of the crisis. Capital outflows spiked significantly in 2015 and 2016 with outflows of USD 715 billion and USD 600 billion, respectively. Other investments (bank loans, trade credit, deposits and currency among others) as well as errors and omissions were those balance-of-payment items, which reflected the capital flow volatility. As the availability of balance-of-payment data is limited, the researchers built a proxy for capital outflows by subtracting the trade, service, and the FDI balances from bank FX settlements. This indication is used as the dependent variable in a regression analysis with interest rate differentials, growth differentials, sentiment, and uncertainty. The interest rate differential is calculated as the difference between the 1m repo rate in China and the US 1m T-bill rate; growth differentials are proxied by the difference between China's industrial production and US output growth; the 12m NDF rate premium is used as a proxy for FX sentiment as a larger gap is a sign of spot depreciation expectations. In addition, China's policy uncertainty index is calculated as 'the ratio of China's policy uncertainty index to that of the world using country-specific policy uncertainty indices that cover fiscal and monetary policies and other economic conditions developed by Baker, Bloom, and Davis' (Chen et al. 2017c). Growth and interest rate differentials predict capital inflows in case the variables are in favour of China and depreciation expectations as well as policy uncertainty depict a negative coefficient with respect to flows as these factors drive capital away. The capital outflows in the second half of 2015 in China were underestimated due to the unexpected change in the FX regime. Chen et al. (2017c) note that this is 'to ease outflow pressure, in our view the most immediate task is to anchor exchange rate expectations, in addition to keeping growth solid and domestic policies stable'. In addition, capital controls were efficient in the sense that the econometric analysis overestimated capital outflows in late 2016, which is examined in detail in the institutional section.

b) Policy-induced Fragilities

i) Development Policies

Transition economies tend to suffer from a lack of inclusion as well as from increasing inequality. 'In many countries, inequality rose substantially at the start of the transition. The experience of such transition countries has shown that reform processes can get stuck, or even go into reverse, in the absence of sufficient inclusion' (EBRD 2016: 8). Reformers must guarantee that the majority of the population supports their policies all the time. In this respect, inequality plays a particular important role. If the majority of the population perceives that the gains from the reforms accrue to a few, even a reversal of the political and economic transformation is possible.

The transition experience has been highly problematic for many countries, as laid out in the historical background section. 'It shows that people born around the beginning of the transition process have grown up to be an average of around 1 cm shorter than their older and younger peers, indicating that the early years of reforms were a period of substantial socioeconomic deprivation' (EBRD 2016: 9). Research by the EBRD shows that inequality of opportunity is still severe among the post-communist transition countries. Before the start of the transition, inequality was very low in these countries. However, the initial failures of the transformations of many Central and Eastern European countries, as well as of the former Soviet Union, led to the concentration of great wealth in the hands of few. As a matter fact, different types of inequality are highly correlated. Inequality of outcomes can lead to inequality of opportunity for the next generation, for instance. This is laid out in detail in the analytical section of this book.

Indeed, the level of inequality that coincided with China's development is significant and is related to many problems China is facing today. For instance, Kumhof et al. (2015: 1217) showed that 'high household leverage and crises can be caused by changes in the income distribution'. Before the two massive financial crises, namely in the periods 1920 to 1929 and 1983 to 2008, inequality in the US increased significantly. The share of income from high-income countries increased at the same time the leverage of low- and middle-income households rose and ultimately, a financial crisis took place. The main argument of the paper from Kumhof et al. (2015: 1219) is that two different strands of literature are linked: 'the literature on income and wealth distribution, and the literature on financial fragility and financial crises'. In addition, Rajan (2010) and Reich (2010) link inequality to long-run fragility to financial crises as well as to the accumulated debt level. This has vital implications for the Chinese leadership; to address the issue of inequality given its importance in early warning analyses should be key.

Moreover, Xu and Zhuang (1998) analyse the role of experimentation in China's trajectory. In general, the main reasons for the country's success include gradualism, the emergence of the nonstate sector as well as experimentation. In addition, Qian and Xu (1993) point to the systemic structure of China as one reason for the successful transformation of the country and the problems Russia faced with its transition from plan to market. The Russian system was described as having a U-form because the economy was highly centralised controlled by the respective ministries. In contrast to this, China was described as having an M-form structure because the ministries had to give up power in favour of the regional governments. This structure was introduced at the end of the 1950s when China split with the Soviet Union and thus, changed its economic model. Regional governments had become the dominant power players in China by the mid-1960s. The decentralised administrative structure had important advantages for the Chinese state, namely better information dissemination due to geographic proximity and the reduction in the likelihood of nation-wide failure of the system in case of an external shock. This also facilitated the introduction of institutional changes with the help of local experimentations without risking the disruption of the whole system. 'Most successful Chinese reform measures were introduced as local experiments by regional governments and only later promoted nationwide by the central government' (Xu and Zhuang1998: 194). In terms of implementation, a bottom-up approach was chosen (McMillan and Naughton 1992).

In contrast to Central and Eastern Europe and the Soviet Union, the Chinese administrative structure greatly facilitated the regional implementation of experiments. The U-form of Russia's set-up made the adoption of experiments quite costly. 'This is because experiments generate shocks and may disturb the normal operations of the economy, regardless of the success or failure of the experiments evaluated locally. This makes the scope of regional experiments more limited and their chances of success smaller' (Xu and Zhuang 1998: 195). The increased rigidity of institutions in case of a U-form makes institutional change via experimentation more difficult. In contrast, an M-form reduces the systemic influence of failed experiments and thus makes this less costly for a nation. The weak regional interdependence hinders the spread of the failure, which increases the success of institutional change with the help of local experiments.

At the same time, successful experiments can be easily transferred to other regions if approved by local and central governments. 'This makes the M-form organization more flexible in the institutional evolutionary process' (Xu and Zhuang 1998: 195). 'Economic transition may be regarded as a process of experimenting with new institutions/laws and the subsequent promotion of successful results' (Xu and Zhuang 1998: 196). China's experimental approach towards development has always distinguished the country from other developing economies and emerging markets. In this respect, the nation started the Free Trade Zone (FTZ) initiative in 2013, a scheme that was further expanded in 2017. These zones play a particular important role in the experimentation with the respect to the RMB internationalisation as 'cross-border RMB-based capital account transactions such as intra-company loans, RMB QDII, and other related capital account transaction items' are facilitated within these zones (Jin and Liu 2017: 12).

Further zones include Tianjin, Fujian, and Guangdong. In March 2017, the State Council decided to expand the original Shanghai Free Trade Zone to another 6 provinces as well as Chongqing municipality, which points to the continued importance of experimentation as a Chinese development policy. In this book, I showed the importance of experimentation with respect to China's economic trajectory.

Apart from the above, experimentation has also been used with respect to urbanisation and population control. 'The PRC's recent urbanization policies and reforms have been fundamental in driving economic growth. However, they have also created additional stress for urban areas because they have encouraged rapid migration from rural to urban areas' (Grable et al. 2017: 2). The Chinese urban population tripled between 2005 and 2014. 'Many rural migrants now live in large cities, putting growing pressure on local governments and the availability and affordability of urban social services. Included are services related to health care, education, and housing, as well as the formal financial sector. It should not be surprising that many of these stressors are infrastructure in nature' (Grable et al. 2017: 2-3). With respect to population control, Guibaud et al. (2014) analyse the abolishment of China's one-child policy in light of the build-up of a social security net in the country. In China, most Chinese elderly still heavily rely on intra-family support. This became more difficult due to decades of China's one-child policy. As previously mentioned, China's implementation of said policy in the early 1980s resulted in a demographic transition in the country and led to a disproportionally strong rise in the percentage of the elderly in comparison to the total population. To address this question, China's institutional set-up is crucial to be taken into account, as children are a vital support for the elderly. The country has no social safety net and thus, retirees have to fully rely on savings as well as on the support of the young. Given the negative repercussions of the one-child policy, China decided on the Third Plenum in 2013 to abolish the policy. In addition, the country aims for building a social safety net to support the elderly population. However, Guibaud et al. (2014) argue that the Chinese government is facing a trade-off in this respect. 'Important feedback loops arise between fertility and social security variables: an expansion of social security benefits reduces fertility – partially offsetting the effects of relaxing the one-child policy' (Guibaud et al. 2014). In addition to the above, 'Yi Fuxian of the University of Wisconsin-Madison believes China's government has overestimated the country's population by about 90m because it has failed to recognise a catastrophic decline in the national fertility rate' (The Economist 2017c). China's population development will pose significant challenges to the country and thus should not be left out from an early warning analysis.

ii) Fiscal and Monetary Policy

In the second half of 2016, fiscal policy became more proactive in China. Infrastructure projects, as well as general budget expenditure implementation were high on the Chinese government's agenda at the same time as monetary policy was not tightened significantly. Indeed, fears of the deflation of the property bubble as well as another wave of capital outflows accompanied by RMB weakness, led the PBoC to refrain from easing policy in order to boost growth. Instead, open market operations and target lending facilities were used to provide liquidity to the market in case of bottlenecks. In December 2016, it was stated at the Central Economic Work Conference that fiscal policy continues to be active, but monetary policy is kept more on the prudent side. One means to estimate the effect of the proactive fiscal policy is via the estimation of fiscal multipliers (Jin and Liu 2017a). This helps to gauge the short-term impact of additional fiscal expenditure or tax cuts on output. Jin and Liu (2017a) use the "rule of thumb" approach from the IMF to come up with their estimation. This approach assigns scores to trade openness, rigidities in the labour market, the level of automatic stabilisers, the FX regime, the ability and willingness to service a country's debt, as well as the effectiveness of fiscal institutions. Due to a relatively low import share to GDP, China gets assigned a binary score of one in this category. In general, the fiscal multiplier should be higher for a closed economy. Given low public spending to GDP, it is assumed that China has a relatively low level of automatic stabilisers, which coincides with a larger fiscal multiplier. The same notion holds for China's quasi-fixed exchange rate. The fiscal multiplier is higher for a nation with capital controls under a fixed exchange rate regime. As China's sovereign debt is below 40 percent, the country also gets assigned a 1 in this category. In addition, given an effective bureaucracy China receives a 1 with respect to fiscal institutions. The only 0 China gets assigned is with respect to labour market rigidities. Furthermore, Jin and Liu (2017a) note that the stage of the business cycle in which a country finds itself plays an important role. The fiscal multiplier is greater in an economic downturn than in an upswing. At the lowest point of an economic decline, any additional fiscal spending has a large impact on output and vice versa. The cyclical coefficient for China is estimated to be between -0.05 to 0.2. Furthermore, monetary policy also affects the fiscal multiplier. A more constrained monetary policy coincides with a higher fiscal multiplier. In general, this coefficient varies between 0 and 0.3 for countries. Given the constraining factors such as fears of capital outflows, monetary policy in China is rather constrained and thus, a coefficient between 0.05 and 0.15 is assigned to this category. Considering the above, researchers from Citi estimate the fiscal multiplier to be between 0.588 and 1.093 for China. In addition, Li et al. (2016) argue that it is fairly difficult to assess China's fiscal stance. 'China's official fiscal balance to GDP ratio has remained in a relatively narrow range, suggesting the fiscal stance has changed little over time, even in 2009, when massive fiscal stimulus was implemented. Meanwhile, off-budget fiscal measures play a key role for the government in maintaining overall growth stability, but are not reflected in the official fiscal data' (Li et al. 2016). Thus, the research adjusts the official fiscal deficit for these items. Sectors such as transport, among others, are taken into account as spending is foremost driven by the state in these areas. Local government financing vehicles carried out off-budget infrastructure investments. 'Compared to the official deficit ratio, the augmented fiscal deficit ratio shows more volatility, which is primarily driven by discretionary expenditure items. A change is shown in fiscal stance from a tightening during the second half of 2014, partly due to the negative impacts of local government debt reform on off-budget activities' (Li et al. 2016). This was one contributor to China's troubles in the second half of 2015 and 2016.

With respect to monetary policy, Chen et al. (2017e) note that commercial banks were provided with temporary liquidity before the Lunar New Year holidays. This temporary liquidity facility was provided in the form of RRR cuts for five large banks, which will be reversed to its initial level after a 28 days period. This is common in China given the higher cash demand ahead of the holidays. Also, increased official TSF growth was observed. However, given the more pronounced focus of the PBoC on managing financial risks as well as reducing capital outflows, the argument for easy monetary policy as well as accommodative credit policy was weak. 'The more interesting question is why the PBOC used temporary, targeted RRR cuts rather than 28-day MLF, as the maturity and funding costs are exactly the same. As background, since 2016, the PBOC has substituted RRR cuts (only one RRR cut in February 2016) with OMOs and other liquidity facilities (SLF/MLF/PSL) to maintain liquidity in the financial system. [...] The main difference between TLF and MLF is that the latter requires banks to provide qualified collateralized assets' (Chen et al. 2017e).

Chen et al. (2017f) further note that the PBoC increased MLF interest rates by 10bp in January 2017. It was the first time since 2013 that the PBoC hiked interest rates; the last time was in October 2013, when the PBoC increased the 7-day reverse repo rate. This showed that monetary policy, even though policy rates - 1-year benchmark lending and deposit rates - were kept unchanged, had a tightening bias in order to contain financial risks and increase macro-prudential measures. This should also be protective of the local exchange rate. 'Since 3Q16, tighter macro-prudential measures have resulted in higher and more volatile money market interest rates (7-day repo and 3-month SHIBOR) and a start of financial de-leveraging as reflected in carry-trade activity in the money market, off-balance sheet WMPs and onshore bond markets, etc' (Chen et al. 2017f). Although this financial deleveraging is positive for China in the longer run, it can lead to increased financial vulnerability in the short-term. In order to prevent such speedy spikes in the repo rates, as in June 2013, the PBoC tries to keep its liquidity operations more diversified (Chen et al. 2017f).

At the beginning of February 2017, the PBoC raised a range of short-term interest rates. Reverse repo rates were increased by 10bp for the 1d, 7d, and 28d tenors. In addition, the upper bound of the interest rate corridor, the standing lending facility rate, was also hiked by 10bp. These measures reflect a continuation of the policy, which started in January, of a more prudent monetary policy. This translates automatically in higher money market funding costs. In particular, the reverse repo rate is perceived as an important guidance for short-term rates. Chang and Zhou (2017b) note on this that 'hiking the range of short-term policy rates (10bp each time, for the first time since 2013 for 7d/14d reverse repos and since 2015 for 28d) rather than the traditional benchmark deposit and lending rates (usually 25bp each) is not unexpected, and [...] the impact on the economy at such magnitude would be small. The bulk of China's total social financing is still dominated by bank lending (1y benchmark rate at 4.35%), and the transmission from the costs of the central banks' liquidity instruments to banks' lending rate will be gradual'. This served the multiple goals of the central bank. On the one hand, the institution tries to contain financial risks by guiding some short-term interest rates higher and on the other hand, growth stability is not curtailed, as benchmark lending rates are kept unchanged.

The PBoC hiked open market reverse repo rates and the Medium-Term Lending Facility by 10bps in March 2017. 'Previously, the PBoC increased the OMO rates by 10bps on 3 Feb and the MLF rates by the same scale on 24 Jan' (Chan and Deng 2017d). Chen et al. (2017a) note on this that 'the comments provided by the PBOC emphasize that the increase in market-based policy rates is an outcome of market auction, reflecting the combined effects of domestic (economic recovery, house price increase and credit growth) and external (upward movements in global yield curve) developments. The PBOC also emphasized that the increase in market interest rates was not a policy rate hike, which should refer to the benchmark deposit and lending rates in the current PBOC monetary policy framework. Recent moves in market interest rates are helpful to address leverage and asset price overvaluation concerns and prevent financial risks. […] The PBOC has developed multiple policy instruments to address multiple policy objectives (monetary stability and financial stability are the two overriding ones)'. According to Suwanapruti and Tilton (2017: 3), the main three key benchmark rates in China are the 1-year lending rate, the 7-day repo rate and the 3M SHIBOR, which form the main point of analysis for the case study.

iii) Soft Factors

In 2014, Wen Jiabao described China's trajectory as 'unsustainable, uncoordinated, unbalanced, and unstable' (De Jonquieres 2014: 1). This has to be seen in light of increased challenges to the Chinese economy. To counter this, Xi Jinping implemented a set of reforms, which were mainly targeted at rebalancing the Chinese economy. These reforms encompassed the partial opening of the capital account (De Jonquieres 2014: 4), which significantly increased the vulnerability of the Chinese economy. Ideational factors played a particular important role in this respect, as described in the conceptual section as well as in the case study of this book. In addition, the SDR inclusion of the Chinese renminbi in the SDR basket of the IMF further enticed China to implement pro-market reforms. The perception of the renminbi was changed due to this and China allowed the market to have a greater say in determining the fixing of the onshore currency. In particular, the IMF played an important role in this as the Fund labelled the Chinese currency as freely convertible (The Economist 2015). Thus, the IMF helped China to escape from its past stigma, which has to be seen in light of China's historical background. In November 2015, the Fund included the RMB as the 5th currency in the SDR basket. The criteria for this were twofold. First, the currency should be used in trade-related transactions, which is clearly the case with respect to the renminbi. Second, the Chinese currency has to be freely convertible, which was questionable in the case of China. The decision to include the RMB in the basket was a political one as the Fund wanted to entice further pro-market reforms by the country. In contrast, for China the inclusion fulfilled the country's demand for status. 'RMB internationalization is partly a vanity project' as Barry Eichengreen put it (Chang and Fernandez 2015: 2). Status in itself can be a goal, even if material rewards would point in a different direction. This has been clearly shown in the case study on China's troubles of 2015 and 2016.

c) Institutional Weaknesses

i) Economic Transition

The transition of China has only been partly achieved and, as Layard (1998: 1) noted, 'sensible strategies for the future depend crucially on learning the right lessons from what has been done so far'. In this respect, this book argues that the events of 2015 and 2016 have not received appropriate attention from an early warning perspective. Indeed, with my research I help stakeholders to gain a better understanding of the holistic picture of China's unfinished transition. To round up, I lay out key insights from transformations of other regions than China, which should help to gain a better understanding of this institutional factor.

Layard (1998) is correct to ask why there was so much pain in the transitions of Eastern Europe and Russia. He put forward six reasons. First, the state power was weak due to the collapse of communism and the energy spent on preventing history from repeating itself. Second, the price liberalisation in these countries was rapid. 'Since governments lacked the authority to undertake a monetary reform and no longer had the power to control prices, they had little option but to free most prices within one or two years of taking power' (Layard 1998: 2). Thus, the transformations happened at an incredible speed; if capital and labour could be swiftly redeployed, the falls in output would not have been that severe. However, transition takes time, particularly given the severe uncertainty of the transformation period. Additionally, the inconvenience of participants to write contracts also led to a slow redeployment of productive factors. Third, the demand from the military fell sharply as the pattern of government spending changed substantially. Fourth, the economic shift resulted in increased unemployment. Previously, the level of monetary demand secured by policy made sure that all products were high in demand given controlled levels of prices. However, the freed prices led to a reallocation of resources, which disadvantaged certain layers of the population. The resulting inflation led to monetary restraint further constraining output and employment. Fifth, inflation was high, as mentioned above. For instance, 'in Russia, unlike China, high inflation and political uncertainty have been major factors retarding output growth' (Layard 1998: 4). Indeed, everybody waits for the uncertainty to vanish. Sixth, privatisations were speedy. To prevent the re-emergence of communism, newly elected governments were selling-off state property at unprecedented speed. In addition, the aim was to generate private property as an essential condition for the efficient allocation of resources. Thus, 'much of the reform policy has been driven by the weakness in government and by the desire to preserve freedom through preventing a return of the Communists' (Layard 1998: 5). In contrast to Central and Eastern Europe and Russia, China's transition experience did not coincide with a collapse in output.

In this respect, Gomulka (1998) analyses the decline in output in Central and Eastern Europe (CEE), as well as in the Former Soviet Union (FSU), in comparison to the trajectories of China and Vietnam. The latter two countries engaged in economic transformation earlier and in a more gradual manner than other regions. The main reasons for the sharp declines in economic performance in CEE and the FSU can be split into two broad categories, namely the initial conditions the countries had to face and the choice of the reform programme. First, the conditions the countries had to burden at the initiation of the transformation vary substantially across countries, which partly explain the wide range of outcomes during the transition process. Moreover, differences in institutional and political determinants were also significant. Second, the reform programmes can be distinguished according to the speed of implementation. A radical transition is mostly known as "Schumpeterian Creative Destruction" in the West and entails 'a costly disruption to the existing economic arrangement in the short run' (Gomulka 1998: 14). However, the researcher argues that the main factors that distinguished the different outcomes of the transformations were related to the initial conditions with the speed of the transition reinforcing these determinants (Gomulka 1998: 15). Kornai (1994) coined these phenomena transformational recession as these are related to changes in the economic system rather than to policies. However, the experience of China and Vietnam teaches us that not only do the initial conditions matter, but the speed of the introduced changes to the system are also important. Gomulka (1998: 28-29) identifies four main reasons for the sharp declines in output, namely, '(1) radical price and foreign trade liberalizations, (2) the elimination of excessive aggregate demand, (3) the collapse of captive markets within the CMEA area, and (4) the near collapse of selected state purchases'. With respect to the recovery, the emergence of the private sector as well as the speed of the trade and price liberalisation and the quality of privatisations played a crucial role (Pohl et al. 1997). In CEE and FSU, the country which came out best of the transformation was Poland with a relatively decent decline in output. Still for most countries, 'the patterns of recession and recovery have been, in the years 1989-1995, largely of the L-curve type' (Gomulka 1998: 18). More recently, China also proclaimed that its economic trajectory has this form. However, the transformations of CEE and the FSU were accompanied by severe disruptions to the system, mostly in the form of high inflation rates from an economic perspective. Thus, the shocks did not only cause output to contract substantially, but also led to a spike in inflation rates. Further features of the transitions included structural changes to the economy as well as a shift in the sectorial composition of GDP in favour of services relative to manufacturing. As mentioned above, Poland did perform better than other CEE countries as well as the FSU. Nonetheless, price liberalisation and a collapse in trade were also the main reason for the transformational recession in Poland. To sum up, 'a radical price liberalization may be viewed as a reform that imposes on the economy, within a short period of time, a large block of "innovations" causing, as any innovations do, the Schumpeterian phenomenon of "creative destruction": declines in most outputs in the short run and increases in the long run' (Gomulka 1998: 24). In contrast to this, the transformations in China and Vietnam aimed at a gradual process, which was in line with the factor endowments of the countries, namely a significant pool of underemployed labour on the countryside, which could be reallocated to more productive means. As mentioned above, the country which did best in the CEE region was Poland. The main reasons for this was that the country aimed at a permanent improvement in its external balance as well as going through a debt reduction process, which helped Poland to start anew. In addition, the privatisation process in Poland took different forms than in other CEE countries or in the FSU (Gomulka 1998: 35).

The transformations in Central and Eastern Europe, as well as in the Former Soviet Union, were preceded by the collapse of the political system. The socialist one-party system ceased to exist and checks and balances stopped working properly. This coincided with a loss of confidence in the local money. The price explosions of the liberalisations were often followed by continued inflation. This is a reflection of the loss in confidence in the whole economic system. The breakdown of the political system significantly contributed to the lack of reforms in many transition countries. Due to the vacuum, which followed the breakdown, old elites as well as rent seekers were able to capture the initiatives at the time of the transformation. Credit issuance by said actors often represented a significant problem for the affected countries. 'When the government is controlled by old elites and rent seekers grabbing for resources, it is no surprise that the politically weak, and particularly those who should benefit from social programs, do not gain from the policies being implemented. The result has been much greater poverty than would otherwise have occurred' (Boone and Hørder 1998: 45). The reinstating of checks and balances was key for the transition economies, which contributed significantly to the reestablishment of confidence.

The initial price jump in these transition countries was due to the price liberalisation and the monetary overhang, which was one legacy of the planned economy. However, the overhang was cleared and inflation often remained high, which reflected a loss in confidence in the system. This resulted in social misery as savings were completely eroded. 'In Russia the IMF estimated that prices would rise by 50 percent after the January 1992 price liberalization. But instead prices would rise by a startling 250 percent. The large rise in prices can be explained by a severe loss in confidence in money as a savings vehicle just before the reforms' (Boone and Hørder 1998: 47). Parallel prices gave an initial estimate where prices would jump to after liberalisation. In addition, the reduction in legal restrictions on monetary transactions should have resulted in a decrease in the parallel rate. Instead, a sharp rise in the parallel market prices was recorded. This was likely caused by the anxieties of the local population of future political and economic policies. It remains the question why local authorities permitted a high rate of inflation to persist. One answer to this is that seigniorage was used as one means of financing. In contrast, those countries, which pursued stabilisation policies, recorded the best economic performance. Powerful vested interests prevented the rein in of inflation. For instance, in Russia, 'in 1992, there was no centralized program for monetary policy, and orders for new credits frequently came from the parliament, government, and president' (Boone and Hørder 1998: 55). In those countries where reformists were able to keep up social consensus, such as in Estonia, Poland, and Czechoslovakia, the credit frenzy could be resisted. In addition, the development of financial markets could help to prevent the erosion of savings via high inflation rates. Why could inflation be tamed in some countries as of 1996? One of the reasons for this is the overall improvement of the political systems in some countries. Free elections led to the articulation of the problem by the local population and thus, it got tackled more efficiently. A functioning political system increases the coordination among decision-makers and thus, has the potential to tackle the inflation problem. In contrast, 'there is no doubt that large seigniorage revenues, a well-organized opposition in favour of loose credit policies, and a corrupt environment reduce the chances that a politician interested in stabilizing an economy will succeed' (Boone and Hørder 1998: 60). One way to prevent the capture of reform initiatives by old elites and rent seekers are currency boards, which help to lock in various macroeconomic policies needed to stabilise the system. For instance, the Bank of Estonia was not permitted to engage in excessive credit issuance. This helped the restructuring of the old industry while at the same time new enterprises were not disadvantaged by the misallocation of credit. In addition, fixed exchange rates were an anchor for domestic prices at the same time as currency convertibility for current account transactions was permitted. Estonia can be classified as one of the rare success stories of Eastern Europe's transition trajectory (Boone and Hørder 1998).

In contrast to the European transition economies and to Russia, the Chinese state did not get undermined by the turmoil of the political and economic transformation. Further to the above, China due to its predominantly agricultural society was relatively poor in comparison to other regions, which offered significant possibilities for catching up. Woo (1998) notes that China's growth can be asserted to a few factors, namely to the advantage of backwardness, to the economic structure of the Chinese economy, as well as to the deregulation of the market sector in the reform period and the emergence of the non-state sector. The first point was already described in previous sections. With respect to the economic structure of China, it has to be noted that the country was based mainly on the agricultural sector. Thus, it was possible that the rural economy was gradually reformed while the SOEs were kept afloat with the help of the Chinese state. This approach contributed to the avoidance of the collapse in output as experienced by Central and Eastern European nations as well as Russia. Furthermore, the deregulation of the market sector led to increased incentives helping to spur output. In addition, the emergence of the non-state sector should be regarded as the success story of the Chinese reform era.

To conclude, it was my aim to reflect on the success of China over the last forty years as well as on the unfinished transformation the country is still facing. I demonstrated that the process of transitioning has to be one key variable in an analytical framework assessing China's strengths and weaknesses. From an early warning perspective, the incremental approach the country chose, which stands in stark contrast to other regions, had many advantages as laid out above. By describing the faults of other models of transformation, the advantages of China's approach became clearer. Nonetheless, China's transition is not yet completed and thus, continues to be one key determinant of the institutional dimension.

ii) Liberalisation

The events of 2015 and 2016 led to a setback regarding renminbi internationalisation. Given the substantial capital outflows during said period, China had to switch from capital account opening to encouraging greater participation of foreigners in Chinese capital markets. This was visible in the removal of entry restrictions as well as in Chinese capital markets being included in major indices, which should help to increase the capitalisation of Chinese markets to the size of US indices by 2025 (Citi Research 2017). According to Jin and Liu (2017: 3), the development of domestic capital markets has become a high priority for the Chinese leadership given the troubles related to capital account liberalisation in 2015 and 2016. These two types of institutional changes are distinctly different, as the latter is related to the IMF Article VIII (IMF 2016) and the former to liberalisation of financial services and capital markets, which is governed by WTO's service trade regime (WTO 2017). As a matter of fact, China's unorthodox sequencing strategy of opening the capital account first before the development of domestic conditions to deal with this had backfired. Now, China aims to develop domestic financial and capital markets more intensively. This is one lesson drawn from the troubles China faced in 2015 and 2016 and indeed, should lower the risk of an ill-sequenced institutional programme that could potentially trigger further one-off adjustments in the exchange rate. In fact, due to the adjustment in China's strategy, the renminbi appreciated significantly in 2017 versus the US dollar. After the launch of the RMB internationalisation strategy in 2009, events culminated in the local currency devaluation in August 2015, which sent shockwaves around the world. The tightening of capital controls in China should represent an automatic circuit breaker preventing self-fulfilling speculative predictions in times of market stress. At the same time, the removal of entry barriers together with the inclusion of Chinese capital markets in major indices will raise foreign participation in Chinese markets. Given the size of Chinese capital markets, institutional, investors do not have the choice of ignoring China altogether (Jin and Liu 2017: 3), which is a positive global development.

In general, one of the first researchers who propagated the important role of finance in a country's development was McKinnon (1973). As more countries opened their capital and financial accounts, crises became more frequent and thus, finance became a new role in research. More recent research supports the view that financial liberalisation entails an increased probability of financial crisis. Therefore, financial liberalisation is in need of a careful strategy, particularly in countries where the institutional development is still on the weak side (Lindgren et al. 1996; Demirgüç-Kunt and Detragiache 1998). Kaminsky and Reinhart (2000) have shown the connection of different types of financial crises when capital accounts are open. It was McKinnon (1973) who already proposed a three-stage sequencing strategy regarding liberalisation in which capital account opening should be among the last institutional changes a country should engage in. Preceding this should be the opening of current accounts as well as the development of domestic financial and capital markets. In addition, the liberalisation of the real economy should be engaged in before the reformation of the financial sector. First, current account liberalisation refers to the removal of any barriers to trade such as tariffs or the facilitation of trade-related foreign exchange transactions as well as the fostering of competition. China opened its current account in 1996. Second, Jin and Liu (2017: 4) name four broad categories of domestic financial liberalisation, namely interest rate liberalisation, the reduction of state involvement, which mainly refers to privatisation of the state-owned enterprise sector in China, removal of entry barriers, and lowering of sector barriers. Third, capital account liberalisation is related to foreign direct investment, portfolio flows, international bank flows as well as derivatives. China opened itself to FDI in the 1980s as part of its development strategy and accelerated other capital account liberalisation measures as of 2009, which backfired in 2015 and 2016 and led to a change in strategy.

China's offshore currency strategy started in the early 2000s. Nonetheless, the direct RMB internationalisations kicked-off in 2009 with the establishment of a pilot project regarding cross-border trade settlement using the renminbi (Goldman Sachs Research 2013b). Further, the former head of the Chinese Central Bank, Zhou Xiaochuan, published three articles regarding the RMB internationalisation with a particular focus on SDR inclusion. This was achieved in 2016; however, it came at a cost as described in the policy section of this book. By 2011, the trade settlement scheme, which started as an experimental institutional innovation, was fully liberalised and could be regarded as a success as trade in goods and services between China and the rest of the world increased significantly. As described in the section on China's troubles in 2015 and 2016, the nation initiated various institutional facilities to promote the use of the RMB such as bilateral swap lines. In addition, clearing bank centres in major financial cities around the world helped to expand trade-related transactions given more prominent access to the onshore market. RMB trade settlement increased significantly until 2015. Furthermore, the RMB was named the most traded currency in the emerging market space by the BIS Triennial Central Bank Survey in 2016 (Jin and Liu 2017: 5-9). China's FX internationalisation strategy came to a sudden stop with the troubles in 2015. The RMB was devalued on August 11, 2015, which shocked the world (Buiter et al. 2015: 2). From August 2015 to June 2017, FX reserves declined by USD 600bn and estimated capital outflows according to the balance of payments amounted to about USD 1.1trn from the second half of 2016 to the second half of 2017. Given the unprecedented troubles China faced during that period, authorities had to tighten capital controls and thus, partially reversed the RMB internationalisation strategy. Jin and Liu (2017: 10) noted that, 'learning from this experience, the authorities have shifted their strategy towards opening China's financial markets to greater foreign participation while slowing capital account liberalization. Globally, foreign participation in both advanced and emerging markets acts as a catalyst in the development of financial markets. Once China has achieved a greater degree of sophistication in its financial and capital markets, liberalization of the capital account will be a natural consequence. This sequencing policy should help China avoid unnecessary mistakes'. Sequencing is a key step towards liberalisation while avoiding a financial crisis (Claessens et al. 2014).

With respect to capital market development, China granted access to its onshore interbank bond market in 2010. 'The PBoC first launched a pilot scheme allowing three types of institutions (foreign central banks, RMB settlement banks and cross-border RMB settlement participating banks) to trade and settle bonds in the interbank bond market' (Jin and Liu 2017: 15). In the period between 2011 and 2015, foreign market participants gained access to the interbank bond market via the QFII and RQFII scheme, in which they were subject to certain quotas as well as to approval by the local authorities (Goldman Sachs Research 2013b). In July 2015, certain participants, such as foreign central banks and sovereign wealth funds, were granted unlimited access and as of February 2016, some mid- and long-term institutional investors were granted the same rights as the aforementioned institutions. As a result of the gradual opening of the bond market the number of foreign participants jumped from 182 in 2014 to 508 in June 2017 (Jin and Liu 2017: 15). This is a reflection of Beijing's new strategy of allowing increased foreign participation in local markets while clamping down on capital flight. In addition, China bonds were included in two new indices in February 2017, namely by Bloomberg – global aggregate + China index and EM local currency government + China index. In the subsequent months, Citi included China bonds in several of its indices. Furthermore, the recent initiation of the Bond Connect programme for Hong Kong-based institutional investors to access the China Interbank Market (CIBM) also supports the inclusion of China bonds into major indices (Suwanapruti and Tilton 2017). In addition to the above, the PBoC clarified its approach towards repatriation of funds, hedging as well as taxation, which include the following measures according to Jin and Liu (2017: 17):

1. Capital repatriation is not restricted as long as there are no significant currency mismatches.
2. The FX hedging market should be opened for foreign participants within a reasonable period of time.
3. At the moment, trading on CIBM is not subject to any taxes.

Nonetheless, Mathur and Sun (2017: 28-30) note that no major bond index provider has yet added China to their flagship products, namely Yieldbook's WGBI, Bloomberg-Barclays' Global Aggregate, and

JPMorgan's GBI-EM Global Diversified. The inclusion of China's bonds could result in notable flows. Hurdles to the index inclusion are the capital gains tax, FX hedging, freely convertible currency and full repatriation flexibility, illiquidity of off-the-run bonds, administrative inconveniences, as well as regulatory uncertainty. However, given China's ambitions, index inclusion in said indices is quite likely in the foreseeable future.

With respect to the liberalisation of Chinese equity markets, the introduction of the QFII scheme in 2002 allowed a restricted number of QFIIs to invest in A-shares. Furthermore, with respect to overseas investment the QDII scheme was launched in 2006, which granted a number of Chinese investors access to overseas financial markets. First, the QDII scheme only covered fixed income and money market products. However, the scheme was expanded to stock products in May 2007. Furthermore, in 2011, China established the RQFII scheme, which allowed for offshore RMB to be used for onshore investments. The investment quotas for all schemes were gradually increased over time and the QFII and RQFII scheme now include 281 and 184 approved institutions, respectively (Goldman Sachs Research 2013b; Jin and Liu 2017: 19). Another means to integrate Chinese equity markets with the global economy is the Stock Connect. The Shanghai-Hong Kong Stock Connect was established in November 2014. Furthermore, the launch of the Shenzen-Hong Kong Stock Connect was only initiated in December 2016 due to concerns of capital outflows. In June 2017, A-shares got included with a 0.7 percent weight in the MSCI. 'MSCI has decided to include A-shares in its major global equity benchmarks, effective from June 1st, 2018. A-shares will initially account for 0.7% of MSCI EM, while China overall will account for 29% of MSCI EM and 3.3% of MSCI AC World as of 2018' (Sun 2017: 40). This entails significant long-term implications for China. 'First, foreign institutional investors will change the investor base in China, which is dominated by retail investors. Second, inclusion will be reviewed periodically and the China weighting could be increased to reflect the size and sophistication of the domestic market. Third, the next stage of China's SOE reform could engender larger foreign participation in China's A-share and Hong Kong's H-share markets' (Jin and Liu 2017: 20).

iii) FX Regime

'I have listened to both sides of this debate. Here is what I think. I think those who call for a fixed exchange rate are right in the short run. And those who call for a floating exchange rate are right in the long run. How long is the short run, you ask? You must understand. China is 8000 years old. So when I say "short run", it could be 100 years' (Li Ruogu 2004).

Yoshino and Asonuma (2017) analyse the optimal path of the transition of an exchange rate regime, which is defined as shift 'from a dollar peg regime to either a basket peg or a floating regime' and the researchers compare 'these policies relative to maintaining the current dollar peg regime'. As laid out in the historical background section, the Asian financial crisis of 1997 and 1998 led to an extensive discussion on the desirable exchange rate regime. Since then, two changes in the FX regimes were recorded. The Republic of Korea and Thailand shifted to managed floating regimes and other countries like China and Malaysia kept their dollar peg regime until 2005. Dynamic transition analysis is used to determine optimal shifts for the FX regime in case of China. Thus, shifts from the current regime to alternatives are evaluated as well as the research 'explores how capital controls are relaxed in order to reach the desired regimes under free capital mobility. This coincides with where the PRC and Malaysia stood in the aftermath of the Asian financial crisis' (Yoshino and Asonuma 2017: 1). The question is, how China can successfully transform its exchange rate regime from the current crawling peg to the US dollar to a basket peg or a floating regime and which of the regimes is more desirable? The researchers conclude that the best option for China is the gradual shift from the current quasi US dollar peg to a basket peg regime. The second-best option is a sudden change in regime towards the basket, which would be still superior in terms of welfare losses than changing to a floating exchange rate regime. Furthermore, McKinnon and Schnabl (2014) recommend the stabilisation of the USD/RMB exchange rate with the help of financial repression and capital controls. The researchers are primarily concerned about the faults of capital flows in case China liberalises its exchange rate and instead recommend a gradual shift with the help of

China's experimental approach, for instance by further expanding the Shanghai Free Trade Zone. Goldstein and Lardy (2006) pointed to the need for gradually widening the exchange rate band and, in contrast to the previous statement, would opt for a removal of capital restrictions with respect to China's exchange rate. Frankel (2005) put forward the idea of establishing a target zone for the RMB exchange rate as well as the introduction of increased exchange rate flexibility. Eichengreen (2006) note on this subject that greater flexibility in the exchange rate would allow the PBoC for increased autonomy regarding its monetary policy, which hints to the monetary trilemma. In a wider context, Shioji (2006) analyses how other Asian currencies would react to a change in the exchange rate regime by China. Gochoco-Bautista and Fabella (2006) note that a shift in China's exchange rate policy may result in an asymmetric response by its neighbours and thus might not be optimal. Volz (2014) speculates that the informal exchange rate cooperation in East Asia would allow for the gradual shift of China's quasi US dollar peg to a basket peg regime.

Regarding the exchange rate history of the RMB, the PBoC fixed the USD/RMB exchange rate at a level of 8.70 in 1994 and allowed for gradual exchange rate appreciation to a rate of 8.28 in 1997. The spot exchange rate was kept stable versus the US dollar from 1999 to 2005. The Chinese government changed the FX regime in mid-2005 by announcing that the RMB would become 'adjustable, based on market supply and demand with reference to exchange rate movements of currencies in a basket' (quoted in Yoshino and Asonuma 2017: 3). The RMB exchange rate appreciated gradually until 2008, when it was re-pegged to the US dollar until 2010 and afterwards the currency resumed its appreciation trend in the years to follow. Given the above, Yoshino and Asonuma (2017: 4-5) distinguish between four subperiods in the sample: '(1) period 1: May 2003-July 2007 [sic], (2) period 2: August 2005-June 2008, (3) period 3: July 2008-May 2010, and (4) period 4: June 2010-June 2012. Period 1 and period 3 coincide with samples under a dollar peg and a temporal recurrence of a dollar peg due to the global financial crisis. In contrast, period 2 and period 4 correspond to a basket peg regime, i.e. departure from dollar peg. In these sample periods (2 and 4), weights on the US dollar in the currency basket are substantially lowered by 0.16 and 0.18 than those in period 1 when the renminbi-US dollar rate was completely fixed (1.00)'. This shows that the Chinese leadership also historically took into account movements of other currencies than the US dollar in certain periods and in doing so, increased the weights of these in a basket exchange rate regime. Nonetheless, 'the PBC has kept China's dollar exchange rate remarkably stable in comparison to other East Asian and emerging market (EM) currencies' (McKinnon and Schnabl 2014: 2), which helped the internationalisation of the RMB over long periods of time.

McKinnon and Schnabl (2014: 2) note that 'the dollar remains the dominant means of settlement for international payments among banks, and is the principal intervention currency used by governments, such as China's, for smoothing exchange rate fluctuations'. It has to be mentioned that if China targets its exchange rate versus the US dollar, triangular arbitrage is the predominant form of cross rate determination of spot and forward rates. Consequently, the United States stays away from official exchange rate interventions via the buying or selling of FX reserves or also by other means.

The peg to the US dollar helped the significant increase in exports of China to the world. The rising current account surplus resulted in global pressure on China, which the country partially gave in in 2005 as it agreed on letting the renminbi appreciate. Western demands to adjust the undervalued currency were also paired with the requests to liberalise the Chinese capital account (Ito 2011). As described in detail in the case study, this contributed to the troubles China faced in the second half of 2015 and 2016. Given the underdeveloped capital markets in China, McKinnon and Schnabl (2014: 3) note that the country has been well-advised not to let the renminbi volatility pick-up. After the troubles of 2015 and 2016, China decided against excessive financial liberalisation. However, the country decided to encourage inflows while discouraging outflows via capital controls, as previously described. In addition, sequencing of the reforms matter. Without the dissolution of financial repression, the exchange rate should not be fully liberalised.

China's experience in the 2000s can be compared to Japan's experience in the 1980s. During this period, the US dollar appreciated against the yen, which coincided with a rising US current account deficit. In addition, Japan's exports to the US mainly came from the automobile and electronic industries. As the US was on a general deindustrialisation trend during this time, resentment against the Japanese exporters emerged. The US government reacted by imposing political pressure on Japan to let its currency appreciate. In 1985, an exchange-rate agreement was struck in the Plaza Hotel in New York, which led to the appreciation of the yen by more than 50 percent within the next years. This entailed to a slowdown in Japan's exports as well as in output, but it did not curtail the Japanese trade surplus due to the further reduction of imports. Only in 1987, which became known as the Louvre Accord, did the Japanese make clear that the appreciation of the yen was excessive. Fiscal policy and lower interests should stop the appreciation trend but had the negative side effects of contributing to asset price bubbles. The deflation of the asset price bubbles in Japan at the end of 1989 entailed long-lasting consequences for the country (McKinnon and Schnabl 2014: 6). China should not only learn from its own history but also from the experience of other countries.

The downfall of Japan led to China being at the centre stage of international attention in East Asia. Similar to the Japanese experience, political pressure on China was levied to let the country's exchange rate appreciate during the 2000s in order to reduce global imbalances. The allegations included that China pursued a mercantilist trade strategy of undervaluing the renminbi. However, this was a result of broad dollar weakness in the 2000s at the same time as China made huge progress in terms of productivity, which was the reason for the appreciation trend of the renminbi as of 2005. It has to be mentioned, however, that given China's history, as laid out in the section 'China's Economic Empowerment', the country is more prone to resisting foreign intervention. The Chinese government only partially gave in to American pressure in 2005. Indeed, as the US induced global financial crisis of 2008 led to a sharp slowdown in Chinese exports, the country decided on temporarily stopping the appreciation trend by re-pegging the renminbi to the US dollar. Thus, in comparison to Japan, China is more autonomous in its decision-making and has the ability to resist international pressure better than other countries.

Inevitably, the theory of optimum currency areas comes to mind given the events described above (Mundell 1961, McKinnon 1963, Kenen 1969). The theory postulates that 'large countries subject to distinctive business-cycle conditions ("asymmetric shocks") will want a more flexible exchange rate, since they can both afford and will wish to tailor monetary policy to domestic conditions. In contrast, relatively open economies with weak financial systems will want a less flexible rate, since volatility will be corrosive to financial stability and export growth' (Eichengreen 2006: 7). With respect to China, 'the country has a high export/GDP ratio and a weak financial system. These considerations point toward a less-flexible rate. Splitting the difference suggests a moderate increase in flexibility, which was precisely the decision taken on July 21st' (Eichengreen 2006: 7). A similar notion can be applied to the events of August 2015, as is laid out in the case study. The other concept that can be applied to both FX debasements in China is sequencing. 'A one-sentence summary of that literature is that exchange rate flexibility should precede capital account convertibility. Exchange rate flexibility should come first to avoid creating one-way bets for speculators, who can force authorities to abandon their exchange rate commitment under duress, at considerable costs to their policy credibility, or to reverse prior measures liberalizing the capital account, which will also raise questions about the consistency of policies' (Eichengreen 2006: 9-10). In addition, the question of interest rate liberalisation has to be touched upon and is addressed in detail in the case study.

Geoffrey Yu analyses the evolution of the Chinese foreign exchange rate regime from 2005 to 2017 published in a special report at LSE IDEAS. In 2005, the PBoC relinquished the USD/RMB peg and replaced the previous regime with a managed floating currency regime. This allowed for a 2.1 percent appreciation of the renminbi versus the US dollar as well as the announcement of daily fixings going forward. Only a few minutes after the Chinese authorities announced the changes, Malaysia also followed suit. Geoffrey Yu identifies four - sometimes overlapping - stages of the evolution of the currency regime in China. First, the appreciation trend of the RMB from 2005 to 2008 and second, the resumption of a strong China trade between 2009 and 2013. Third, the establishment of the offshore market between 2010 and 2016 as well as, fourth, the end of the RMB appreciation trend and the accompanied currency troubles from 2014 to the present. The accession of China to the WTO in 2001 and the accompanied productivity gains led to the build-up of significant FX reserves in China, which served the country as a 'status symbol for mercantilist behaviour' (Yu 2017: 30). The Bush government demonstrated their discontent with the Chinese foreign exchange strategy in 2003, but it took until 2005 for China to accommodate its strategy slightly. Demands for greater currency flexibility within China emerged and thus, the de-pegging of 2005 was seen positively across the spectrum of observers. However, the trading band versus the US dollar was set at the narrow daily range of 0.5 percent around the central parity. The PBoC secured this via daily FX interventions. Nonetheless, 'there was no guarantee that there would be any alignment between the last trade of the current trading day and the fixing on the following day' (Yu 2017: 31). Apart from the adjustment in 2005, no further large one-off RMB changes happened as the currency set on a gradual appreciation trend. Nonetheless, due to strong growth in the US and good global conditions, the Chinese current account peaked nearly at 10 percent of GDP in 2007, just before the great financial crisis disturbed the boom years of the 2000s. This stopped any liberalising steps as global demand collapsed in the crisis years leading to distortions in the balance-of-payments of China. Therefore, the peg of the renminbi versus the US dollar was re-established in July 2008. In addition, the Chinese leadership engaged in massive credit stimulus as of the second quarter of 2009. Loan quotas for banks were issued and fixed asset investment growth was spurred to above 30 percent in 2009. The situation calmed down and 'in June 2010, the PBoC announced that markets were once again to play a role in price formation and the dollar-renminbi peg started moving again' (Yu 2017: 32). Furthermore, the Eurozone crisis of 2010 led Beijing to embrace the opportunity to push for a greater say in the global monetary and financial system as well as go ahead with its liberalisation strategy. 'China had in Hong Kong the luxury of possessing a separate jurisdiction with the ability to experiment' (Yu 2017: 33). The offshore yuan market plays a crucial role in the Chinese internationalisation of the renminbi. Between 2009 and 2011, the offshore market took off, which contributed to the positive sentiment towards the yuan. By 2014, the Chinese exchange rate had appreciated nearly 30 percent in nominal terms and 40 percent in real terms, which led to the question of the sustainability of the Chinese exchange rate policy. Indeed, the Chinese current account fell in the first quarter of 2014 at the same time as developed markets started to reflate. The Chinese economic picture further worsened and the Fed talked about raising interest rates. Thus, the renminbi started to depreciate versus the US dollar (Yu 2017: 34). This culminated in the RMB devaluation in August 2015, which is examined in detail in the case study.

Chang et al. (2017a) reported that the PBoC is contemplating introducing a counter-cyclical adjustment factor in the calculation of the CNY fixing rate. 'The current fixing regime takes into account the previous day's close (4.30pm local time) and changes in a basket of currencies. [...] A counter-cyclical factor in the daily fixing mechanism would provide the PBoC with discretion to both adjust the fixing and smooth excessive volatility in the exchange rate if it thought the spot rate had been excessively driven by market forces (ie, "cyclical factor") and was deviating from its fundamental value' (Chang et al. 2017a). Since the beginning of 2017, the CFETS NEER depreciated as other Asian currencies were outperforming the CNY. This is a sign that the Chinese leadership is not really sticking to its basket rule and that the bilateral USD/CNY exchange rate remains the most important target for the PBoC. Since the troubles in the second half of 2015, there have been three milestones with respect to the reform of the CNY fixing mechanism: '1) On 11 August 2015, the PBoC announced that market forces (previous day's closing rate) would drive the daily fixing rate. 2) In December 2015, the PBoC launched the CFETS basket to shift market attention away from bilateral USDCNY rate. 3) Since January 2016, [...] the USDCNY fixing rate has been based on: i) the previous day's close spot rate (4:30pm); ii) major cross-currency movements, and iii) a need to stabilise market sentiment towards the USDCNY, of necessary' (Chang et al. 2017a). According to J.P. Morgan (2017), the CFETS announced the above-mentioned adjustment on May 26. This should tackle the problem of pro-cyclicality as the closing spot level of the previous day usually strongly influences the next day's fixing level. Indeed, when US dollar demand is on the strong side and CNY spot trades weaker, this is reflected in the next day's fixing. This policy was announced by China in 2015 in order to give the market a greater say in determining the local exchange rate. Now, 'the concern of policymakers is that there is a "pro-cyclical" component in the FX market, which is driven by "sticky irrational expectations" that exacerbate one-sided market expectations and cause over-shooting in CNY adjustments' (J.P. Morgan 2017). The counter-cyclical adjustment factor aims to better incorporate macro fundamentals in the determination of the spot exchange rate. 'The adjustment seems to have existed for a while, as hinted from official communication' (J.P. Morgan 2017). The announcement immediately affected the USD/CNY exchange rate. However, the new rule will be fairly difficult to track for investors and thus, as happened in previous changes of the FX regime, the bilateral exchange rate versus the US dollar is the most important indication to watch.

iv) State-owned Enterprises, Governance and the Rule of Law

At the Communist Party's congress in October 2017, which takes place every five years, Xi Jinping declared that, 'socialist modernisation would be realised' by 2025. Through these reform announcements, the Chinese President aimed to secure himself a prominent position in China's history. 'In 2013 Mr Xi promised to give the market "a decisive role" in the economy and approved a list of 60 or so reforms to implement that idea. At the congress he turned to the theme of "ensuring the market-based allocation of resources". A burst of this sort of liberalisation cannot be entirely ruled out. But in the past three years, the politics of reform has moved strongly against the idea' (The Economist 2017a). Since giving the market a greater say would push back the influence of the CCP, reformists will be disappointed in the second term of Xi

Jinping. The Economist (2017a) put this as follows: 'a new round of "reform with Chinese characteristics" will therefore mean more party control over companies, more state-directed industrial subsidies, the merger, and transformation of SOEs into national champions and tighter supervision of the online economy'.

Private ownership hardly existed in communism and was de facto non-existent outside the agricultural sector. Privatisation fulfils the goals 'of developing private ownership and the market system generally, and of motivating and enabling restructuring in the former state-owned sector' (Estrin 1998:96). Therefore, privatisation was high on the agenda for many reformists. This was embedded into a wider set of reforms, such as price liberalisation, the build-up of a legal system, or the removal of trade restrictions. Given the breakdown of the political system at the time of the transformation, many countries had to innovate with respect to privatisation, and the outcome was the method of mass privatisation. In theory, privatisation should help to resolve the conflict of interest issues with for efficiency due to an asymmetric information problem. In a market, this conflict can be resolved in a number of ways. For instance, competition and regulation limit firm-specific rents and thus, the magnitude of the harm a single manager can do. The capital market serves as a constraining factor, as it exercises scrutiny. Regarding ownership of the state, Estrin (1998) notes that 'ownership and control are still separate, with the resulting conflict of interest and informational asymmetry between managers and the state. However, the state as owner may have multiple objectives – for example, creating employment in depressed regions, holding prices below average costs as an element of a prices and income policy, or satisfying service criteria. Profits can become secondary'. Kornai (1980) noted that these problems of asymmetric information led to very low levels of efficiency and innovations in state-led enterprises.

The usual form of privatisation to deal with these issues is an auction system to allocate assets. 'In practice, the collapse of Communism has left state-owned firms with few or no resources, a weak internal structure to handle the new demands of the marketplace, and a few mechanisms for the state to enforce governance' (Estrin 1998: 76). This made the option to privatise SOEs via auctions impossible to pursue. However, the path via rapid privatisations was equally bad for the transition economies. In principle, mass privatisation should guarantee an egalitarian distribution of former state-owned assets. Vouchers were often used to perform this task. The success of this is partly related to who will be the new majority owner of the firms. With respect to the privatisation of state-owned enterprises, Berglof (1997) points out that 'the very weak or non-existent legal protection for shareholders leaves managers in control unless a strategic investor can be found with a big enough stake to force his interests upon the manager'. In general, the idea behind privatisation was the notion that privately-owned enterprises would perform better than government-owned firms, which partially depends on the budget constraint. 'If budget constraints continue to be soft, it is unlikely that ownership changes will divert managerial behaviour from the fruitful path of pursuing greater subsidies to the infinitely tougher task of restructuring. Conversely, the hardening of hitherto soft budget constraints is likely to lead to fundamental changes' (Estrin 1998: 84). Apart from the voucher method to privatise companies, management and employee buyouts were a common form. This had the severe disadvantage that managers often undervalued assets in order to make a bargain.

A matter closely related to the firm reforms is the restructuring of banks. 'Firms in distress stop servicing their loans, and nonperforming loans are at the root of the commercial banks' troubles. In turn, unreformed banks' failure to enforce loan contracts adequately gives firms incentives for lax loan servicing' (Wijnbergen 1998: 99). Therefore, supervision of banks is as crucial as improvements in accounting, and certain standards were identified as important steps to address these issues. Indeed, weaknesses in regulation as well as in accounting provide for bad incentives, i.e. banks conceal loan problems. The situation gets even more complicated in transition economies as nearly the entire manufacturing sector faced distress in Central and Eastern Europe as well as in the Former Soviet Union. Furthermore, a Western style commercial banking system was entirely unknown in communism, as a sole monobank existed. Early in the process, bankruptcy was identified as an inadequate means to deal with the problem of government-owned firms and thus, restructuring programmes were set-up. Generally, banking distress emerges at the point when nonperforming loans do threaten the liquidity of the bank and thus, problems can no longer be disguised. 'The standard approach consists of incentive reform, management change, wholesale removal of nonperforming loans from the banks involved, with control typically transferred to a bank rehabilitation agency' (Wijnbergen 1998: 100). In the case of China, these agencies were so-called asset management companies and the process of freeing the newly emerging banking sector from its debt legacy was relatively successful. In many cases, the post-Communist trauma with respect to legacy debt can be classified as a one-off problem and thus, any restructuring does not send any signals to future creditors (Wijnbergen 1998: 105-106).

Additionally, Knaack and Gruin (2017) stated in their paper that, 'As a representative of the developing world, China has taken the lead in promoting a regulatory approach to shadow banking that strikes a balance between development and risk control' (Knaack and Gruin 2017: 16). However, the Chinese government has not succeeded in altering the global regulatory framework. For decades, developed countries primarily drove financial regulation; representatives of standard-setting bodies (SSB) were mainly chosen from said nations. However, these global standards often have to be adopted by a wider set of countries, which did not get a voice in this process. Knaack and Gruin (2017: 2) describe China's approach towards challenging key players in the Financial Stability Board (FSB) with respect to non-bank financial intermediaries (NBFI). Given that the FSB has not included the suggestions of China and other Asian nations in its framework, the researchers see certain developments evolving going forward. The most important development is that 'Chinese regulatory authorities have sharply limited their degree of cooperation with the FSB in the field of shadow banking, sharing only a modicum of financial data with their peers' (Knaack and Gruin 2017: 2). In general, the term shadow banking was first coined by Paul McCulley from PIMCO, who used the phrase in relation to the US subprime mortgage crisis. This is also the reason for the negative connotation of the term. The FSB notes on this subject that the great financial crisis showed that shadow banking could entail systemic risk. In contrast, for many developing countries shadow banking also relates to vehicles supporting the trajectory of the respective countries. This is seen in light of financial inclusion, which should help to narrow the development gap. In addition, there are various reasons for the speedy growth of non-bank credit intermediaries, particularly in China. In general, the system of financial repression entails the disadvantage that small borrowers find it hard to obtain funding for their projects. Thus, in many developing and emerging countries shadow banking is often related to financial inclusion (Knaack and Gruin 2017: 5-8).

Citi (2017c) describes the risk of regulatory tightening to local Chinese capital markets in their research note 'Why tighter regulations will not choke off economy/markets'. Guo Shuqing, the head of the China Bank Regulatory Commission (CBRC), has tightened regulations significantly since he took up office in February 2017. Seven new documents were released between 26 March 2017 and 7 April 2017, which described tighter regulatory measures as well as enforcements. The new regulations can be classified into four themes, namely 'cracking down 'three violations', stemming 'three arbitrages', rectifying 'four irregularities', and re-assessing key risks' (Citi 2017c). This has led to uncertainty in local capital markets, sparking a selloff in commodity, bond, and equity markets. Before the tightening move, the PBoC already hiked onshore money market rates to manage financial risks without changing the official one-year benchmark lending and deposit rates. Indeed, the above is a strong message to the banking sector. The trend is that banks have to refocus their lending to the real economy. A selloff resulting in higher rates could lead to a decline in funding sources and higher credit risk, which in return would hurt the Chinese banking system. However, 'in the long term, vulnerable companies with high leverage will be forced to exit once shadow banking finance has been cut' (Citi 2017c).

v) Technology and Productivity

Given capital and labour, improvements in technology lead to a higher output. While in developed countries research and development is the main source of sustainable growth, most developing countries tend to be importers of new technologies and thus, rather users than producers of technology. The adoption of imported technologies leads to productivity growth over time. Therefore, the source of productivity growth in developed and developing countries is fundamentally different (Blanchard and Johnson 2013: 249-260). Patent protection is generally very weak in developing countries due to a different growth model than in advanced nations. However, as these countries develop such topics become more important (Yueh 2013). As described in the conceptual section, growth accounting can serve to assess the main drivers of a country's economic performance. The method dates back to Solow (1957), who showed that a sustainable growth path is only related to improvements in technology. Indeed, for developed countries the main source of growth is productivity. Thus, there are two ways how developing countries can catch-up with more advanced nations. First, fast capital accumulation can lead to a temporary growth spurt. Second, the adoption of new technologies leads to progress in terms of productivity (Blanchard and Johnson 2013: 261). What can be said about China's trajectory with the help of growth accounting? Technological progress was the main source of growth from the beginning of the reform period since the mid-1990s. Speedy capital accumulation was the primary driver of growth since the mid-1990s until the country's accession to the WTO (Zheng and Hu 2006; Zheng et al. 2009). Thus, China's successful trajectory is described well by both factors.

Part 6: Concluding Remarks on this Book

In conclusion, it should be clear that the transition of China is not yet complete. The troubles China faced in the second half of 2015 and 2016 are partly symptoms of the unfinished shift from plan to market and thus, stakeholders should pay proper attention to the unfolding of this period. China's success has been tremendous over the past forty years; however, this does not mean that the successful trajectory will continue. The Chinese government has not yet addressed financial distortions. Instead, a misguided belief has led China to partially liberalise the economy without thinking about the correct sequence of said project. Capital markets are underdeveloped and banks dominate the financial sector. Therefore, reforms should start with the repressive system. Households should be given a fair interest on their savings and should be provided with alternative vehicles other than deposits. A fair and equitable distribution of income should be possible.

The imbalance between households and the state secured cheap costs of funding for the reallocation of productive factors. Hence, China is facing a systemic problem, which cannot be simply tackled with individual reforms. To dissolve this system, the correct sequencing of reforms is crucial, which has been neglected so far by the Chinese government. Deng Xiaoping coined development as the only hard truth. Now, it is time for China to go through a second ideological shift. A systematic array of reforms has to be undertaken; reducing policy-induced uncertainty as well as building inclusive institutions is key for the country's trajectory in the future. My triangular analytical approach helps stakeholders to better understand the holistic picture of the country's struggles. Indeed, a unified framework consisting of a fundamental, policy and institutional dimension leads to a better understanding of outcomes from an early warning perspective, in particular of the events unfolding in China in the second half of 2015 and 2016. It demonstrates that the policy efforts of China should aim at addressing underlying vulnerabilities.

List of Abbreviations

ABC	Agricultural Bank of China
ADB	Asian Development Bank
AFD	Augmented Fiscal Deficit
AIIB	Asian International Infrastructure Bank
AMCs	Asset Management Companies
ARA	Assessing Reserve Adequacy
AREAER	Annual Report on Exchange Arrangements and Exchange Restrictions
ASEAN	Association of Southeast Asian Nations
BEER	Behavioural Equilibrium Exchange Rate
BIC	Brazil, India and China
BIS	Bank for International Settlements
BoAML	Bank of America Merrill Lynch
BOC	Bank of China
BoP	Balance-of-Payments
BRIC	Brazil, Russia, India, China
CA	Current Account
CAS	Chinese Academy of Science
CBRC	China Bank Regulatory Commission
CCB	China Construction Bank
CCP	Chinese Communist Party
CEE	Central and Eastern Europe
CFETS	China Foreign Exchange Trading System
CFLP	China Federation of Logistics and Purchasing
CIBM	China Interbank Market
CIC	China Investment Corporation
CIRC	China Insurance Regulatory Commission
CMI	Chang Mai Initiative
CMIM	Chang Mai Initiative Multilateralization
CMU	Central Moneymarket Unit
CNH	Chinese Yuan Offshore
CNY	Chinese Yuan Onshore
CPC	Communist Party of China
CPI	Consumer Price Index
CSRC	China Securities Regulatory Commission

DCSD	Developed Country Studies Division
DS	Developmental State
DTCs	Developing and Transition Countries
DXY	US Dollar Index
E&Os	Errors and Omissions
EBRD	European Bank for Reconstruction and Development
EM	Emerging Market
ETFs	Exchange Traded Funds
EU	European Union
EUR	Euro
EWS	Early Warning Systems
FDI	Foreign Direct Investment
FDIC	Federal Deposit Insurance Corporation
FEER	Fundamental Equilibrium Exchange Rate
FSB	Financial Stability Board
FSU	Former Soviet Union
FTZ	Free Trade Zone
FX	Foreign Exchange
G20	Group of Twenty
G7	Group of Seven
G8	Group of Eight
GATT	General Agreement on Tariffs and Trade
GDP	Gross Domestic Product
GLF	Great Leap Forward
GNP	Gross National Product
GS	Goldman Sachs
HIBOR	Hong Kong Interbank Offered Rate
HKMA	Hong Kong Monetary Authority
IBL	Institutionalisation Before Liberalisation
ICBC	Industrial and Commercial Bank of China
ICs	Industrial Countries
IDA	International Development Association
IIP	International Investment Position
IMF	International Monetary Fund
INR	Indian Rupee
IOER	Interest Rate on Banks' Excess Reserves

IP	Industrial Production
IPO	Initial Public Offering
IPR	Intellectual Property Rights
ISI	Import-Substitution Industrialisation
ISM	Institute of Supply Management
ITC	International Trade Commission
JPY	Japanese Yen
JSCB	Joint-Stock Commercial Bank
KLR	Kaminsky, Lizondo and Reinhart
KRW	Korean Won
LGFV	Local Government Financing Vehicle
LGFVs	Local Government Financing Vehicles
LIBOR	London Interbank Offered Rate
LLC	Limited Liability Company
LTP	Lewis Turning Point
M&A	Mergers & Acquisitions
MITI	Ministry of International Trade and Industry
MLF	Medium-term Lending Facility
MNE	Multinational Enterprise
MoF	Ministry of Finance
MPA	Macro Prudential Assessment
MPL	Marginal Product of Labor
MXN	Mexican Peso
NBFI	Non-Bank Financial Intermediaries
NBS	National Bureau of Statistics
NDF	Non-Deliverable Forward
NDRC	National Development and Reform Commission
NEER	Nominal Effective Exchange Rate
NIC	National Intelligence Council
NPC	National People's Congress
NPL	Non-Performing Loan
NRC	National Resource Commission
OCA	Optimal Currency Area
ODIs	Outward Direct Investments
OECD	Organisation for Economic Co-operation and Development
OFA	Optimal Financial Area

OMOs	Open Market Transactions
OPEC	Organization of the Petroleum Exporting Countries
PBoC	People's Bank of China
PCA	Principal Component Analysis
PDR	Policy Development and Review
PLA	People's Liberation Army
PMI	Purchasing Manager Index
PPP	Purchasing Power Parity
PRC	People's Republic of China
PSDS	Post-Socialist Developmental State
PSL	Pledged Supplementary Lending
QDII	Qualified Domestic Institutional Investor
QDII2	Qualified Domestic Individual Investor
QFII	Qualified Foreign Institutional Investor
R&D	Research and Development
REER	Real Effective Exchange Rate
RER	Real Exchange Rate
RMB	Renminbi
RMSE	Root Mean Square Error
RQFII	Renminbi Qualified Foreign Institutional Investor
RRR	Reserve Requirement Ratio
SAFE	State Administration of Foreign Exchange
SASAC	State-Owned Assets Supervision and Administration Commission
SDR	Special Drawing Rights
SEZ	Special Economic Zone
SEZs	Special Economic Zones
SFTZ	Shanghai Free Trade Zone
SHIBOR	Shanghai Interbank Offered Rate
SLF	Standard Lending Facility
SME	Small- and Medium-Sized Enterprises
SOE	State-Owned Enterprise
SSB	Standard-Setting Bodies
Std	Standard Deviation
SWF	Sovereign Wealth Fund
TAA	Tactical Asset Allocation
TFP	Total Factor Productivity

TLF	Temporary Liquidity Facility
TMA	Treasury Markets Association
TRY	Turkish Lira
TSF	Total Social Financing
TVEs	Township and Village Enterprises
TWD	Taiwan Dollar
UBS	Union Bank of Suisse
UNCTAD	United Nations Conference on Trade and Development
US	United States
USD	United States Dollar
WB	World Bank
WMP	Wealth Management Product
WTO	World Trade Organisation
WW	World War
YoY	Year-on-Year
ZAR	South African Rand

Bibliography

Introduction

Acemoglu, D., & Robinson, J. A. (2013). Why nations fail: The origins of power, prosperity, and poverty. Crown Business.

Acemoglu, D. (2004). Understanding Institutions - Lionel Robbins Lecture at LSE. MIT Department of Economics [Online] February 2004 http://economics.mit.edu/files/1353 [Accessed: September 2017].

Chamon, M., Ghosh, A., & Kim, J. (2012). Are All Emerging Market Crises Alike?. Global Economic Crisis: Impacts, Transmission, Recovery, Cheltenham, UK: Edward Elgar.

Drazen, A. (2000). Political contagion in currency crises, in Krugman P. (ed) Currency crises (Chicago: University of Chicago Press), 47-67.

Feenstra, R. C., & Taylor, A. M. (2014). International economics. 3rd Edition. New York: Worth Macmillan.

Frankel, J. A., & Rose, A. K. (1996). Currency crashes in emerging markets: An empirical treatment. Journal of international Economics, 41(3), 351-366.

Goldstein, M. (1998). The Asian financial crisis: Causes, cures, and systemic implications (Vol. 55). Peterson Institute.

Goldstein, M., Kaminsky, G. L., & Reinhart, C. M. (2000). Assessing financial vulnerability: an early warning system for emerging markets. Peterson Institute.

Gong, G. W. (2001). The beginning of history: Remembering and forgetting as strategic issues. Washington Quarterly, 24(2), 45-57.

Ghosh, S. R., & Ghosh, A. R. (2003). Structural vulnerabilities and currency crises. IMF Staff Papers, 481-506.

Ghosh, M. A. R., Zalduendo, M. J., Thomas, M. A. H., Kim, M. J. I., Ramakrishnan, M. U., & Joshi, B. (2008). IMF Support and Crisis Prevention (No. 262). International Monetary Fund.

Heilmann, S. (2008). Policy Experimentation in China's Economic Rise, In: Studies in Comparative International Development (SCID), Vol. 43, No. 1 (Januar 2008): p. 1-26.

Hurrell, A. (2014). Rising Powers and the Emerging Global, in Baylis, J., Smith, S., & Owens P. (eds.), The Globalization of World Politics: an introduction to international relations, 6th Edition. Oxford: Oxford University Press, 80-94.

Kaufmann, D., Kraay, A., & Mastruzzi, M. (2006). Governance matters V: Governance indicators for 1996-2005.

Lardy, N. R. (2012). Sustaining China's economic growth after the global financial crisis. Peterson Institute.

McNally, C. A., & Gruin, J. (2017). A novel pathway to power? Contestation and adaptation in China's internationalization of the RMB. Review of International Political Economy, 1-30.

North, D. C. (1990). Institutions, institutional change and economic performance. Cambridge university press.

Reinhart, C. M. (2002). Default, currency crises, and sovereign credit ratings. the world bank economic review, 16(2), 151-170.

Reinhart, C. M., & Rogoff, K. S. (2009). This time is different: Eight centuries of financial folly. Princeton University Press.

Sharma, R. (2016). The Rise and Fall of Nations: Forces of Change in the Post-crisis World. WW Norton & Company.

Fundamental Vulnerabilities

Acemoglu, D. (2004). Understanding Institutions - Lionel Robbins Lecture at LSE. MIT Department of Economics [Online] February 2004 http://economics.mit.edu/files/1353 [Accessed: September 2017].

Acemoglu, D., & Robinson, J. A. (2013). Why nations fail: The origins of power, prosperity, and poverty. Crown Business.
Ades, A., Masih, R., & Tenengauzer, D. (1998). GS Watch: A New Framework for Predicting Financial Crises in Emerging Markets. New York: Goldman Sachs.

Allen, R. C. (2003). Farm to factory: a reinterpretation of the Soviet industrial revolution. Princeton University Press.

Angkinand, A., Li, J., & Willett, T. (2006). Measures of currency crises: A survey. Forthcomming in: International Interaction.

Baron, M., & Xiong, W. (2017). Credit expansion and neglected crash risk. The Quarterly Journal of Economics, 132(2), 713-764.

Barro, R. J. (1979). On the determinants of the public debt. Journal of Political Economy 87(5): 940-71.

Barro, R. J. (1988). The Ricardian approach to budget deficits.

Beavan, A. (2013). Macro drivers of asset performance and global TAA strategy. London Financial Studies.

Bellas, D., Papaioannou, M. G., & Petrova, I. (2010). Determinants of emerging market sovereign bond spreads. Sovereign debt and the financial crisis. IMF, Washington, DC, 77-101.

Berg, A., & Pattillo, C. (1999). Are currency crises predictable? A test. IMF staff papers, 46(2), 107-138.

Bernanke, B. S., & Blinder, A. S. (1992). The federal funds rate and the channels of monetary policy transmission. American Economic Review 82(4): 901-21.

Blanchard, O. J., & Johnson, D. (2013). Macroeconomics. Sixth Edition. Pearson Education.

Brüggemann, A., & Linne, T. (1999). How good are leading indicators for currency and banking crises in Central and Eastern Europe? An empirical test (No. 95). IWH Discussion Papers.

Brüggemann, A., & Linne, T. (2002). Are the Central and Eastern European transition countries still vulnerable to a financial crisis? Results from the signals approach.

Calomiris, C. W., & Gorton, G. (1991). The origins of banking panics: models, facts, and bank regulation. In Financial markets and financial crises (pp. 109-174). University of Chicago Press.

Calvo, G. (2003). Explaining Sudden Stop. In Growth Collapse and BOP Crisis: The Case of Discretionary Output Tax, The Mundell Fleming Lecture for the Third Annual IMF Research Conference, Washington, DC.

Calvo, G. A. (2005). Emerging capital markets in turmoil: bad luck or bad policy?. MIT Press Books, 1.

Calvo, G. A., & Mendoza, E. G. (1996). Petty crime and cruel punishment: lessons from the Mexican debacle. The American Economic Review, 86(2), 170-175.

Calvo, G. A., Leiderman, L. and Reinhart, C.M. (1994) 'The capital inflows problem: Concepts and issues' Contemporary Economic Policy (12:3), 54-66.

Calvo, G., & Reinhart, C. (2000). When capital inflows come to a sudden stop: Consequences and policy options.

Calvo, G., Goldstein, M., & Hochreiter, E. (1996). Private capital flows to emerging markets after the Mexican crisis. Peterson Institute for International Economics.

Catão, L., & Sutton, B. (2002). Sovereign defaults: the role of volatility. International Monetary Fund.

Chamon, M., Ghosh, A., & Kim, J. (2012). Are All Emerging Market Crises Alike?. Global Economic Crisis: Impacts, Transmission, Recovery, Cheltenham, UK: Edward Elgar.

Checherita, C., and Rother, P. (2010). The impact of high and growing government debt on economic growth: An empirical investigation for the euro area. Working paper 1237, European Central Bank.

Cheremukhin, A., Golosov, M., Guriev, S., & Tsyvinski, A. (2017). The Industrialization and Economic Development of Russia through the Lens of a Neoclassical Growth Model. The Review of Economic Studies, 84(2), 613-649.

Chinn, M. D., & Ito, H. (2008). A new measure of financial openness. Journal of comparative policy analysis, 10(3), 309-322.

Clark, P. B., & MacDonald, R. (1999). Exchange rates and economic fundamentals: a methodological comparison of BEERs and FEERs. In Equilibrium exchange rates (pp. 285-322). Springer Netherlands.

Comelli, F. (2012). Emerging market sovereign bond spreads: Estimation and back-testing. Emerging Markets Review, 13(4), 598-625.

De la Rocha, M. M., Perrelli, M. R., & Mulder, M. C. B. (2002). The role of corporate, legal and macroeconomic balance sheet indicators in crisis detection and prevention (No. 2-59). International Monetary Fund.

Debelle, G., & Galati, G. (2005). Current Account Adjustment and Capital Flows (BIS Working Paper 169). Basel, Switzerland.

DeRosa, D. F. (2009). Central Banking and Monetary Policy in Emerging-Markets Nations.

Dornbusch, R. (1976). Expectations and exchange rate dynamics. Journal of political economy, 84(6), 1161-1176.

Dornbusch, R., Goldfajn, I., Valdés, R. O., Edwards, S., & Bruno, M. (1995). Currency crises and collapses. Brookings Papers on Economic Activity, 1995(2), 219-293.

Edwards, S. (2004). Thirty years of current account imbalances, current account reversals and sudden stops (No. w10276). National Bureau of Economic Research.

Eggertsson, G. B., & Krugman, P. (2012). Debt, deleveraging, and the liquidity trap: A Fisher-Minsky-Koo approach. The Quarterly Journal of Economics, 127(3), 1469-1513.

Eichengreen, B., & Hausmann, R. (1999). Exchange rates and financial fragility (No. w7418). National bureau of economic research.

Eichengreen, B., & Rose, A. K. (1999). Contagious currency crises: Channels of conveyance. In Changes in exchange rates in rapidly developing countries: Theory, practice, and policy issues (NBER-EASE volume 7) (pp. 29-56). University of Chicago Press.

Eichengreen, B., Rose, A. K., & Wyplosz, C. (1994). Speculative attacks on pegged exchange rates: an empirical exploration with special reference to the European Monetary System (No. w4898). National Bureau of economic research.

Eichengreen, B., Rose, A. K., & Wyplosz, C. (1995). Exchange market mayhem: The antecedents and aftermath of speculative attacks. Economic Policy, 249-312.

Feenstra, R. C., & Taylor, A.M. (2014). International economics. 3rd Edition, New York: Worth Macmillan.

Freund, C. L. (2000). Current account adjustment in industrial countries. International Finance Discussion Paper 692, Board of Governors of the Federal Reserve System.

Fuster, A., Laibson, D., & Mendel, B. (2010). Natural expectations and macroeconomic fluctuations. The Journal of Economic Perspectives, 24(4), 67-84.

Galbis, V. (1993). High Real Interest Rates Under Financial Liberalization Is There a Problem?.

Galor, O., & Weil, D. N. (2000). Population, technology, and growth: From Malthusian stagnation to the demographic transition and beyond. American economic review, 806-828.

Gertler, M. (1988). Financial structure and aggregate economic activity: an overview. Journal of Money, Credit and Banking 20(3): 559-88.

Ghosh, A. R., Ostry, J. D., & Tamirisa, N. (2009). Anticipating the Next Crisis-What can early warning systems be expected to deliver?. Finance & Development, 46(3), 35-37.

Ghosh, M. A. R., Zalduendo, M. J., Thomas, M. A. H., Kim, M. J. I., Ramakrishnan, M. U., & Joshi, B. (2008). IMF Support and Crisis Prevention (No. 262). International Monetary Fund.

Ghosh, S. R., & Ghosh, A. R. (2003). Structural vulnerabilities and currency crises. IMF Staff Papers, 481-506.

Goldfajn, I., & Valdés, R. (1997). Balance of Payments Crises and Capital Flows: The Role of Liquidity (No. 11). Central Bank of Chile.

Goldman Sachs (2015). Untangling China's credit conundrum.

Goldstein, M. (1998). The Asian financial crisis: Causes, cures, and systemic implications (Vol. 55). Peterson Institute.

Goldstein, M., Kaminsky, G. L., & Reinhart, C. M. (2000). Assessing financial vulnerability: an early warning system for emerging markets. Peterson Institute.

Gruber, J. W., & Kamin, S. B. (2007). Explaining the global pattern of current account imbalances. Journal of International Money and Finance, 26(4), 500-522.

Hall, R. E., & Jones, C. I. (1999). Why do some countries produce so much more output per worker than others?. The quarterly journal of economics, 114(1), 83-116.

International Monetary Fund (2002). Global Financial Stability Report. Early Warning System Models: The Next Steps Forward. International Monetary Fund, Publication Services, Washington.

International Monetary Fund (2017). Global financial stability report. Is growth at risk?. World Economic and Financial Surveys, October 2017.

J.P. Morgan (2015). Keeping a wary eye on the EM credit cycle.

Jordà, Ò., Schularick, M., & Taylor, A. M. (2016). The great mortgaging: housing finance, crises and business cycles. Economic Policy, 31(85), 107-152.

Kaminsky, G. L., & Reinhart, C. M. (1998). Financial crises in Asia and Latin America: Then and now. The American Economic Review, 88(2), 444-448.

Kaminsky, G. L., & Reinhart, C. M. (1999). The twin crises: the causes of banking and balance-of-payments problems. American economic review, 473-500.

Kaminsky, G. L., Reinhart, C.M. and Végh, C.A (2004) 'When it rains, it pours: procyclical capital flows and macroeconomic policies'. National Bureau of Economic Research No. w10780

Kaminsky, G., Lizondo, S., & Reinhart, C. M. (1998). Leading indicators of currency crises. Staff Papers, 45(1), 1-48.

Kindleberger, C. P. (1978). Manias, panics, and crashes: A history of financial crises. New York: Basic Books.

Kiyotaki, N., & Moore, J. (1997). Credit cycles. Journal of political economy, 105(2), 211-248.

Korinek, A., & Simsek, A. (2016). Liquidity trap and excessive leverage. The American Economic Review, 106(3), 699-738.

Krugman, P. (1979). A model of balance-of-payments crises. Journal of money, credit and banking, 11(3), 311-325.

Krugman, P. (2001). Crises: the next generation. Razin Conference, Tel Aviv University.

Krugman, P. R., Obstfeld, M., & Melitz, M. (2015). International Economics, 10th. Edition, Prentice Hall.

Kumar, M., & Woo, J. (2010). Public debt and growth. IMF working paper WP/10/174.
Lal, D. (1992). Development economics. Volume 1. The international library of critical writings in economics 18.

Lewis, W. A. (1954). Economic development with unlimited supplies of labour. The manchester school, 22(2), 139-191.

Lucas, R. E. (1990). Why doesn't capital flow from rich to poor countries?. The American Economic Review, 80(2), 92-96.

Lucas, R. E. (1998). On the mechanics of economic development. Econometric Society Monographs, 29, 61-70.

MacDonald, R., & Dias, P. (2007). Behavioural equilibrium exchange rate estimates and implied exchange rate adjustments for ten countries. Peterson Institute of International Economics Working Paper, February.

Mahoney, J., and Terrie, P.L. (2008) 'Comparative-historical analysis in contemporary political science' Oxford handbook of political methodology, 741-749.

Manasse, P., Roubini, N., & Schimmelpfennig, A. (2003). Predicting sovereign debt crises.

Mankiw, N. G., Romer, D., & Weil, D. N. (1992). A contribution to the empirics of economic growth. The quarterly journal of economics, 107(2), 407-437.

McKinnon, R. I., & Pill, H. (1996). Credible Liberalizations and International Capital Flows: The" Overborrowing Syndrome". In Financial Deregulation and Integration in East Asia, NBER-EASE Volume 5 (pp. 7-50). University of Chicago Press.

McKinsey Global Institute (2015). Debt and (not much) deleveraging. McKinsey&Company.

McNally, C. A., & Gruin, J. (2017). A novel pathway to power? Contestation and adaptation in China's internationalization of the RMB. Review of International Political Economy, 1-30.

Mendoza, E. G., & Terrones, M. E. (2012). An anatomy of credit booms and their demise (No. w18379). National Bureau of Economic Research.

Mian, A., & Sufi, A. (2011). House prices, home equity–based borrowing, and the us household leverage crisis. The American Economic Review, 101(5), 2132-2156.

Mian, A., Rao, K., & Sufi, A. (2013). Household balance sheets, consumption, and the economic slump. The Quarterly Journal of Economics, 128(4), 1687-1726.

Mian, A., Sufi, A., & Verner, E. (2017). Household debt and business cycles worldwide. The Quarterly Journal of Economics.

Milesi-Ferretti, G. M., & Razin, A. (1998). Sharp reductions in current account deficits an empirical analysis. European Economic Review, 42(3), 897-908.

Minsky, H., P. (1977). The financial instability hypothesis: an interpretation of Keynes and alternative to standard theory. Challenge (March-April): 20-27.

Mishkin, F., S. (1978). The household balance sheet and the great depression. Journal of Economic History 38: 918-37.

Mundell, R. A. (1961). A theory of optimum currency areas. The American economic review, 51(4), 657-665.

Mundell, R. A. (1963). Capital mobility and stabilization policy under fixed and flexible exchange rates. Canadian Journal of Economics and Political Science/Revue canadienne de economiques et science politique, 29(4), 475-485.

Mussa, M. M., Dell'Ariccia, M. G., Eichengreen, M. B. J., & Detragiache, M. E. (1998). Capital account liberalization: theoretical and practical aspects (No. 172). International Monetary Fund.

Naughton, B. (2007). The Chinese economy: Transitions and growth. MIT press.

Ngai, L. R. (2004). Barriers and the transition to modern growth. Journal of Monetary Economics, 51(7), 1353-1383.

Olson, M. (1996). Distinguished lecture on economics in government: big bills left on the sidewalk:

why some nations are rich, and others poor. The Journal of economic perspectives, 10(2), 3-24.
Panizza, U., & Presbitero, A. F. (2012). Public debt and economic growth: is there a causal effect?. Money & Finance Research Group, Working Paper n. 65.

Park, Y. C. (2006). Economic liberalization and integration in East Asia: a post-crisis paradigm. Oxford University Press on Demand.

Pattillo, C., Poirson, H., & Ricci, L., A. (2011). External debt and growth. Review of economics and institutions 2(3): Article 2.

Prasad, E. S., Rajan, R. G., & Subramanian, A. (2007). Foreign capital and economic growth (No. w13619). National Bureau of Economic Research.

Quinn, D. (1997). The correlates of change in international financial regulation. American Political science review, 91(3), 531-551.

Quinn, D. P. (2003). Capital account liberalization and financial globalization, 1890–1999: a synoptic view. International Journal of Finance & Economics, 8(3), 189-204.

Reinhart, C. M. (2002). Default, currency crises, and sovereign credit ratings. the world bank economic review, 16(2), 151-170.

Reinhart, C. M., & Rogoff, K. S. (2004). The modern history of exchange rate arrangements: a reinterpretation. the Quarterly Journal of economics, 119(1), 1-48.

Reinhart, C. M., & Rogoff, K. S. (2009). This time is different: Eight centuries of financial folly. Princeton University Press.

Reynolds, L. G. (1983). The spread of economic growth to the Third World: 1850-1980. Journal of economic literature, 21(3), 941-980.

Rodrik, D. (2008). The real exchange rate and economic growth. Brookings Papers on Economic Activity 39(2 (Fall)): 365-439.

Rostow, W. W. (1956). The take-off into self-sustained growth. The Economic Journal, 66(261), 25-48.

Sahay, R., Čihák, M., N'Diaye, P., & Barajas, A. (2015). Rethinking financial deepening: Stability and growth in emerging markets. Revista de Economía Institucional, 17(33), 73-107.

Schmitt-Grohé, S., & Uribe, M. (2016). Downward nominal wage rigidity, currency pegs, and involuntary unemployment. Journal of Political Economy, 124(5), 1466-1514.

Schularick, M., & Taylor, A. (2012). Credit booms gone bust: monetary policy, leverage cycles, and financial crises, 1870-2008. American Economic Review 102(2): 1029-61.

Sharma, R. (2016). The Rise and Fall of Nations: Forces of Change in the Post-crisis World. WW Norton & Company.

Shiller, R. J. (2014). Why Is Housing Finance Still Stuck in Such a Primitive Stage?. The American Economic Review, 104(5), 73-76.

Shiller, R. J. (2015). Irrational exuberance. Princeton University Press.

Solow, R. (1957). Technical change and the aggregate production function.

Stern, N. (1991). The determinants of growth. The Economic Journal, 101(404), 122-133.

Syrquin, M., & Chenery, H. (1989). Three decades of industrialization. The World Bank Economic Review, 3(2), 145-181.

The Economist (2017a). A rash of bankruptcies hits Chinese lenders backed by state firms. The Economist [Online] 21 October. https://www.economist.com/news/finance-and-economics/21730441-government-struggles-control-firms-it-owns-rash-bankruptcies-hits [Accessed: October 2017].

The Economist (2017b). Asian households binge on debt. The Economist [Online] 2 November. https://www.economist.com/news/finance-and-economics/21730932-what-should-be-good-news-global-economy-has-its-downsides-asian-households [Accessed: November 2017].

The Economist (2017c). Close to retiring, China's central-bank chief warns of financial risk. The Economist [Online] 9 November. https://www.economist.com/news/china/21731180-zhou-xiaochuan-trying-burnish-his-legacy-close-retiring-chinas-central-bank-chief-warns [Accessed: November 2017].

The Economist (2017d). What there is to learn from the Soviet economic model. The Economist [Online] 9 November. https://www.economist.com/news/finance-and-economics/21731113-even-today-some-see-it-way-kick-start-industrialisation-what-there [Accessed: November 2017].

Valdés, R. (1997). Emerging markets contagion: evidence and theory.

Williamson, J. (1985). The Exchange Rate System, policy analyses in international economics. Institute for International Economics, Washington, DC.

Williamson, S. D. (2014). Macroeconomics. Pearson Education Limited.

World Bank (1997). China 2020. Washington, DC: World Bank.

Yueh, L. (2013). China's growth: The making of an economic superpower. Oxford University Press.

Zheng, J., Bigstein, A., & Hu, A. (2009). Can China´s growth be sustained? A productivity perspective. World Development (Special issue on law, finance, and economic growth in China), 37/4: 874-88.

Zheng, J., Hu, A. (2006). An empirical analysis of provincial productivity in

China 1979-2001. Journal of Chinese Economic and Business Studies, 4/3: 221-39.

Zheng, J., Liu, X, & Bigsten, A. (2003). Efficiency, technical progress, and best practice in Chinese state enterprises 1980-1994. Journal of Comparative Economics, 31/1: 134-52.

The Policy Dimension

Areddy, J., King, N., Kissel, M., & Dean, J. (2005). Behind yuan move, open debate and closed doors. Wall Street Journal, 25 July 2005.

Atkinson, A. B. (2015). Inequality: what can be done?. Harvard University Press.

Banerjee, A., Duflo, E., Glennerster, R., & Kinnan, C. (2015). The miracle of microfinance? Evidence from a randomized evaluation. American Economic Journal: Applied Economics, 7(1), 22-53.

Barnett, M., & Finnemore, M. (2004). Rules for the world: international organizations in global politics. Ithaca, NY: Cornell University Press, p. 45-72.

Barnett, S., & Brooks, R. (2011). Does Government Spending on Health and Education Raise Consumption. Rebalancing Growth in Asia: Economic Dimensions for China, 129-38.

Beachy, B. (2012). A Financial Crisis Manual Causes, Consequences, and Lessons of the Financial Crisis (No. 12-06). GDAE, Tufts University.

Bergsten, C. F., Freeman, C., Lardy, N. R., & Mitchell, D. (2008). China's rise: challenges and opportunities. Washington: Peterson Institute for International Economics and Center for Strategic and International Studies.

Blyth, M. (2002). Great transformations: economic ideas and institutional change in the twentieth century. Cambridge University Press.

Bongaarts, J., & Greenhalgh, S. (1985). An alternative to the one-child policy in China. Center for Policy Studies. Working Papers. New York: Population Council.

Bunce, V. (1999). Subversive Institutions: the Design and the Destruction of Socialism and the State. Cambridge University Press.

Cao, Y., Qian, Y., & Weingast, B. R. (1999). From federalism, Chinese style to privatization, Chinese style. Economics of Transition, 7(1), 103-131.

Chamon, M., Ghosh, A., & Kim, J. (2012). Are All Emerging Market Crises Alike?. Global Economic Crisis: Impacts, Transmission, Recovery, Cheltenham, UK: Edward Elgar.

Chung, J. H. (1999). Preferential policies, municipal leadership, and development strategies. Cities in China, 103.

Chwieroth, J. (2007). Neoliberal economists and capital account liberalization in emerging markets. International organization, 61(2), 443-463.

Dabla-Norris, E., Kochhar, K., Ricka, F., Suphaphiphat, N., & Tsounta, E. (2015). Causes and consequences of income inequality; a global perspective. IMF Staff Discussion Note.

Das, M., & N'Diaye, M. P. M. (2013). Chronicle of a Decline Foretold: Has China Reached the Lewis Turning Point? (No. 13-26). International Monetary Fund.

De Soto, H. (1993). The missing ingredient. The Economist, 328(7828), 8-10.

De Soto, H. (2000). The mystery of capital: Why capitalism triumphs in the West and fails everywhere else. Basic Civitas Books.

DeRosa, D. F. (2009). Central Banking and Monetary Policy in Emerging-Markets Nations.

Dornbusch, R. (2001). A primer on emerging market crises. No. w8326, National Bureau of Economic Research.

Dornbusch, R., Goldfajn, I., Valdés, R. O., Edwards, S., & Bruno, M. (1995). Currency crises and collapses. Brookings Papers on Economic Activity, 1995(2), 219-293.

Eichengreen, B. (1993). The endogeneity of exchange rate regimes (No. w4361). National Bureau of Economic Research.

Eichengreen, B., Rose, A. K., & Wyplosz, C. (1994). Speculative attacks on pegged exchange rates: an empirical exploration with special reference to the European Monetary System (No. w4898). National Bureau of economic research.

Eichengreen, B., Rose, A. K., & Wyplosz, C. (1995). Exchange market mayhem: The antecedents and aftermath of speculative attacks. Economic Policy, 249-312.

Evans, P. (2004). Development as institutional change: the pitfalls of monocropping and the potentials of deliberation. Studies in comparative international development, 38(4), 30.

Evans, P. (2005). The challenges of the institutional turn: new interdisciplinary opportunities in development theory. The economic sociology of capitalism, 90-116.

Fan, G. (1994). Incremental change and dual-track transition: understanding the case of China. Economic Policy, 19/Supp: 99-122.

Fearon, J. D. (1991). Counterfactuals and hypothesis testing in political science. World Politics 43 (2).

Feenstra, R. C., and Taylor, A.M. (2014) International Economics 3rd Edition (New York: Worth Macmillan).

Frankel, J. A. (2005) 'Contractionary Currency Crashes in Developing Countries' The 5th Mundell-Fleming Lecture IMF Annual Research Conference

Fravel, M. T., & Medeiros, E. S. (2003). China's New Diplomacy. Foreign Affairs, 82(6), 22-35.

Friedman, M. (1972). Have monetary policies failed? American Economic Review, vol. 62, no. 2 (May):11-18.

Ghosh, M. A. R., Zalduendo, M. J., Thomas, M. A. H., Kim, M. J. I., Ramakrishnan, M. U., & Joshi, B. (2008). IMF Support and Crisis Prevention (No. 262). International Monetary Fund.

Ghosh, S. R., & Ghosh, A. R. (2003). Structural vulnerabilities and currency crises. IMF Staff Papers, 481-506.

Gilpin, R. (1983). War and change in world politics. Cambridge University Press.

Goldstein, M., & Lardy, N. R. (2008a). China's exchange rate policy: an overview of some key issues. In Goldstein, M., & Lardy, N. R. (2008). Debating China's exchange rate policy. Peterson Institute, p. 1-76.

Goldstein, M., & Lardy, N. R. (2008b). Debating China's exchange rate policy. Peterson Institute.

Green, S. (2004). The development of China's stockmarket, 1984-2002: equity politics and market institutions. Routledge.

Haas, P. (1992). Introduction: epistemic communities and international policy coordination. International Organization 46:1 (1992).

Hall, P. (1993). Policy paradigms, social learning, and the state: the case of economic policymaking in Britain. Comparative Politics 25, April 1993, p. 275-296.

Hardoon, D., Ayele, A., & Fuentes-Nieva, R. (2016). An economy for the 1%. Oxfam Briefing Paper.

He, J., & Kujis, L. (2007). Rebalancing China's economy – modelling a policy package. World Bank Research Paper No. 7 (September). Beijing: World Bank.

Heilmann, S. (2008a). From local experiments to national policy: The origins of China's distinctive policy process. The China Journal, (59), 1-30.

Heilmann, S. (2008b). Policy Experimentation in China's Economic Rise, In: Studies in Comparative International Development (SCID), Vol. 43, No. 1 (Januar 2008): p. 1-26.

Heilmann, S., Shih, L., & Hofem, A. (2013). National planning and local technology zones: Experimental governance in China's Torch Programme. The China Quarterly, 216, 896-919.

Hirschman, A. O., & Rothschild, M. (1973). The changing tolerance for income inequality in the course of economic development with a mathematical appendix. The Quarterly Journal of Economics, 87(4), 544-566.

Hokenson, R. F. (2004). Retiring the current model of retirement. Hokenson Research.

Hopper, T. (2015). A history of the baby bonus: Tories now tout benefits of program they once axed. National Post, July 13, 2015.

Howell, J. (2012). Civil society, corporatism and capitalism in China. Journal of Comparative Asian Development, 11(2), 271-297.

Huang, Y. (2003). One country, two systems: foreign-invested enterprises and domestic firms in China. China Economic Review, 14/4: 404-16.

Hurrell, A. (2009). Rising powers and the question of status in international society. In Annual Meeting of the International Studies Association (pp. 15-18).

Hurrell, A. (2014). Rising Powers and the Emerging Global, in Baylis, J., Smith, S., & Owens P. (eds.), The Globalization of World Politics: an introduction to international relations, 6th Edition. Oxford: Oxford University Press, 80-94.

Ikenberry, G. J., & Kupchan, C. (1990). Socialization and hegemonic power. International Organization 44:3.

Jacobson, H., & Oksenberg, M. (1990). China's participation in the IMF, the World Bank, and GATT: toward a global economic order. University of Michigan Press.

Jiabao, W. (2011). Report on work of the government. March 5, 2011.

Jianmin, W. (2015). Inside the dragon: chinese perspectives on the world. LSE IDEAS on 7 November.

Kamin, S., Turner, P., & Van 't dack (1998). The transmission mechanism of monetary policy in emerging market economies: an overview. Overview paper for BIS policy paper No. 3. Bank for International Settlements, Basle, Switzerland.

Khan, A., & Riskin, C. (2005). China's household income and its distribution, 1995 and 2002. China Quarterly, no. 182, 356-84.

Krugman, P. (2001). Analytical afterthoughts on the Asian crisis. Economic Theory, Dynamics and Markets: Essays in Honor of Ryuzo Sato, 5, 243.

Krugman, P. R. (1998). It's baaack: Japan's slump and the return of the liquidity trap. Brookings Papers on Economic Activity, 1998(2), 137-205.

Krugman, P. R., Obstfeld, M., & Melitz, M. (2015). International Economics, 10th. Edition, Prentice Hall.

Kuznets, S. (1955). Economic growth and income inequality. American Economic Review, 45(1), 1-28.

Lardy, N. R. (1998). China's unfinished economic revolution. Washington, D.C.: Brookings Institution Press.

Lardy, N. R. (2002). Integrating China into the global economy. Washington: Brookings

Institution.

Lardy, N. R. (2012). Sustaining China's economic growth after the global financial crisis. Peterson Institute.

Liew, L. H. (2004). Policy elites in the political economy of China's exchange rate policymaking. Journal of Contemporary China 13, February 2004.

Maddison, A. (2007). Chinese Economic Performance in the Long Run. Development Center of the OECD.

Mason, A. (2005). Demographic transitions and demographic dividends in developing and developed countries. United Nations Expert Group Meeting on Social and Economic Implications of Changing Population Age Structures, August 31 – September 2, 2005.

Mason, A., & Kinugasa, T. (2005). East Asian economic development: two demographic dividends. East-West Center Working Papers: Economics Series, No. 83, Honolulu.

McNally, C. A., & Gruin, J. (2017). A novel pathway to power? Contestation and adaptation in China's internationalization of the RMB. Review of International Political Economy, 1-30.

McNamara, K. (1999). The currency of ideas. Ithaca, NY: Cornell University Press.

McNamara, K. (2002). Rational fictions: Central bank independence and the social logic of delegation. West European politics, 25(1), 47-76.

Meyer, M. W. (2008). China's second economic transition: Building national markets. Management and Organization Review, 4(1), 3-15.

Milanovic, B. (2016). Global inequality: a new approach for the age of globalization. The Belknap Press of Harvard University Press.

Minkin, R., & Lau, K. (2013). The offshore renminbi. The rise of the Chinese currency and its global future. John Wiley & Sons Singapore.

Montinola, G., Qian, Y., & Weingast, B. R. (1995). Federalism, Chinese style: the political basis for economic success in China. World politics, 48(1), 50-81.

Mukand, S., & Rodrik, D. (2002). In search of the holy grail: policy convergence, experimentation, and economic performance (No. w9134). National Bureau of Economic Research.

National Intelligence Council (2012). Global trends 2030: alternative worlds. December 2012.

Naughton, B. (1995). Growing out of the plan: Chinese economic reform, 1978-1993. Cambridge University Press.

Naughton, B. (2007). The Chinese economy: Transitions and growth. MIT press.

North, D. C. (2006). Understanding the process of economic change. Academic Foundation.

Obstfeld, M. (2013). On keeping your powder dry: fiscal foundations of financial and price stability. Centre for Economic Policy Research.

OECD (2012). OECD employment outlook 2012. OECD Publishing.

Park, A., Wang, S., & Wu, G. (2002). Regional poverty targeting in China. Journal of Public Economics, vol. 86, issue 1 (October), pp. 123-53.

Pearson, C. S. (2015). On the cusp: from population boom to bust. Oxford University Press.

Peng, X. (2005). Is it time to change China's population policy? China: An International Journal, 2(1), March, 135-49.

Pesenti, P. A., & Tille, C. (2000). The economics of currency crises and contagion: An introduction.

Phillips, N. (2017). Power and inequality in the global political economy. International Affairs 93: 2, 2017.

Piketty, T. (2014). Capital in the twenty-first century. Cambridge, Massachusetts: The Belknap Press of Harvard University Press.

Piketty, T., & Saez, E. (2006). The evolution of top incomes: a historical and international perspective. American Economic Review, 96 (2): 200-205.

Prasad, E. S. (2017). Gaining currency. The rise of the renminbi. Oxford University Press.

Ravallion, M., & Chen, S. (2004). China's (uneven) progress against poverty. World Bank Policy Research Working Paper 3408, September.

Rawski, T. G. (1995). Implications of China'Reform Experience. The China Quarterly, 144, 1150-1173.

Retherford, R. D., Kim Choe, M, Chen, J., Xiru, L., & Hongyan, C. (2005). How far has fertility in China really declined? Population and Development Review 31(1), March 57-84.

Roland, G. (2000). Transition and economics: Politics, markets, and firms. MIT press.

Scharping, T. (2003). Birth Control in China, 1949-2000: Population Policy and Demographic Development.

Segal, P., & Sudhir, A. (2017). Who are the global top 1%?. Working Paper 8, LSE International Inequalities Institute.

Sharma, R. (2016). The Rise and Fall of Nations: Forces of Change in the Post-crisis World. WW Norton & Company.

Shirk, S. L. (1994). How China opened its door: the political success of the PRC's foreign trade and investment reforms. Brookings Institution Press.

Sims, C. A. (2013). Paper money. The American Economic Review, 103(2), 563-584.

Smith, A. (1776). The wealth of nations.

Spence, M. (2008). The growth report: Strategies for sustained growth and inclusive development. Commission on Growth and Development Final Report, Washington, DC.

Steinfeld, E. S. (1998). Forging reform in China: The fate of state-owned industry. Cambridge University Press.

Stiglitz, J. E. (2008). The Washington consensus reconsidered: towards a new global governance. Oxford University Press.

Stiglitz, J. E. (2012). The price of inequality: How today's divided society endangers our future. WW Norton & Company.

The Economist (2013). Monks without a temple. The Economist [Online] 16 March. http://www.economist.com/news/china/21573579-china-may-have-begun-long-end-game-its-one-child-policy-experts-say-it-cannot-end-soon [Accessed: October 2017].

The Economist (2017a). Local-government finances in China are a dangerous mess. The Economist [Online] 18 November. http://www.economist.com/news/leaders/21731389-best-fix-political-one-local-government-finances-china-are-dangerous-mess?frsc=dg%7Ce [Accessed: November 2017].

The Economist (2017b). What a debt crisis in the provinces says about governing China. The Economist [Online] 16 November. http://www.economist.com/news/china/21731406-xi-jinpings-enormous-power-still-has-limits-what-debt-crisis-provinces-says-about?frsc=dg%7Ce [Accessed: November 2017].

The World Bank (2007). The global family planning revolution. Three decades of population policies and programs. Washington D.C.

The World Bank Group (2016). Taking on inequality. Poverty and shared prosperity 2016. Washington D.C.

Todaro, M. P. (2000). Economic development. Seventh Edition. Pearson Education Limited.

Walter, C. E., & Howie, F. (2006). Privatizing China: inside China's stock markets. Singapore: Wiley & Sons.

Weil, D. N. (2008) Economic Growth. Third edition. Routledge.

Wohlforth, W. C., & Kang, D. C. (2009). Hypotheses on status competition. Toronto Meeting Paper.

Wohlforth, W. C., & Kang, D. C. (2009). Hypotheses on status competition. Toronto Meeting Paper.

Woo, W. T. (1999). The real reasons for China's growth. The China Journal, (41), 115-137.

Woodford, M. (2010). Optimal monetary stabilization policy. No. w16095, National Bureau of Economic Research.

Woods, N. (1995). Economic ideas and international relations: beyond rational neglect. International Studies Quarterly 39 (1995), p. 161-180.

World Bank (2005). SOE dividends: how much and to whom? Policy Note (October). Washington: World Bank.

World Bank (2007). Water supply pricing in China: economic efficiency, environment, and social affordability. Policy Note (December). Washington: World Bank.

World Bank (2008). Mid-term evaluation of China's 11th five-year plan, Washington.

World Bank (2009). Effective discipline with adequate autonomy: the direction for further reform of China's SOE dividend policy. Policy Note (November). Washington: World Bank.

Wright, L. H. (2009). The elusive price of stability: ideas and interests in the reform of China's exchange rate regime. Dissertation at The George Washington University.

Wu, J. (2005). Understanding and interpreting Chinese economic reform. Texere.

Xing, W. (2011). Income tax threshold in surprise increase. China Daily, July 1-3, 2011, 2.

Yang, D. L. (1997). Beyond Beijing: Liberalization and the regions in China. Routledge.

Young, S. (1995). Private business and economic reform in China. ME Sharpe.

Yueh, L. (2010). The economy of China. Cheltenham: Edward Elgar.

Yueh, L. (2013). China's growth: The making of an economic superpower. Oxford University Press.

Zweig, D. (2002). Internationalizing China: domestic interests and global linkages. Cornell University Press.

Institutions

Acemoglu, D. (2004). Understanding Institutions - Lionel Robbins Lecture at LSE. MIT Department of Economics [Online] February 2004 http://economics.mit.edu/files/1353 [Accessed: September 2017].

Acemoglu, D., & Robinson, J. A. (2002). Economic Backwardness in Political Perspective. National Bureau of Economic Research.

Acemoglu, D., Johnson, S., & Robinson, J. A. (2005). Institutions As a Fundamental Cause of Long-Run Growth. Handbook of Economic Growth, 1, 385-472.

Aizenman, J., & Sengupta, R. (2013). Financial Trilemma in China and a Comparative Analysis with India. Pacific Economic Review 18(2): 123-46.

Allen, F., Qian, J., & Qian, M. (2005). Law, Finance, and Economic Growth in China. Journal of Financial Economics, 77(1), 57-116.

Ariyoshi, M. A., Kirilenko, M. A., Ötker, M. I., Laurens, M. B., Kriljenko, M. J. I. C., & Habermeier, M. K. F. (2000). Capital Controls: Country Experiences With Their Use and Liberalization (No. 190). International Monetary Fund.

Bai, C, Li, D. D., Tao, Z., & Wang, Y. (2000). A Multitask Theory of State Enterprise Reform. Journal of Comparative Economics, 28/4: 716-38.

Banerjee, A. V., & Duflo, E. (2005). Growth Theory Through the Lens of Development Economics. Handbook of Economic Growth, 1, 473-552.

Barnett, M. N., & Finnemore, M. (1999). The politics, power, and pathologies of international organizations. International organization, 53(4), 699-732.

Barton, J. H., Goldstein, J. L., Josling, T. E., & Steinberg, R. H. (2006). The Evolution of the Trade Regime: Politics, Law, and Economics of the GATT and the WTO. Princeton University Press, pp. 10-11.

Baumol, W. J. (1996). Entrepreneurship: Productive, Unproductive, and Destructive. Journal of Business Venturing (11:1), 3-22.

Bayne, N. (2016). The New Economic Diplomacy: Decision-Making and Negotiation in International Economic Relations. Taylor and Francis, pp. 15-37.

Bayoumi, M. T., & Ohnsorge, F. (2013). Do Inflows or Outflows Dominate? Global Implications of Capital Account Liberalization in China (No. 13-189). International Monetary Fund.

Berglof, E., & Bolton, P. (2001). The Great Divide and Beyond: Financial Architecture in Transition. William Davidson Working Paper Number 414, December 2001.

Bhagwati, J. (1998). The Capital Myth: The Difference Between Trade in Widgets and Trade in Dollars. Foreign Affairs, 77, 7-12.

Biggeri, M. (2003). Key Factors of Recent Chinese Provincial Economic Growth. Journal of Chinese Economic and Business Studies, 1(2), 159-183.

Blagden, D., Gruin, J., & Xu, J. (2011). International Financial Institutions in an Age of Crisis. St Antony's International Review, 7(1), 3-10.

Blanchard, O. J., & Johnson, D. (2013). Macroeconomics. Sixth Edition. Pearson Education.

Böhmer, M., Funke, C., Sachs, A., Weinelt, H., & Weiss, J. (2016). Globalization Report 2016. Who Benefits Most from Globalization?. Bertelsmann Stiftung.

Bowles, P., & Wang, B. (2013). Renminbi Internationalization: A Journey to Where?. Development and Change 44(6): 1363-85.

Boyreau-Debray, G., & Wei, S. J. (2005). Pitfalls of a State-Dominated Financial System: The Case of China (No. w11214). National Bureau of Economic Research.

Brandt, L., & Zhu, X. (2000). Redistribution in a Decentralized Economy: Growth and Inflation in China Under Reform. Journal of Political Economy, 108(2), 422-439.

Buzan, B., & Lawson, G. (2014). Capitalism and the Emergent World Order. International Affairs, 90(1), 71-91.

Byrd, W. (1987). The Impact of the Two-Tier Plan/Market System in Chinese Industry. Journal of Comparative Economics, vol. 13, pp. 177-204.

Byrd, W. A. (1991). The Market Mechanism and Economic Reforms in China. ME Sharpe Incorporated.

Calvo, G. (1998). Capital Flows and Capital-Market Crises: The Simple Economics of Sudden Stops. Journal of Applied Economics, Vol. 1, No. 1, November 1998, pp. 35-54.

Calvo, G. (2005). Emerging Capital Markets in Turmoil: bad luck or bad policy?. MIT Press Books.

Calvo, G. (2011). On Capital Inflows, Liquidity and Bubbles. New York, United States: Columbia University.

Calvo, G. A., Izquierdo, A., & Mejia, L. F. (2004). On the Empirics of Sudden Stops: The Relevance of Balance-Sheet Effects (No. w10520). National Bureau of Economic Research.

Calvo, G., & Reinhart, C. (1999). Capital Flow Reversals, the Exchange Rate Debate, and Dollarization. Finance & Development, September 1999.

Calvo, G., & Reinhart, C. (2002). Fear of Floating. Quarterly Journal of Economics, no 117(2), pp 379-408.

Calvo, G., & Reinhart, C. M. (1999). When Capital Inflows Come to a Sudden Stop: Consequences and Policy Options.

Caprio Jr, G., & Levine, R. (1994). Reforming Finance in Transitional Socialist Economies. The World Bank Research Observer, 9(1), 1-24.

Caprio, G. (1997). Safe and Sound Banking in Developing Countries: We're Not in Kansas Anymore. Research in Financial Services: Private and Public Policy, 9, 79-97.

Chamon, M., & Prasad, E. (2010). Why Are Savings Rates of Urban Households in China Rising?. American Economic Journal: Macroeconomics, 21, 93-130.

Chang, E. C., & Wong, S. M. (2004). Political Control and Performance in China's Listed Firms.

Journal of Comparative Economics, 32(4), 617-636.

Chen, B., & Feng, Y. (2000). Determinants of Economic Growth in China: Private Enterprise, Education, and Openness. China Economic Review, 11(1), 1-15.

Chen, C., Chang, L., & Zhang, Y. M. (1995). The Role of Foreign Direct Investment in China Post-1978 Economic Development. World Development, 23/4: 691-703.

Chen, K., Jefferson, G., & Singh, I. (1992). Lessons from China's Economic Reform. Journal of Comparative Economics.

Chen, Z. (2003). Capital Markets and Legal Development: The China Case. China Economic Review, 14(4), 451-472.

Chinn, M. D., & Ito, H. (2008). A New Measure of Financial Openness. Journal of Comparative Policy Analysis, 10(3), 309-322.

Choo, C., & Yin, X. (2000). Contract Management Responsibility System and Profit Incentives in China's State-Owned Enterprises. China Economic Review, 11/1: 98-112.

Chwieroth, J. M. (2014a). Controlling Capital: The International Monetary Fund and Transformative Incremental Change From Within International Organisations. New Political Economy, 19(3), 445-469.

Chwieroth, J. M. (2014b). Managing Capital Inflows in East Asia: An Exercise in Productive Power. In Benjamin J. Cohen and Eric M.P. Chiu, eds, Power in a Changing World Economy: Lessons from East Asia. London: Routledge.

Claessens, S., & Laeven, L. (2003). Financial Development, Property Rights, and Growth. Journal of Finance 58 (6), 2401-2436.

Clarke, D. C. (2003a). Corporate Governance in China: An Overview. China Economic Review, 14(4): 494-507.

Clarke, D. C. (2003b). Economic Development and the Rights Hypothesis: The China Problem. Am. J. Comp. L., 51, 89.

Cliff, R. (1998). China's Potential for Developing Advanced Military Technology. July 8, Santa Monica: RAND Corporation.

Coase, R. H. (1937). The Nature of the Firm. Economica, 4(16), 386-405.

Cooper, R. N. (1998). Should Capital Account Convertibility Be a World Objective?. Essays in International Finance No. 207.

Cull, R., & Xu, L. C. (2005). Institutions, Ownership, and Finance: the Determinants of Profit Reinvestment Among Chinese Firms. Journal of Financial Economics, 77(1), 117-146.

Dahl, R. A. (1957). The Concept of Power. Systems Research and Behavioral science, 2(3), 201-215.

Demirgüç-Kunt, A., & Detragiache, E. (1998). Financial Liberalization and Financial Fragility. In Proceedings of Annual Bank Conference on Development Economics, Washington, DC, 20-21 April.

DeRosa, D. F. (2009). Central Banking and Monetary Policy In Emerging-Markets Nations.

Dinç, I. S. (2005). Politicians and Banks: Political Influences on Government-Owned Banks in Emerging Markets. Journal of Financial Economics, 77(2), 453-479.

Drezner, D. W. (2012). The Irony of Global Economic Governance. The System Worked. Council of Foreign Relations.

Drezner, D. W. (2015). Is There an Exceptional American Approach to Global Economic Governance?. In Ikenberry, G. J., Feng, Z., & Jisi, W. (Eds.). (2015). America, China, and the Struggle for World Order: Ideas, Traditions, Historical Legacies, and Global Visions. Springer.

Du, J., & Xu, C. (2009). Which Firms Went Public in China? A study of Financial Market Regulation. World Development, 37(4), 812-824.

Easterly, W., Islam, R., & Stiglitz, J. (1999). Shaken and Stirred: Volatility and Macroeconomic Paradigms for Rich and Poor Countries. Given as Michael Bruno Memorial Lecture, International Economics Association World Congress, Buenos Aires.

Edison, H., & Reinhart, C. M. (2001). Stopping Hot Money. Journal of Development Economics, 66(2), 533-553.

Edwards, S. (1999). How Effective Are Capital Controls? (No. w7413). National Bureau of Economic Research.

Eichengreen, B. (2011). Exorbitant Privilege: The Rise and Fall of the Dollar and the Future of the International Monetary System. New York: Oxford University Press.

Eichengreen, B., & Kawai, M. (2014). Issues for Renminbi Internationalization: An Overview. TADBI Working Paper Series 454, Tokyo: Asian Development Bank Institute.

Eichengreen, B., & Wyplosz, C. (1993). The Unstable EMS. Brookings Papers on Economic Activity, 51-143.

Evans, P. (1989). Predatory, Developmental and Other Apparatuses: A Comparative Political Economy Perspective on the Third World State. Sociological Forum, 4(4): 561-587.

Fan, G. (1994). Incremental Changes and Dual-Track Transition: Understanding the Case of China. Economic Policy, 100-122.

Fan, J. P., Morck, R., Xu, L. C., & Yeung, B. (2009). Institutions and Foreign Direct Investment: China Versus the Rest of the World. World Development, 37(4), 852-865.

Feenstra, R. C., & Taylor, A. M. (2014). International Economics. New York: Worth Macmillan.

Feigenbaum, E. (1999). Soldiers, Weapons and Chinese Development Strategy: the Mao Era Military in China´s Economic and Institutional Debate. China Quarterly, 158 (June), 285-313.

Feinstein, C., & Howe, C. (1997). Chinese Technology Transfer in the 1990s. Edward Elgar Publishing.

Felmingham, B. S., & Zhang, Q. (2002). The Role of FDI, Exports and Spillover Effects in the Regional Development of China. Journal of Development Studies, 38/4: 157-78.

Filardo, A. J., Yetman, J., Lee, S. I., Gudmundsson, M., Kenen, P. B., Munro, A., … & Gao, H. (2011). Currency Internationalisation: Lessons from the Global Financial Crisis and Prospects for the Future in Asia and the Pacific. BIS Papers No 61.

Fischer, W. A., & Von Zedtwitz, M. (2004). Chinese R&D: Naissance, Renaissance, or Mirage?. R&D Management, 34(4), 349-365.

Fisher-Vanden, K., & Jefferson, G. H. (2008). Technology Diversity and Development: Evidence from China's Industrial Enterprises. Journal of Comparative Economics, 36(4), 658-672.

Frankel, J. (2012). Internationalization of the RMB and Historical Precedents. Journal of Economic Integration, 27(3), 329-365.

Frankel, J., & Wei, S-J. (2007). Assessing China's Exchange Rate Regime. Economic Policy, vol 22, no 51, pp 575-672.

Franks, J. R., Mayer, C., & Rossi, S. (2009). Ownership: Evolution and Control. Review of Financial Studies, 22(10), 4009-56.

Fry, M. (1997). In Favour of Financial Liberalization. Economic Journal, Vol. 107, pp. 754-770.

Gagnon, J. E., & Troutman, K. (2014). Internationalization of the Renminbi: The Role of Trade Settlement.

Garber, P. M. (1998). Buttressing Capital Account Liberalization with Prudential Regulation and Foreign Entry. Essays in International Finance No. 207.

Garnaut, R., Song, L., Yao, Y., & Wang, X. (2014). Private enterprise in China. ANU Press.

Gelb, A., Jefferson, G., & Singh, I. (1993). The Chinese and East European Routes to Reform. Manuscript, NBER Eighth Annual Macroeconomics Conference.

Gerschenkron, A. (1962). Economic Backwardness in Historical Perspective. Praeger New York.

Ghani, A., & Lockhart, C. (2009). Fixing Failed States: A Framework for Rebuilding a Fractured World. Oxford University Press.

Gilboy, G. J. (2004). The Myth Behind China's Miracle. Foreign Affairs, 33-48.

Green, S. (2004). Enterprise Reform and Stock Market Development in Mainland China.

Deutsche Bank Research, China Special.

Green, S. (2004). The Development of China's Stock Market, 1984-2002. London and New York: Routledge.

Greif, A. (1993). Contract Enforceability and Economic Institutions in Early Trade: the Maghribi Traders' Coalition. American Economic Review, 83/3: 525-48.

Grossman, G. M., & Helpman, E. (1991). Innovation and Growth in the Global Economy. Cambridge, Massachusetts: MIT Press.

Groves, T., Hong, Y., McMillan, J., & Naughton, B. (1995). China's Evolving Managerial Labor Market. Journal of Political Economy, 103(4), 873-892.

Gruin, J. (2011). 'Freedom' Through Repression: Epistemic Closure in Agricultural Trade Negotiations. Review of International Studies 37(5): 2465-2490.

Gruin, J. (2013). Asset or Liability? The Role of the Financial System in the Political Economy of China's Rebalancing. Journal of Current Chinese Affairs, (42:4), 73-104.

Gruin, J. (2016). The Social Order of Chinese Capitalism: Socio-Economic Uncertainty, Communist Party Rule and Economic Development, 1990-2000. Economy & Society 45(1): 24-50.

Gruin, J. (2017). Financial Centers and RMB internationalization. Prospects for a post-American Monetary order?. in James Parisot and Santino Regilme (eds.) American Hegemony and the Rise of Emerging Powers: Cooperation or Conflict. Abingdon, UK: Routledge.

Gylfason, T. (1999). Exports, Inflation and Growth. World Development, 27/6: 1031-57.

Haggard, S., & Simmons, B. A. (1987). Theories of international regimes. International organization, 41(3), 491-517.

Hall, P. A. (1983). Policy innovation and the structure of the State: The politics-administration nexus in France and Britain. The Annals of the American Academy of Political and Social Science, 466(1), 43-59.

Hall, R., & Jones, C. I. (1999). Why Do Some Countries Produce So Much More Output Per Worker Than Others? Quarterly Journal of Economics 114, 83-116.

Hart, H. L. (1961). The Concept of Law. Chap. II, 9-11.

Hay, D., Morris, D., Liu, G., & Yao, S. (1994). Economic Reform and State-Owned Enterprises in China 1979-1987. Oxford University Press.

He, D., & McCauley, R. (2010). Offshore Markets for the Domestic Markets: Monetary and Financial Stability Issues. BIS Working Paper, no 320.

He, D., Cheung, L., Zhang, W., & Wu, T. (2012). How Would Capital Account Liberalization

Affect China's Capital Flows and the Renminbi Real Exchange Rates?. China & World Economy, 20(6), 29-54.

Hellmann, T., Murdock, K., & Stiglitz, J. (1997). Financial Restraint: Toward a New Paradigm. The Role of Government in East Asian Economic Development: Comparative Institutional Analysis, 163-207.

Hellmann, T., Murdock, K., & Stiglitz, J. (2000). Liberalisation, Moral Hazard, in Banking and Prudential Regulation: Are Capital Controls Enough?. American Economic Review, Vol. 90, pp. 147-165.

Himmelberg, C. P., Hubbard, R. G., & Palia, D. (1999). Understanding the Determinants of Managerial Ownership and the Link Between Ownership and Performance. Journal of Financial Economics, 53: 353-84.

Ho, P. (2006). Institutions in Transition: Land Ownership, Property Rights and Social Conflict in China. Oxford University Press.

Hoff, K., & Stiglitz, J. E. (2004). After the Big Bang? Obstacles to the Emergence of the Rule of Law in Post-Communist Societies. The American Economic Review, 94(3), 753-763.

Holz, C. A. (2003). China's Industrial State-Owned Enterprises: Between Profitability and Bankruptcy. Singapore: World Scientific.

Hooley, J. (2013). Bringing Down the Great Wall? Global Implications of Capital Account Liberalisation in China.

Hu, A. G., & Jefferson, G. H. (2009). A Great Wall of Patents: What Is Behind China´s Recent Patent Explosion. Journal of Development Economics, 90/1: 57-68.

Hu, A. G., Jefferson, G. H., & Jinchang, Q. (2005). R&D and Technology Transfer: Firm-Level Evidence from Chinese Industry. The Review of Economics and Statistics, 87(4), 780-786.

Huang, Y, & Wang, X. (2011). Does Financial Repression Inhibit or Facilitate Economic Growth? A Case Study of Chinese Reform Experience. Oxford Bulletin of Economics and Statistics, 736, 833-855.

Huang, Y. (2003). One Country, Two Systems: Foreign-Invested Enterprises and Domestic Firms in China. China Economic Review, 14/4: 404-16.

Huwart, J.-Y., & Verdier, L. (2013). A Global or Semi-global Village? Globalisation: Origins and Consequences. OECD Publishing Paris.

International Monetary Fund (1997). World Economic Outlook. IMF May 1997. Washington DC.

International Monetary Fund (2006). World Bank Plenary Remarks. September 19, 2006. http://www.ustreas.gov/press/releases/hp116.htm.

International Monetary Fund (2007). World Economic Outlook. IMF October 2007. Washington DC.

International Monetary Fund (2012). The Liberalization and Management of Capital Flows: An Institutional View. Washington DC.

International Monetary Fund (2015). Statement by the Honorable Zhou Xiaochuan Governor of the IMF for China to the Thirty-First Meeting of the International Monetary and Financial Committee. [Online] 18 April http://www.imf.org/external/spring/2015/imfc/statement/eng/chn.pdf [Accessed: 31 October 2017].

Ito, H. (2006). Financial Development and Financial Liberalization in Asia: Thresholds, Institutions and the Sequences of Liberalization. The North American Journal of Economics and Finance, Vol. 17, pp. 303-327.

Jefferson, G. H., & Rawski, T. G. (2002). China's Emerging Market for Property Rights: Theoretical and Empirical Perspectives. Economics of Transition, 10(3), 585-617.

Jensen, N., Biglaiser, G., & Li, Q. (2012). Politics and Foreign Direct Investment. University of Michigan Press.

Johansson, A., & Wang, X. (2012). Financial Repression and External Imbalances. Working Paper No. 2012-20, Beijing: China Economic Research Center.

Jones, E., & Underhill, G. R. (2014). Theory of Optimum Financial Areas: Retooling the Debate on the Governance of Global Finance.

Kahler, M. (2013). Rising Powers and Global Governance: Negotiating Change in a Resilient Status Quo. International Affairs 89: 3, 711-729.

Kaminsky, G. L., Reinhart, C. M., & Végh, C. A. (2004). When It Rains, It Pours: Procyclical Capital Flows and Policies in Mark Gertler and Kenneth S. Rogoff, eds. NBER Macroeconomics Annual 2004. Cambridge, Mass: MIT Press, 11-53.

Kaufmann, D., Kraay, A., & Mastruzzi, M. (2006). Governance Matters V: Governance Indicators for 1996-2005.

Kaufmann, D., Kraay, A., & Zoido-Lobaton, P. (1999). Governance Matters. World Bank Working Paper No. 2196, October.

Kenen, P. B. (2011). Currency Internationalization: An Overview. BIS Papers, 61, 9-18.

Keynes, J. M. (1935). The General Theory of Employment, Interest and Money. University of Adelaide Library Etext Version.

Keynes, J.M. (1937). Some Economic Consequences of a Declining Population. The Eugenics Review, (29:1).

Kindleberger, C. P. (1986). The World in Depression, 1929-1939: Revised and Enlarged Edition (Vol. 4). University of California Press.

Koo, A. Y. (1990). The contract responsibility system: Transition from a planned to a market economy. Economic Development and Cultural Change, 38(4), 797-820.

Kornai, J. (1979). Resource-Constrained Versus Demand-Constrained Systems. Econometrica, 47: 801-19.

Kornai, J. (1980). Economics of Shortage. Amsterdam: North-Holland.

Kornai, J. (1992). The Socialist System. Oxford: Clarendon Press.

Kornai, J. (1994). Transformational Recession: the Main Causes. Journal of Comparative Economics 19, 39-63.

Kornai, J. (2000). Ten Years After 'The Road to a Free Economy': the Author's Self-Evaluation. In Annual Bank Conference on Development Economics 2000 (pp. 49-66).

Krugman, P. (1998). Saving Asia: It's Time to Get Radical. Fortune, September 7, p. 74-80.

Krugman, P. R., Obstfeld, M., & Melitz, M. (2015). International Economics, 10th. Edition, Prentice Hall.

Kuo, C. C., & Yang, C. H. (2008). Knowledge Capital and Spillover on Regional Economic Growth: Evidence from China. China Economic Review, 19/4: 594-604.

La Porta, R. L., Lopez-de-Silanes, F., Shleifer, A., & Vishny, R. W. (1998). Law and Finance. Journal of Political Economy, 106(6), 1113-1155.

La Porta, R., Lopez-de-Silanes, F., Shleifer, A., & Vishny, R. (1997). Legal Determinants of External Finance. Journal of Finance, 54/20: 1113-50.

La Porta, R., Lopez-de-Silanes, F., Shleifer, A., & Vishny, R. (2000). Investor Protection and Corporate Governance. Journal of Financial Economics, 58(1), 3-27.

Laban, R., & Larrain, F. (1994). Can a Liberalization of Capital Outflows Increase Net Capital Inflows?. Santiago de Chile, Pontificia Universidad Catolica de Chile.

Laffont, J. J., & Martimort, D. (1999). Separation of Regulators Against Collusive Behavior. The Rand Journal of Economics, 232-262.

Lai, M., Peng, S., & Bao, Q. (2006). Technology Spillovers, Absorptive Capacity and Economic Growth. China Economic Review, 17/3: 300-20.

Lardy, N. (2008). Financial Repression in China. Peterson Institute Working Paper.

Lardy, N. R. (2012). Sustaining China's Economic Growth After the Global Financial Crisis. Peterson Institute.

Lardy, N., & Douglass, P. (2011). Capital Account Liberalization and the Role of the Renminbi. Peterson Institute for International Economics.

Lau, L. J., Qian, Y., & Roland, G. (2001). Reform Without Losers: An Interpretation of China's Dual-Track Approach to Transition. Journal of Political Economy, 108/1: 120-43.

Levine, R. (1997). Financial Development and Economic Growth: Views and Agenda. Journal of Economic Literature, XXXV(June), 688-726.

Li, D. (2001) Beating the Trap of Financial Repression in China. Cato Journal, 211, 77-90.

Lin, C. (2001). Corporatisation and Corporate Governance in China's Economic Transition. Economics of Planning, 34: 5-35.
Lin, J. Y. (2012). Demystifying the Chinese economy. Cambridge University Press.

Lin, J. Y., Cai, F., & Zhou, L. (2003). The China Miracle: Development Strategy and Economic Reform. Hong Kong: Chinese University Press.

Lin, J., Cai, F., & Li, Z. (1996). The China Miracle. Hong Kong: The Chinese University Press.

Lin, Y. M., & Zhu, T. (2001). Ownership Restructuring in Chinese State Industry: An Analysis of Evidence on Initial Organizational Changes. The China Quarterly, 166, 305-341.

Lindblom, C. E. (1959). The science of" muddling through". Public administration review, 79-88.

Linz, J. J. (1990). The Perils of Presidentialism. Journal of Democracy, 1(1), 51-69.

Liu, X., & White, S. (2001). Comparing Innovation Systems: A Framework and Application to China's Transitional Context. Research policy, 30(7), 1091-1114.

Lu, S. F., & Yao, Y. (2009). The Effectiveness of Law, Financial Development, and Economic Growth In An Economy of Financial Repression: Evidence From China. World Development, 37(4), 763-777.

Lucas, R. (1990). Why Doesn't Capital Flow From Rich to Poor Countries?. American Economic Review Papers and Procedings, 80(2), May 1990, 92-96.

Ma, G., & Yi, W. (2010). China's High Savings rate: Myth and Reality. BIS Working Paper No. 312, Basel: Bank for International Settlement.

Ma, G., & Zhou, H. (2009). China's Evolving External Wealth and Rising Creditor Position. BIS Working Paper.

Magud, N. E., Reinhart, C. M., & Rogoff, K. S. (2011). Capital Controls: Myth and Reality-a Portfolio Balance Approach (No. w16805). National Bureau of Economic Research.

Magud, N. E., Reinhart, C. M., & Vesperoni, E. R. (2014). Capital Inflows, Exchange Rate Flexibility and Credit Booms. Review of Development Economics, 18(3), 415-430.

Mainwaring, S., & Pérez-Liñán, A. (2013). Democratic Breakdown and Survival. Journal of Democracy, 24(2), 123-137.

Mainwaring, S., & Shugart, M. S. (1997). Juan Linz, Presidentialism, and Democracy: A Critical Appraisal. Comparative Politics, 449-471.

McKinnon, R, & Schnabl, G. (2004). The Return to Soft Dollar Pegging in East Asia Mitigating Conflicted Virtue. International Finance, vol 7, no 2, pp 169-201.

McKinnon, R. (1973). Money and Capital in Economic Development. Washington, DC: Brookings Institution.

McKinnon, R. (1993). The Order of Economic Liberalization: Financial Control in the Transition to a Market Economy. Baltimore: Johns Hopkins University Press.

McMillan, J., & Naughton, B. (1992). How to Reform a Planned Economy: Lessons from China. Oxford Review of Economic Policy, 8(1), 130-143.

McMillan, J., & Woodruff, C. (2002). The central role of entrepreneurs in transitional economies. Journal of Economic Perspectives 16 (3), 153-170.

McNally, C. A. (2012). Sino-Capitalism: China's Reemergence and the International Political Economy. World Politics 64(4): 741-76.

McNally, C. A. (2015). The Political Economic Logic of RMB Internationalization: A Study in Sino-Capitalism. International Politics 52(6): 704-23.

McNally, C. A., & Gruin, J. (2017). A Novel Pathway to Power? Contestation and Adaptation in China's Internationalization of the RMB. Review of International Political Economy, 1-30.

Megginson, W. L., & Netter, J. M. (2001). From State to Market: A Survey of Empirical Studies on Privatization. Journal of Economic Literature, 39(2), 321-389.

Minikin, R., & Lau, K. (2012). The Offshore Renminbi: The Rise of the Chinese Currency and Its Global Future. John Wiley & Sons.

Mitchell, J. (1998). The Problem of Bad Debts: Clearing Banks' Balance Sheets in Economies in Transition. CEPR Discussion Papers, No. 1977, London: CEPR.

Murphy, K. M., Shleifer, A., & Vishny, R. W. (1992). The Transition to a Market Economy: Pitfalls of Partial Reform. The Quarterly Journal of Economics, 107(3), 889-906.

National Intelligence Council (2012). Global Trends 2030: Alternative Worlds. December 2012.

Naughton, B. (1996). Growing Out of the Plan: Chinese Economic Reform, 1978-1993. Cambridge University Press.

Naughton, B. (2007). The Chinese Economy: Transitions and Growth. MIT press.

Ngai, R. (2015). Growth and Development Accounting. Lecture at The London School of Economics and Political Science on 22 October 2015.

Nolan, P. (2002). China and the Global Business Revolution. Cambridge Journal of Economics, 26(1): 119-37.

North, D. C. (1990). Institutions, Institutional Change and Economic Performance. Cambridge University Press.

North, D. C. (1991). Institutions. The Journal of Economic Perspectives, 5(1), 97-112.
OECD (2002). Foreign Direct Investment for Development. Paris.

Oi, J. C. (1999). Rural China Takes Off: Institutional Foundations of Economic Reform. University of California Press.

Olson, M. (1971). The Logic of Collective Action: Public Goods and the Theory of Groups. Cambridge, Mass.: Harvard University Press.

Olson, M. (1982). The Rise and Decline of Nations. Yale University Press.

Olson, M. (1996). Distinguished Lecture on Economics in Government: Big Bills Left on the Sidewalk: Why Some Nations are Rich, and Others Poor. The Journal of Economic Perspectives, 3-24.

Otero-Iglesias, M., & Vermeiren, M. (2015). China's State-Permeated Market Economy and Its Constraints to the Internationalization of the RMB. International Politics 52(6): 684-703.

Paris, R. (2004). At War's End: Building Peace After Civil Conflict. Cambridge University Press.

Park, Y. C. (2006). Economic Liberalization and Integration in East Asia. A Post-Crisis Paradigm. Oxford University Press.

Persson, T., & Tabellini, G. (2006). Democracy and Development: The Devil in the Details (No. w11993). National Bureau of Economic Research.

Pickford, S., & Subacchi, P. (2015). International Economic Governance: Last Chance for the G20? Chatham House.

Popov, V. (2000). Shock Therapy Versus Gradualism: The End of the Debate (Explaining the Magnitude of Transformational Recession).

Prasad, E. S. (2017). Gaining Currency: The Rise of the Renminbi. Oxford University Press.

Prasad, E. S., Rogoff, K., Wei, S., & Kose, M. A. (2003). Effects of Global Financial Globalization in Developing Countries: Some Empirical Evidence. Washington, DC: International Monetary Fund.

Prasad, M. E., & Rajan, R. (2006). Modernizing China's Growth Paradigm. International Monetary Fund.

Qian, Y., & Xu, C. (1993). The M-Form Hierarchy and China's Economic Reform. European Economic Review, 37(2-3), 541-548.

Qian, Y., Lau, L., & Roland, G. (2000). Reform Without Losers: An Interpretation of China's Dual Track Approach to Transition. Journal of Political Economy, 2000.

Rajan, R., & Zingales, L. (1998). Financial Dependence and Growth. American Economic Review 88 (3), 559-586.

Reinhart, C. (2012). Capital Inflows, Credit Booms and Their Risks. MPRA Paper 50981, in China Finance 40 Forum Report, March 2012.

Reinhart, C. M., & Reinhart, V. (1998). Some Lessons for Policy Makers Who Deal with the Mixed Blessing of Capital Inflows. Capital Flows and Financial Crises, 93-127.

Reinhart, C. M., & Reinhart, V. R. (2008). Capital Flow Bonanzas: An Encompassing View of the Past and Present (No. w14321). National Bureau of Economic Research.

Reinhart, C. M., & Reinhart, V. R. (2015). Financial Crises, Development, and Growth: A Long-Term Perspective. The World Bank Economic Review, 29, 53-S76.

Rey, H. (2015). Dilemma not trilemma: the global financial cycle and monetary policy independence. NBER Working Paper No. 21162. Cambridge, MA: National Bureau of Economic Research.

Riskin, C. (1987). China's Political Economy: The Quest for Development Since 1949. Oxford: Oxford University Press.

Rodrik, D. (1996). Coordination failures and government policy: A model with applications to East Asia and Eastern Europe. Journal of International Economics, 40(1), 1-22.

Rodrik, D. (1999). The New Global Economy and Developing Countries: Making Openness Work. Overseas Development Council (Baltimore, Maryland) Policy Essay No. 24.

Rodrik, D. (2000). Institutions for High-Quality Growth: What They Are and How to Acquire Them. Studies in Comparative International Development, Vol. 35, No. 3, Fall.

Rodrik, D. (2011), The Future of Economic Convergence. Harvard University, Faculty Research Working Paper Series no. RWP 11-033, Aug. 2011.

Rodrik, D., Subramanian, A., & Trebbi, F. (2004). Institutions Rule: the Primacy of Institutions Over Geography and Integration in Economic Development. Journal of Economic Growth, 9(2), 131-165.

Roland, G. (2000). Transition and Economics: Politics, Markets, and Firms. MIT Press.

Roland, G. (2002). Ten Years After … Transition and Economics. IMF Staff Papers vol. 48, Special Issue, 2002, pp. 29-52.

Roland, G. (2005). Understanding Institutional Change: Fast-Moving and Slow-Moving Institutions.

Roland, G., & Verdier, T. (1997). Transition and the Output Fall. William Davidson Working Paper Number 37, March 1997.

Rosen, D. H. (2003). Low-tech bed, high-tech dreams. China Economic Quarterly Q, 4, 20-40.

Roubini, N., & Sala-I-Martin, X. (1992). Financial Repression and Economic Growth. Journal of Development Economics, 39, 5-30.

Sedik, T. S., & Sun, T. (2012). Effects of Capital Flow Liberalization: What is the Evidence from Recent Experiences of Emerging Market Economies? (No. 12-275). International Monetary Fund.

Sharma, P. (2015). How Does Capital Market Opening Affect Investment Choices? Evidence from China's Qualified Foreign Institutional Investor Scheme. Cornell University.

Sharma, R. (2016). The Rise and Fall of Nations: Forces of Change in the Post-crisis World. WW Norton & Company.

Shaw, E. (1973). Financial Deepening in Economic Development. New York: Oxford University Press.

Shen, X. (1999). The Chinese Road to High Technology: Telecommunications Switching Technology in the Economic Transition. Springer.

Shen, Y., Shen, M., Xu, Z., and Bai, Y. (2009). Bank Size and Small and Medium-Sized Enterprise (SME) Lending: Evidence from China. World Development (Special Issue on Law, Finance, and Economic Growth in China), 37/4: 800-11.

Shepsle, K. A., & Weingast, B. R. (1987). The institutional foundations of committee power. American Political Science Review, 81(1), 85-104.

Shu, C., Chow, N., & Chan, J-Y. (2007). Impact of the renminbi exchange rate on Asian currencies. China Economic Issues, no 3/07, Hong Kong Monetary Authority, January.

Shu, C., He, D., & Cheng, X. (2014). One Currency, Two Markets: the Renminbi's Growing Influence in Asia-Pacific. China Economic Review, 33, 163-178.

Solow, R. (1957). Technical Change and the Aggregate Production Function.

Spiegel (2010). Norway takes aim at G20: One of the Greatest Setback Since World War II. Interview with Jonas Gahr Støre, in Der Spiegel, 22 June 2010.

Stiglitz, J. (1994). The Role of the State in Financial Markets. In Bruno M. and Pleskovic B. (eds.), Proceeding of the World Bank Annual Conference on Development Economics, 1993: Supplement to the World Bank Economic Review and the World Bank Research Observer, Washington DC: World Bank, pp. 19-61.

Stiglitz, J. (2000). Capital Market Liberalization, Economic Growth, and Instability. World Development, 28, 1075-1086.

Stokes, S. (2009). Political Clientelism. In the Oxford Handbook of Comparative Politics.

Sun, Q., & Tong, W. H. (2003). China Share Issue Privatization: the Extent of Its Success. Journal of Financial Economics, 70/2: 183-222.

Svejnar, J. (2007). China in Light of the Performance of Central and East European Economies. IZA DP No. 2791.

The World Bank (2005). A Better Investment Climate for Everyone. World Development Report 2005. Oxford University Press and the World Bank.

The World Bank Group (2017). Governance and the law. World Development Report.

Thelen, K. (1999). Historical institutionalism in comparative politics. Annual review of political science, 2(1), 369-404.

Tirole, J. (1994). The Internal Organization of Government. Oxford Economic Papers, 1-29.

Tobin, J. (1978). A Proposal for International Monetary Reform. Eastern Economic Journal, 4(3/4), 153-159.

Tsebelis, G. (1995). Decision making in political systems: Veto players in presidentialism, parliamentarism, multicameralism and multipartyism. British journal of political science, 25(3), 289-325.

Underhill, G. R. (2003). States, Markets and Governance for Emerging Market Economies: Private Interests, the Public Good and the Legitimacy of the Development Process. International Affairs, 79(4), 755-781.

Underhill, G. R. (2016). Markets, Institutions, and Transaction Costs: the Endogeneity of Governance.

Vestergaard, J., & Wade, R. H. (2012). Establishing a New Global Economic Council: Governance Reform at the G20, the IMF and the World Bank. Global Policy Volume 3, Issue 3, September 2012.

Vestergaard, J., & Wade, R. H. (2013). Protecting Power: How Western States Retain the Dominant Voice in the World Bank's Governance. World Development Vol. 46, pp. 153-164.

Wade, R. H. (2013). The United States and the World. The Art of Power Maintenance. How Western States Keep the Lead in Global Organizations. Challenge, vol. 56, no. 1, January/ February 2013, pp. 5-39.

Walter, C. E., & Howie, F. (2011). Red Capitalism: The Fragile Financial Foundation of China's Extraordinary Rise. Singapore: Wiley & Sons.

Wei, L. (2015). IMF move would pressure China on management of yuan. The Wall Street Journal.

Wei, S. J. (1993). The Open Door Policy and China´s Rapid Growth: Evidence from City-Level Data. NBER Working Paper, 4602.

Weil, D. N. (2008). Economic Growth. 3rd edition. Routledge.

Williamson, O. (1975). Markets and Hierarchies. Free Press, New York.

Williamson, O. (1985). The Economic Institutions of Capitalism. Free Press, New York.
Wolf, M. (2004). Sweep Away the Barriers to Growth. The Financial Times.

Woo, W. T. (1995). Comments on Wei´s (1995) Foreign Direct Investment in China: Sources and Consequences. In A. Krueger (ed.), Financial Deregulation and Integration in East Asia. University of Chicago Press, 166-89.

Woods, N. (2003). The United States and the international financial institutions: Power and influence within the World Bank and the IMF. Foot, McFarlane and Mastanduno (Eds.), US Hegemony and International Organizations, Oxford, 92-114. World Bank (2005). A better investment climate for everyone. World Development Report 2005.

World Bank (1997). China 2020. Washington, DC: World Bank.

World Bank and Development Research Center of the State Council (2012). China 2030: Building a Modern, Harmonious and Creative High-Income Society. Washington, DC: World Bank.

Wright, J. (2008). Do Authoritarian Institutions Constrain? How Legislatures Affect Economic Growth and Investment. American Journal of Political Science, 52(2), 322-343.

Wright, L. (2009). The Elusive Price of Stability: Ideas and Interests in the Reform of China's Exchange Rate Regime. Doctoral Dissertation, George Washington University.

Wu, J. (2005). Understanding and Interpreting Chinese Economic Reform. Texere.

Xielin, L. (2005). China's Development Model: An Alternative Strategy for Technological Catch-Up. Research Institute of Economy, Trade and Industry.

Yao, Y., & Yueh, L. (2009). Law, Finance, and Economic Growth in China: An Introduction. World Development, 37(4), 753-762.

Yueh, L. (2004). Wage Reforms in China During the 1990s. Asian Economic Journal, 18(2), 149-164.

Yueh, L. (2013). China's Growth: The Making of an Economic Superpower. Oxford University Press.

Yusuf, S., Nabeshima, K., & Perkins, D. H. (2006). Under New Ownership: Privatizing China's State-Owned Enterprises. World Bank Publications.

Zhang, W. (1993). Decision Rights, Residual Claim and Performance: a Theory of How Chinese

Economy Works. Nuffield College, Oxford.

Zheng, J., Bigstein, A., & Hu, A. (2009). Can China's Growth Be Sustained? A productivity perspective. World Development (Special issue on law, finance, and economic growth in China), 37/4: 874-88.

Zheng, J., Hu, A. (2006). An Empirical Analysis of Provincial Productivity in China 1979-2001. Journal of Chinese Economic and Business Studies, 4/3: 221-39.
Zheng, J., Liu, X, & Bigsten, A. (2003). Efficiency, Technical Progress, and Best Practice in Chinese State Enterprises 1980-1994. Journal of Comparative Economics, 31/1: 134-52.

Zoellick, R. (2010). The end of the third world? Address to Woodrow Wilson Center for International Scholars, Washington. DC, 14 April.

Zweig, D. (2005). Competing for Talent: China's Strategies to Reverse the Brain Drain. International Labour Review, 145, 65-90.

FX Crises and Early Warning Systems

Acemoglu, D. (2004). Understanding Institutions - Lionel Robbins Lecture at LSE. MIT Department of Economics [Online] February 2004 http://economics.mit.edu/files/1353 [Accessed: September 2017].

Acemoglu, D., & Robinson, J. A. (2013). Why nations fail: The origins of power, prosperity, and poverty. Crown Business.

Ades, A., Masij, R., & Tenengauzer, D. (1998). GS-Watch: a new framework for predicting financial crisis in emerging markets. Goldman Sachs, December 1998.

Berg, A., & Pattillo, C. (1999a). Are currency crises predictable? A test. IMF Staff papers, 46(2), 107-138.

Berg, A., & Pattillo, C. (1999b). Predicting currency crises: The indicators approach and an alternative. Journal of international Money and Finance, 18(4), 561-586.

Berg, M. A., Borensztein, M. E., & Pattillo, M. C. A. (2004). Assessing early warning systems: how have they worked in practice? (No. 4-52). International Monetary Fund.

Blanco, H., & Garber, P. M. (1986). Recurrent devaluation and speculative attacks on the Mexican peso. Journal of political economy, 94(1), 148-166.

Bussiere, M., & Fratzscher, M. (2006). Towards a new early warning system of financial crises. journal of International Money and Finance, 25(6), 953-973.

Calvo, G. A. (1995). Varieties of capital-market crises. Working Paper 15. Center for International Economics, University of Maryland.

Corsetti, G., Pesenti, P., & Roubini, N. (1999). Paper tigers?: A model of the Asian crisis. European Economic Review, 43(7), 1211-1236.

Demirgüç-Kunt, A., & Detragiache, E. (1997). The determinants of banking crises-evidence from developing and developed countries (Vol. 106). World Bank Publications.

Dooley, M. P. (2000). A model of crises in emerging markets. The economic journal, 110(460), 256-272.

Eichengreen, B., & Rose, A. K. (2003). Does it pay to defend against a speculative attack?. In Managing currency crises in emerging markets (pp. 61-86). University of Chicago Press.

Eichengreen, B., Rose, A. K., & Wyplosz, C. (1995). Exchange market mayhem: the antecedents and aftermath of speculative attacks. Economic Policy, 10(21), 249-312.

Flood, R. P., & Garber, P. M. (1984). Collapsing exchange-rate regimes: some linear examples. Journal of international Economics, 17(1-2), 1-13.

Frankel, J. A., & Rose, A. K. (1996). Currency crashes in emerging markets: An empirical treatment. Journal of international Economics, 41(3-4), 351-366.

Frieden, J. A. (1991). Invested interests: the politics of national economic policies in a world of global finance. International Organization, 45(4), 425-451.

Kamin, S. B., Schindler, J. W., & Samuel, S. L. (2001). The contribution of domestic and external factors to emerging market devaluation crises: An early warning systems approach.

Kaminsky, G. L., & Reinhart, C. M. (1999). The twin crises: the causes of banking and balance-of-payments problems. American economic review, 89(3), 473-500.

Kaminsky, G., Lizondo, S., & Reinhart, C. M. (1998). Leading indicators of currency crises. Staff Papers, 45(1), 1-48.

Krugman, P. (1979). A model of balance-of-payments crises. Journal of Money, Credit and Banking, 11(3), 311-325.

Kumar, M. M. S., Perraudin, M. W., & Moorthy, M. U. (2002). Predicting Emerging Market Currency Crashes (No. 2-7). International Monetary Fund.

Leblang, D. (2003). To devalue or to defend? The political economy of exchange rate policy. International Studies Quarterly, 47(4), 533-559.

Leblang, D. A. (2002). The political economy of speculative attacks in the developing world. International Studies Quarterly, 46(1), 69-91.

Leblang, D., & Satyanath, S. (2006). Institutions, expectations, and currency crises. International Organization, 60(1), 245-262.

Obstfeld, M. (1996). Models of currency crises with self-fulfilling features. European Economic Review, 40(3-5), 1037-1047.

Roy, A., & Tudela, M. M. (2001). Emerging Market Risk Indicator (EMRI): re-estimated version

September 2000. Credit Suisse, February 2001.

Schnatz, B. (1998). Macroeconomic Determinants of currency turbulences in emerging markets (No. 1998, 03e). Discussion paper, Economic Research Group of the Deutsche Bundesbank.

Van den Berg, J. J. F. (2011). Currency crises and their early warning systems. Doctoral dissertation, Maastricht university.

Crises in Perspective

Acemoglu, D., & Robinson, J. A. (2013). Why nations fail: The origins of power, prosperity, and poverty. Crown Business.

Ackerman, R. A., Fries, G., & Windle, R. A. (2012). Changes in US family finances from 2007 to 2010: Evidence from the Survey of Consumer Finances. Federal Reserve Bulletin, 100, 1-80.

Ades, A., Masih, R., & Tenengauzer, D. (1998). GS Watch: A New Framework for Predicting Financial Crises in Emerging Markets. New York: Goldman Sachs.

Aghion, P., & Blanchard, O. J. (1994). On the speed of transition in Central Europe. NBER macroeconomics annual, 9, 283-320.

Aghion, P., Bacchetta, P., & Banerjee, A. (2001). Currency crises and monetary policy in an economy with credit constraints. European economic review, 45(7), 1121-1150.

Akerlof, G. A., Romer, P. M., Hall, R. E., & Mankiw, N. G. (1993). Looting: The economic underworld of bankruptcy for profit. Brookings papers on economic activity, 1993(2), 1-73.

Alba, P., Bhattacharya, A., Claessens, S., Ghosh, S., & Hernandez, L. (1998). Volatility and contagion in a financially integrated world: lessons from East Asia's recent experience (No. 2008). World Bank, Poverty Reduction and Economic Management Network, Economic Policy Unit.

Alejandro, C. F. D. (1983). Stories of the 1930s for the 1980s. In Financial policies and the world capital market: The problem of Latin American countries (pp. 5-40). University of Chicago Press.

Almansour, A., Aslam, A., Bluedorn, J., & Duttagupta, R. (2014). On the receiving end? External conditions and emerging market growth before, during and after the global financial crisis. IMF, World Economic Outlook, 113-151.

Angkinand, A., Li, J., & Willett, T. (2006). Measures of currency crises: A survey. Forthcomming in: International Interaction.

Åslund, A. (1991). Principles of privatization. Systemic change and stabilization in Eastern Europe, 17-31.

Balassa, B., & McCarthy, F. (1984). Adjustment policies in developing countries, 1979-83: An update. The World Bank.

Beachy, B. (2012). A Financial Crisis Manual Causes, Consequences, and Lessons of the Financial Crisis (No. 12-06). GDAE, Tufts University.

Bellas, D., Papaioannou, M. G., & Petrova, I. (2010). Determinants of emerging market sovereign bond spreads. Sovereign debt and the financial crisis. IMF, Washington, DC, 77-101.

Berg, A., & Pattillo, C. (1999). Are currency crises predictable? A test. IMF Staff papers, 46(2), 107-138.

Berg, A., & Sachs, J. (1992). Structural adjustment and international trade in Eastern Europe: The case of Poland. Economic Policy, 7(14), 117-173.

Berg, C. (2011, May). The Global Financial Crisis and the Great Recession: Causes, Effects, Measures and Consequences for Economic Analysis and Policy. In Presented at a Workshop on Monetary Policy.

Berglof, E., & Bolton, P. (2004). The great divide and beyond: Financial architecture in transition. In Financial Development and Economic Growth (pp. 106-134). Palgrave Macmillan UK.

Bergsten, C. F. (1998). The trade implications of the Asian financial crisis. Statement before the Committee on finance, United States' Senate.

Bisignano, J. (1999). Precarious credit equilibria: reflections on the Asian financial crisis. BIS Working Paper No. 64.

Bordo, M. D., & Jeanne, O. (2002). Boom-busts in asset prices, economic instability, and monetary policy (No. w8966). National Bureau of Economic Research.

Brüggemann, A., & Linne, T. (1999). How good are leading indicators for currency and banking crises in Central and Eastern Europe? An empirical test (No. 95). IWH Discussion Papers.

Brüggemann, A., & Linne, T. (2002). Are the Central and Eastern European transition countries still vulnerable to a financial crisis? Results from the signals approach.

Brunnermeier, M. K., & Schnabel, I. (2015). Bubbles and central banks: Historical perspectives.

Calomiris, C. W., & Gorton, G. (1991). The origins of banking panics: models, facts, and bank regulation. In Financial markets and financial crises (pp. 109-174). University of Chicago Press.

Calvo, G. A., & Mendoza, E. G. (1996). Petty crime and cruel punishment: lessons from the Mexican debacle. The American Economic Review, 86(2), 170-175.

Calvo, G. A., & Reinhart, C. M. (2000). Fear of floating. The Quarterly Journal of Economics, 117(2), 379-408.

Calvo, G., Goldstein, M., & Hochreiter, E. (1996). Private capital flows to emerging markets after the Mexican crisis. Peterson Institute for International Economics.

Caprio, G., & Klingebiel, D. (2003). Episodes of Systemic and Borderline Financial Crises.

World Bank, January 22.

Cashin, P., McDermott, C. J., & Scott, A. (2002). Booms and slumps in world commodity prices. Journal of Development Economics, 69(1), 277-296.

Catão, L., & Sutton, B. (2002). Sovereign defaults: the role of volatility. International Monetary Fund.

Chamon, M., Ghosh, A., & Kim, J. (2012). Are All Emerging Market Crises Alike?. Global Economic Crisis: Impacts, Transmission, Recovery, Cheltenham, UK: Edward Elgar.

Chamon, M., Ghosh, A., Habermeier, K., Ostry, J., Qureshi, M., & Reinhart, B. (2010). Capital inflows: the role of controls. IMF Staff Position Note, 2010.

Chang, R., & Velasco, A. (1998). Financial crises in emerging markets (No. w6606). National Bureau of Economic Research.

Comelli, F. (2012). Emerging market sovereign bond spreads: Estimation and back-testing. Emerging Markets Review, 13(4), 598-625.

Corsetti, G., Pesenti, P., & Roubini, N. (1999). What caused the Asian currency and financial crisis?. Japan and the world economy, 11(3), 305-373.

Cowan, K., Levy-Yeyati, E. L., Panizza, U., & Sturzenegger, F. (2006). Sovereign debt in the Americas: new data and stylized facts.

Das, U. S., Papaioannou, M. G., & Trebesch, C. (2012). Sovereign Debt Restructurings 1950-2010: Literature Survey, Data, and Stylized Facts. International Monetary Fund.

Dewatripont, M., & Roland, G. (1995). The design of reform packages under uncertainty. The American Economic Review, 1207-1223.

Dewatripont, M., & Roland, G. (1996). Transition as a process of large-scale institutional change. Economics of Transition, 4(1), 1-30.

Diaz-Alejandro, C. F. (1984). Latin American debt: I don't think we are in Kansas anymore. Brookings papers on economic activity, 1984(2), 335-389.

Dornbusch, R., Goldfajn, I., Valdés, R. O., Edwards, S., & Bruno, M. (1995). Currency crises and collapses. Brookings Papers on Economic Activity, 1995(2), 219-293.

Drazen, A. (2000). Political contagion in currency crises. In Currency crises (pp. 47-67). University of Chicago Press.

Edison, H., & Reinhart, C. M. (2001). Stopping hot money. Journal of Development Economics, 66(2), 533-553.

Eichengreen, B. (1991). Historical research on international lending and debt. The Journal of Economic Perspectives, 5(2), 149-169.

Eichengreen, B., & Hausmann, R. (1999). Exchange rates and financial fragility (No. w7418). National bureau of economic research.

Eichengreen, B., & Rose, A. K. (1999). Contagious currency crises: Channels of conveyance. In Changes in exchange rates in rapidly developing countries: Theory, practice, and policy issues (NBER-EASE volume 7) (pp. 29-56). University of Chicago Press.

Eichengreen, B., Hausmann, R., & Panizza, U. (2002). Original Sin: The Pain, the Mystery and the Road to Redemption, paper presented at a conference on "Currency and Maturity Matchmaking: Redeeming Debt from Original Sin". Inter-American Development Bank.

Eichengreen, B., Rose, A. K., & Wyplosz, C. (1994). Speculative attacks on pegged exchange rates: an empirical exploration with special reference to the European Monetary System (No. w4898). National Bureau of economic research.

Eichengreen, B., Rose, A. K., & Wyplosz, C. (1995). Exchange market mayhem: The antecedents and aftermath of speculative attacks. Economic Policy, 249-312.

Epstein, R. A. (2014). Overcoming 'economic backwardness' in the European Union. JCMS: Journal of Common Market Studies, 52(1), 17-34.

Federal Deposit Insurance Corporation (1997). The LDC Debt Crisis. Chap. 5 in History of the Eighties - Lessons for the Future, Volume I: An Examination of the Banking Crises of the 1980s and Early 1990s. Federal Deposit Insurance Corporation Washington.

Flood, R. P., & Garber, P. M. (1984). Collapsing exchange-rate regimes: some linear examples. Journal of international Economics, 17(1-2), 1-13.

Frankel, J. A., & Rose, A. K. (1996). Currency crashes in emerging markets: An empirical treatment. Journal of international Economics, 41(3), 351-366.
Galbis, V. (1993). High Real Interest Rates Under Financial Liberalization Is There a Problem?.

Gerschenkron, A. (1962). Economic backwardness in historical perspective: a book of essays (No. 330.947 G381). Cambridge, MA: Belknap Press of Harvard University Press.

Ghosh, A. R., Ostry, J. D., & Tamirisa, N. (2009). Anticipating the Next Crisis-What can early warning systems be expected to deliver?. Finance & Development, 46(3), 35-37.

Ghosh, A. R., Zalduendo, M. J., Thomas, M. A. H., Kim, M. J. I., Ramakrishnan, M. U., & Joshi, B. (2008). IMF Support and Crisis Prevention (No. 262). International Monetary Fund.

Ghosh, S. R., & Ghosh, A. R. (2003). Structural vulnerabilities and currency crises. IMF Staff Papers, 481-506.

Glick, R. (1999). Thoughts on the origins of the Asian crisis: Impulses and propagation mechanisms. The Asian Financial Crisis: Origins, Implications, and Solutions (pp. 33-63).

Goldfajn, I., & Valdés, R. (1997). Balance of Payments Crises and Capital Flows: The Role of Liquidity (No. 11). Central Bank of Chile.

Goldstein, M. (1998). The Asian financial crisis: Causes, cures, and systemic implications (Vol. 55). Peterson Institute.

Goldstein, M., Kaminsky, G. L., & Reinhart, C. M. (2000). Assessing financial vulnerability: an early warning system for emerging markets. Peterson Institute.

Guscina, A., & Jeanne, M. O. (2006). Government debt in emerging market countries: A new data set (No. 6-98). International Monetary Fund.

Harberger, A. (1985a). Observations on the Chilean economy, 1973-1983. Economic Development and Cultural Change, 33(3), 451-462.

Harberger, A. (1985b). Lesson for debtor-country managers and policymakers. International Debt and the Developing Countries, The World Bank, Washington DC, USA, 236-257.

Hughes, A., & Singh, A. (1991). The world economic slowdown and the Asian and Latin American economies: a comparative analysis of economic structure, policy and performance. Economic Liberalization: No Panacea The Experiences of Latin America and Asia, 57-99.

Hunter, W. C., Kaufman, G. G., & Krueger, T. H. (Eds.). (1999). The Asian financial crisis: origins, implications, and solutions. Springer Science & Business Media.

Hurrell, A. (2014). Rising Powers and the Emerging Global, in Baylis, J., Smith, S., & Owens P. (eds.), The Globalization of World Politics: an introduction to international relations, 6th Edition. Oxford: Oxford University Press, 80-94.

International Monetary Fund (2002). Global Financial Stability Report. Early Warning System Models: The Next Steps Forward. International Monetary Fund, Publication Services, Washington.

Kaminsky, G. L., & Reinhart, C. M. (1998). Financial crises in Asia and Latin America: Then and now. The American Economic Review, 88(2), 444-448.

Kaminsky, G. L., & Reinhart, C. M. (1999). The twin crises: the causes of banking and balance-of-payments problems. American economic review, 473-500.

Kaminsky, G., Lizondo, S., & Reinhart, C. M. (1998). Leading indicators of currency crises. Staff Papers, 45(1), 1-48.

Keynes, J. M. (1935). The general theory of employment, interest and money. University of Adelaide Library Etext version.

Kincaid, M. G. R., & Collyns, M. C. (2003). Managing financial crises: recent experience and lessons for Latin America (No. 217). International Monetary Fund.

Kornai, J. (1980). " Hard" and" Soft" budget constraint. Acta Oeconomica, 231-245.

Kornai, J. (1992). The socialist system: The political economy of communism. Oxford University Press.

Kornai, J. (1998). From Socialism to Capitalism: What is Meant by the Change of System'?. London: Social Market Foundation.

Kornai, J. (2000). Ten years after 'the road to a free economy': the author's self-evaluation. In Annual Bank Conference on Development Economics 2000 (pp. 49-66).

Kornai, J. (2000). What the change of system from socialism to capitalism does and does not mean. The journal of Economic perspectives, 14(1), 27-42.

Kornai, J. (2006). The great transformation of central eastern Europe. Economics of transition, 14(2), 207-244.

Kornai, J. (2014). Példaképünk: Kína? (Can China Set Us an Example?) In: Kolosi, T. Társadalmi riport, 603-616.

Krishnamurthy, A., & Vissing-Jorgensen, A. (2011). The effects of quantitative easing on interest rates: channels and implications for policy (No. w17555). National Bureau of Economic Research.

Krugman, P. (1979). A model of balance-of-payments crises. Journal of money, credit and banking, 11(3), 311-325.

Krugman, P. (1979). A model of balance-of-payments crises. Journal of money, credit and banking, 11(3), 311-325.

Krugman, P. (1998a). Free Advice: A Letter to Malaysia's Prime Minister. Fortune (138:6), 35-37.

Krugman, P. (1998b). Saving Asia: It's time to get radical. Fortune, September, 7, 74-80.

Krugman, P. (2001). Crises: the next generation. Razin Conference, Tel Aviv University.

Lardy, N. R. (1998). China's unfinished economic revolution. Brookings Institution Press.

Lardy, N. R. (2012). Sustaining China's economic growth after the global financial crisis. Peterson Institute.

Lin, J. Y. (2012). Demystifying the Chinese economy. Cambridge University Press.

Lissakers, K. (1999). The IMF and the Asian crisis: A view from the executive board. The Asian Financial Crisis: Origins, Implications, and Solutions, 1. Springer US.

Litwack, J. M., & Qian, Y. (1998). Balanced or unbalanced development: special economic zones as catalysts for transition. Journal of Comparative Economics, 26(1), 117-141.

Liu, L. G., Noland, M., Robinson, S., & Wang, Z. (1998). Asian competitive devaluations (No. wp98-2).

Maddison, A. (1985). Two Crises: Latin America and Asia 1929-38 and 1973-83.

Maddison, A. (2007a). Chinese Economic Performance in the Long Run. Development Center of the OECD.

Maddison, A. (2007b). Contours of the world economy 1-2030 AD: Essays in macro-economic history. Oxford University Press.

Manasse, P., Roubini, N., & Schimmelpfennig, A. (2003). Predicting sovereign debt crises.

McKinnon, R. I., & Pill, H. (1996). Credible Liberalizations and International Capital Flows: The" Overborrowing Syndrome". In Financial Deregulation and Integration in East Asia, NBER-EASE Volume 5 (pp. 7-50). University of Chicago Press.

McMillan, J., & Naughton, B. (1992). How to reform a planned economy: lessons from China. Oxford Review of Economic Policy, 8(1), 130-143.

Milesi-Ferretti, M. G. M., & Lane, M. P. R. (2010). The cross-country incidence of the global crisis (No. 10-171). International Monetary Fund.

Moskow, M. H. (1999). The Asian financial crisis. The Asian Financial Crisis: Origins, Implications, and Solutions (pp. 11-14). Springer US.

Muchhala, B. (Ed.). (2007). Ten Years After: Revisiting the Asian Financial Crisis: Essays. Woodrow Wilson International Center for Scholars, Asia Program.

Murphy, K. M., Shleifer, A., & Vishny, R. W. (1992). The transition to a market economy: Pitfalls of partial reform. The Quarterly Journal of Economics, 107(3), 889-906.

Obstfeld, M. (1986). Rational and self-fulfilling balance-of-payments crises. American economic review, 76, No. 1, pp. 161-177.

Orenstein, M. A. (2013). Reassessing the neo-liberal development model in Central and Eastern Europe. Resilient Liberalism in Europe's Political Economy, 374.

Park, Y. C. (2006). Economic liberalization and integration in East Asia: a post-crisis paradigm. Oxford University Press on Demand.

Pauly, L. W. (2008). The political economy of global financial crisis. Global Political Economy, 198-222.

Perry, G., & Lederman, D. (1998). Financial Vulnerability, Spillover Effects, and Contagion: Lessons from the Asian Crises for Latin America. World Bank Publications.

Popov, V. (2000). Shock therapy versus gradualism: the end of the debate (explaining the magnitude of transformational recession).

Purcell, J. F., & Kaufman, J. A. (1993). The Risks of Sovereign Lending: Lessons from History.

Qian, Y., Roland, G., & Xu, C. (1999). Why is China different from Eastern Europe? Perspectives from organization theory. European Economic Review, 43(4), 1085-1094.

Reinhart, C. M. (2002). Default, currency crises, and sovereign credit ratings. the world bank economic review, 16(2), 151-170.

Reinhart, C. M., & Rogoff, K. S. (2004). The modern history of exchange rate arrangements: a reinterpretation. the Quarterly Journal of economics, 119(1), 1-48.

Reinhart, C. M., & Rogoff, K. S. (2008). Is the 2007 US sub-prime financial crisis so different? An international historical comparison (No. w13761). National Bureau of Economic Research.

Reinhart, C. M., & Rogoff, K. S. (2009). This time is different: Eight centuries of financial folly. Princeton University Press.

Reis, R. (2010). Interpreting the unconventional us monetary policy of 2007-09 (No. w15662). National Bureau of Economic Research.

Rodrik, D. (2000). Institutions for high-quality growth: what they are and how to acquire them (No. w7540). National bureau of economic research.

Rogoff, K. (1999). International institutions for reducing global financial instability (No. w7265). National bureau of economic research.

Roland, G. (2000). Transition and economics: Politics, markets, and firms. MIT Press.

Roland, G. (2005). Understanding Institutional Change: Fast Moving and Slow Moving Institutions. Unpublished paper.

Roland, G., & Verdier, T. (1997). Transition and the output fall. Economics of transition, 7(1), 1-28.

Sachs, J. D. (1989). Developing Country Debt and Economic Performance. The International Financial System. In Developing Country Debt and Economic Performance, Volume 1: The International Financial System (pp. 12-0). University of Chicago Press.

Sachs, J. D., & Williamson, J. (1985). External debt and macroeconomic performance in Latin America and East Asia. Brookings Papers on Economic Activity, 1985(2), 523-573.

Sachs, J., & Woo, W. T. (1994). Structural factors in the economic reforms of China, Eastern Europe, and the former Soviet Union. Economic policy, 9(18), 101-145.

Sharma, R. (2012). Broken BRICs: Why the rest stopped rising. Foreign Affairs, 2-7.

Sharma, R. (2016). The Rise and Fall of Nations: Forces of Change in the Post-crisis World. WW Norton & Company.

Singh, A. (1993). Asian economic success and Latin American failure in the 1980s: new analyses and future policy implications. International Review of Applied Economics, 7(3), 267-289.

Stiglitz, J. E. (2002). Globalization and its Discontents (Vol. 500). Norton: New York.

Sturzenegger, F., & Zettelmeyer, J. (2006). Debt defaults and lessons from a decade of crises. MIT Press.

Taylor, A. M. (1999). Latin America and foreign capital in the twentieth century: economics, politics, and institutional change (No. w7394). National bureau of economic research.

Turley, G., & Luke, P. J. (2011). Transition economics: Two decades on. Routledge.

Velloso, H., & Bustillo, I. (2013). Debt financing rollercoaster: Latin American and Caribbean access to international bond markets since the debt crisis, 1982-2012. United Nations.

Wade, R. (1990). Governing the market: Economic theory and the role of government in East Asian industrialization. Princeton University Press.

Walter, S. (2013). Financial crises and the politics of macroeconomic adjustments. Cambridge University Press.

Wei, S. J. (1997). Gradualism versus big bang: Speed and sustainability of reforms. Canadian Journal of Economics, 1234-1247.

Woo, W. T. (1994). The art of reforming centrally planned economies: Comparing China, Poland, and Russia. Journal of comparative economics, 18(3), 276-308.

Woods, N. (2014). International political economy in an age of globalization, in Baylis, J., Smith, S., & Owens P. (eds.), The Globalization of World Politics: an introduction to international relations, 6th Edition. Oxford: Oxford University Press, 243-257.

Zecchini, S. (Ed.). (2013). Lessons from the economic transition: Central and Eastern Europe in the 1990s. Springer Science & Business Media.

China's Economic Empowerment

Acemoglu, D., & Robinson, J. A. (2013). Why nations fail: The origins of power, prosperity, and poverty. Crown Business.

Beachy, B. (2012). A Financial Crisis Manual Causes, Consequences, and Lessons of the Financial Crisis (No. 12-06). GDAE, Tufts University.

Berg, C. (2011). The Global Financial Crisis and the Great Recession: Causes, Effects, Measures and Consequences for Economic Analysis and Policy. In Presented at a Workshop on Monetary Policy.

Blanchard, O. & Johnson, D. R. (2013). Macroeconomics. Sixth Edition. Addison-Wesley Longman.

Brandt, L. (1989). Commercialization and Agricultural Development: Central and Eastern China, 1870-1937. Cambridge University Press.

Byrd, W. A. (1991). The market mechanism and economic reforms in China. ME Sharpe

Incorporated.

Cabestan, J. P., Di Meglio, J. F., & Richet, X. (Eds.). (2012). China and the global financial crisis: a comparison with Europe (Vol. 48). Routledge.

Cai, F., Du, Y., Giles, J., Park, A. & Wang, M. (2010). Shock and Recovery in China's Labor Market: Flexibility in the Face of a Global Financial Crisis. Review Paper for East Asia PREM, World Bank.

Cheng, L. (2003). Banking in modern China: entrepreneurs, professional managers, and the development of Chinese banks, 1897-1937. Cambridge University Press.

Dreyer, J. T. (2004). China's Political System. Routledge.

Fairbank, J. K., & Goldman, M. (2006). China: A new history. Harvard University Press.

Gong, G. W. (2001). The beginning of history: Remembering and forgetting as strategic issues. Washington Quarterly, 24(2), 45-57.

Hayek, F. A. (1944). The road to serfdom. Dymock's Book Arcade.

Heilbroner, R. L. (1986). The Essential Adam Smith. Oxford: Oxford University Press.

Howell, J. (2012) 'Civil society, corporatism and capitalism in China' Journal of Comparative Asian Development (11:2), 271-297

Hurrell, A. (2014). Rising Powers and the Emerging Global, in Baylis, J., Smith, S., & Owens P. (eds.), The Globalization of World Politics: an introduction to international relations, 6th Edition. Oxford: Oxford University Press, 80-94.

Jing, R. (2012). The collapse speed of China's exports in the 2008–2009 financial crisis. CESifo Economic Studies, 58(4), 650-670.

Kim, S. & Yamakawa, T. (2005). The "ABC" of Asia's FX Regime Shift. Goldman Sachs.

Lague, D. (2002). Asset-management companies could drag down the central bank: A government move to clean up loans backfires. Far Eastern Economic Review, 165(45), 35-35.

Lardy, N. R. (2012). Sustaining China's economic growth after the global financial crisis. Peterson Institute.

Lardy, N. R. (2014). Markets over Mao: The rise of private business in China. Columbia University Press.

Lau, L. J., Qian, Y., & Roland, G. (1997). Pareto-improving economic reforms through dual-track liberalization. Economics Letters, 55(2), 285-292.

Lau, L. J., Qian, Y., & Roland, G. (2000). Reform without losers: An interpretation of China's dual-track approach to transition. Journal of Political Economy, 108(1), 120-143.

Li, X., & Hu, B. (2011). China's New Deal: Economic Development Under International Financial Crisis. Nova Science Publishers.

Li, Z., Song, Y., Tang, M., Tilton, A. & Wei, M. (2016b). SOE reform in China – potentially powerful, practically challenging. Goldman Sachs.

Lieberthal, K. (1995). Governing China: From revolution through reform. WW Norton.

Lin, J. Y. (1992). Rural reforms and agricultural growth in China. The American economic review, 34-51.

Lin, J. Y. (2012). Demystifying the Chinese economy. Cambridge University Press.

Lin, J. Y., Cai, F., & Li, Z. (1996). The China Miracle: Development Strategy and Economic Reform, The Hong Kong Centre for Economic Research and The International Center for Economic Growth.

Maddison, A. (1998). Chinese Economic Performance in the Long Run. Development Center of the OECD.

Maddison, A. (2007a). Chinese Economic Performance in the Long Run. Development Center of the OECD.

Maddison, A. (2007b). Contours of the world economy 1-2030 AD: Essays in macro-economic history. Oxford University Press.

McMillan, J. (2004). Avoid Hubris and other lessons for reformers. Finance and Development, 41, 34-37.

McMillan, J., & Naughton, B. (1992). How to reform a planned economy: lessons from China. Oxford Review of Economic Policy, 8(1), 130-143.

Naughton, B. (1988). The Third Front: defence industrialization in the Chinese interior. The China Quarterly, 115, 351-386.

Naughton, B. (1996). Growing out of the plan: Chinese economic reform, 1978-1993. Cambridge university press.

Naughton, B. (2007). The Chinese economy: Transitions and growth. MIT press.

Nolan, P. (2015). Re-balancing China: Essays on the Global Financial Crisis, Industrial Policy and International Relations. Anthem Press.

Pang, K. (2016). China SOE: Taking a closer look at China's Debt-to-Equity Swap Plan. Morgan Stanley.

Pauly, L. W. (2005). The political economy of international financial crises. Global Political Economy, 176-203.

Qian, Y. (2001). How reform worked in China. William Davidson Institute Working Paper Number 473.

Qian, Y., & Wu, J. (2000). China's transition to a market economy: How far across the river?. Stanford Center for International Development.

Rawski, T. G. (1989). Economic growth in prewar China. University of California Press.

Rawski, T. G. (2001). What is happening to China's GDP statistics?. China Economic Review, 12(4), 347-354.

Reinhart, C. M., & Rogoff, K. S. (2009). This time is different: Eight centuries of financial folly. Princeton University Press.

Riskin, C. (1987). China's political economy: the quest for development since 1949. Oxford University Press.

Roland, G. (2000). Transition and economics: Politics, markets, and firms. MIT Press.

Rostow, W. W. (1960). The stages of economic growth: A non-communist manifesto, 3rd edn. New York: Cambridge University Press.

Shaoguang, W., Angang, H., & Yuanzhu, D. (2002). Behind China's Wealth Gap. South China Morning Post, 31.

Spence, J. D. (1990). The search for modern China. WW Norton & Company.

Stavis, B. (1982). Rural institutions in China. Barker, Sinha and Rose.

Sun, Q., & Fu, X. (2012). China's battle against the global economic crisis in

Fu, X. (ed.), China's Role in Global Economic Recovery. Routledge.

Wen, G. J. (1993). Total factor productivity change in China's farming sector: 1952-1989. Economic Development and Cultural Change, 42(1), 1-41.

Woo, W. T. (2012). Sense and sensibility in the reduction of US–China trade tension at the G20 Summit in Cannes in 2012 in Fu, X. (ed.), China's Role in Global Economic Recovery. Routledge.

Woods, N. (2014). International political economy in an age of globalization, in Baylis, J., Smith, S., & Owens P. (eds.), The Globalization of World Politics: an introduction to international relations, 6th Edition. Oxford: Oxford University Press, 243-257.

Wu, J. (2005). Understanding and interpreting Chinese economic reform. Texere.

Yang, J. (2011). China's International Coordination in Policy Response to the 2008 Financial Crisis. Whitehead Journal of Diplomacy and International Relations, 12, 73-88.

Young, A. N. (1971). China's nation-building effort, 1927-1937. Hoover Press.

The Developmental State

Acemoglu, D. (2004). Understanding Institutions - Lionel Robbins Lecture at LSE. MIT Department of Economics [Online] February 2004 http://economics.mit.edu/files/1353 [Accessed: September 2017].

Acemoglu, D., & Robinson, J. A. (2013). Why nations fail: The origins of power, prosperity, and poverty. Crown Business.

Amsden, A. H. (1992). Asia's next giant: South Korea and late industrialization. Oxford University Press.

Baek, S. W. (2005). Does China follow "the East Asian development model"?. Journal of Contemporary Asia, 35(4), 485-498.

Balassa, B. A. (1981). The process of industrial development and alternative development strategies (No. 141). International Finance Section, Dept. of Economics, Princeton University.

Balassa, B. A. (1982). Development strategies in semi-industrial economies. Published for the World Bank [by] the Johns Hopkins University Press.

Bates, R. (1981). Markets and states in tropical Africa. Berkeley. Cal.: University of California Press.

Beeson, M. (2009). Developmental states in East Asia: a comparison of the Japanese and Chinese experiences. Asian Perspective, 5-39.

Bhagwati, J. N. (1986). Rethinking trade strategy. Development Strategies Reconsidered, 91-104.

Bishop, M. L., Payne, A., Sen, K., Breslin, S., Öniş, Z., Muzaka, V., & Yeung, H. W. C. (2018). Revisiting the developmental state. The University of Sheffield, SPERI Paper No. 43.

Bolesta, A. (2015). Creating a post-socialist developmental state: the political economy of China's transformation and development. Studia z Polityki Publicznej/Szkoła Główna Handlowa, (4), 107-127.

Bradford, C. I. (1987). Trade and structural change: NICs and next tier NICs as transitional economies. World Development, 15(3), 299-316.

Brownbridge, M., & Kirkpatrick, C. (1999). Financial sector regulation: The lessons of the Asian crisis. Development Policy Review, 17(3), 243-266.

Cerny, P. G. (1997). Paradoxes of the competition state: The dynamics of political globalization. Government and opposition, 32(2), 251-274.

Cumings, B. (1984). The origins and development of the Northeast Asian political economy: industrial sectors, product cycles, and political consequences. International Organization, 38(1), 1-40.

Deyo, F. C. (Ed.). (1987). The political economy of the new Asian industrialism. Cornell University Press.

Evans, P. (1989). Predatory, developmental, and other apparatuses: A comparative political economy perspective on the third world state. In Sociological forum (Vol. 4, No. 4, pp. 561-587). Kluwer Academic Publishers-Plenum Publishers.

Evans, P. (1995). Embedded autonomy: States and industrial transformation. Princeton University Press.

Gerschenkron, A. (1962). Economic backwardness in historical perspective. Cambridge, MA: Belknap.

Haggard, S. (1990). Pathways From The Periphery: The Politics of Growth in the Newly Developing Countries.

Hamilton, C. (1986). Capitalist industrialization in South Korea. Boulder: Westview.

Hasan, P. (1976). Korea-Problems and issues in a rapidly growing economy. The World Bank.

Hirschmann, A. (1958). The strategy of economic development. New Haven: Yale University Press.

Howell, J. (1998). An unholy trinity? Civil society, economic liberalization and democratization in post-Mao China. Government and Opposition, 33(1), 56-80.

Howell, J. (2006). Reflections on the Chinese state. Development and Change, 37(2), 273-297.

Huang, Y. (2010). China's great ascendancy and structural risks: consequences of asymmetric market liberalisation. Asian-Pacific Economic Literature, 24(1), 65-85.

Johnson, C. (1982). MITI and the Japanese miracle: the growth of industrial policy: 1925-1975. Stanford University Press.

Jones, L. P., & Sakong, I. (1980). Government, business and entrepreneurship in economic development: the case of Korea.

Knight, J. B. (2014). China as a developmental state. The World Economy, 37(10), 1335-1347.

Lal, D. (1983). The poverty of development economics. London. Institute of Economic Affairs.

Lardy, N. R. (1998). China's Unfinished Economic Revolution. Washington: Brookings Institution.

Lardy, N. R. (2014). Markets over Mao: The rise of private business in China. Columbia University Press.

Lee, K., & Mathews, J. A. (2010). From Washington consensus to BeST consensus for world development. Asian-Pacific Economic Literature, 24(1), 86-103.

Leftwich, A. (1995). Bringing politics back in: Towards a model of the developmental state. The journal of development studies, 31(3), 400-427.

Lin, J. Y. (2009). Economic development and transition: thought, strategy, and viability. Cambridge University Press.

List, F., & Colwell, S. (1885). National system of political economy. New York: A.M. Kelley.

Mann, M. (1994). The autonomous power of the state: Its origins, mechanisms and results. The State: Critical Concepts, 331-53.

Mason, E. S. (1980). The economic and social modernization of the Republic of Korea (No. 92). Harvard University.

Naughton, B. (2007). The Chinese economy: Transitions and growth. MIT Press.

Naughton, B. (2008). A political economy of China's economic transition. China's great economic transformation, 91-135.

North, D. (1990). Institutions, institutional change and economic performance. Cambridge: Cambridge University Press.

Önis, Z. (1991). The Logic of the Developmental State, Review Article. Comparative Politics, October.

Pack, H., & Westphal, L. E. (1986). Industrial strategy and technological change: theory versus reality. Journal of development economics, 22(1), 87-128.

Ping, J. H. (2011). The Chinese development model: international development and hegemony.
Polanyi, K. (1944). The great transformation. Boston: Beacon Press.

Polidano, C. (2001). Don't discard state autonomy: Revisiting the East Asian experience of development. Political Studies, 49(3), 513-527.

So, A. (2002). Guest editor's introduction. Chinese Economy, vol. 35, No. 3.

Wade, R. (1990). Governing the market: Economic theory and the role of government in East Asian industrialization. Princeton University Press.

Wade, R. H. (2018). The developmental state: dead or alive?. Development and Change, 49(2), 518-546.

Weber, M. (1968). Economy and society. Eds. Guenther Roth and Claus Wittich. New York: Bedminster Press.

Weiss, L. (2000). Developmental states in transition: adapting, dismantling, innovating, not 'normalizing'. The Pacific Review, 13(1), 21-55.

White, G. (1984). Developmental states and socialist industrialisation in the Third World. The Journal of Development Studies, 21(1), 97-120.

White, G., & Wade, R. (1988). Developmental states and markets in East Asia: An introduction. In Developmental States in East Asia (pp. 1-29). Palgrave Macmillan, London.

Wong, J. (2004). The adaptive developmental state in East Asia. Journal of East Asian Studies, 4(3), 345-362.

Wu, J., & Zhao, R. (1987). The dual pricing system in China's industry. Journal of Comparative Economics, 11(3), 309-318.

Xu, C. (2011). The fundamental institutions of China's reforms and development. Journal of economic literature, 49(4), 1076-1151.

Young, S. (1984). Trade Policy Reform in Korea: Background and Prospect. Seoul: Korea Development Institute, mimeo.

Yusuf, S., & Peters, R. K. (1984). Is capital accumulation the key to economic growth? Neoclassical models and development economics on Korea's investment policies. World Bank, Washington, D.C.

China's Vulnerabilities

Abiad, A., Lee, M., Pundit, M., & Ramayandi, A. (2016). Structural change and moderating growth in the People's Republic of China: Implications for developing Asia and beyond. ADB Briefs No. 53, March 2016.

Acemoglu, D., & Robinson, J. A. (2013). Why nations fail: The origins of power, prosperity, and poverty. Crown Business.

Arora, R., Chang, J., Fernandez, D., Kotecha, M., Lee, J., & Zhou, Y. (2015). Strong signal sent on CNY basket. Barclays.

Atkinson, A. B. (2015). Inequality: what can be done?. Harvard University Press.

Aziz, J, Ng, G., & Zhu, H. (2015). China: the future of monetary policy. J.P. Morgan.

Baba, N., & Tilton, A. (2016). Lessons for China from Japan (part 2): Learning from Japan's non-performing loan problems. Goldman Sachs.

Baba, N., Ota, T., & Tilton, A. (2016). Lessons for China from Japan's experience (part 1): Exploring similarities and differences. Goldman Sachs.

Bank of America Merrill Lynch (2016). 2016 EM Local Markets Guide. GEMs Paper #27.

Barclays (2012). CNH Market Primer: Casting a Wider Net. Cross Asset Research September 2012.

Barro, R. J. (1991). Economic growth in a cross section of countries. The quarterly journal of economics, 106(2), 407-443.

Barro, R. J. (1997). Getting it right: markets and choices in a free society. MIT Press.

Barro, R. J. (1998). Determinants of economic growth: a cross-country empirical study (No. w5698). National Bureau of Economic Research.

Barro, R. J., & Lee, J. W. (1994, June). Sources of economic growth. In Carnegie-Rochester conference series on public policy (Vol. 40, pp. 1-46). North-Holland.

Barro, R. J., & Ursúa, J. F. (2017). Stock-market crashes and depressions. Research in Economics.

Binici, M., Hutchison, M., & Schindler, M. (2010). Controlling capital? Legal restrictions and the asset composition of international financial flows. Journal of International Money and Finance, 29(4), 666-684.

Bisignano, J. (1999). Precarious credit equilibria: reflections on the Asian financial crisis. BIS Working Paper No. 64.

Blanchard, O. J., & Johnson, D. (2013). Macroeconomics. Sixth Edition. Pearson Education.

Bloomberg (2015a). A timeline: The Chinese yuan's journey to global reserve status. Bloomberg [Online] 30 November. http://www.bloomberg.com/news/articles/2015-11-30/a-timeline-the-chinese-yuan-s-journey-to-global-reserve-status [Accessed: October 2017].

Bloomberg (2015b). Offshore yuan tumbles as China unveils multi-currency index. [Online] 11 December. http://www.bloomberg.com/news/articles/2015-12-11/offshore-yuan-weakens-as-china-unveils-multi-currency-index [Accessed: October 2017].

Bloomberg (2015c). China loses another economic indicator as Minxin suspends PMI. Bloomberg [Online] 21 December. http://www.bloomberg.com/news/articles/2015-12-21/china-loses-another-economic-indicator-as-minxin-suspends-pmi [Accessed: October 2017].

Blyth, M. (2002). Great transformations: economic ideas and institutional change in the twentieth century. Cambridge University Press.

Breslin, S. (2013a). China and the global order. International Affairs (89:3), 615-634.

Breslin, S. (2013b). Xi-ing believes in political and economic reforms under China's new leadership. Analysis No. 210 [Online] November 2013. http://www.ispionline.it/sites/default/files/pubblicazioni/analysis_210_2013.pdf [Accessed: October 2017].

Breslin, S. (2014). China plays politics with debt while the West holds its breath. [Online] 13 February. http://theconversation.com/china-plays-politics-with-debt-while-the-west-holds-its-breath-22374 [Accessed: October 2017].

Buiter, W., Chua, J., Shen, M., Mondino, G., & Rahbari, E. (2015). Global economics view: What does the Chinese devaluation mean for the world?. Citi Research.

Buzan, B., & Cox, M. (2013). China and the US: Comparable cases of 'peaceful rise'?. Chinese

Journal of International Politics, 6(2), 109-132.

Buzan, B., & Lawson, G. (2014). Capitalism and the emergent world order. International Affairs, 90(1), 71-91.

Callaghy, T. M. (1993). Political passions and economic interests: economic reform and political structure in Africa. Hemmed in: Responses to Africa's economic decline, 463-519.
Calvo, G. A. (1991). The perils of sterilization. Staff Papers, 38(4), 921-926.

Cavenagh, J., & Gu, Y. (2016). CNY valuation in the trade-weighted index (TWI) regime. J.P. Morgan.

Chang, J., & Fernandez D. (2015). Putting SDR inclusion in perspective. A conference call with Barry Eichengreen. Barclays.

Chang, J., Chatterjee, A., Kotecha, M., Tan, D., Wang, S., & Zhou, Y. (2015a). China – Leaky capital account: Estimating outflows and policy implications. Barclays.

Chang, J., Fernandez, D. & Zhou, Y. (2016). Alternative credit aggregates. Barclays.

Chang, J., Fernandez, D., Kotecha, M., Lee, J., & Wang, S. (2015b). RMB in the SDR: Initial thoughts. Barclays.

Chang, J., Kotecha, M., & Zhou, Y. (2016b). China - Rising outflows; stepped-up controls. Barclays.

Chang, J., Kotecha, M., & Zhou, Y. (2016c). Sharp fall in FX reserves amid capital outflow pressure. Barclays.

Chang, J., Kotecha, M., Tan, D. & Zhou, Y. (2016a). China - CNY FX basket gets a refresh. Barclays.

Chang, J., Wang, S. & Zhou, Y. (2015c). PBoC lowers SLF rates in move to build a new policy framework. Barclays.

Chen, J. (2016). Housing system an urbanization in the People's Republic of China. ADBI Working Paper Series.

Chen, L., Kwok, D., Wang, T., Zhang, N., & Zhong, J. (2017). China Economic Perspectives – Understanding China (Part I-IV): FX, Debt, Monetary Policy and Property Bubble. UBS.

Chen, M., Ng, G. & Zhu, H. (2016e). Greater China Quarterly Issues. J.P. Morgan.

Chen, M., Ng, G., & Zhu, H. (2015a). China: IMF staff recommended RMB inclusion in the SDR. J.P. Morgan.

Chen, M., Ng, G., & Zhu, H. (2015b). China's two-speed economy. J.P. Morgan.

Chen, M., Ng, G., & Zhu, H. (2015c). China: the full report of the Party recommendation for the next Five-Year Plan. J.P. Morgan.

Chen, M., Ng, G., & Zhu, H. (2015d). PBOC started to release a trade-weighted basket exchange rate. J.P. Morgan.

Chen, M., Ng, G., & Zhu, H. (2016a). China: First working day is a stress test on the new trading mechanism in equity and FX markets. J.P. Morgan.

Chen, M., Ng, G., & Zhu, H. (2016b). China's Financial Regulatory Reform (1): Macro-Prudential Assessment (MPA) framework. J.P. Morgan.

Chen, M., Ng, G., & Zhu, H. (2016c). China's Financial Regulatory Reform (2): Macro-Prudential Assessment (MPA) framework. J.P. Morgan.

Chen, M., Ng, G., & Zhu, H. (2016d). Economic Research Note: China's saving rate. J.P. Morgan.

Chinn, M. D., & Ito, H. (2008). A new measure of financial openness. Journal of comparative policy analysis, 10(3), 309-322.

Chua, J., Lubin, D., Mondino, G., & Willer, D. (2016). Emerging markets economic outlook & strategy: Has China fixed its capital account problem. Citi Research.

Claessens, S., Kose, M. M. A., Laeven, M. L., & Valencia, F. (2014). Financial crises: Causes, consequences, and policy responses. International Monetary Fund.

Claessens, S., Underhill, G. R., & Zhang, X. (2006). The Political Economy of Global Financial Governance: the costs of Basle II for poor countries.

Clark, P. B., & MacDonald, R. (1999). Exchange rates and economic fundamentals: a methodological comparison of BEERs and FEERs. In Equilibrium exchange rates (pp. 285-322). Springer Netherlands.

Coale, A., & Hoover, E. (1958). Population growth and economic development in low-income countries. Princeton: Princeton University Press.

Cox, M. (2012). Power shifts, economic change and the decline of the West?. International Relations, 26(4), 369-388.

Cox, M. (2014). From the end of the cold war to a new global era. John Baylis, Steve Smith & Patricia Owens, The Globalization of World Politics. An Introduction to International Relations, Oxford University Press, 73-74.

Daniel, M. J. (2016). Debt Equity Conversions and NPL Securitization in China: Some Initial Considerations. International Monetary Fund.

De Jonquières, G. (2013). Is power really shifting to China?. Journal of Economic Diplomacy.

De Jonquières, G. (2014). The problematic politics of China's economic reform plans. European

Centre for International Political Economy (ECIPE), (5/2014), 1-8.

Deng, W., & Tao, D. (2016). China: Premier reveals 2016 macro target. Credit Suisse.

DeRosa, D. F. (2009). Central Banking and Monetary Policy in Emerging-Markets Nations.

Evans, P. (2004). Development as institutional change: the pitfalls of monocropping and the potentials of deliberation. Studies in comparative international development, 38(4), 30.

Evans, P. (2005). The challenges of the institutional turn: new interdisciplinary opportunities in development theory. The economic sociology of capitalism, 90-116.

Farris, R., & Deng, W. (2016). China: Policy is tightening. Credit Suisse.

Feenstra, R. C., & Taylor, A.M. (2014). International Economics. 3rd Edition, New York: Worth Macmillan.

Feng, W., Cai, Y., & Gu, B. (2013). Population, Policy, and Politics: How Will History Judge China's One-Child Policy?. Population and Development Review, 38(s1), 115-129.

Gill, I. S., Kharas, H. J., & Bhattasali, D. (2007). An East Asian renaissance: ideas for economic growth. World Bank Publications.

Goldman Sachs Research (2013a). EM Macro Daily: Capital account reforms – charting a roadmap. Goldman Sachs.

Goldman Sachs Research (2013b). EM Macro Daily: RMB internationalization to power ahead. Goldman Sachs.

Goldman Sachs Research (2015). EM Macro Daily: The impact of recent equity, credit and FX moves on China risk. Goldman Sachs.

Goldstein, M., & Lardy, N. R. (2008a). China's exchange rate policy: an overview of some key issues. In Goldstein, M., & Lardy, N. R. (2008). Debating China's exchange rate policy. Peterson Institute, p. 1-76.

Goldstein, M., & Lardy, N. R. (2008b). Debating China's exchange rate policy. Peterson Institute.

Goldstein, M., Kaminsky, G. L., & Reinhart, C. M. (2000). Assessing financial vulnerability: an early warning system for emerging markets. Peterson Institute.

Gong, G (2016). Two stages of economic development. ADBI Working Paper Series.

Greenhalgh, S. (2008). Just one child: Science and policy in Deng's China. University of California Press.

Gruin, J. (2013). Asset or liability? The role of the financial system in the political economy of China's rebalancing. Journal of Current Chinese Affairs, 42(4), 73-104.

Gruin, J. (2016). The social order of Chinese capitalism: socio-economic uncertainty, communist party rule and economic development, 1990–2000. Economy and Society, 45(1), 24-50.

Gruin, J., Toohey, L., Picker, C. B., & Greenacre, J. (2015). Contesting the Liberal Imaginary? China's Role in the International Monetary System. China in the International Economic Order: New Directions and Changing Paradigms, 189-210.

Gu, Y. (2015). China FX: Key Q&As following recent USD/CNH volatility. J.P. Morgan.

Gu, Y., & Cavenagh, J. (2016). CNY: Why is the TWI depreciating, despite the straightforward $CNY fixing mechanism laid out by PBoC?. J.P. Morgan.

Hauner, D. (2006). A fiscal price tag for international reserves. International Finance, 9(2), 169-195.

He, D., Cheung, L., Zhang, W., & Wu, T. (2012). How would capital account liberalization affect China's capital flows and the renminbi real exchange rates?. China & World Economy, 20(6), 29-54.

Heep, S. (2014). China in global finance: domestic financial repression and international financial power. Springer Science & Business Media.

Heilmann, S. (2008a). From local experiments to national policy: The origins of China's distinctive policy process. The China Journal, (59), 1-30.

Heilmann, S. (2008b). Policy Experimentation in China's Economic Rise, In: Studies in Comparative International Development (SCID), Vol. 43, No. 1 (Januar 2008): p. 1-26.

Heilmann, S. (2017). China's Political System. Mercator Institute for China Studies.

Holz, C. A. (2014). The quality of China's GDP statistics. China Economic Review, 30, 309-338.

Hsieh, C. T., & Song, Z. M. (2015). Grasp the large, let go of the small: the transformation of the state sector in China (No. w21006). National Bureau of Economic Research.

Hurrell, A. (2009). Rising powers and the question of status in international society. In Annual Meeting of the International Studies Association (pp. 15-18).

International Monetary Fund (2016a). Assessing Reserve Adequacy. IMF [Online] 20 May http://www.imf.org/external/np/spr/ara/ [Accessed: October 2017].

International Monetary Fund (2016b). Guidance note on the assessment of reserve adequacy and related considerations. IMF Strategy, Policy and Review Department.

International Monetary Fund (2017). People's Republic of China. IMF Country Report No. 17/247.

J.P. Morgan (2015a). China: PBoC weakened yuan reference rate by 1.86%. Asia Pacific Economic Research.

J.P. Morgan (2015b). EM debt overhang: Mostly domestic, private and in loans. J.P. Morgan European Emerging Markets Research.

J.P. Morgan (2015c). Who's funding China's external borrowing?. J.P. Morgan Economic Research.

Jones, E., & Underhill, G. R. (2014). Theory of optimum financial areas: retooling the debate on the governance of global finance.

Kaminsky, G. L., & Reinhart, C. M. (1999). The twin crises: the causes of banking and balance-of-payments problems. American economic review, 473-500.

Keynes, J. M. (1937). The general theory of employment, interest and money. University of Adelaide Library Etext version.

Kim, O., Maasry, C., Ozerov, M., Tomb, I., Trivedi, K., & Wei, J. (2016). The search for external balance in EM Asia. Goldman Sachs.

Kim, S., & Yamakawa, T. (2005). The "ABC" of Asia's FX regime shift. Goldman Sachs.

Kotecha, M., & Pepper, H. (2014). CNY – Crossing the river by feeling the stones. Barclays.

Krugman, P. R., Obstfeld, M., & Melitz, M. (2015). International Economics, 10th. Edition, Prentice Hall.

Kurumlu, E., Li, S., Hsu, G., & Chu, D. (2015). Baby boosts and consumption – Part II. J.P. Morgan.

Lei, K., Tsui, S., & Rajat, A. (2016). China Financials - China corporate bond defaults: A constructive thought. J.P. Morgan.

Lewis, W. A. (1954). Economic development with unlimited supplies of labour. The manchester school, 22(2), 139-191.

Li, Z., Song, Y., Tang, M., Tilton, A., & Wei, M. (2016a). China's credit boost to growth – How long and how strong? Goldman Sachs.

Li, Z., Song, Y., Tang, M., Tilton, A., & Wei, M. (2016b). SOE reform in China – potentially powerful, practically challenging. Goldman Sachs.

Li, Z., Song, Y., Tang, M., Tilton, A., & Wei, M. (2016c). Sources and sizes of China's capital outflows. Goldman Sachs.

Liu, L. (2016). China: Liberalization bond market access. Deutsche Bank Markets Research.

Liu, L., & Jin, X. (2016a). China Economics View - PBoC reported to have injected RMB3.4trn into policy banks, fiscal policy to stabilize the economy. Citi Research.

Liu, L., & Jin, X. (2016b). China has tightened capital controls again. Citi Research.

Liu, L., & Jin, X. (2016c). How large has the monetary stimulus been so far this year? Citi Research.

Liu, L., & Jin, X. (2016d). RMB's daily fixing rate: Which currency basket does it follow? Citi

Research.

Liu, L., Jin, X., & Ho-Por Lam, K. (2016). China's encumbered FX reserve and reserve adequacy: a reassessment. Citi Research.

Lusardi, A., & Mitchell, O. S. (2011). Financial literacy and planning: Implications for retirement wellbeing (No. w17078). National Bureau of Economic Research.

Ma, G., & Yi, W. (2010). China's high saving rate: myth and reality. Economie internationale, (2), 5-39.

McKinnon, M., (1973). Money and capital in economic development. The Brookings Institute, Washington DC.

McNally, C. A., & Gruin, J. (2017). A novel pathway to power? Contestation and adaptation in China's internationalization of the RMB. Review of International Political Economy, 1-30.

Minkin, R., & Lau, K. (2013). The offshore renminbi. The rise of the Chinese currency and its global future. John Wiley & Sons Singapore.

Mukand, S., & Rodrik, D. (2002). In search of the holy grail: policy convergence, experimentation, and economic performance (No. w9134). National Bureau of Economic Research.

Naughton, B. (2007). The Chinese economy: Transitions and growth. MIT Press.

Nishimura, K. G. (2012). Ageing, Finance and Regulations. In Keynote Address at the Joint Forum Meeting, Tokyo, November (pp. 14-15).

North, D. C. (1990). Institutions, Institutional Change and Economic Performance. Cambridge University Press.

Nurkse, R. (1944). International currency experience: lessons of the interwar period (No. 4). League of Nations.

O'Neill, J. (2001). Building better global economic BRICs. London: Goldman Sachs Economics Research, Global Economics Paper No. 66.

Orlik, T. (2012). Understanding China's economic indicators: Translating the data into investment opportunities. Pearson Education.

Pang, K. (2016). China SOE: Taking a closer look at China's debt-to-equity swap plan. Morgan Stanley.

Paris, R. (2004). At war's end: building peace after civil conflict. Cambridge University Press.

Park, A., Wang, S., & Wu, G. (2002). Regional poverty targeting in China. Journal of Public Economics, vol. 86, issue 1 (October), pp. 123-53.

Quah, D. (2011). The global economy's shifting centre of gravity. Global Policy, 2(1), 3-9.

Quah, D. (2013). Is China's economy crashing?. BOAO Review (October): 18–21.

Quinn, D. (1997). The correlates of change in international financial regulation. American Political science review, 91(3), 531-551.

Quinn, D. P. (2003). Capital account liberalization and financial globalization, 1890–1999: a synoptic view. International Journal of Finance & Economics, 8(3), 189-204.

Ravallion, M., & Chen, S. (2004). China's (uneven) progress against poverty. World Bank Policy Research Working Paper 3408, September.

Rawski, T. G. (2001). What is happening to China's GDP statistics?. China Economic Review, 12(4), 347-354.

Reinhart, C. M., & Rogoff, K. S. (2009). This time is different: Eight centuries of financial folly. Princeton University Press.

Roland, G. (2000). Transition and Economics: Politics, Markets, and Firms. MIT Press.

Saborowski, C., Sanya, S., Weisfeld, H., & Yepez, J. (2014). Effectiveness of Capital Outflow Restrictions (No. 14-18). International Monetary Fund.

Schlichting, S. (2008). Internationalising China's financial markets. Springer.

Sedik, T. S., & Sun, T. (2012). Effects of Capital Flow Liberalization: What is the Evidence from Recent Experiences of Emerging Market Economies? (No. 12-275). International Monetary Fund.

Sen, K. (2016). The determinants of structural transformation in Asia: A review of the literature. ADB Economics Working Paper Series No. 478.

Sequeira, J., & Tilton, A. (2016). Lessons for China from 150 Years of Debt Booms. Goldman Sachs.

Shambaugh, D. (2014). The illusion of Chinese power. The National Interest [Online] http://nationalinterest.org/feature/the-illusion-chinese-power-10739 [Accessed: October 2017].

Sharma, R. (2012). Broken BRICs: Why the rest stopped rising. Foreign Affairs, 2-7.

Stiglitz, J. E. (2003). Globalization and its discontents. London: Penguin Books.

Subramanian, A. (2011). The inevitable superpower: Why China's dominance is a sure thing. Foreign Affairs.

Tao, D. & Deng, W. (2015). China: The PBoC devalues the CNY by 1.9%. Credit Suisse.

The Economist (2013). Monks without a temple. The Economist [Online] 16 March. http://www.

economist.com/news/china/21573579-china-may-have-begun-long-end-game-its-one-child-policy-experts-say-it-cannot-end-soon [Accessed: October 2017].

The Economist (2015a). Pulled back in. The Economist [Online] 14 November http://www.economist.com/news/briefing/21678215-world-entering-third-stage-rolling-debt-crisis-time-centred-emerging [Accessed: October 2017].

The Economist (2015b). Pricing risk. The Economist [Online] 28 November. http://www.economist.com/news/21679097-debt-issuance-booms-despite-wave-defaults-chinese-bond-market-bubbling [Accessed: October 2017].

The Economist (2015c). Maiden Voyage. The Economist [Online] 5 December. http://www.economist.com/news/business-and-finance/21679341-its-new-status-might-make-weaker-yuan-chinese-renminbi-joins-imfs [Accessed: October 2017].

The Economist (2016a). Three wise men. The Economist [Online] 9 January. http://www.economist.com/news/china/21685511-ageing-reformists-diagnose-economys-ills-three-wise-men [Accessed: October 2017].

The Economist (2016b). A crisis of faith. The Economist [Online] 16 January http://www.economist.com/news/briefing/21688399-their-response-wobbly-markets-chinas-leaders-reveal-their-fears-crisis-faith [Accessed: October 2017].

The Economist (2016c). The yuan and the markets. The Economist [Online] 16 January. http://www.economist.com/news/leaders/21688396-strains-currency-suggest-something-very-wrong-chinas-politics-yuan-and [Accessed: October 2017].

The Economist (2017a). A big Chinese province admits faking its economic data. The Economist [Online] 26 January. https://www.economist.com/news/finance-and-economics/21715688-typical-say-cynics-cleaning-up-last-say-optimists-big-chinese-province [Accessed: October 2017].

The Economist (2017b). China's state enterprises are not retreating but advancing. The Economist [Online] 20 July. China's state enterprises are not retreating but advancing. The Economist [Accessed: October 2017].

The Economist (2017c). The link between poor harvests and violence. The Economist [Online] 27 July. https://www.economist.com/news/finance-and-economics/21725593-historically-there-were-more-anti-semitic-attacks-when-crops-failed-link [Accessed: October 2017].

The Economist (2017d). How crisis-hit economies become investment darlings. The Economist [Online] 3 August. https://www.economist.com/news/finance-and-economics/21725777-basket-cases-frontier-economies-how-about-phoenixes-how-crisis-hit-economies [Accessed: October 2017].

The Economist (2017e). China modernises its monetary policy. The Economist [Online] 17 August. https://www.economist.com/news/finance-and-economics/21726723-little-imperial-inspiration-china-shifts-more-market-based [Accessed: October 2017].

The Economist (2017f). Making sense of capacity cuts in China. The Economist [Online] 9 September. https://www.economist.com/news/leaders/21728640-investors-have-been-cheeredsweeping-cutbacks-they-should-look-more-closely-making-sense [Accessed: October 2017].

The Economist (2017g). China's demographic divisions are getting deeper. The Economist [Online] 21 September. https://www.economist.com/news/china/21729573-no-province-has-many-babies-some-shortfalls-are-much-worse-others-chinas-demographic [Accessed: October 2017].

The Economist (2017h). How China is battling ever more intensely in world markets. The Economist [Online] 23 September. https://www.economist.com/news/leaders/21729430-does-it-play-fair-how-china-battling-ever-more-intensely-world-markets [Accessed: October 2017].

Tilton, A., Kwon, G., Poddar, T., Song, Y., Tang, M., Siregar, R., Droumaguet, M., Sequeira, J., Wei, M., Vaibhaw, V., Chawla, M., & Choi, I. (2015). Asia Economics Analyst, China's bumpy deceleration continues, pulling region along for the ride. Goldman Sachs.

Viñals, J., & Singh, A. (2011). People's Republic of China: Financial system stability assessment. In IMF Country Report No. 11/321.

Wang, V., & Zhao, Y. (2016). CSRC announces new rules to curb sales of A-shares by major shareholders.

Wilson, D., & Purushothaman, R. (2003). Dreaming with BRICs: The path to 2050 (Vol. 99). New York, NY: Goldman, Sachs & Company.

Wohlforth, W. C., & Kang, D. C. (2009). Hypotheses on status competition. APSA 2009 Toronto Meeting Paper.

Wong, C., & Bird, R. (2008). China's fiscal system: a work in progress. China's great economic transformation, 429-466.

Woods, N. (1995). Economic ideas and international relations: beyond rational neglect. International Studies Quarterly 39 (1995), p. 161-180.

Wright, L. H. (2009). The elusive price of stability: ideas and interests in the reform of China's exchange rate regime. Dissertation at The George Washington University.

Wu, H. X. (2014, January). China's Growth and Productivity Performance Debate Revisited. In The Conference Board Economics Working Papers (No. 14-01).

Zeng, L., & Zhang, Z. (2016a). China: Unveiling the channels of capital outflows. Deutsche Bank Research.

Zeng, L., & Zhang, Z. (2016b). China tail series IV: Credit tightening started. Deutsche Bank Research.

Quantitative Case Study

Areddy, J., King, N., Kissel, M., & Dean, J. (2005). Behind yuan move, open debate and closed doors. Wall Street Journal, 25 July 2005.

Barnett, M., & Finnemore, M. (2004). Rules for the world: international organizations in global politics. Ithaca, NY: Cornell University Press, p. 45-72.

Beachy, B. (2012). A Financial Crisis Manual Causes, Consequences, and Lessons of the Financial Crisis (No. 12-06). GDAE, Tufts University.

Blyth, M. (2002). Great transformations: economic ideas and institutional change in the twentieth century. Cambridge University Press.

Chamon, M., Ghosh, A., & Kim, J. (2012). Are All Emerging Market Crises Alike?. Global Economic Crisis: Impacts, Transmission, Recovery, Cheltenham, UK: Edward Elgar.

Chwieroth, J. (2007). Neoliberal economists and capital account liberalization in emerging markets. International organization, 61(2), 443-463.

Eichengreen, B. (1993). The endogeneity of exchange rate regimes (No. w4361). National Bureau of Economic Research.

Fearon, J. D. (1991). Counterfactuals and hypothesis testing in political science. World Politics 43 (2).

Fravel, M. T., & Medeiros, E. S. (2003). China's New Diplomacy. Foreign Affairs, 82(6), 22-35.

Ghosh, M. A. R., Zalduendo, M. J., Thomas, M. A. H., Kim, M. J. I., Ramakrishnan, M. U., & Joshi, B. (2008). IMF Support and Crisis Prevention (No. 262). International Monetary Fund.

Ghosh, S. R., & Ghosh, A. R. (2003). Structural vulnerabilities and currency crises. IMF Staff Papers, 481-506.

Goldstein, M., & Lardy, N. R. (2008a). China's exchange rate policy: an overview of some key issues. In Goldstein, M., & Lardy, N. R. (2008). Debating China's exchange rate policy. Peterson Institute, p. 1-76.

Goldstein, M., & Lardy, N. R. (2008b). Debating China's exchange rate policy. Peterson Institute.

Haas, P. (1992). Introduction: epistemic communities and international policy coordination. International Organization 46:1 (1992).

Hall, P. (1993). Policy paradigms, social learning, and the state: the case of economic policymaking in Britain. Comparative Politics 25, April 1993, p. 275-296.

Ikenberry, G. J., & Kupchan, C. (1990). Socialization and hegemonic power. International Organization 44:3.

Jacobson, H., & Oksenberg, M. (1990). China's participation in the IMF, the World Bank, and GATT: toward a global economic order. University of Michigan Press.

Liew, L. H. (2004). Policy elites in the political economy of China's exchange rate policymaking. Journal of Contemporary China 13, February 2004.

McNamara, K. (1999). The currency of ideas. Ithaca, NY: Cornell University Press.

McNamara, K. (2002). Rational fictions: Central bank independence and the social logic of delegation. West European politics, 25(1), 47-76.

Minkin, R., & Lau, K. (2013). The offshore renminbi. The rise of the Chinese currency and its global future. John Wiley & Sons Singapore.

Prasad, E. S. (2017). Gaining currency. The rise of the renminbi. Oxford University Press.

Wohlforth, W. C., & Kang, D. C. (2009). Hypotheses on status competition. Toronto Meeting Paper.

Woods, N. (1995). Economic ideas and international relations: beyond rational neglect. International Studies Quarterly 39 (1995), p. 161-180.

Wright, L. H. (2009). The elusive price of stability: ideas and interests in the reform of China's exchange rate regime. Dissertation at The George Washington University.

Acemoglu, D. (2004). Understanding Institutions - Lionel Robbins Lecture at LSE. MIT Department of Economics [Online] February 2004 http://economics.mit.edu/files/1353 [Accessed: September 2017].

Acemoglu, D., & Robinson, J. A. (2013). Why nations fail: The origins of power, prosperity, and poverty. Crown Business.

Ades, A., Masih, R., & Tenengauzer, D. (1998). GS Watch: A New Framework for Predicting Financial Crises in Emerging Markets. New York: Goldman Sachs.

Aghion, P., Bacchetta, P., & Banerjee, A. (2001). Currency crises and monetary policy in an economy with credit constraints. European economic review, 45(7), 1121-1150.

Alba, P., Bhattacharya, A., Claessens, S., Ghosh, S., & Hernandez, L. (1998). Volatility and contagion in a financially integrated world: lessons from East Asia's recent experience (No. 2008). World Bank, Poverty Reduction and Economic Management Network, Economic Policy Unit.

Angkinand, A., Li, J., & Willett, T. (2006). Measures of currency crises: A survey. Forthcomming in: International Interaction.

Atkinson, A. B. (2015). Inequality: what can be done?. Harvard University Press.

Berg, A., & Pattillo, C. (1999). Are currency crises predictable? A test. IMF Staff papers, 46(2), 107-138.

Blyth, M. (2002). Great transformations: economic ideas and institutional change in the twentieth century. Cambridge University Press.

Bordo, M. D., & Jeanne, O. (2002). Boom-busts in asset prices, economic instability, and monetary policy (No. w8966). National Bureau of Economic Research.

Breslin, S. (2014). China plays politics with debt while the West holds its breath. [Online] 13 February. http://theconversation.com/china-plays-politics-with-debt-while-the-west-holds-itsbreath-22374 [Accessed: October 2017].

Brüggemann, A., & Linne, T. (1999). How good are leading indicators for currency and banking crises in Central and Eastern Europe? An empirical test (No. 95). IWH Discussion Papers.

Brüggemann, A., & Linne, T. (2002). Are the Central and Eastern European transition countries still vulnerable to a financial crisis? Results from the signals approach.

Brunnermeier, M. K., & Schnabel, I. (2015). Bubbles and central banks: Historical perspectives.

Callaghy, T. (1993) 'Political passions and economic interests: economic reform and political structure in Africa' in Callaghy T. M. and Ravenhill J. (eds.) Hemmed in: Responses to Africa's Economic Decline (New York: Columbia University Press)

Calvo, G. A., Leiderman, L. and Reinhart, C.M. (1994) 'The capital inflows problem: Concepts and issues' Contemporary Economic Policy (12:3), 54-66.

Calvo, G., & Reinhart, C. (1999). Capital flow reversals, the exchange rate debate, and dollarization. Finance & Development, September 1999.

Calvo, G., Goldstein, M., & Hochreiter, E. (1996). Private capital flows to emerging markets after the Mexican crisis. Peterson Institute for International Economics.

Caprio, G., & Klingebiel, D. (2003). Episodes of Systemic and Borderline Financial Crises. World Bank, January 22.

Catão, L., & Sutton, B. (2002). Sovereign defaults: the role of volatility. International Monetary Fund.

Chamon, M., Ghosh, A., & Kim, J. (2012). Are All Emerging Market Crises Alike?. Global Economic Crisis: Impacts, Transmission, Recovery, Cheltenham, UK: Edward Elgar.

Chamon, M., Ghosh, A., Habermeier, K., Ostry, J., Qureshi, M., & Reinhart, B. (2010). Capital inflows: the role of controls. IMF Staff Position Note, 2010.

Chang, R., & Velasco, A. (1998). Financial crises in emerging markets (No. w6606). National Bureau of Economic Research.

Chen, M., Ng, G., & Zhu, H. (2016a). China: First working day is a stress test on the new trading mechanism in equity and FX markets. J.P. Morgan.

CQF Lectures, 2013. Certificate in Quantitative Finance. Fitch Learning. CQF Institute.

DeRosa, D. F. (2009). Central Banking and Monetary Policy in Emerging-Markets Nations.

Diamond, R. (2013). Introduction to principal component analysis (PCA). Certificate in Quantitative Finance. Fitch Learning. CQF Institute.

Dornbusch, R., Goldfajn, I., Valdés, R. O., Edwards, S., & Bruno, M. (1995). Currency crises and collapses. Brookings Papers on Economic Activity, 1995(2), 219-293.

Drazen, A. (2000). Political contagion in currency crises. In Currency crises (pp. 47-67). University of Chicago Press.

Eichengreen, B., & Hausmann, R. (1999). Exchange rates and financial fragility (No. w7418). National bureau of economic research.

Eichengreen, B., & Wyplosz, C. (1993). The Unstable EMS. Brookings Papers on Economic Activity, 51-143.

Eichengreen, B., Rose, A. K., & Wyplosz, C. (1994). Speculative attacks on pegged exchange rates: an empirical exploration with special reference to the European Monetary System (No. w4898). National Bureau of economic research.

Eichengreen, B., Rose, A. K., & Wyplosz, C. (1995). Exchange market mayhem: The antecedents and aftermath of speculative attacks. Economic Policy, 249-312.

Eichengreen, B., Rose, A. K., & Wyplosz, C. (1996). Contagious currency crises (No. w5681). National bureau of economic research.

Fairbank, J. K., & Goldman, M. (2006). China: A new history. Harvard University Press.

Feenstra, R. C., and Taylor, A.M. (2014) International Economics 3rd Edition (New York: Worth Macmillan).

Flood, R. P., & Garber, P. M. (1984). Collapsing exchange-rate regimes: some linear examples. Journal of international Economics, 17(1-2), 1-13.

Frankel, J. A., & Rose, A. K. (1996). Currency crashes in emerging markets: An empirical treatment. Journal of international Economics, 41(3), 351-366.

Gerring, J. (2008). Case selection for case-study analysis: qualitative and quantitative techniques. In The Oxford Handbook of Political Methodology, 645-684.

Ghosh, A. R., Ostry, J. D., & Tamirisa, N. (2009). Anticipating the next crisis - What can early warning systems be expected to deliver?. Finance & Development, 46(3), 35-37.

Ghosh, M. A. R., Zalduendo, M. J., Thomas, M. A. H., Kim, M. J. I., Ramakrishnan, M. U., & Joshi, B. (2008). IMF Support and Crisis Prevention (No. 262). International Monetary Fund.

Ghosh, S. R., & Ghosh, A. R. (2003). Structural vulnerabilities and currency crises. IMF Staff Papers, 481-506.

Goldfajn, I., & Valdés, R. (1998). Balance of Payments Crises and Capital Flows: The Role of Liquidity (No. 11). Central Bank of Chile.

Goldstein, M. (1998). The Asian financial crisis: Causes, cures, and systemic implications (Vol.

55). Peterson Institute.

Goldstein, M., Kaminsky, G. L., & Reinhart, C. M. (2000). Assessing financial vulnerability: an early warning system for emerging markets. Peterson Institute.

Gruin, J. (2013) 'Asset or liability? The role of the financial system in the political economy of China's rebalancing' Journal of Current Chinese Affairs,(42:4), 73-104

Gruin, J. (2016) 'The social order of Chinese capitalism: socio-economic uncertainty, communist party rule and economic development, 1990–2000', Economy and Society, 45(1), 24-50

Hardoon, D., Ayele, A., & Fuentes-Nieva, R. (2016). An economy for the 1%. Oxfam Briefing Paper.

Heilmann, S. (2008). Policy Experimentation in China's Economic Rise, In: Studies in Comparative International Development (SCID), Vol. 43, No. 1 (Januar 2008): p. 1-26.

Hurrell, A. (2009) 'Rising Powers and the Question of Status in International Society' in Annual Meeting of the International Studies Association (February 2009: 5-18)

Hurrell, A. (2014). Rising Powers and the Emerging Global, in Baylis, J., Smith, S., & Owens P. (eds.), The Globalization of World Politics: an introduction to international relations, 6th Edition. Oxford: Oxford University Press, 80-94.

International Monetary Fund (1998). World Economic Outlook. Washington: IMF.

International Monetary Fund (2002). Global Financial Stability Report. Early Warning System Models: The Next Steps Forward. International Monetary Fund, Publication Services, Washington.

Jones, E., & Underhill, G. R. (2014). Theory of Optimum Financial Areas: Retooling the Debate on the Governance of Global Finance.

J.P. Morgan (2015a). China: PBoC weakened yuan reference rate by 1.86%. Asia Pacific Economic Research.

J.P. Morgan (2015b). EM debt overhang: Mostly domestic, private and in loans. J.P. Morgan European Emerging Markets Research.

J.P. Morgan (2015c). Who's funding China's external borrowing?. J.P. Morgan Economic Research.

Kaminsky, G. L., & Reinhart, C. M. (1998). Financial crises in Asia and Latin America: Then and now. The American Economic Review, 88(2), 444-448.

Kaminsky, G. L., & Reinhart, C. M. (1999). The twin crises: the causes of banking and balance-of-payments problems. American economic review, 473-500.

Kaminsky, G. L., Lizondo, S., & Reinhart, C. M. (1998). Leading indicators of currency crises. Staff Papers, 45(1), 1-48.

Kaminsky, G. L., Reinhart, C.M. and Végh, C.A (2004) When it rains, it pours: procyclical capital flows and macroeconomic policies. National Bureau of Economic Research No. w10780

Kindleberger, C. P. (1978). Manias, panics, and crashes: A history of financial crises. New York: Basic Books.

Kornai, J. (1994). Transformational recession: the main causes. Journal of Comparative Economics 19, 39-63.

Krugman, P. (1979). A model of balance-of-payments crises. Journal of money, credit and banking, 11(3), 311-325.

Krugman, P. (2001). Crises: the next generation. Razin Conference, Tel Aviv University.

Krugman, P. R., Obstfeld, M., & Melitz, M. (2015). International Economics, 10th. Edition, Prentice Hall.

Lardy, N. (2008). Financial Repression in China. Peterson Institute Working Paper.

Lardy, N. R. (2012). Sustaining China's economic growth after the global financial crisis. Peterson Institute.

Manasse, P., Roubini, N., & Schimmelpfennig, A. (2003). Predicting sovereign debt crises.

McKinnon, R. (1973). Money and Capital in Economic Development. Washington, DC: Brookings Institution.

McKinnon, R. I., & Pill, H. (1996). Credible Liberalizations and International Capital Flows: The" Overborrowing Syndrome". In Financial Deregulation and Integration in East Asia, NBER-EASE Volume 5 (pp. 7-50). University of Chicago Press.

McNally, C. A., & Gruin, J. (2017). A novel pathway to power? Contestation and adaptation in China's internationalization of the RMB. Review of International Political Economy, 1-30.

Meese, R. A., & Rogoff, K. (1983). Empirical exchange rate models of the seventies: Do they fit out of sample?. Journal of International Economics, 14(1-2), 3-24.

Minsky, H., P. (1977). The financial instability hypothesis: an interpretation of Keynes and alternative to standard theory. Challenge (March-April): 20-27.

Mukand, S., & Rodrik, D. (2002). In search of the holy grail: policy convergence, experimentation, and economic performance (No. w9134). National Bureau of Economic Research.

Naughton, B. (2007). The Chinese Economy: Transitions and Growth. MIT press.

North, D. C. (1990). Institutions, institutional change and economic performance. Cambridge university press.

North, D. C. (2006). Understanding the process of economic change. Academic Foundation.

Obstfeld, M. (1986). Rational and self-fulfilling balance-of-payments crises. American economic review, 76, No. 1, pp. 161-177.

OECD (2012). OECD employment outlook 2012. OECD Publishing.

Orlik, T. (2012). Understanding China's Economic Indicators: Translating the Data into Investment Opportunities. Pearson Education.

Paris, R. (2004) At war's end: building peace after civil conflict (Cambridge: Cambridge University Press).

Pesenti, P. A., & Tille, C. (2000). The economics of currency crises and contagion: An introduction.
Prasad, E. S. (2017). Gaining Currency: The Rise of the Renminbi. Oxford University Press.

Reinhart, C. M. (2002). Default, currency crises, and sovereign credit ratings. the world bank economic review, 16(2), 151-170.

Reinhart, C. M., & Rogoff, K. S. (2004). The modern history of exchange rate arrangements: a reinterpretation. the Quarterly Journal of economics, 119(1), 1-48.

Reinhart, C. M., & Rogoff, K. S. (2009). This time is different: Eight centuries of financial folly. Princeton University Press.

Reynolds, L. G. (1983). The spread of economic growth to the Third World: 1850-1980. Journal of economic literature, 21(3), 941-980.

Roland, G. (2000). Transition and Economics: Politics, Markets, and Firms. MIT Press.

Schularick, M., & Taylor, A. (2012). Credit booms gone bust: monetary policy, leverage cycles, and financial crises, 1870-2008. American Economic Review 102(2): 1029-61.

Sharma, R. (2016). The Rise and Fall of Nations: Forces of Change in the Post-crisis World. WW Norton & Company.

Solow, R. (1957). Technical change and the aggregate production function.

Stiglitz, J. (2000). Capital market liberalization, economic growth, and instability. World Development, 28, 1075-1086.

Stiglitz, J. E. (2002) Globalization and its Discontents (London: Penguin Books)

Woods, N. (2014). International political economy in an age of globalization, in Baylis, J., Smith, S., & Owens P. (eds.), The Globalization of World Politics: an introduction to international relations, 6th Edition. Oxford: Oxford University Press, 243-257.

China in Constant Transition

Amsden, A. H. (1992). Asia's next giant: South Korea and late industrialization. Oxford University Press on Demand.

Asian Development Bank (2017a). The Asian bond markets initiative. Policy makers achievements and challenges. Manila, Philippines.

Asian Development Bank (2017b). Transforming toward a high-income people's republic of China. Challenges and recommendations.

Bai, C.-E., & Zhang, Q. (2017). Is the People's Republic of China's current slowdown a cyclical downturn or a long-term trend? A productivity based analysis. ADBI Working Paper Series.

Barnett, M. N., & Finnemore, M. (1999). The politics, power, and pathologies of international organizations. International organization, 53(4), 699-732.

Bayoumi, T., & Eichengreen, B. (1997). Optimum currency areas and exchange rate volatility: theory and evidence compared. In Cohen, B. (ed.). International trade and finance: new frontiers of research. Cambridge University Press, pp. 184-215.

Berglof, E. (1997). Boardrooms: reforming corporate governance in Europe. Economic Policy, vol. 24. (Apr): 91-123. Centre for Economic Policy Research.

Besley, T., & Kudamatsu, M. (2007). Making autocracy work. London School of Economics and Political Science

Blanchard, O. J., & Johnson, D. (2013). Macroeconomics. Sixth Edition. Pearson Education.

Bloomberg (2012). China's urban population exceeds countryside for first time. https://www.bloomberg.com/news/articles/2012-01-17/china-urban-population-exceeds-rural

Boone, P., & Hørder, J. (1998). Inflation: causes, consequences, and cures. In: Boone, P., Gomulka, S., & Layard, R. (Eds.). (1998). Emerging from Communism: Lessons from Russia, China, and Eastern Europe. MIT Press.

Boone, P., Gomulka, S., & Layard, R. (Eds.). (1998). Emerging from Communism: Lessons from Russia, China, and Eastern Europe. MIT Press.

Caprio, G., Honohan, P., & Stiglitz, J. E. (Eds.). (2006). Financial liberalization: how far, how fast?. Cambridge University Press.

Chen, C., Chang, L., & Zhang, Y. M. (1995). The Role of Foreign Direct Investment in China Post-1978 Economic Development. World Development, 23/4: 691-703.

Citi Research (2017). China economics & multi-asset view. Capital markets opening: what it means for assets/financials.

Claessens, S., Kose, M. M. A., Laeven, M. L., & Valencia, F. (2014). Financial crises: Causes, consequences, and policy responses. International Monetary Fund.

Cliff, R. (1998). China´s Potential for Developing Advanced Military Technology. July 8, Santa Monica: RAND Corporation.

De Jonquières, G. (2014). The problematic politics of China's economic reform plans. European Centre for International Political Economy (ECIPE), (5/2014), 1-8.

Demirgüç-Kunt, A., & Detragiache, E. (1998). Financial liberalization and financial fragility. IMF Working Paper 98/83.

DeRosa, D. F. (2009). Central Banking and Monetary Policy in Emerging-Markets Nations.

Detragiache, E., & Spilimbergo, A. (2001). Crises and liquidity: evidence and interpretation. IMF Working Paper 01/2. Washington, DC: International Monetary Fund.

Detragiache, E., & Spilimbergo, A. (2004). Empirical models of short-term debt and crises: Do they test the creditor run hypothesis?. European Economic Review, 48(2), 379-389.

Deyo, F. C. (Ed.). (1987). The political economy of the new Asian industrialism. Cornell University Press.

Eichengreen, B. (2006). China's exchange rate regime: the long and short of it. University of California, Berkeley.

Eichengreen, B., Park, D., & Shin, K. (2011). When fast growing economies slow down: international evidence and implications for China. NBER Working Paper Series.

Eichengreen, B., Park, D., & Shin, K. (2013). Growth slowdown redux: new evidence on the middle-income trap. NBER Working Paper Series.

Estrin, S. (1998). Privatization and restructuring in Central and Eastern Europe. In: Boone, P., Gomulka, S., & Layard, R. (Eds.). (1998). Emerging from Communism: Lessons from Russia, China, and Eastern Europe. MIT Press.

European Bank for Reconstruction and Development (2016). Transition Report 2016-17. Transition for all: equal opportunities in an unequal world.

Evans, P. B. (2012). Embedded autonomy: States and industrial transformation. Princeton University Press.

Feigenbaum, E. (1999). Soldiers, Weapons and Chinese Development Strategy: the Mao Era Military in China´s Economic and Institutional Debate. China Quarterly, 158 (June), 285-313.

Feinstein, C., & Howe, C. (1997). Chinese Technology Transfer in the 1990s. Edward Elgar Publishing.

Felipe, J., & McCombie, J. (2017). The debate about the sources of growth in East Asia after a quarter of a century: much ado about nothing. Asian Development Bank.

Felmingham, B. S., & Zhang, Q. (2002). The Role of FDI, Exports and Spillover Effects in the Regional Development of China. Journal of Development Studies, 38/4: 157-78.

Fischer, W. A., & Von Zedtwitz, M. (2004). Chinese R&D: Naissance, Renaissance, or Mirage?. R&D Management, 34(4), 349-365.

Fisher-Vanden, K., & Jefferson, G. H. (2008). Technology Diversity and Development: Evidence from China's Industrial Enterprises. Journal of Comparative Economics, 36(4), 658-672.

Frankel, J. (2005). On the renminbi: the choice between adjustment under a fixed exchange rate and adjustment under a flexible rate. NBER WP No. 11274, National Bureau of Economic Research, Cambridge, MA.

Gerschenkron, A. (1964). Economic backwardness in historical perspective. Cambridge: Harvard University Press.

Gilboy, G. J. (2004). The Myth Behind China's Miracle. Foreign Affairs, 33-48.

Gill, I., & Kharas, H. (2007). An East Asian renaissance. The World Bank.

Glawe, L., & Wagner, H. (2017). The people's republic of China? In the middle-income trap?. Asian Development Bank.

Gochoco-Bautista, M. S., & Fabella, R. V. (2006). What type of monetary and exchange rate cooperation do China's Asian neighbours want from China?. University of the Philippines Discussion Paper, no. 2006, 04.

Goldstein, M., & Lardy, N. (2006). China's exchange rate policy dilemma. American Economic Review, vo. 96(2), pp. 422-26.

Gomulka, S. (1998). Output: causes of the decline and the recovery. In: Boone, P., Gomulka, S., & Layard, R. (Eds.). (1998). Emerging from Communism: Lessons from Russia, China, and Eastern Europe. MIT Press.

Grable, J. E., Lyons, A. C., & Zeng, T. (2017). Infrastructure, urbanization, and demand for bank and non-bank loans of households in the people's republic of China. Asian Development Bank Institute.

Grossman, G. M., & Helpman, E. (1991). Innovation and Growth in the Global Economy. Cambridge, Massachusetts: MIT Press.

Guibaud, S., Jin, K., & Coeurdacier, N. 2014). Fertility policies and social security reforms in China.

Gylfason, T. (1999). Exports, Inflation and Growth. World Development, 27/6: 1031-57.

Haggard, S. (1990). Pathways from the periphery: The politics of growth in the newly industrializing countries. Cornell University Press.

Haggard, S., & Simmons, B. A. (1987). Theories of international regimes. International organization, 41(3), 491-517.

Hall, P. A. (1983). Policy innovation and the structure of the State: The politics-administration nexus in France and Britain. The Annals of the American Academy of Political and Social Science, 466(1), 43-59.

Hall, P. A. (1993). Policy paradigms, social learning, and the state: the case of economic policymaking in Britain. Comparative politics, 275-296.

Heilmann, S. (2008a). From local experiments to national policy: The origins of China's distinctive policy process. The China Journal, (59), 1-30.

Heilmann, S. (2008b). Policy Experimentation in China's Economic Rise, In: Studies in Comparative International Development (SCID), Vol. 43, No. 1 (Januar 2008): p. 1-26.

Heilmann, S., Shih, L., & Hofem, A. (2013). National planning and local technology zones: Experimental governance in China's Torch Programme.
The China Quarterly, 216, 896-919.

Henning, C. R. (2012). Choice and coercion in East Asian exchange rate regimes. Peterson Institute for International Economics Working Paper. WP 12-15.

Hu, A. G., & Jefferson, G. H. (2009). A Great Wall of Patents: What Is Behind China´s Recent Patent Explosion. Journal of Development Economics, 90/1: 57-68.

Hu, A. G., Jefferson, G. H., & Jinchang, Q. (2005). R&D and Technology Transfer: Firm-Level Evidence from Chinese Industry. The Review of Economics and Statistics, 87(4), 780-786.

Huang, Q., Huang, Y., He, J., Jiang, F., & Liu, G. (2017). The middle-income trap and the manufacturing transformation of the people's republic of China (PRC): Asian experience and the PRC's industrial policy orientation. Asian Development Bank.

Hurrell, A. (2009). Rising powers and the question of status in international society. In Annual Meeting of the International Studies Association, pp. 15-18.

Ikenberry, G. J. (1994). History's heavy hand: institutions and the politics of the state.

Ilzetzki, E., Reinhart, C., & Rogoff, K. (2010). Exchange rate arrangements entering the 21st century: which anchor will hold?. London School of Economics.

International Monetary Fund (1999). Capital market development, Washington D.C.

International Monetary Fund (2014). Annual report on exchange rate arrangements and exchange restrictions (ARREAR). Washington, DC: IMF.

International Monetary Fund (2016). Articles of agreement. IMF Washington, D.C.

Ito, T. (2011). The internationalization of the renminbi: opportunities and pitfalls. Council of

Foreign Relations, Washington D.C.

Jin, K. (2016). Clear and present challenges to the Chinese economy. Public lecture LSE on 9 March 2016.

Jin, X., & Liu, L.-G. (2017). Economics view. In Citi Research (2017). China economics & multi-asset view. Capital markets opening: what it means for assets/financials, 3-24.

Jin, X., & Liu, L.-G. (2017). Economics view. In Citi Research (2017). China economics & multi-asset view. Capital markets opening: what it means for assets/financials, 3-24.

Jones, C. I. (2011). Misallocation, economic growth, and input-output economics. National Bureau of Economic Research Working Paper w16742. Cambridge: MA: NBER.

Kaminsky, G. L., & Reinhart, C. M. (1999). The twin crises: the causes of banking and balance-of-payments problems. American Economic Review, 473-500.

Katzenstein, P. J. (1996). Cultural norms and national security: Police and military in postwar Japan. Cornell University Press.

Kenen, P. (1969). The theory of optimum currency areas: an eclectic view. In Mundell, R., & Swoboda, A. (eds.). Monetary problems of the international economy. University of Chicago Press, pp. 41-60.

Knaack, P., & Gruin, J. Y. (2017). From shadown banking to digital financial inclusion: regulatory framework contestation between China and the FSB. GEG Working Paper 134, Oxford.

Kornai, J. (1980). Economics of shortage. Amsterdam: North Holland.

Kornai, J. (1994). Transformational recession: the main causes. Journal of Comparative Economics 19(1) 39-63.

Krugman, P. R., Obstfeld, M., & Melitz, M. (2015). International Economics, 10th. Edition, Prentice Hall.

Kumhof, M., Rancière, R., & Winant, P. (2015). Inequality, leverage, and crises. American Economic Review 2015, 105(3): 1217-1245.

Kuo, C. C., & Yang, C. H. (2008). Knowledge Capital and Spillover on Regional Economic Growth: Evidence from China. China Economic Review, 19/4: 594-604.

Lai, M., Peng, S., & Bao, Q. (2006). Technology Spillovers, Absorptive Capacity and Economic Growth. China Economic Review, 17/3: 300-20.

Lam, D. (2017). Insurance sector implications & outlook. In Citi Research (2017). China economics & multi-asset view. Capital markets opening: what it means for assets/financials, 54-70.

Lardy, N. R. (2012). Sustaining China's economic growth after the global financial crisis. Peterson Institute.

Layard, R. (1998). Why so much pain? Overview. In: Boone, P., Gomulka, S., & Layard, R. (Eds.). (1998). Emerging from Communism: Lessons from Russia, China, and Eastern Europe. MIT Press.

Liao, T. X. (2017). Commodities market implications & outlook. In Citi Research (2017). China economics & multi-asset view. Capital markets opening: what it means for assets/financials, 35-39.

Lin, J. Y. (2012). Demystifying the Chinese economy. Cambridge University Press.

Lindblom, C. E. (1959). The science of' muddling through". Public administration review, 79-88.

Lindgren, C. J., Garcia, G. G., & Saal, M. I. (1996). Bank soundness and macroeconomic policy. International Monetary Fund.

Lissakers, K. (1999). The IMF and the Asian crisis: A view from the executive board. The Asian Financial Crisis: Origins, Implications, and Solutions, 1. Springer US.

Liu, X., & White, S. (2001). Comparing Innovation Systems: A Framework and Application to China's Transitional Context. Research policy, 30(7), 1091-1114.

Mathur, S., & Sun, L. (2017). Rates market implications & outlook. In Citi Research (2017). China economics & multi-asset view. Capital markets opening: what it means for assets/ financials, 25-34.

McKinnon, R. (1963). Optimum currency areas. American Economic review 53, pp. 717-725.

McKinnon, R. (1973). Money and capital in economic development. Washington, DC: Brookings Institution.

McKinnon, R., & Schnabl, G. (2014). China's exchange rate and financial repression: the conflicted emergence of the renminbi as an international currency. China & World Economy, vol. 22(2), pp. 1-35.

McMillan, J., & Naughton, B. (1992). How to reform a planned economy: lessons from China. Oxford Review of Economic Policy, 8(1), 130-143.

McNally, C. A., & Gruin, J. (2017). A novel pathway to power? Contestation and adaptation in China's internationalization of the RMB. Review of International Political Economy, 1-30.

Milesi-Ferretti, M. G. M., & Lane, M. P. R. (2010). The cross-country incidence of the global crisis (No. 10-171). International Monetary Fund.

Mundell, R. (1961). Optimum currency areas. American Economic Review 51, pp. 657-665.

Naughton, B. (2007). The Chinese economy: Transitions and growth. MIT press.

Nolan, P. (2002). China and the Global Business Revolution. Cambridge Journal of Economics, 26(1): 119-37.

North, D. C. (1990). Institutions, Institutional Change and Economic Performance. Cambridge University Press.

Nurkse, R. (1944). International currency experience: lessons of the interwar period (No. 4). League of Nations.

Park, Y. C., & Bea, K. H. Financial Liberalisation and Integration in East Asia. Financial Stability and Growth in Emerging Economies, 149.

Persson, T., & Tabellini, G. (2007). Political regimes and economic growth.

Pohl, G., Anderson, R., Claessens, S., & Djankov, S. (1997). Privatisation and restructuring in Central and Eastern Europe: evidence and policy options. World Bank Technical Paper no. 368. Washington, DC: World Bank.

Poon, D., & Zhang, J. (2017). Banking sector implications & outlook. In Citi Research (2017). China economics & multi-asset view. Capital markets opening: what it means for assets/ financials, 71-74.

Pritchett, L., & Summers, L. H. (2014). Asiaphoria meets regression to the mean. No. w20573,

Qian, Y., & Xu, C. (1993). Why China's economic reforms differ: the M-form hierarchy and entry/expansion of the non-state sector. Economics of Transition 1(2): 135-170.

Rajan, R. (2010). Fault lines: how hidden fractures still threaten the world economy. Princeton University Press.

Reich, R. B. (2010). Aftershock: the next economy and America's future. New York: Random House.

Rodrik, D. (1999). The New Global Economy and Developing Countries: Making Openness Work. Overseas Development Council (Baltimore, Maryland) Policy Essay No. 24.

Roland, G. (2000). Transition and economics: Politics, markets, and firms. MIT Press.

Rosen, D. H. (2003). Low-tech bed, high-tech dreams. China Economic Quarterly Q, 4, 20-40.

Rueschemeyer, D., Stephens, E. H., & Stephens, J. D. (1992). Capitalist development and democracy. Cambridge, UK.

Shambaugh, D. (2014). The Illusion of Chinese Power. The National Interest [Online] http:// nationalinterest.org/feature/the-illusion-chinese-power-10739 [Accessed: October 2017].

Sharma, R. (2016). The rise and fall of nations: forces of change in the post-crisis world. WW Norton & Company.

Shen, X. (1999). The Chinese Road to High Technology: Telecommunications Switching Technology in the Economic Transition. Springer.

Shepsle, K. A., & Weingast, B. R. (1987). The institutional foundations of committee power. American Political Science Review, 81(1), 85-104.

Shioji, T. (2006). Chinese exchange rate regimes and the optimal basket weights for the rest of East Asia. RIETI Discussion Paper Series 06-E-024.

Solow, R. (1957). Technical Change and the Aggregate Production Function.
Solow, R. (1957). Technical Change and the Aggregate Production Function.
Stark, D., & Bruszt, L. (1998). Postsocialist pathways: Transforming politics and property in East Central Europe. Cambridge University Press.

Sturzenegger, F., & Zettelmeyer, J. (2006). Debt defaults and lessons from a decade of crises. MIT Press.

Sun, J. (2017). Equity market implications & outlook. In Citi Research (2017). China economics & multi-asset view. Capital markets opening: what it means for assets/financials, 40-51.

Sun, Q., & Fu, X. (2012). China's battle against the global economic crisis in Fu, X. (ed.), China's Role in Global Economic Recovery. Routledge.

The Economist (2015). Maiden Voyage. The Economist [Online] 5 December. http://www.economist.com/news/business-and-finance/21679341-its-new-status-might-make-weaker-yuan-chinese-renminbi-joins-imfs [Accessed: October 2017].

The Economist (2016). The yuan and the markets. The Economist [Online] 16 January. http://www.economist.com/news/leaders/21688396-strains-currency-suggest-something-very-wrong-chinas-politics-yuan-and [Accessed: October 2017].

The Economist (2017a). It's my party. Xi Jinping has announced a new era. It won't be an era of reform in the Western sense. The Economist [Online]. http://www.theworldin.com/article/14429/edition2018its-my-party [Accessed: December 2017].

The Economist (2017b). L for longer. Growth will disappoint, but the outlook for China's economy is still strong. The Economist [Online]. http://www.theworldin.com/article/14431/edition2018l-longer [Accessed: December 2017].

The Economist (2017c). The China bet. Will it have both the biggest economy and the largest population, asks Simon Cox. The Economist [Online]. http://www.theworldin.com/article/14391/edition2018china-bet [Accessed: December 2017].

The Economist Intelligence Unit (2017). The world in 2018. The Economist.
Thelen, K. (1999). Historical institutionalism in comparative politics. Annual review of political science, 2(1), 369-404.

Tsebelis, G. (1995). Decision making in political systems: Veto players in presidentialism, parliamentarism, multicameralism and multipartyism. British journal of political science, 25(3), 289-325.

Volz, U. (2014). RMB internationalisation and currency cooperation in East Asia. In Hilpert ,H. G., & Rovekamp, F. (eds). Currency cooperation in East Asia (pp. 57-81). Springer.

Wade, R. (1990). Governing the market: Economic theory and the role of government in East Asian industrialization. Princeton University Press.

Wei, S. J. (1993). The Open Door Policy and China´s Rapid Growth: Evidence from City-Level Data. NBER Working Paper, 4602.

Weir, M. (1992). Politics and jobs: the boundaries of employment policy in the United States. Princeton University Press.

Wijnbergen, S. v. (1998). Bank restructuring and enterprise reform. In: Boone, P., Gomulka, S., & Layard, R. (Eds.). (1998). Emerging from Communism: Lessons from Russia, China, and Eastern Europe. MIT Press.

Wohlforth, W. C., & Kang, D. C. (2009). Hypotheses on status competition. APSA 2009 Toronto Meeting Paper.

Woo, T. W. (1998). Why China grew. In: Boone, P., Gomulka, S., & Layard, R. (Eds.). (1998). Emerging from Communism: Lessons from Russia, China, and Eastern Europe. MIT Press, pp. 154-181.

Woo, W. T. (1995). Comments on Wei´s (1995) Foreign Direct Investment in China: Sources and Consequences. In A. Krueger (ed.), Financial Deregulation and Integration in East Asia. University of Chicago Press, 166-89.

World Bank (1997). China 2020. Washington, DC: World Bank.

World Trade Organisation (2017). General agreement on trade and services.

Xielin, L. (2005). China's Development Model: An Alternative Strategy for Technological Catch-Up. Research Institute of Economy, Trade and Industry.

Xu, C., & Zhuang, J. (1998). Why China grew: the role of decentralization. In: Boone, P., Gomulka, S., & Layard, R. (Eds.). (1998). Emerging from Communism: Lessons from Russia, China, and Eastern Europe. MIT Press, pp. 154-181.

Yoshino, N., & Asonuma, T. (2017). Optimal dynamic path during the transition of exchange rate regime: analysis of the People's Republic of China (PRC), Malaysia, and Singapore. ADBI Working Paper Series.

Yoshino, N., Kaji, S., & Suzuki, A. (2014). Dynamic transition of exchange rate regime in China. China and World Economy, vol. 22(3). pp. 36-55.

Yu, G. (2017). The evolution of the renminbi 2005-present: a market participant's perspective.

LSE IDEAS Special Report. May 2017, 30-35.

Yueh, L. (2013). China's growth: The making of an economic superpower. Oxford University Press.

Zheng, J., Bigstein, A., & Hu, A. (2009). Can China´s Growth Be Sustained? A productivity perspective. World Development (Special issue on law, finance, and economic growth in China), 37/4: 874-88.

Zheng, J., Hu, A. (2006). An Empirical Analysis of Provincial Productivity in China 1979-2001. Journal of Chinese Economic and Business Studies, 4/3: 221-39.

Zheng, J., Liu, X, & Bigsten, A. (2003). Efficiency, Technical Progress, and Best Practice in Chinese State Enterprises 1980-1994. Journal of Comparative Economics, 31/1: 134-52.

Zweig, D. (2005). Competing for Talent: China's Strategies to Reverse the Brain Drain. International Labour Review, 145, 65-90.

Other Research

Ahya, C., Cheung, J., Kam, D. Y., & Lai, H. (2017). Identifying inflection. Asian exports – inflecting higher. Morgan Stanley Research.

Aziz, J., Liao, C. W., & Zhu, H. (2017). China's debt: the sum of all fears. J.P. Morgan Economic Research.

Barclays (2017). China. Ratings down; limited impact. Barclays Credit Strategy.

Buiter, W., Chua, J., Shen, M., Mondino, G., & Rahbari, E. (2015). Global economics view: What does the Chinese devaluation mean for the world?. Citi Research.

Chan, V. (2017). Quick take: China announces the start of Bond Connect. Credit Suisse Fixed Income Research.

Chan, V. (2017). Quick take: credit warning on selected groups. Credit Suisse Fixed Income Strategy.

Chan, V. (2017). Quick take: Moody's downgrades China. Credit Suisse Fixed Income Research.

Chan, V., & Deng, W. (2017a). China: leverage and de-leveraging. Credit Suisse Fixed Income Research.

Chan, V., & Deng, W. (2017b). Quick take: China announced to establish Xiongan New Area. Credit Suisse Fixed Income Research.

Chan, V., & Deng, W. (2017c). Quick take: China economics. Credit Suisse Fixed Income Research.

Chan, V., & Deng, W. (2017d). Quick take: the PBoC increased the OMO rates, again. Credit Suisse Fixed Income Research.

Chan, V., Deng, W., & Farris, R. (2017a). China: focus on stability. Credit Suisse Fixed Income Research.

Chan, V., Deng, W., & Farris, R. (2017b). Quick take: China- the premier reveals macro targets for 2017. Credit Suisse Fixed Income Research.

Chang, J., & Fernandez D. (2015). Putting SDR inclusion in perspective. A conference call with Barry Eichengreen. Barclays.

Chang, J., & Fernandez, D. (2017). Questions beyond China's current period of macro stability. Barclays Emerging Market Research.

Chang, J., & Zhou, Y. (2017a). National Finance Work Conference emphasized deleveraging and risk control. Barclays Emerging Markets Research.

Chang, J., & Zhou, Y. (2017b). PboC hikes policy rates and sends more tightening signals. Barclays Emerging Markets Research.

Chang, J., Fernandez, D., Kotecha, M., Lee, J., & Wang, S. (2015). RMB in the SDR: Initial thoughts. Barclays.

Chang, J., Kotecha, M., Tan, D., & Zhou, Y. (2017a). China. Reportedly fine tuning the CNY fixing mechanism. Barclays Foreign Exchange Research.

Chang, J., Kotecha, M., Tan, D., & Zhou, Y. (2017b). FX reserves edge below USD3trn. Barclays Emerging Markets Research.

Chen, M. M., Liao, C. W. Ng, G., & Zhu, H. (2017a). China: another 10bp hike in market-based policy rate. J.P. Morgan Asia Pacific Economic Research.

Chen, M. M., Liao, C. W. Ng, G., & Zhu, H. (2017b). China: January FX reserves fell a touch below $3 trillion. J.P. Morgan Asia Pacific Emerging Markets Research.

Chen, M. M., Liao, C. W. Ng, G., & Zhu, H. (2017c). Economic Research Note. China's capital flows: a tug-of-war. J.P. Morgan Economic Research.

Chen, M. M., Liao, C. W., Ng, G., & Zhu, H. (2017c). China: July FX reserves turning up further to $3.081 trillion. J.P. Morgan Asia Pacific Emerging Markets Research.

Chen, M. M., Liao, C. W., Ng, G., & Zhu, H. (2017d). Greater China quarterly issues. J.P. Morgan.

Chen, M. M., Ng, G., & Zhu, H. (2017e). China: PBOC provides temporary liquidity for large banks. J.P. Morgan Economic Research.

Chen, M. M., Ng, G., & Zhu, H. (2017f). China: PBOC raises MLF interest rates by 10bp. J.P. Morgan Economic Research.

Chen, M. M., Ng, G., & Zhu, H. (2017g). Ten questions about China in 2017. J.P. Morgan

Economic Research.

Chen, M., Ng, G., & Zhu, H. (2015a). China: IMF staff recommended RMB inclusion in the SDR. J.P. Morgan.

Citi (2017a). Asia economic outlook & strategy. What if we get a summer of discontent? Citi Research Economics.

Citi (2017b). China economics & multi-asset view. Capital markets opening: what it means for assets/financials. Citi Research Multi-Asset.

Citi (2017c). China economics & multi-asset views. Why tighter regulation will not choke off economy/ markets. Citi Research Multi-Asset.

Deng, W. (2017). Quick take: Moody's downgrades Hong Kong. Credit Suisse Fixed Income Research.

Deutsche Bank (2017). Emerging markets monthly. Half full … Deutsche Bank Markets Research.

Fan, Q., He, L., Wu, Y., Xu, E. H., & Yu, J. (2017). China's transition to high income. At a crossroads of transportation industry reform. Morgan Stanley Research.

Goldman Sachs (2017). The (tr)end of globalization. Goldman Sachs Emerging Market Analyst.

Goldman Sachs Research (2013a). EM Macro Daily: Capital account reforms – charting a roadmap. Goldman Sachs.

Goldman Sachs Research (2013b). EM Macro Daily: RMB internationalization to power ahead. Goldman Sachs.

Gu, Y. K., & Zhu, H. (2017). Bond Connect: a milestone in China's capital market development. J.P. Morgan Asia Pacific Emerging Markets Research.

Ho, R., Kelleher, B., & Topiwalla, H. (2017). China Summit 2017. Day 1: Keep calm, (markets) carry on. Morgan Stanley Research.

Ho, R., Kelleher, B., & Topiwalla, H. (2017). China Summit 2017. Day 2: Invest in consumption. Morgan Stanley Research.

Ho, R., Kelleher, B., & Topiwalla, H. (2017). China Summit 2017. Day 3: Focus on the bottom-up opportunities. Morgan Stanley Research.

Hu, L., & Peng, J. (2016). China debt: myth and realities. Macquarie Research.

International Monetary Fund (2017). Asia and Pacific preparing for choppy seas. Regional Economic Outlook, April 2017.

International Monetary Fund (2017). Getting the policy mix right. Global Financial Stability Report, April 2017.

J.P. Morgan (2017). China: lower capital outflows to reduce pressure on CNY and money market rates. J.P. Morgan Asia Pacific Economic Research.

Jin, X., & Liu, L.-G. (2017a). China economic view. How large is the fiscal multiplier for China? Citi Research Economics.

Jin, X., & Liu, L.-G. (2017b). China economic view. NPC outlook: steady growth, strengthening regulation, and containing risk. Citi Research Economics.

Jin, X., & Liu, L.-G. (2017c). China economic view. NPC policy targets and priorities – no surprises in a political transition year. Citi Research Economics.

Jin, X., & Liu, L.-G. (2017d). China economic view. PBoC's mixed monetary policy signal: what does the MCI tell us? Citi Research Economics.

Jin, X., & Liu, L.-G. (2017e). China economic view. Q4 GDP growth quickens on service industry, challenges ahead. Citi Research Economics.

Jin, X., & Liu, L.-G. (2017f). China economics view. 2H outlook: unleashing some instability for greater stability. Citi Research Economics.

Jin, X., & Liu, L.-G. (2017g). China economics view. Alert: China to confront financial risks; key takeaways from 5th National Financial Work Conference. Citi Research Economics.

Jin, X., & Liu, L.-G. (2017h). China economics view. Beware a regulation led monetary tightening. Citi Research Economics.

Jin, X., & Liu, L.-G. (2017i). China economics view. Robust 1Q growth with limited CPI inflationary pressure, sustainability remains a concern. Citi Research Economics.

Jin, X., & Liu, L.-G. (2017j). China economics view. Surprisingly robust 2Q growth, export 6.8% growth in 2017E. Citi Research Economics.

Jin, X., & Liu, L.-G. (2017k). China economics view. Tracking SOE reforms: mixed ownership reform treads (slowly) ahead.

Jin, X., Liao, T. X. & Liu, L.-G. (2017l). China economics view. Xiong-An: a new district – how big an impact on the economy? Citi Research Economics.

Jin, X., Liu, L.-G., & Yu, X. (2017e). China economics view. Will renminbi's strength be sustained? Citi Research Economics.

Jin, X., Liu, L.-G., & Yu, X. (2017m). China economics flash. Alert: continued FX reserves rise should support the RMB. Citi Research Economics.

Jin, X., Liu, L.-G., & Yu, X. (2017n). China economics view. How might China react to the US section 301 trade inquiry and what are the implications? Citi Research Economics.

Kalani, G. (2017). What is driving EM FX? Deutsche Bank Research.

Lau, K., Moe, T., Tang, M., & Tilton, A. (2017). China's 19th party congress and its economic and policy significance. Goldman Sachs Asia Economics Analyst.

Lee, J., & Del-Rosario, D. (2017). Asia vulnerability monitor: caution over higher rates. Deutsche Bank Research.

Li, Z., Song, Y., Tang, M., Tilton, A., & Wei, M. (2016). Tracking China's fiscal stance: beyond the official fiscal balance. Goldman Sachs Asia Economics Analyst.

Li, Z., Song, Y., Tang, M., Tilton, A., & Wei, M. (2017a). China infrastructure investment: is the high growth sustainable? Goldman Sachs Asia Economics Analyst.

Li, Z., Song, Y., Tang, M., Tilton, A., & Wei, M. (2017b). Risks to China's growth in the year of the rooster. Goldman Sachs Asia Economics Analyst.

Lubin, D., Willer D., & Chua, J. (2017). Emerging markets economic outlook & strategy. How to think about EM's 'trade revival'. Citi Research Economics.

Lubin, D., Willer D., & Chua, J. (2017). Emerging markets economic outlook & strategy. On EM's 'China dependence'. Citi Research Economics.

Morgan Stanely (2017). China's transition to high income. Chinese capital market liberalization and implications for asset allocators. Morgan Stanley Research.

Pang, K. (2017). China credit risk back in vogue. Morgan Stanley Research.

Siddharth, M., (2017). Emerging markets rates strategy focus. Impact of China's inclusion into EM-GBI. Citi Research Multi-Asset.

Suwanapruti, D., & Tilton, A. (2017). What China's inclusion into global bond indices would mean for capital flows. Goldman Sachs Asia Economics Analyst.

The World Bank Group (2017a). Global economic prospects. A fragile recovery. June 2017.

The World Bank Group (2017b). Global economic prospects. Weak investments in uncertain times. January 2017.

The World Bank Group (2017c). Governance and the law. Washington D.C.

The World Bank Group (2017d). International debt statistics 2017. Washington D.C.

The World Bank Group (2017e). World development indicators 2017. Washington D.C.

Zhang Z., & Zeng, L. (2017a). China: prelude to a US-China trade war. Deutsche Bank Research.

Zhang, Z. (2017). China macro in charts (CMC). Deutsche Bank Research.

Zhang, Z., & Zeng, L. (2017b). China's indispensable property bubble. Deutsche Bank Research.

Made in the USA
Monee, IL
12 November 2026

e6053ec1-eaea-445e-a49b-fbec5514313eR01